CULTURAL SPORT PSYCHOLOGY

Robert Schinke, EdD
Laurentian University, Canada

Stephanie J. Hanrahan, PhD
University of Queensland, Australia

Editors

Human Kinetics

Library of Congress Cataloging-in-Publication Data

Library of Congress Cataloging-in-Publication Data
Cultural sport psychology / Robert Schinke and Stephanie J. Hanrahan, editors.
    p. cm.
 Includes bibliographical references and index.
 ISBN-13: 978-0-7360-7133-8 (hard cover)
 ISBN-10: 0-7360-7133-4 (hard cover)
 1. Sports--Psychological aspects. 2. Sports--Social aspects. I. Schinke, Robert, 1966-
II. Hanrahan, Stephanie J., 1961-
 GV706.4.C85 2009
 796.01--dc22

                          2008023294

ISBN-10: 0-7360-7133-4
ISBN-13: 978-0-7360-7133-8

The Web addresses cited in this text were current as of May 2008, unless otherwise noted.

Acquisitions Editors: Myles S. Schrag and Laura Pierce; **Developmental Editor:** Elaine H. Mustain; **Managing Editor:** Melissa J. Zavala; **Copyeditor:** Jocelyn Engman; **Proofreader:** Joanna Hatzopoulos Portman; **Indexer:** Nancy Ball; **Permission Manager:** Dalene Reeder; **Graphic Designer:** Nancy Rasmus; **Graphic Artist:** Dawn Sills; **Cover Designer:** Bob Reuther; **Photos (interior):** © Human Kinetics, unless otherwise noted; **Photo Asset Manager:** Laura Fitch; **Photo Office Assistant:** Jason Allen; **Art Manager:** Kelly Hendren; **Associate Art Manager:** Alan L. Wilborn; **Illustrator:** Bullseye Studio; **Printer:** Sheridan Books

Printed in the United States of America   10 9 8 7 6 5 4 3 2 1

Human Kinetics
Web site: www.HumanKinetics.com

United States: Human Kinetics
P.O. Box 5076
Champaign, IL 61825-5076
800-747-4457
e-mail: humank@hkusa.com

Canada: Human Kinetics
475 Devonshire Road Unit 100
Windsor, ON N8Y 2L5
800-465-7301 (in Canada only)
e-mail: info@hkcanada.com

Europe: Human Kinetics
107 Bradford Road
Stanningley
Leeds LS28 6AT, United Kingdom
+44 (0) 113 255 5665
e-mail: hk@hkeurope.com

Australia: Human Kinetics
57A Price Avenue
Lower Mitcham, South Australia 5062
08 8372 0999
e-mail: info@hkaustralia.com

New Zealand: Human Kinetics
Division of Sports Distributors NZ Ltd.
P.O. Box 300 226 Albany
North Shore City
Auckland
0064 9 448 1207
e-mail: info@humankinetics.co.nz

CONTENTS

PART III   APPLIED PRACTICE

PREFACE

This book began many years before Human Kinetics was approached with a formal proposal. In the autumn of 1996, I (Rob) began consulting with the Canadian National Boxing Team. That experience quickly taught me that applied sport psychology requires a flexible approach based on people in relation to their backgrounds. In the multicultural training ground of boxing, clients wanted to be approached thoughtfully depending on what they valued most: family, religion, finance, or accolades. Some years later, when I attended the 2002 Commonwealth Games as a sport psychology consultant, each day I traveled to the competition venue with athletes from different countries. The Canadian athletes often sat alone, listened to their music with headphones, and spent their travel time either psyching up or maintaining composure. In contrast, the South African athletes immediately moved to the back of the bus, with three people crammed into seating typically intended for only two. Before long, the athletes and coaching staff would start singing a melody. As the trip proceeded, the melody would gain momentum until many of the African athletes from other countries joined in. To the African athletes, precompetition preparation was achieved as a group rather than in isolation. This experience was a defining moment for me, one that spurred me to think about a new approach to applied practice, teaching, and research.

I (Stephanie) am an avid traveler and international practitioner of sport and exercise psychology who has long been fascinated by culturally reflexive practice. After growing up in a White middle-class neighborhood, my first interactions with people who were different from me were in sixth grade, when I moved from the West to the East Coast of the United States and for the first time had African American classmates. My learning curve really began at age 17, when I worked as a counselor at a camp in Arkansas for juvenile offenders, abandoned and abused kids, and kids who were just plain poor. While working at this camp, which was about 90% Black, I had time to attend a Southern Black Baptist church and a rally against the Ku Klux Klan, among other things. I took advantage of many other opportunities to experience different ways of living, but my interest in cultural sport psychology (CSP) as a formal pursuit was solidified when I began working with Aboriginal

performing artists in the 1990s. For the first time I realized that even with my genuine appreciation of multiple cultures, I had naively excluded culture as an influence on service delivery in sport psychology. Although cultural awareness had been part of my personal life, my work as a sport psychologist was an academically determined compartment of my life in which culture was never mentioned. In short, I finally learned that sport psychology had to be applied to all clients in relation to their cultures.

In 2004, the two of us began conversing when Rob was developing a special issue about CSP for a journal, and before long we began discussing the possibility of a book devoted to the topic. Next, we started searching for like-minded contributors, and in the process we struck up new friendships and rekindled a few established ones. It seemed that everyone we spoke with believed we were onto something. Slowly, the structure of the present book formed with the help of Myles Schrag from Human Kinetics. What follows is the first edition in what we hope is a burgeoning new area of applied sport psychology.

This text is the first book-length attempt to focus entirely on a challenging line of discussion that we have called *cultural sport psychology* (CSP). Clearly it is not a definitive effort but rather a catalytic work, intended to spur development of a nascent field. Part I provides an introduction to CSP. In chapter 1, along with Peter Catina, we introduce concepts, terms, and characteristics of culture. In chapter 2, Heather Peters and Jean Williams use preexisting sport psychology paradigms and concepts to provide strategies from which to consider culture. We call this general approach the *sport psychology perspective*. In chapter 3, Leslee Fisher, Emily Roper, and Ted Butryn address a second viewpoint that we have named the *cultural studies perspective*. Neither set of authors endorses one approach over the other; we all realize that the questions asked and the strategies used to understand culture will vary depending on which perspective is chosen, with both providing valuable insights.

In part II, the authors move beyond generalities into more precise reflections on what to consider from the vantage point of the athlete or sport scientist engaged in cross-cultural understanding. In chapter 4, Tatiana Ryba considers the importance of the sport psychologist's cultural identity as part of the athlete-practitioner dyad. In chapter 5, Diane Gill and Cindra Kamphoff shift the focus of attention to understanding the client's identity. In chapter 6, Kerry McGannon and Christina Johnson suggest various ways to approach CSP research using generally defined worldviews. Together, the chapters that compose part II go from the conceptual to the methodological and provide a foundation for part III.

Part III is devoted entirely to applied practice. The contributors to this part use several approaches. Considered in the context of both the places of practice and the cultures of the contributors themselves, each chapter can provide something useful even if some practitioners find themselves disagreeing with the approaches taken. We are hopeful that scholars and practitioners can put themselves into the worldviews of other cultures and perhaps in the process even modify their own perspectives.

Several of the chapters in part III feature multiple minority cultures within one nation, and others focus on one specific culture. The author of chapter 7, Peter Terry, is an English applied sport psychologist currently working in Australia who has extensive multinational experience. He introduces effective multicultural practice and reflects on how such practice works in different regions of the world. Chapter 8 features one of the editors of this text (Rob) and his coauthors speaking about their experiences working with Canadian Aboriginal athletes. In chapter 9, Anthony Kontos considers athletes from minority populations in the United States. In chapter 10, Luis Carlos Moraes and John Salmela share their views as applied sport psychologists observing and working with Brazilian athletes. Natalia Stambulova, Urban Johnson, and Alexander Stambulov are applied practitioners with extensive experience working with athletes in their respective countries, and chapter 11 compares the cultural strategies they employed with athletes from two different countries, Sweden and Russia.

In chapter 12, Ronnie Lidor and Boris Blumenstein share their experiences working with elite Jewish, Arab, and foreign athletes in Israel. Chapter 13 presents the experiences of Shaun Galloway, a Canadian sport psychologist currently based in England who consulted with Muslim athletes in Kuwait as part of an overseas teaching experience. Philomena Ikulayo and J. Semidara from Nigeria authored chapter 14, in which they consider strategies for integrating traditional beliefs with contemporary sport. In chapter 15, Caren Diehl, Anna Hegley, and Andrew Lane share strategies that enabled them to work successfully with athletes in Ghana. One of the editors of this text (Stephanie) authored chapter 16 based on her experiences consulting with Australian Aboriginal athletes and performing artists. In chapter 17, Kaori Araki and Govindasamy Balasekaran discuss their perceptions of working with Chinese, Malay, and Indian athletes in the multicultural society of Singapore. Finally, chapter 18 reflects the experiences of Yoichi Kozuma, an applied consultant living in Japan.

We conclude this book with suggestions for sport psychology educators, consultants, and researchers. These parting words are meant to encourage ongoing CSP discourse and catalyze new discussions among sport enthusiasts interested in effective CSP.

ACKNOWLEDGMENTS

This book brings a new dimension to sport psychology. We conceived of the idea based on discussions with and guidance from many people. Collectively, we would like to thank the athletes and coaches with whom we have worked. Clients and students from many cultures have encouraged us to consider diversity in our applied practice, teaching, and research. Additionally, Rob would like to thank the people from Wikwemikong Unceded First Nations Indian Reserve for their ongoing collaboration and his wife, Erin, for her encouragement and support as a sounding board and partner.

PART I

NEW DIMENSION IN SPORT PSYCHOLOGY

Cultural sport psychology (CSP) is a burgeoning area in sport psychology. Until now, only a few articles have been available to the reader interested in knowing more about CSP. Part I reflects the work of three sets of authors, each with a specific purpose. Chapter 1 unpacks and explains the parameters of CSP. As part of the process, the authors also provide factors to consider when working as a researcher or a practitioner in a multi-cultural setting. Chapters 2 and 3 provide distinct approaches to considering culture within sport psychology: CSP and the cultural studies approach to sport psychology. The CSP approach, building upon work in cultural psychology, emphasizes learning about new cultures with the understanding that through conscientiously chosen strategies, the sport psychology practitioner can gain insight into another person in a multicultural exchange. The cultural studies approach presents a slightly different view, and in chapter 3, the authors integrate strategies based in cultural studies. The focus is on the exchanges that happen between people and how, for example, power and privilege can influence multicultural exchanges.

The approaches offered in part I are meant to reflect some of the diversity (and therefore multiple possibilities) available to the sport psychologist working in multicultural contexts. Additionally, at the end of each chapter the authors offer general suggestions in relation to their discussion. These suggestions are meant to inform CSP research and practice based on the authors' views. However, the final considerations of the authors in this section of the book, as well as in the sections that follow, are suggestions and not directives. The nuances and distinctions of each culture are what need to be considered when one embraces culture in sport psychology.

INTRODUCTION TO CULTURAL SPORT PSYCHOLOGY

Robert J. Schinke, EdD; Stephanie J. Hanrahan, PhD; and Peter Catina, PhD

Sport psychologists are increasingly working with athletes and coaches from a wide variety of cultural backgrounds. American mainstream sport psychology interns at a large university may work with international scholarship athletes on the tennis team. In Canada, sport psychologists regularly consult with Anglophone and Francophone athletes, and previous athletes on the national boxing team have come from Barbados, Jamaica, Nigeria, Kenya, Afghanistan, Guatemala, and Iran (Schinke, 2007). Professionals in Singapore are likely to consult with athletes of Chinese, Malaysian, and Indian descent, as well as those from other countries. In such situations, the most effective strategies are tailored to the client's cultural identity—an identity that reflects nationality, religion, race, and ethnicity (Hill, 1993; Kontos & Breland-Noble, 2002; Martens, Mobley, & Zizzi, 2000). With the globalization of sport and society, teams and clubs are increasingly likely to include athletes and coaches (and perhaps sport psychologists) from multiple cultures (Maguire, 1999). It would be remiss for the field of sport psychology to ignore the influence of culture on communication, motivation, and the process and meaning of achievement.

Though it is easy to suppose that mental training skills are transferable across regions and regional groups, effective communication strategies are consistent among all people, and all athletes are inspired by similar motives, we already know from the sport literature that these assumptions are unfounded. All cultures have many nuances that make them unique. For example, eye contact during communication among most North Americans is a sign of interest, engagement, transparency, and politeness. However, when communicating with traditional Australian Aborigines, the same tactic could be regarded as a sign of aggression or even promiscuity (Schinke & Hanrahan, 2006). Similarly, whereas some people regard time as precise and rely on a watch to punctually attend appointments (clock-based time), others follow different guidelines for punctuality, arriving and departing after the designated time (event-based time) (Hanrahan, 2005a; Levine, 1988). As this book will show, these are only two examples among others that underscore the intricacies of effective practice in cross-cultural sport psychology.

The intersection of sport psychology and culture is not a new discussion point in the literature. As early as 1990, authors including Duda and Allison (1990) and Danish, Petipas, and Hale (1993) recognized that there is no universal approach to applied sport psychology, and there is little understanding among sport psychologists regarding how to work with clients of cultures different from their own. Nearly 10 years ago, Duda and Hayashi (1998) identified a decade-long void in cross-cultural considerations in research writings, although racial and ethnic differences definitely existed in sport. None of the theoretical and empirical articles examined in the *Journal of Sport and Exercise Psychology* between 1979 and 1987 used race or ethnicity, two aspects of culture, as independent variables. This omission was not a reflection of the journal but rather an indication of a pervasive monocultural approach among sport psychology authors. Affirming Duda and Hayashi's report, others (e.g., Fisher, Butryn, & Roper, 2003; Kontos & Breland-Noble, 2002; Ryba & Wright, 2005) have indicated that culture-specific aspects for those outside of White Eurocentric society have also been overlooked in the sport psychology literature.

In cultural sport psychology (CSP), sociocultural aspects of athletes' environments are considered as gateways to mutual understanding and subsequently motivation and performance (Kontos & Arguello,

2005; Martens et al., 2000). Cultural reflections are believed to enhance the understanding of those who already practice sport psychology and other sport sciences. In addition, they can provide valuable insight for academic and sport institutions wishing to incorporate multicultural awareness into their training and to improve cultural competence of staff.

Although it is entirely plausible that effective practice must take into account the cultural identities of prospective clients, many sport professionals use approaches that they regard as effective with all people (Martens et al., 2000). The authors of this chapter, for example, were taught to deliver the skills of imagery, goal setting, relaxation, focusing, and planning in much the same way regardless of the client. Each of us soon realized, however, that effectively delivering, implementing, and monitoring skills sometimes requires cultural understanding.

This view is especially important when working with athletes from backgrounds other than one's own. For example, Schinke (2007) learned from a traditional Canadian aboriginal athlete that precompetition preparation on the day of performance may require cultural strategies including the burning of sweetgrass, sage, or tobacco. Many aboriginal athletes employ this strategy to pray to their Creator for personal health and success for themselves and for their opponents. By understanding the importance of sacred medicines and also what is being prayed for, Schinke was better equipped to work with aboriginal athletes, employing discussion points that were relevant from their standpoint.

In a culturally diverse sport environment, athletes and sport science professionals must try to understand each other despite potential nuances in customs, values, and language, including different interpretations of eye contact, physical space (proxemics), time, and how individuals relate to the group. Though the task of achieving cross-cultural competence might seem daunting given the differences that can exist from one group to the next—and even in the same group—the chapters that follow will help

This diving award ceremony features athletes from Canada, Mexico, and the United States. What mental training skills could each of these women have used to earn these medals?

© AP Photo/Dario Lopez-Mills

demystify the process. Before going forward, however, let's consider some of the terminology and strategies that frame this book.

DEFINING CULTURE

The term *culture* has only recently gained traction in the sport psychology literature, though it has a strong presence in anthropology and psychology (see Kral, Burkhardt, & Kidd, 2002; Shweder, 1990) and intersects both domains in the field of cultural psychology. Cultural psychology developed out of the ethnocentric approach of psychology (Seeley, 2000) and the way cross-cultural psychology represented culture as an independent variable rather than as a process (Greenfield, 1997), focusing on "the understanding of not only how mind constitutes culture but more importantly of how culture constitutes mind" (Kral et al., 2002, p. 155). The views found in cultural psychology have only begun to surface in sport psychology. At the heart of this shift is the recognition that culture has always played a large part in sport psychology (Ryba & Wright, 2005).

Though some might dispute this view, consider how (and by whom) our domain has come to be. At the forefront of the discussion are power and privilege (Butryn, 2002). In the origin of sport psychology in mainstream North America and Europe, there is a strong emphasis on theories of self, including self-efficacy, self-concept, self-esteem, and self-determination. Each framework reflects cultural values that promote the individual as the focal point and the world as extending outward from the individual to community and society. It makes sense, then, that mental training skills, such as goal setting, attribution retraining, competition plans, and post-performance debriefs, reflect self-promoting qualities. And yet personal goals, or at least how they are pursued, might be viewed differently depending on how one views oneself (as primary or secondary) in relation to family, peers, and community (Hanrahan, 2004). If the goal is to work effectively with athletes, practitioners need to understand who the athletes are, where they come from, and how they were socialized—in summary, what is important to them.

In addition, as Butryn (2002) has suggested, sport psychology professionals also must understand who they are. The omission of understanding one's own enculturation is common when the practitioners come from the dominant culture. Everyone is a cultural being with norms, values, and opinions that stem in part from ancestry and socialization (see Cowlishaw, 2000). When students are asked to consider the role of culture on their identity as

developing academics during a CSP course, I (Rob S.) often remind them of their willingness to engage in academic banter with their instructors as a culturally accepted behavior in their institution. For many Chinese students, on the other hand, the questioning of authority may be considered disrespectful, even when studying in countries where such behaviors are encouraged (Holmes, 2006). Sport psychologists need to consider the role of cultural backgrounds if the intent is to understand others and oneself.

Triandis (1994) defined culture as a set of human-made objective and subjective elements that in the past increased the probability of survival. As part of the larger definition, we can include the following terms in relation to the client and oneself: *mainstream* or *minority, ethnicity, race,* and *religion.* Combined, these aspects provide a system of information that helps describe how a group of people, a society, or a nation lives in its social and physical environment (Reber, 1995). Each of these aspects will be considered in turn:

- Several of the applied chapters in this book present athletes from geographical regions where a certain culture is prevalent (e.g., Muslim athletes in Kuwait, Chinese athletes in Singapore). These examples reflect the aspects of a mainstream culture, race, and in at least one example, religion.

- In other instances, groups reflect cultural communities other than the predominate culture in a region (e.g., Latin American baseball players in the United States, aboriginal athletes in Canada). This text refers to such examples of culture as *ethnic groups,* meaning groups of people (majority or minority in a society) with common traditions (religious and otherwise) and a shared sense of identity.

- Adding texture to the discussion is the term *race.* From a biological vantage, race differences were considered on the basis of inherited physical characteristics, including skin color and hair texture (Myers & Spencer, 2003). Many people realize that physical traits do not demarcate race; for example, it is possible to be an olive-complexioned Caucasian or a light-skinned African American. Some have also suggested (e.g., Cowlishaw, 2000) that race is at least partially a socially constructed phenomenon whereby people act or are expected to act in accordance with their biological attributes. Consequently, race is regarded by some as fixed and by others as fluid, with people self-identifying based on physical characteristics or sociocultural and political grounds.

- Religion provides another underpinning, with its basis of traditionally defined patterns and ceremonies. This fourth aspect contributes a universal dimension to the larger discussion, with its overall objective being the need to understand the human condition. Typically associated with religion are beliefs related to one or more supreme beings, worship, and moral guidelines.

Because these underpinnings contribute to clients' and practitioners' identities in varying degrees, they will play a part in the forthcoming chapters, and more importantly, in the relationships practitioners develop with clients.

CULTURAL CHARACTERISTICS

Following are additional considerations that can guide effective multicultural practice, with each contributing to clients' cultural identities. They include

- norms, values, beliefs, and behaviors;
- enculturation and acculturation;
- collectivism and individualism;
- goal-directed behavior;
- space;
- time; and
- gender (masculinity and femininity).

NORMS, VALUES, BELIEFS, AND BEHAVIORS

What athletes and sport psychologists regard as cultural is a reflection of their affiliations with one or several of the aforementioned cultural underpinnings, perhaps stemming from their family heritage as well as their current cultural community. We all exhibit telltale signs that reflect our norms, values, and beliefs.

Norms are standards, models, or patterns regarded as typical in a particular group. As indicated earlier, the amount of eye contact during communication will vary as a norm from one cultural group to the next both in how often and when it is used. A second cultural norm is the amount of physical space between people during informal and formal exchanges, as well as the type or absence of physical contact when communicating. Among some cultures putting a hand on another person's arm while engaged in conversation indicates attention and respect, whereas in others the same physical contact could be regarded as condescending when the people involved do not know each other well.

Values are the ideals, customs, standards, or qualities toward which the people of a group have an affective regard. These values may be positive (e.g., freedom, cleanliness, education) or negative (e.g.,

United States athletes Tommie Smith and John Carlos raise their fists during an awards ceremony at the 1968 Summer Olympics. Why is this gesture widely misinterpreted due to cultural differences?
© AP Photo

blasphemy, cruelty, crime). How and when people communicate illustrates whether a group values circular, top-down, or bottom-up decisions. Similarly, the evaluation of wisdom—by life experience, formal education, or a combination of both—is based on cultural values.

Every culture also has its own set of beliefs, or the mental acceptance of and conviction in what is the truth. Some of these beliefs are cross-cultural, such as the existence of God, and yet the term for and representation of God varies by culture. Other beliefs are culture specific, including the respect of elders or the right to free speech.

Culture can also involve behaviors or objective elements such as eating, including the use of hands (left, right, or both) and various types of cutlery or none at all. A related objective element is food, which is a salient facet of cultural identification; for instance, restaurants are often identified by their cultural connection (e.g., Chinese, Italian, Mexican). Additional objective aspects of culture are the design and placement of residences (e.g., on stilts, at the top of a hill to avoid flooding); dress code, including what is fashionable; and language.

The differences and interconnectedness among norms, values, beliefs, and behaviors can be illustrated by hypothetical team meetings (see table 1.1). The first example reflects an egalitarian approach and the second a more hierarchical formation.

ENCULTURATION AND ACCULTURATION

All people have been enculturated or socialized—everyone has gone through the process of learning to live in a particular culture. Some people have also engaged in acculturation, or adopting a culture other than their original culture. This additional culture may be the mainstream culture where one has grown up as a minority member of society, the introduction of a new culture through adoption, or moving either through personal choice or forced relocation (e.g., war or famine). How people integrate their culture into their lives and which aspects of culture are more pertinent to a given situation provide a useful starting point for awareness of individual differences in a culture. In addition, as Kontos and Breland-Noble (2002) have indicated, general cultural practices do not take into account whether and to what extent athletes practice their original culture, particularly when it is not the mainstream culture (see chapter 9).

Based on experience working with Native Americans, Thomason (1991), a clinical counselor who specializes in cross-cultural consultation, provided four general groupings of clients:

1. Clients who retain all of their practices and live in their cultural communities
2. Clients who retain their languages and customs but also integrate some mainstream language and customs into the household
3. Bicultural clients who balance two cultures in their daily existence
4. Acculturated clients who exemplify the mainstream culture even within the household

Given these possibilities of where clients are situated on this continuum, it would appear that reflective practice requires a multitude of considerations beyond the general grouping strategy (e.g., all African Americans or Caucasian Americans as exhibiting common behaviors based on their respective stereotypes) that Andersen (1993) has cautioned sport psychologists to avoid. The following chapters propose several guidelines to consider when taking a cultural approach.

COLLECTIVISM AND INDIVIDUALISM

Extensive literature in psychology differentiates among cultures in terms of whether they are collectively or individually minded. The importance of self-identity has been more closely associated with individualistic rather than with collectivistic societies (Norenzayan & Nisbett, 2004; Williams, Satterwhite, & Saiz, 1998). Individualistic societies such as Canada, the United States, and England seem to foster a unique sense of self and autonomy, clearly delineating boundaries between oneself and others and encouraging the needs, wishes, and desires of individuals over group or collective concerns (Myers & Spencer, 2003). In contrast, collectivistic societies, such as China and Japan, value needs, wishes, and desires of groups over those of individuals and emphasize harmony, cooperation, cohesion, and conformity (e.g., Holmes, 2006).

The relevance of the collectivistic–individualistic continuum has begun to surface in sport psychology. Consider, for example, how success is defined. In a cross-cultural analysis of team sports, Catina (2006) found that the characteristic of personal optimism, defined as the tendency to interpret and explain one's daily experiences positively through personally controllable aspects, was extremely prevalent among

TABLE 1.1 NORMS, VALUES, BELIEFS, AND BEHAVIORS IN RELATION TO TEAM MEETINGS

	Values	Beliefs	Behaviors
Team 1	The time of each team member is equally valuable.	All team members (e.g., athletes, coaches, manager) are to be treated equally.	All members arrive on time, and the team meeting begins punctually.
Team 2	The time of senior group members is more valuable than the time of junior members.	Team members have different levels of status, with senior athletes and staff regarded as most critical to team decisions.	Junior members arrive before senior members, and the team meeting begins only when senior members arrive.

Norwegian, Croatian, and American mainstream athletes. Given this evidence, we could reasonably speculate that the cultures of these countries are individualistic, leading the majority of people from them to think, interpret, and explain their experiences individualistically. It is reasonable to assume that the majority of athletes from these individualistic cultures will interpret both success and failure primarily in terms of their own efforts.

People from collectivist societies, in contrast, typically evaluate their success in relation to their peers (e.g., Kashima, Yamaguchi, Kim, Choi, Gelfand, & Yuki, 1995) and attribute their successes to group-related factors (Miller, 1984; Norenzayan & Nisbett, 2004). Thus it is believed that how people define success may be influenced by whether they come from a collectivistic or an individualistic culture. This characteristic also could have some bearing on whether one-on-one or group-based sport psychology sessions are most effective with a given group.

Determining whether a society and its cultural groups are collectivistic or individualistic is not as easy as it might first appear. In the United States, for example, the mainstream culture is Eurocentric and individual in emphasis, but not all people share this characteristic. In chapter 9, Anthony Kontos illustrates the extensive relationship of self to community among Latin American athletes who migrate to pursue professional baseball careers. In the chapter 9 case example, Stress of Acculturation (page 107), Kontos describes how an athlete from a collective culture struggled to adapt to diverging individualistic values such as personal pursuits. The solution for such athletes, Kontos suggests, is to reconnect with their cultural communities, in this instance a pocket of collective-minded Dominican immigrants living in the United States. In a predominantly individualistic society, then, intervention strategies sometimes require refinements to suit the needs of clients originally from a collectivistic culture. Following this line of thinking, intervention strategies in collectivistic societies might also need to be tailored to align with pockets of individually oriented clients who integrate Eurocentric practices. In short, countries have mainstream cultures that might fall at a certain point on the individualistic–collectivistic continuum, but not every country is represented by one culture and one point on the continuum.

GOAL-DIRECTED BEHAVIOR

People participate in sport and competition for various reasons. The literature on achievement goal orientation in sport strongly supports the existence of task and ego orientations (e.g., Duda & Hall, 2001). Some primarily strive to improve their performance, whereas others are mostly driven to win. Many clients may neatly fit into one or both of these orientations. That being said, some athletes have culturally based definitions of success. For example, some might feel successful when they represent their cultural community or when community members are in attendance at their competitions (Schinke, Eys, et al., 2006). Others might place more weight on community ties than competition, resulting in a premature withdrawal from sport when they believe that those ties are severed (Schinke, Michel, et al., 2006). Reflective CSP practitioners need to uncover what their clients value and then try to understand situations from the client's cultural standpoint as opposed to their own.

Two personality measures have been linked with goal-directed behavior: hope and optimism. The sport literature has made the case that optimism is associated with success (Rettew & Reivich, 1995). It is commonly assumed that optimists (athletes and coaches included) explain success by attributing the outcome to personal and permanent characteristics, and they explain setbacks using a style that is often impermanent, external in accountability, and situational (Peterson, 2000; Seligman, 1991). As indicated in the previous section about individualism and collectivism, however, culture needs to be integrated in this discussion. Not every athlete will attribute success to internally controllable factors. For example, in chapter 10, Moraes and Salmela explain how Brazilian athletes who are members of a group called *Athletes of Christ* often attribute success to God in place of personal efforts and abilities. Such athletes garner hope from a power higher than themselves. Outside of sport, it has been indicated that Hindus ascribe success to contextual factors including the benevolence of those in the environment (Miller, 1984). Attempting to reinforce optimism using conventional Eurocentric wisdom and theoretical frameworks with a client from this culture is likely to fail due to the absence of shared understanding.

PERSONAL SPACE AND CONCEPTS OF TIME

It is well documented that personal space is a culturally informed phenomenon. Work in this area was pioneered by Edward T. Hall (1966). His research noted four zones or distances at which North Americans communicate with others. The zone of intimacy includes distances that range from actual body contact to 18 inches (46 centimeters). This zone is typically reserved for a person's most intimate acquaintances. The zone of personal distance extends from 18 inches to 4 feet (46 centimeters-1 meter). Conversation between close friends or trusted acquaintances occurs at this distance. Social distance ranges from 4 to 12 feet (1-3.5 meters), a zone that is appropriate for impersonal relationships, casual acquaintances, and formal work settings. Public distance includes all space beyond 12 feet (3.5 meters). Formal exchanges, such as a speaker addressing an audience, as well as interactions with strangers, occur at this distance. These ranges were based on research in mainstream North America.

The interpersonal space that is considered to be comfortable in different social situations varies among cultures and subcultures. For example, the zone of personal distance may be 18 inches to 4 feet (46 centimeters-1 meter) in mainstream North American culture, but it may be considerably less than that in some Latin American countries and considerably more in some North African and Asian countries. In addition, subcultural components may be involved, such as in the subculture of dance, where physical touching is common when communicating (Hanrahan, 2005b). This book, however, is limited to cultural considerations and does not include subcultural nuances. It is beyond the scope of this book to consider the role of the subcultures inherent in many sports (e.g., surfing, cricket, sumo wrestling).

Sport scientists and practitioners, of course, use culturally determined space parameters (proxemics) when meeting with athletes and coaches. In view of increasing globalization, however, they need to become aware of how cultural attitudes toward personal space can affect their interactions. In the course of international consulting, the authors of this chapter have found that our proxemic norms sometimes vary from those of our clients. For example, in Latin America, we have found that people typically communicate at slightly closer physical distances than those to which we are accustomed. When working with some indigenous clients, we discovered a second proxemic nuance: Clients may be more comfortable sitting alongside and at a slight angle to the sport psychologist during communication instead of face to face (Schinke & Hanrahan, 2006). Thus we have learned that in some cultures not only the appropriate size of personal space but also the appropriate positions of conversational participants are affected by both the nature of the relationship (e.g., formal versus informal) and proxemic norms.

Another culturally bound consideration is the concept of time. Some people organize their days in accordance with clock time, which might include 15-, 30-, or 60-minute slots. Others organize their days with a number of meetings planned, but their understanding of chronology might reflect a rela-

tional strategy where one event follows the other with no clear tie to a clock. When people with such contrasting strategies must meet together, they often experience frustration that stems from different conceptions of what time means and how it is kept. Some of the authors of this book have spoken elsewhere about the importance of viewing time through a cultural lens. For example, when Hanrahan (2005a) worked with orphans in Mexico, she found that they were often tardy for scheduled workshops. Similarly, Peter Terry (chapter 7) found that meeting times were relative when he consulted with athletes from India. His clients assumed that it was normal to arrive 30 minutes late and that given Terry's stature as a sport psychologist, he would arrive even later.

Western mainstream clients and consultants adhere to clock-based time. The strength of this approach to scheduling and its emphasis on punctuality is also its weakness. When people expect to begin and end discussions by the clock, their exchanges can be hurried, and it may seem that time is prioritized over the process of meeting and exchanging ideas, especially from the perspective of those who take an event-based approach. There is no easy solution to multicultural exchanges where people share differing notions of time. However, engaging in CSP requires an understanding and appreciation of how others regard time. If the consultant is event based and the client is time based, they should discuss which approach they will follow. Understanding often comes from clarification, and some of the initial CSP literature indicates that the negotiation of time can be an important part of cross-cultural relations.

GENDER AND CULTURE

Gender-based literature is an essential part of the CSP puzzle, and it has already made several important contributions. One contribution from the feminist sport psychology literature has been the call for diverse practices and more general ways of knowing (see Gill, 2000). Feminism has been defined as "a movement to end sexism, sexist exploitation, and oppression" (Hooks, 2000, p. viii) of women. Feminism also takes in account males and their enculturation, the silencing of men's emotions, and the personal and interpersonal costs for males living in sexist societies. As Ryba and Wright (2005) have noted, feminism offers CSP a great deal in terms of its interdisciplinary approach, acknowledgment of social differences, and movement toward increased power and representation (multiple voices) in research. The strategies proposed by women can also be considered as a general tactic with underrepresented cultural groups in sport. To do otherwise would parallel the limited approaches that were once taken to understanding and representing women, reductionist strategies that trivialized intuition and qualitative research, among other factors.

Discussions about gender intersect with CSP in a second way—each cultural group regards gender and gender-appropriate behavior in its own way. For example, in Vanuatu it is not uncommon to see heterosexual young men holding hands while walking down the road engaged in conversation, a behavior that would have a different connotation in many cultures. Myers and Spencer (2003) proposed that cultures are best understood in terms of a masculinity–femininity continuum, and cultures rated as low on the masculinity continuum tend to have flexible sex roles. For example, in mainstream Canadian culture, partners share housework, cooking, and family duties, and it is also common for families to be represented by two full-time wage earners. When consulting with Latin American male athletes, Kontos and Arguello (2005) found that their values reflected a high level of machismo, which presented a challenge for female consultants to overcome when working with male athletes. Awareness of diverse gender roles and behaviors within and across cultures has opened an important discussion that needs to be extended to multicultural sport settings. It seems, then, that gender provides an important

piece to the CSP puzzle both in terms of how to gain information and what may be considered as gender-appropriate behavior.

MOVING FORWARD

As indicated earlier, the majority of this book is devoted to applied practice with specific cultural groups. These groups reflect one or several of the following aspects: the mainstream culture of a region, ethnicity, race, and religion. Admittedly, this is a limited classification system, and there are many more factors to consider than this book, the first on CSP, can possibly cover. This text has been designed as a starting point in a larger discussion where the ultimate objective is cross-cultural understanding.

A summary of the main issues presented in this chapter appear in Cultural Awareness Basics for Sport Psychology. Some of the suggested strategies are not based on research characterized by exacting scientific rigor because such studies are not yet available; the field is too new to have produced a large body of such work. Rather, these strategies are meant to stimulate discussion, enhance understanding based on cross-cultural and in-cultural considerations, and stimulate researchers to the work necessary to provide more reliable results than anecdotal evidence can. Aside from these long-term goals, our immediate aim is to help readers develop a deepened appreciation of

CULTURAL AWARENESS BASICS FOR SPORT PSYCHOLOGY

Below are a few considerations proposed as starting points for those interested in multicultural exchanges in their research and practice.

- Sport psychologists need to account for themselves and their athletes in relation to the cultures of both parties.
- Athletes from cultures outside the mainstream vary along a continuum in terms of whether they have retained their cultural background or have assimilated into mainstream cultural norms, values, beliefs, and behaviors.
- There are as many within-culture nuances as between-culture nuances for sport psychologists to consider when working with athletes from cultures other than their own.
- Time and space (proxemics) are culturally bound, and their integration in multicultural exchanges contributes to effective CSP practice.
- Views of self and the collective hold varying amounts of weight by culture, though weighting must also allow for within-culture variations.
- Gender roles are culturally bound and vary from clearly defined to flexible.
- Cultural awareness is a skill that can be developed with exposure to multicultural settings, sensitivity, and practice.

the topic as well as to present some coherent and substantive CSP strategies.

We hope that readers will use this book as a reference guide to assist with culturally competent practice. The populations covered in the present edition are only a small representation of the many cultures and subcultures encountered by sport psychology consultants or coaches. That being said, many of the guiding principles discussed by the authors can provide helpful tips for engaging in culturally competent practice. It is hoped that the discussions inside (and as a result of) this book affirm the need for a culturally sensitive sport psychology that is modified in relation to each client's cultural identity.

A final note is necessary for our American readers in particular: In keeping with the spirit of the book, *football* refers to what Americans call *soccer*, and *American football* is used when referring to what Americans call *football*.

Rationale for Developing a Cultural Sport Psychology

Heather J. Peters, PhD, and Jean M. Williams, PhD

In this chapter we examine cultural sport psychology (CSP) from a sport psychology perspective in an attempt to answer the question, "Where has culture in sport psychology been hiding?" This perspective is not to be equated with a cultural studies approach to sport psychology (see chapter 3); instead, it employs preexisting sport psychology paradigms and concepts to examine cultural background. Throughout the chapter, we outline guidelines for working from this perspective and provide examples. Additionally, we discuss potential consequences of sport psychology consultants practicing without multicultural competence.

This chapter is written from a viewpoint of cultural influence, which suggests that culture influences behavior in sport settings (Chelladurai, Imamura, Yamaguchi, Oinuma, & Miyauchi, 1988). We believe that distinctions between collectivist and individualist cultural backgrounds are important in theorizing about sport psychology. Furthermore, we contend that sport psychology researchers, trainers (e.g., graduate school advisers, mentors), and practitioners should consider cultural contexts in attempting to understand psychological processes and that researchers need to compare sport psychology concepts across cultures to gain this understanding (Si & Lee, 2007).

CSP BASICS

Before we can answer the question of where culture in sport psychology has been hiding, we need to define the individual terms *culture, sport,* and *psychology.* In

addition, we need to review the current status of the field and outline a rationale for CSP.

DEFINITIONS

Culture was defined in the first chapter of this book, and many topics are included under the term. For example, socioeconomic status, gender, sexual orientation, race, cultural background, and disability status are some of the variables represented by culture. This chapter will focus on the variable of cultural background and refer to it as a set of behaviors, attitudes, and traditions that are shared by a group of people and passed down from one generation to the next (Myers, 2005).

Just as the term *culture* can have many meanings, so can *sport.* In the United States, sport represents an activity that involves physical exertion, has a set form, and has a set of rules (Berube et al., 1994). Internationally, sport is defined more broadly. For example, competition, exercise, physical activity, physical rehabilitation, and youth activities often fit under the umbrella of sport. In this chapter we use the broader meaning of the term. Finally, for the purpose of this chapter, the term *psychology* refers to the science that deals with mental processes and behavior of individuals and groups (Berube et al., 1994).

CURRENT PRACTICE IN RELATION TO CULTURE

Examination of the sport psychology literature has revealed a dearth of attention to cultural factors, particularly cultural background. From 1979 to

1987, authors in only 3.8% of empirical papers in the *Journal of Sport Psychology* identified participants' cultural backgrounds (e.g., race and ethnicity), and no authors addressed cultural background as a main component of their theoretical framework (Duda & Allison, 1990). Ram, Starek, and Johnson (2004) conducted a content analysis of the *Sport Psychologist, Journal of Applied Sport Psychology,* and *Journal of Sport and Exercise Psychology* from 1987 to 2000 and found that authors in only 11.5% of the articles identified participants' cultural backgrounds. Of those authors, only 1.5% examined cultural background as a main component of their theoretical framework.

The authors of this chapter conducted a content analysis of the article titles and abstracts of the three previously mentioned journals from 2001 to 2006. We found that the authors of only 4.8% of the articles used cultural background as a main component of their theoretical framework. Although this reflects a 320% improvement over the past six years, the end result is still grossly inadequate. Additionally, Gill (2004) indicated that no research or theoretical work has looked at culture in relation to developmental sport and exercise psychology. Thus sport psychology researchers are negligent when it comes to examining cultural background and its influence on sport psychology. Furthermore, because research typically influences practice or is representative of sport consultants' current practices, it would seem that many applied practitioners are also negligent.

RATIONALE FOR CSP

Authors both inside and outside of sport psychology have indicated why cultural background is important to the study and practice of sport psychology. Gill (2004) stated, "We can only make important contributions to the real world of developing sport and exercise participants when we incorporate gender and cultural analyses" (p. 497). Researchers in psychology have indicated that ethnic minorities typically respond differently to treatment than nonminorities, and these differences are probably attributable to cultural background (Bernal & Saez-Santiago, 2006).

Additionally, researchers in cultural psychology suggest that findings once thought to be universal are culturally bound (Hofstede, 1980), and although some theories may be universal, cultural background shapes the expression of the theory (Chang, Arkin, Leong, Chan, & Leung, 2004; Cheung & Leung, 1998). For example, later in the chapter we will discuss an article we published on a study involving college students from both East Asian and European American backgrounds (Peters & Williams, 2006). We found that although participants from both backgrounds

engaged in self-talk, their cultures influenced how self-talk related to performance. Thus, unless sport psychology takes a cultural approach to both research and practice, it will stay a unidemensional science at risk of becoming culturally obsolete (see also Sue, Bingham, Porche-Burke, & Vasquez, 1999).

Our warnings are in line with Duda and Allison (1990), who called the field of sport psychology to task and stated that failure to consider variability among cultural groups not only diminishes the importance of nondominant group experiences but also produces biased theoretical understandings. They cited Jackson (1989), who described the importance of research that considers ethnic and racial variation in human behavior. Jackson's point is so important that we cite it here again because, unfortunately, it has not been heeded by the majority of sport psychologists:

> Some recent literature emphasizes the role of race and ethnicity as resources which form a context for behavior. An even stronger observation is that racial and ethnic experiences may affect the very nature of social and psychological processes of interest. . . . In this latter view, race and ethnicity are not merely independent variables defining group membership and structural position, but instead more fundamentally may be related to basic psychological processes of perception, cognition, intellectual functioning, value acquisition, personality development and expression, and social interaction. Based upon this view, psychological theories . . . that claim universality should include as integral components how the nature of race and ethnicity may influence these basic psychological processes. (1989, p. 1)

In addition to the minimal attention given to cultural background in sport psychology research, attention to multicultural training in applied sport psychology is also lacking. In 2000, a review of sport psychology graduate training programs by Martens, Mobley, and Zizzi revealed an almost complete absence of multicultural training. Such training is important for properly preparing not only future researchers but also sport consultants. Sue (2006) states that sport consultants can become multiculturally competent by gaining cultural awareness, cultural knowledge, and cultural skills. First, he says that sport consultants need to be sensitive to their personal beliefs, values, and biases and how these may influence perceptions of the client, the client's problem, and the counseling relationship. Second, sport consultants should develop knowledge of the client's worldview, culture, and expectations for the counseling relationship. Finally, the sport consultant needs the ability to intervene in a manner that is culturally relevant and sensitive. Sue (2006), Kontos and Arguello (2005), and this book provide much useful information regarding how to become a multiculturally competent sport consultant.

For practitioners to become multiculturally competent, sport psychology needs to develop multicultural training that is based on multicultural research. Given this need for multicultural training and research, there is little excuse for cultural background being examined as a main component of an author's theoretical framework in only 1.5% of articles in three popular sport psychology journals from 1987 to 2000 (Ram et al., 2004). In an attempt to understand how cultural background has been examined in other journals, we conducted a preliminary review of article titles in the *International Journal of Sport and Exercise Psychology*. We found that the percentage of authors examining cultural background as a main component of their theoretical framework (e.g., Geisler & Kerr, 2007; Morgan, Sproule, McNeill, Kingston, & Wang, 2006) was higher (12.61%) than in the three sport psychology journals mentioned previously. Further, in this journal a section editor is specifically assigned to address cross-cultural concerns.

Although these findings are encouraging, it is inadequate to only discuss culture in select journals. Cultural background needs to be considered when designing, conducting, discussing, and applying all research because sport psychology does not take place in a vacuum outside the influence of cultural background. In the next section we will highlight three articles that demonstrate how culture influences theories and applications of sport psychology principles.

In summary, CSP is needed to increase our understanding of theories and sport psychology interventions that were previously thought to be universal. For example, in the next section we discuss how children from different cultural backgrounds are all motivated to participate in physical activity but have different participation motives (Yan & McCullagh, 2004). Thus, interventions for these different populations should be adapted accordingly. Additionally, CSP is needed to examine aspects of concepts that are not observed in the majority culture. For instance, in the next section we discuss a goal orientation derived from research that focuses on African Americans rather than European Americans (Gano-Overway & Duda, 1999). Increasing our understanding of theories and sport psychology interventions and identifying concepts pertinent to people from nondominant

cultural backgrounds will increase the multicultural competencies of researchers and practitioners.

TRADITIONAL TOOLS FOR UNCOVERING CULTURE

In this section we highlight three studies (i.e., Gano-Overway & Duda, 1999; Peters & Williams, 2006; Yan & McCullagh, 2004) that demonstrate what CSP from a sport psychology perspective should look like and the benefits that come from such work. The key to this approach is examining cultural background by employing preexisting sport psychology paradigms and concepts. The articles come from a sport psychology perspective because all of the authors

- identified a relevant idea in sport psychology,
- discussed a lack of attention in the literature to different cultural backgrounds,
- identified how findings in cultural and general psychology suggest that cultural background may affect the idea,
- conducted a study to test the effect of cultural background on the idea, and
- discussed the results and relevant applications for sport consultants.

Although the three articles are consistent in their approach to CSP, each has limitations. For example, Gano-Overway and Duda's (1999) results, though significant, did not report an effect size. Yan and McCullagh (2004) had a large sample size, which could have increased the likelihood of a type I error. Our study (Peters & Williams, 2006) combined people from various East Asian cultural backgrounds into one group for analyses, thus falling prey to the outgroup homogeneity bias (i.e., perceiving members of another group as more similar than members of one's own group). Furthermore, these three articles deal with non-elite populations (i.e., young children, high school athletes, and college students); however, other chapters within this book focus on elite populations.

In spite of these shortcomings, we believe that much can be learned from these studies. For example, these three articles were chosen because the authors considered the variability among cultural groups, recognized the importance of nondominant group experiences, and helped decrease biases and distorted theoretical understandings of sport psychology concepts (e.g., goal orientations, physical activity motivation, self-talk, practice persistence). The articles also contributed to the cultural awareness, cultural knowledge, and cultural skills of sport psychology researchers and practitioners. Following a general overview of the three articles, we summarize their implications for practitioners in an attempt to highlight why CSP is necessary and how it has direct implications for practitioners, coaches, and athletes.

GANO-OVERWAY AND DUDA (1999)

Gano-Overway and Duda proposed a new goal orientation derived from literature relating to African Americans. Their 1999 article indicated that although sport psychology researchers have explored many factors that affect motivation, the role of ethnicity and race in both central motivation concepts and the relationships among motivation-related variables has not been examined. The authors posited that in addition to learned drives and personality characteristics, personal factors, such as cultural background and gender, affect achievement motivation (Maehr, 1974; Maehr & Nicholls, 1980). For example, to date the majority of research on African American cultural values has compared African Americans with European Americans in relation to values exhibited by European Americans, not values exhibited by African Americans (Gano-Overway & Duda, 1999).

Gano-Overway and Duda examined theories related to African Americans and found that African Americans are influenced by both the European American ethos and their African heritage, which produces an African American culture that consists of nine realms, such as communalism, expressive individualism, harmony, movement, and spirituality (Boykin, 1983). Furthermore, similar to European American athletes, African American athletes have the goal of winning, but unlike European Americans they also have a desire to perform in a way that is shaped by individual style (Kochman, 1981). Thus, Gano-Overway and Duda posited a new goal orientation, expressive individualism (i.e., feeling successful when one's performance is not only skillful but also a unique and creative portrayal of oneself), and concluded that it is relevant to African Americans' motivation in sport.

Gano-Overway and Duda reached these conclusions by having 55 African American and 116 European American high school track athletes respond to instruments that examined task and ego goal orientations, expressive individualism, cooperation goal orientation (i.e., working with others to achieve success), and work-avoidance goal orientation (i.e., avoiding effort to achieve a goal). According to goal perspective theory, people with a task orientation

African American football players perform endzone dances, like "the squirrel" by Kelley Washington of the Cincinatti Bengals, to express individuality.
© AP Photo/David Kohl

derive perceptions of competence and ability from improving their performance, whereas people with an ego orientation derive perceptions of competence and ability from succeeding or failing in relation to others (Nicholls, 1984).

Results indicated that expressive individualism was a salient and multidimensional goal perspective among both the African American and European American athletes. Expressive individualism appears to include personal expression (i.e., expressing a unique style) and personal appearance (i.e., being innovative in outward appearance compared with others). As hypothesized, personal expression and cooperation were higher among African Americans than European Americans. Gano-Overway and Duda concluded that "athletes may come to the playing field with a tendency toward a particular motivational perspective that is in line with their cultural values" (p. 559).

Further analyses showed that, regardless of cultural background, personal expression related positively to task, ego, and cooperation orientations. This suggests that personal expression is a valuable goal orientation meriting examination in future motivation studies. In addition, personal expression was more strongly associated with the task factor for African Americans and the ego factor for European Americans. It was concluded that "personal expression seems to be a more task-related or intrinsic characteristic for African American athletes and suggests that African American athletes not only wish to master sport skills but also exhibit a creative and personal style in doing so" (p. 560). Therefore, personal expression may not conflict with hard work, personal improvement, and cooperative team effort.

The authors concluded that "these results, in combination with the expansive literature on the motivational significance of task versus ego goal perspectives, suggest that coaches should not attempt to diminish the value placed on (personal) expressive goals by African American athletes; rather, they should foster them in conjunction with task-involving goals" (p. 561). This work is a great example of how sport psychology should allow theories and ideas "to emanate from the values of the culture rather than via the imposing of variables pertinent only to the mainstream culture" (p. 561).

YAN AND MCCULLAGH (2004)

Yan and McCullagh (2004) compared young people from three cultural backgrounds (Chinese, Chinese American, and non-Chinese American) regarding their motivation to participate in physical activity. Yan and McCullagh stated that it is not known why children from individualistic and collectivist cultural backgrounds choose to participate in physical activities, even though Hayashi and Weiss (1994) and Yan and Thomas (1995) have suggested that cultural background might influence participation motivation. Such knowledge is important for promoting an active lifestyle for children in multicultural societies such as the United States.

Yan and McCullagh (2004) collected data from a physical activity motivation questionnaire provided to two age groups (i.e., 12-13 years, 14-16 years) for Chinese children from the metropolitan area of Guangzhou in mainland China (n = 155;), Chinese American children born in the United States (n = 122), and non-Chinese American children born in the United States (n = 147). Results indicated that Chinese American and non-Chinese American children participated in sport or physical activities for the competition and skills improvement whereas

Chinese children were motivated by getting fit and socializing. Furthermore, Chinese American children were motivated to participate by significantly more reasons than children from the other two groups. This finding may perhaps be attributed to acculturation in that two cultures rather than one influence Chinese American children. No age- or gender-associated differences occurred.

The authors suggested that the differences between the sociocultural and natural environments of Chinese and American cultures (e.g., history, lifestyle, values system, surroundings, climate) may have influenced motivation. The authors continued that "cultural differences, rather than gender- or age-related differences, may affect the motivation for sport participation" (p. 383). They concluded that "a cross-cultural approach may facilitate our understanding of youths' participatory motives for sports or physical activities, which can be helpful in organizing sports or physical activities for a diverse population" (p. 384).

PETERS AND WILLIAMS (2006)

We recently published the third and final article to be highlighted (Peters & Williams, 2006). We examined how people from collectivist and individualistic cultural backgrounds engaged in negative self-talk, how self-talk tied to performance, and how cultural background influenced practice persistence following positive and negative feedback. We pointed out that sport psychology researchers have invested considerable effort in examining the effects of self-talk on performance, and the majority have found negative self-talk to be associated with poorer performance (e.g., McPherson, 2000; Van Raalte, Brewer, Rivera, & Petitpas, 1994) and positive self-talk with better performance (e.g., Eklund, 1996; Gould, Eklund, & Jackson, 1992; Van Raalte, Brewer, Lewis, Linder, Wildman, & Kozimor, 1995). These findings have led to the implementation of cognitive self-talk interventions designed to decrease athletes' negative self-talk and foster positive self-talk (e.g., Williams & Leffingwell, 2002; Zinsser, Bunker, & Williams, 2001). Unfortunately, researchers who have studied self-talk have failed to consider whether differences in cultural background might affect their findings.

We suggested that the failure to investigate how cultural background influences self-talk and its relationship to performance and other behavioral and psychological constructs is problematic considering the cultural psychology literature on individualistic and collectivist cultural backgrounds (Peters & Williams, 2006). For example, cultural psychology research shows that a self-critical orientation is characteristic of people from collectivist cultural backgrounds, such as Japanese, Chinese, and Singaporeans, whereas positive self-regard is characteristic of people from individualistic cultural backgrounds, such as European Americans, Canadians, and Australians (e.g., Heine, 2001; Heine, Lehman, Markus, & Kitayama, 1999; Kitayama, 2002). Research also indicates that cultural background influences not only self-evaluations, it also influences motivation after receiving negative and positive feedback. For example, Japanese were motivated by correcting their shortcomings, but Canadians were motivated by thinking about success (Heine et al., 2001).

We compared the actual self-talk of East Asians and European Americans during performance on a dart-throwing task, determined the relationship of that self-talk to performance, and examined the effects of positive and negative feedback on practice persistence (Peters & Williams, 2006). Data on self-talk, dart-throwing performance, and practice persistence were collected from 26 East Asian participants who lived in the United States for 3 or fewer years and 54 European American participants who were born and raised in the United States.

Cultural background affected participants' responses to feedback in that European Americans who received positive feedback persisted longer than those who received negative feedback. This finding, taken together with previous research (Kamal & Blais, 1992), suggests that European Americans perceive negative feedback as unfavorable and inaccurate and thus are less motivated to persist at a task. The same cannot be said for East Asians because their practice persistence was not influenced by receiving different types of feedback.

As hypothesized, East Asians had a higher proportion of negative to positive self-talk than European Americans, and cultural background influenced the relationship between self-talk and performance. As East Asians' proportion of negative to positive self-talk increased, their dart-throwing performance improved. In contrast, for European Americans larger proportions of negative to positive self-talk were associated with poorer dart-throwing performance. We believe that a negative self-orientation among East Asians contributed to this finding. For example, the Japanese culture encourages the practice of *hanse*, which is the act of routinely reflecting on one's shortcomings and problems to increase the awareness that is thought to be instrumental for self-improvement (Kitayama, 2002).

In the article, we cautioned against using interventions to stop negative thinking or change negative self-talk to positive when working with athletes from East Asian cultural backgrounds until more research is conducted (Peters & Williams, 2006). Specifically, researchers need to determine whether cognitive interventions designed to increase positive self-talk and decrease negative self-talk facilitate the performance of athletes from collectivist cultural backgrounds, as they have been shown to do for athletes from individualistic cultural backgrounds (e.g., Highlen & Bennett, 1979; McPherson, 2000; Van Raalte et al., 1994). The findings in our study reinforced the importance of increasing cultural awareness in sport psychology research and consulting. We reiterated the need to "pay attention to Hofstede (1980) and others who believe that research findings once thought to be universal (e.g., the present belief that negative self-talk relates to poorer performance) are culturally bound" (p. 251).

IMPLICATIONS FOR CONDUCTING CSP

Findings from the previous three studies have implications for sport psychology researchers and practitioners and reinforce the need for approaching CSP using traditional sport psychology paradigms. The implications can be divided into those that highlight the advantages of the CSP approach and those that highlight the disadvantages of ignoring that approach.

ADVANTAGES OF IMPLEMENTING CSP

First, Gano-Overway and Duda (1999) derived a new goal orientation—expressive individualism—that is relevant to both African Americans and European Americans and that furthers our understanding of goal orientations. These findings can help coaches, commentators, and sport consultants more accurately interpret African American athletic behavior and encourage goal orientations that facilitate both individual and group performance.

Second, Yan and McCullagh (2004) proposed that knowledge about differences in motivation for participating in physical activity among young people from different cultural backgrounds may increase the effectiveness of outreach programs in multicultural societies. For example, after-school programs and recreational organizations might be able to increase attendance and the physical activity levels of young people, which could lead to benefits such as a decrease in childhood obesity.

Third, the present authors (Peters & Williams, 2006) provided evidence suggesting that sport consultants and coaches who work with East Asian athletes should use caution when implementing interventions designed to stop negative thinking or change negative self-talk to positive because their negative self-talk might actually improve performance. Additionally, when providing athletes with feedback, coaches should remember that European American athletes may be less motivated to participate following negative feedback compared with positive feedback and that feedback type does not appear to affect the practice persistence of East Asians.

These three examples of CSP reinforce the need for scientists and practitioners to become aware of how their cultural backgrounds influence their own values, worldviews, and beliefs. Furthermore, scientists and practitioners need to think about how these factors may influence not only their actions, thoughts, feelings, and behaviors but also the actions, thoughts, feelings, and behaviors of others. For instance, European American sport consultants or coaches may perceive an African American's attempt at expressive individualism as showboating instead of an attempt to feel successful through a skillful performance that is also unique and creative self-expression. This inaccurate perception could in turn negatively influence interactions and interventions with the athlete (Gano-Overway & Duda, 1999). More research similar to that described in the three articles will increase our understanding of constructs (e.g., goal orientations, participation motivation, self-talk, practice persistence), effectiveness of interventions, and multicultural competencies.

CONSEQUENCES OF IGNORING CSP

Because limited research has been done on sport psychology and cultural background, the consequences of practicing sport psychology without multicultural competency are unknown. For this reason we turn to findings from counseling psychology that are likely to apply to sport psychology.

Minority clients' perceptions of their therapists' multicultural counseling and general competency predicted their satisfaction with therapy (Constantine, 2002). For example, African American college students rated counselors with low racial consciousness less favorably than counselors with high racial consciousness, regardless of race. In addition, counseling literature shows that attrition rates following the first session of counseling are 25% to 43% higher for minority clients compared with majority clients (Rudolfa, Rappaport, & Lee, 1983; Sue & Sue, 1999). Following are six possible factors that may contribute to the discrepancy in attrition rates:

1. Counselors are at risk of misinterpreting emotional expressions, verbal styles, or mannerisms if they are unfamiliar with cultural norms, which could in turn affect the treatment outcome (Barona & Santos de Barona, 2003). For example, in some collectivist cultures an athlete who maintains direct eye contact with a coach or a sport psychology consultant could be perceived as aggressive or rude, whereas the same behavior could be perceived as attentive and respectful in some individualistic cultures.

2. A sport consultant's credibility can be reduced if the client's problem, treatment plan, and therapeutic goals are communicated in a way that is incongruent with the client's cultural values (Bernal & Saez-Santiago, 2006). For example, some consultants may find it beneficial to understand the relationship between athletes and their parents. However, this line of questioning could lead to premature termination by athletes from collectivist cultural backgrounds because the athlete may perceive the therapist as blaming the parents and thus bringing shame to the athlete's family.

3. A lack of cultural awareness can inhibit a sport consultant from structuring the consulting relationship in a way that is acceptable to both the consultant and the client. For instance, Latino clients have discontinued therapy because their therapist would not accept an invitation to socialize with them and their family. This invitation is related to *personalismo*, a cultural value suggesting that the therapist should be a constant presence of assistance and support (Barona & Santos de Barona, 2003). Thus, a multiculturally competent sport consultant working with Latinos would clarify the client's expectations at the beginning of the therapeutic process (Echeverry, 1997), including the limitations of their relationship, thus avoiding misunderstandings that could lead to early termination (Bernal & Saez-Santiago, 2006).

4. Attrition can occur if sport consultants are not aware of their own cultural beliefs, biases, and values and have not evaluated how these factors influence their clients. For example, the authors of this chapter are European American, and thus our cultural values promote an individualistic value system. We may be more inclined to promote differentiation and individuation (i.e., separation of self from others) with clients versus exploring interdependent values such as familialism (i.e., focus on connections with others), which is more common in some minority communities in the United States.

5. Early termination can occur if sport consultants have not explored the stereotypes they hold regarding different cultural backgrounds. These

beliefs can unintentionally influence the therapeutic working alliance, which has been found to significantly influence the effectiveness of consulting relationships (Martin, Garske, & Davis, 2000). Constantine (2007) wrote that "White therapists' conscious or unconscious displays of racial micro-aggressions against African American clients could create relationship difficulties in the form of poor counseling relationship bonds, therapeutic impasses, premature termination from counseling, and/or client dissatisfaction with treatment (Helms & Cook, 1999)" (p. 3).

6. Practicing under the guise of color blindness or the notion of treating everyone the same can facilitate early termination. For example, Constantine (2007) found support for the belief that attempting to minimize or ignore cultural and racial concerns negatively affects counseling outcomes for African American clients. Furthermore, African American participants became frustrated when counselors avoided racial issues in a counseling situation (Thompson & Jenal, 1994). If a highly skilled African American athlete presents with complaints regarding playing time, a so-called color-blind counselor might fail to consider that external factors (e.g., racial discrimination) could be contributing to the client's lack of playing time and put full responsibility on the athlete for the situation. This inaccurate perception could lead to client frustration and, in turn, early termination.

FUTURE DIRECTIONS

With globalization increasing not only the diversity of countries but also the diversity of people participating in sport, it is important that sport psychology practitioners and researchers become multiculturally competent. Becoming familiar with the main points

WHY A CULTURAL PSYCHOLOGY OF SPORT IS NEEDED

Sport psychology research, training, and practice lack sufficient attention to culture. As such, provided are a few key suggestions that we believe explain the need for CSP as part of the larger domain.

- Research in general psychology, cultural psychology, and sport psychology indicates that culture is an important factor in sport.
- We need to increase our understanding of theories and sport psychology interventions once thought to be universal.
- We need to examine aspects of sport psychology concepts that are not observed in the majority culture.
- CSP from a sport psychology perspective should
  - identify a relevant concept in sport psychology,
  - discuss a lack of attention in the literature on the chosen concept to different cultural backgrounds,
  - identify how findings in cultural and general psychology suggest that cultural background may affect the concept,
  - conduct a study to test effect of the cultural background on the concept, and
  - discuss the results and relevant applications for sport psychology consultants.
- CSP is necessary for practitioners to increase their cultural awareness, knowledge, and skills in order to increase their multicultural competency.
- Consequences of ignoring CSP include decreased perceived competency of the sport consultant by the client and decreased client satisfaction.
  - Theory-driven CSP instead of atheoretical cultural comparisons are needed in sport psychology research.
  - Assume neither that culture does not matter nor that everyone from a particular cultural background is the same; rather, use cultural awareness, knowledge, and skills to increase sensitivity to each individual while avoiding stereotyping.

of this chapter will be a small but helpful first step (See Why a Cultural Psychology of Sport Is Needed). In addition, practitioners and researchers cannot begin to move toward increased multicultural competency without grasping and applying the following three concepts:

1.   Sport psychology researchers and practitioners should resist generalizing findings from one cultural background to another. The literature on cultural psychology is rich with information suggesting that cultural background affects principles in sport psychology. For example, cultural background has been found to influence achievement motivation (e.g., Church & Katigbak, 1992; Kirkby, Kolt, & Liu, 1999; Ramirez & Price-Williams, 1976; Salili, 1996), the relationship between performance and self-efficacy (e.g., Eaton & Dembo, 1997; Kwok, 1995; Stigler, Smith, & Mao, 1985), the relationship between fear of failure and performance (e.g., Eaton & Dembo, 1997; Steinberg, Dornbusch, & Brown, 1992), internal and external sources of control (e.g., Iyengar & Lepper, 1999; Salili, Chiu, & Lai, 2001), attributions for success (e.g., Heine et al., 2001; Stevenson & Stigler, 1992; Yan & Gaier, 1994), and achievement prediction (e.g., Basow, 1984; Fryberg & Markus, 2008).

2.   Sport psychology researchers need to conduct theory-driven research rather than randomly comparing people from different cultural backgrounds. Kim, Williams, and Gill (2003) indicated that "cross-cultural studies in sport and exercise psychology have focused on the comparative study of psychological phenomena, without much emphasis on theoretical implications" (p. 170-171). Conducting atheoretical cultural research is similar to throwing darts in the dark and hoping that one lands on the dartboard. This type of guesswork is unnecessary because theories in psychology and cultural psychology can guide theoretical explorations of cultural differences pertinent to sport.

3.   Practitioners and researchers need to be wary of applying their newfound understanding of different cultural backgrounds in a blanket fashion with disregard for individual differences. The purpose of CSP is not for practitioners to group people into categories and to assume that everyone in a category is identical. Rather, the purpose of CSP is to provide sport consultants with cultural awareness, knowledge, and skills so that they have the foundation to work competently with clients from various cultural backgrounds while remaining sensitive to individual differences.

Culture in sport psychology has not been hiding; it has always been present. Unfortunately, most sport psychology researchers and consultants have been unaware of or indifferent to the existence of different cultures. Cultural psychology provides a framework that will aid sport psychologists interested in conducting culturally sensitive research and applied practice. The foundation for CSP is available, as evidenced in this chapter and the rest of this book. Will sport psychology build upon this foundation, or will it continue to ignore the influence of cultural background and persist in putting forth information that applies to only a portion of the world and provides a limited picture of reality?

Engaging Cultural Studies and Traditional Sport Psychology

Leslee A. Fisher, PhD; Emily A. Roper, PhD; and Ted M. Butryn, PhD

What kind of relationship between (political) community and its individual members should we privilege? Or, to put it succinctly: What model of citizenship should we privilege? (Duhacek, 2006, p. 15)

What type of sport psychology do we want to have? For example, what kind of athlete do we want to emerge after our work with a client is finished? In two recent papers (Fisher, Butryn, & Roper, 2003, 2005) we argued that questions such as these can be explored through exposure to the cultural studies literature. Such literature can enhance the effectiveness of sport psychology professionals whether they are conducting research, teaching, or consulting. We suggest that although scholars (e.g., Green, 1996) have posited an uneasy relationship between cultural studies and other disciplines in the academy, such tensions are necessary to move disciplines such as sport psychology forward to a cultural study of sport psychology. In our previous work, we hoped to begin this movement forward with three interrelated projects:

- Interrogating and critiquing dominant sport psychology practices
- Encouraging personal examination and reflection by sport psychology professionals regarding the settings in which we work (i.e., universities, sporting organizations, or private practice), particularly institutional structures; legal, political, and financial conditions of existence; and the flows of power and knowledge that emanate from them

- Working with local or national constituencies that connect social justice and sport (e.g., Nike's Educating for Justice campaign, Schinke and Hanrahan's [2006] work with aboriginal peoples and sport)

The task of this chapter is to examine our first project in more depth: to explore what sport psychology researchers and practitioners can gain from cultural studies of sport psychology based on a critique of dominant sport psychology practices. We introduce six sections, each of which integrates traditional sport psychology and cultural studies:

1. The dominant underpinnings of sport psychology versus a postmodern way of thinking

2. Typical research focuses in sport psychology based on these orthodoxies

3. Sport psychology theories and methods versus the intellectual sensibilities of cultural studies

4. Personality research versus a cultural studies approach that recognizes constructions and locations of identity

5. Eurocentrism versus nationalism, postmodernism, postcolonialism, and globalization

6. How we might reconstruct sport psychology as cultural sport psychology (CSP)

We end with conclusions and suggestions for future research and practice.

POSITIVISM VERSUS POSTMODERNISM

According to Brustad (2002), although the subdiscipline of sport psychology is relatively new, its foundations rest on traditional scientific paradigms, particularly positivism. This chapter has limited space for delving into the history of positivism, and many sport studies scholars are moving beyond it at the same time that they recognize their training was based in it. However, a brief discussion of positivism is warranted here. Brustad suggests that philosophers such as John Stuart Mills contributed to this theory of knowledge as the orthodox science in Europe before the 18th century (Martens, 1987). Brustad critiques positivism as the "most trustworthy form of inquiry" (p. 24), especially given that it is only one form of knowledge development. As he states, beliefs such as the possibility of objectivity, a focus on reductionist practices, and dependence on quantifiable forms of knowledge are major characteristics of positivism.

A CSP theorist or practitioner could contrast such positivist beliefs with postmodern beliefs in at least four major areas: self-concept, moral and ethical discourse, art and culture, and globalization. For example, a researcher of cultural studies of sport psychology could examine how athletes construct and reconstruct their identities from a variety of subcultural sources and locations—an athlete is not just an athlete but a gendered, raced, classed, sexually oriented, able-bodied human being. Such a poststructural theoretical orientation assumes that athletes' identities are multiple, fragmented, and dependent upon location rather than fixed or unchangeable (see figure 3.1).

Such researchers could also explore how athletes' moral and ethical selves are socially constructed and shift depending upon the worldviews of those in power around them, especially athletic officials, coaches, and administrators. Sport could be scrutinized as a cultural entity to include a focus on a new definition of *athlete* that does not privilege one sport over another or one type of athlete over another, and such definitions could be constantly renegotiated. And because of the continually changing nature of our world as globalization advances, researchers could investigate how quick and unprecedented access to people and information through the Internet and other technology destabilizes boundaries between countries and people and how this affects athletes' experiences of sport participation.

FIGURE 3.1 Just as you can see either a vase or two faces in this picture, so the athlete's identity will shift depending on the eye of the beholder.

FOCUSES OF TRADITIONAL SPORT PSYCHOLOGY RESEARCH

A postmodern viewpoint enables us to deconstruct the previous one-size-fits-all theoretical stance of sport psychology. Cultural studies enables us to dismantle traditional disciplinary boundaries and put a new frame in place for describing everyday practices related to sport and exercise in more complex ways.

CURRENT FOCUSES

Extending our previous work (Fisher et al., 2003, 2005) where we examined the forms of knowledge that have been used the most in sport psychology, the politics that inform such knowledge, and how cultural studies could help us interrogate those forms of knowledge, we began by reviewing introductory texts in sport psychology to determine which topics make up the established boundaries of knowledge of the discipline and which disciplinary homes they originate in (H. Wright, personal communication, November 12, 2003).

For example, when we examined textbooks written by Duda (1998), Gill (2000), and Weinberg and Gould (2003, 2007)—all prominent sport psychology researchers—we discovered that sport psychology is bounded by such constructs as group dynamics, aggression, anxiety, motivation, psychological skills and skills training, self-concept, body image, affect, mood, emotion, and morality. In addition, special considerations consisting of gender, race, class, sexual orientation, disability, ethics, developmental issues, and cross-cultural concerns are tacked on, usually near the end of the text, or worse yet, they are mentioned only in passing (see, for example, Cox, 2006).

Already we see that certain constructs in sport psychology are *primary* or privileged (e.g., motivation and anxiety) whereas others are *marginal* or special (e.g., gender, race, sexual orientation, and disability). Introductory textbooks for exercise psychology fare no better. In the exercise psychology textbook written by Berger, Pargman, and Weinberg (2002) and in the sections on exercise psychology in Weinberg and Gould's text (2007), we found similar disciplinary boundaries with a focus on exercise and enhanced self-concept, personality, mood and mood alteration, quality of life, motivation, and injury, as well as similar special concerns such as children and exercise, older age, eating disorders, exercise addiction and dependence, and substance abuse. Again, we see that motivation, personality, and self-concept, all of which are based on modernism with static views of the self and truth with a capital *T*, define exercise psychology whereas the experiences of younger people, older people, people with disabilities, and so-called disordered people are outside the normal frame of study.

EXPANDING OUR VIEW

Such framing in sport and exercise psychology has been heavily influenced by the discipline of psychology (and its foundations in liberal humanism and social democratic orthodoxies) with a focus on controlling variables and psychological constructs through scientific study and the establishment of laboratories within which to manipulate and observe human behavior (Fisher et al., 2005; Gill, 2000). As we mentioned before, the goal appears to be to master the scientific method, systematically examine and describe phenomena, and refine and develop theory. However, as Gill (2000) intimated, this framing leaves out other sources of knowledge such as intuition, tenacity, logic, and authority (see Thomas & Nelson, 1996, for further discussion).

In addition, feminist postmodern scholars such as Fernandes (2003) have proposed that knowledge "is not a neutral entity, but a set of practices that produce relationships of power" (p. 79). Certain fields of inquiry (knowledges) in the academy in general—and in sport and exercise psychology in particular—are therefore marginalized and deemed unimportant (e.g., intuition). Of interest to feminist and postmodern scholars is the fact that such marginalized fields of inquiry are primarily connected to those who deviate from social norms, such as gay, lesbian, bisexual, transgendered, and transsexual people; women; people of color; and native peoples.

Cultural studies of sport psychology could help us examine how certain fields of inquiry in sport psychology have been privileged over others and how these established, power-filled, and dominant fields of inquiry have profoundly shaped the structure of sport psychology as well as framed the way we view its practice. For example, employing a traditional sport psychology framework (e.g., assuming that athletes will come see us because we have certain knowledge) with a nontraditional population (e.g., an athlete from another culture who does not believe in psychology or sport psychology) is not as effective as matching our practices to our constituents. Therefore, following our initial inquiry into privileged traditional fields of inquiry in sport psychology, we must also examine how such fields have come to be defined by certain theories and methods.

DIVERGENT APPROACHES

In 2003, we suggested that cultural studies is not a "monolithic body of theories and methods" (using Storey, 1996, p. 1), but rather a blurring of interdisciplinary boundaries and an integration and appropriation of theories and methods from a variety of fields such as anthropology, communication studies, film and music studies, history, literary criticism, sociology, and women's studies. Such integration allows researchers to maintain an intellectual sensibility revolving around a certain theoretical orientation or critical stance such as postmodernism, for example, rather than adherence to strict disciplinary boundaries. In contrast, the field of sport psychology has been organized around a traditional set of theoretical and methodological practices and, until recently, has awarded little attention to cultural studies (Fisher et al., 2003, 2005; Krane, Waldron, Michalenok, & Stiles-Shipley, 2001; Ryba & Wright, 2005).

Giroux (1994), in her critique of education, proposes the following, which also aligns with our perspective:

While other disciplines have appropriated, engaged, and produced new theoretical languages in keeping with changing historical conditions, colleges of education [and sport psychology programs] have maintained a deep suspicion of theory and intellectual dialogue and thus have not been receptive to the introduction of cultural studies. (p. 278)

THEORIES AND METHODS APPROACH

Borrowing further from Giroux (1994) and applying that work to sport psychology, we argue that cultural sport psychologists may encounter resistance when attempting to incorporate cultural studies into their research or applied work. We suspect, as does Giroux, that this potential resistance will be due in part to the "narrow technocratic models that dominate" the field (p. 278; see also Ryba & Wright, 2005; Wright, 2007). Due to our alignment with psychology and kinesiology—disciplines in which studying the self often becomes separated from social context—we must consider what knowledge is potentially missing and what we can learn from theoretical frameworks outside the traditional parent disciplines. As Giroux argues, "The slavish adherence to structuring the curriculum around the core disciplinary subjects is at odds with the field of cultural studies whose theoretical energies are largely focused on interdisciplinary issues" (p. 278).

Disciplinary coursework, not intellectual sensibilities, is rewarded in the practice of sport psychology. For example, examination of the coursework requirements for Association for Applied Sport Psychology (AASP) certification reveals that students in sport psychology may have few opportunities to study or emphasize theoretical work outside their core subject areas. Courses on topics such as women, sport, and culture; critical race and postcolonial theory; and theorizing bodies (graduate courses offered at many U.S. universities) are considered valuable sources of theoretical knowledge for the sport and exercise psychology professional, but they are not required. A course with a theme such as women, sport, and culture often draws heavily upon theoretical and methodological analyses from cultural studies, feminist theory and women's studies, sport sociology, and history, encouraging students to critically examine the historical and social context in which women and men participate in and make sense of their sporting experiences. One goal of such a course is to enhance students' awareness of the complex relationships among gender, sport, history, and society so that they

can become critical sport professionals, consumers, and participants.

INTELLECTUAL SENSIBILITIES APPROACH

In terms of intellectual sensibilities used in research (when researchers employ a certain theoretical orientation or critical stance such as postmodernism, for example, rather than adhering to strict disciplinary boundaries), one example of a cultural studies approach is Krane and colleagues' (2001) examination of body image among female exercisers and athletes. Employing a feminist cultural studies framework, focus groups were conducted with 8 female collegiate athletes and 10 female exercisers regarding their ideal body image and their feelings and behaviors surrounding exercise and eating. The researchers found that the majority of participants compared themselves against an unrealistic ideal body. For the athletes, two distinct body images emerged—an athletic female body image and a culturally ideal female body image. The female athletes' perceptions of each body image depended on the social context. For instance, in the sport context of competition and practice, the athletes understood the function and purpose of their bodies, expressing positive attitudes toward their athletic physiques. Outside the sport domain, however, these same athletes expressed dissatisfaction with their bodies, indicating that they deviated from the culturally ideal body.

In addition, body image fluctuated depending upon athletes' daily eating and exercise patterns. As Krane and colleagues (2001) suggested, the findings present "a need for concern among sport psychology professionals regarding the eating and exercise patterns of female athletes" (p. 25), and, we would add, a concern regarding which body images are privileged over others. Previous research regarded body image as a stable attribute, but Krane et al. focused on body image as culture bound, exploring the ways in which the social context may influence female athletes' perceptions of and experiences in the female athletic body. These findings also point toward a reconsideration of existing methods for measuring body image due to the fluctuation that may occur. Finally, both researchers and practitioners need to consider the multidimensional nature of body image among female athletes, paying close attention to the context in which female athlete identity is defined and situated. This example of a cultural studies of psychology approach to research shows how the ways in which studying the social environment and its meaning become critical to understanding athletes' sport experiences (see figure 3.2).

FIGURE 3.2 A cultural studies of psychology approach pre-supposes that self-identity may change from one sociocultural context to another.

Lastly, although many in sport psychology may experience discomfort when attempting to incorporate the tenets of cultural studies into their research or applied work, it is helpful to note the positive value of such discomfort when employing new strategies. This discomfort or tension is necessary to advance our knowledge. Cultural studies presents vast opportunities for sport psychology students and professionals to reconsider the nature of theory and practice as well as what it means to educate and certify future professionals.

DIVERGENT ASSUMPTIONS ABOUT THE SELF

Traditional sport psychology and CSP also diverge in their views of self. As an example, let's imagine we are working with a collegiate athlete transitioning out of sport. If we are traditional sport psychologists, our ideas about the self are shaped by three basic but incomplete assumptions about the nature of the self:

- Multiple selves exist and vary as a function of context or domain, which means this transitioning athlete has an athlete self, an academic self, and so on (Brewer, Van Raalte, & Petitpas, 2000).

- Athletic identity is malleable. In other words, when competing in sport, this athlete had

significantly more athletic identity than now, and the athlete can transfer mental skills learned on the playing field to the work environment.

- A decrease or ending of the athlete self directly relates to emotions or behavior, albeit in individually experienced ways. For example, for this athlete, the transition out of sport will result in significant distress whereas for others it will come as a relief (see Fisher, 2001, p. 451, for a similar discussion).

A cultural studies of sport psychology approach would push us to reckon with our understanding of power as we choose theories related to the self to explain this athlete's transition out of sport and also our intervention techniques. Such an approach would emphasize power dynamics and relationships as central to its mission by seeing theoretical and intervention choices and definitions of the self as advantaging some people and disadvantaging others.

For example, if the athlete self is a cultural and historical invention located in a particular time and space, then a cultural studies of sport psychology approach would go beyond what traditional sport psychology researchers have done to incorporate an analysis of power as it relates to athletic transition and identity during this transition. Such a power analysis might include questions regarding who has the power in this collegiate sport organization to determine who transitions out of sport and who doesn't; how this power is created, maintained, and negotiated and how it affects athletes' transition out of sport; what role gender, race, class, type of sport, ethnicity, and sexual orientation play in transitions out of sport; what role nationhood and national identity play; how the sport subculture that this athlete was a part of and its work ethic relate to the athlete's experience of what is expected during the transition; and perhaps most importantly, what social functions are served by proposing that the transitioning athlete self has particular characteristics that the sport psychology consultant needs to address.

In other words, if we locate the problem of athlete transitioning and the subsequent intervention within the athlete—for example, teaching the athlete how to manage emotions, reframing the sport experience, exploring a new identity postathletics—might we also be colluding in the power dynamic of the sport organization if we don't interrogate the institution of sport itself and how it has influenced a transitioning athlete?

At the same time, postmodern and poststructural theorists have wrestled with the idea of self, and it is important to use their insights in our work with athletes and exercisers. Ward (1997) posited that postmodernism examines the "various ways that self-identity is something fabricated 'on the outside'" (p. 138). Further, he suggested that postmodernism reveals how "appearance and behavior *produce* the self as well as express it" (p. 138). Sport sociologists such as M. Ann Hall (1996) and Pirkko Markula (2003) took up these notions to unravel the ways in which women struggle with their physical selves. Hall cited studies such as Frigga Haug's (1986) collective work on how females' bodies serve as the axis around which their own sexuality is conceptualized and how they learn to be girls, and Markula explicated how a Foucauldian framework (based on the work of Michel Foucault; see Foucault, 1976) might help us help clients challenge the practices of domination they experience by critically reflecting on power, self, and ethics. At present, we know of no work in sport psychology that uses such theories as a framework.

EUROCENTRISM AND THE POLITICS OF SPORT PSYCHOLOGY IN ACADEMIA

Raymond Williams (1960) suggested that during the 1800s, the predominant definition of *culture* was disrupted. What had once been defined as "coming to mean what was most elevated, sensitive, essential, and precious" about "high society" related to "the best creations of modern Europe" (Clifford, 1999, p. 69) was dismantled as globalization began to occur. In an anthropological sense, culture was revealed in other countries as alternative ways of life with other art forms and so on. However, Eurocentrism still had a hold on the academy.

EUROCENTRISM

CSP might provide insight into, and perhaps a critique of, this Eurocentrism and how it has formed the basis of mainstream psychology and, by extension, sport psychology. As defined by Delgado and Stefancic (2001), "Eurocentrism is the tendency to interpret the world in terms of European values and perspectives and the belief that they are superior" (p. 146). Many of the issues that sport psychology, especially applied sport psychology, addresses are framed in Eurocentric terms. Thus, cultural studies frameworks can help us more closely interrogate the underlying assumptions of taken-for-granted concepts, such as competitiveness, mental toughness, and confidence, and consider how they might be read through other cultural lenses. As Barker (2003) pointed out, global cultural flows have affected our lives in fundamental ways such that the networks we engage in extend across cultural and national boundaries. We need to ask how a term such as *mental toughness* is read by athletes from different cultures and how ideas about competition and group dynamics are interpreted by athletes with differing belief systems.

Various examples of national and cultural differences might relate directly to athletes working with practitioners. The entire notion of applied sport psychology with its focus on the mental aspect of performance and well-being does not fit well with traditional Eastern conceptualizations of the mind–body connection. Some Asian American groups, for example, appear to engage in somatization (i.e., expressing psychological distress in the form of physical symptoms) more than other racial and ethnic groups do, in part due to cultural differences over what constitutes mental, emotional, and physical ailments (Chun, Enomoto, & Sue, 1996). Further, some traditional Asian cultural values such as community and cooperation may be in tension with Western sport psychology approaches to focus, competitiveness, and so on.

For example, in California in early 2007, the Monta Vista High School boys' basketball team in the San Francisco Bay Area made headlines because the starting five players were all Asian American athletes, an uncommon phenomenon in local high school basketball leagues. Cultural norms and stereotypes were woven into the discourse surrounding the team, from the players' need to balance sport with academics due to family expectations to the racialized notions of having to "play the game smarter" in order to compensate for a lack of height (Kiefer, 2007, p. 1D). A traditional, ethnocentric approach to sport psychology consulting may be effective in such multicultural settings, but it may also result in poor service. Our hope is that this book prompts further research on the complex relationship between sport psychology interventions and multiculturalism.

Aside from intervention strategies, even sport metaphors and examples used by academics and practitioners may be problematic because young athletes in diverse regions have little in common with respect to cultural background, language, and identity. In short, although some work on multicultural issues in sport psychology has been done, the overarching Eurocentric approach to working with athletes is worthy of much more critique and research using a cultural studies approach.

POLITICS OF RACE AND CLASS

Not only are the concepts discussed in mainstream sport psychology textbooks and literature worthy of critical examination, but so are the sites where sport psychology research is practiced (i.e., professional and college environments). Although precise numbers are elusive, it appears that applied sport psychology has gained steam in college environments. In previous work (Fisher et al., 2003, 2005), we address the need for sport psychology consultants and academics working in higher educational settings to adopt an athlete-as-citizen model of consulting. One topic we have not discussed in terms of the college setting, however, is the politics of race and class and their relationship with sport psychology consultants.

In their theoretical discussion on sport, identity, and cultural politics as they relate to U.S. urban areas, Giardina and McCarthy (2005) provided a useful critique of sport films, particularly Spike Lee's (1998) basketball drama, *He Got Game*. They argued that Lee's film, though seemingly critical, is mired in neoliberal notions of meritocracy and what sport sociologist Jay Coakley (2007) would call *functionalist perspectives* that center not on power and transformative justice but on using sport as a way out of poverty. So, how do the comments of Giardina and McCarthy relate to sport psychology? As numerous scholars in sport sociology, critical race theory, and cultural studies have noted, minority athletes at many National Collegiate Athletic Association (NCAA) Division I institutions (i.e., large universities) face stressors that other athletes do not, particularly when they

participate in revenue-producing sports (which only holds true at a select number of schools).

Critical sport sociologists such as Coakley (2007) have outlined issues that some minority athletes face, such as social isolation, and Eitzen (2000) termed the structural inequities experienced by Black athletes in major college programs as the *college sport plantation*. According to these scholars, many Black college athletes face stressors that are different from those that White athletes face, including a lack of campus activities representing the interests of Black students, cultural differences between themselves and White athletes and coaches, and the confrontation of other students' racial stereotypes, including athletes. Further, Eitzen (2000) and other scholars have argued that Black athletes in revenue-producing sports such as American football and basketball have become commodities that, if injured, become disposable. Although the work on cultural competency and multicultural consulting done by scholars such as Kontos and Breland-Noble (2002) is encouraging and its inclusion in the 2007 sport psychology textbook by Cox is noteworthy, the larger systems of power within which Black athletes exist have not been recognized or analyzed as thoroughly as they might be.

Cultural studies scholars critique the demonization of so-called inappropriate forms of culture and expression, as do numerous sport studies scholars (e.g., Hughes, 2004; Majors, 1998; Walton, 2001). Several recent examples involving African American basketball and American football players (male and female, college and professional) provide a useful entrée into a larger discussion of how the broad concept of the mental game relates to culturally contingent and individually mediated means of self-expression. The mainstream media have criticized players such as National Football League (NFL) wide receiver Terrell Owens for postscore celebrations (e.g., Owens taking a marker from his sock in a 2002 game and signing the football in the end zone), but we would look to Majors' (1998) notion of the *cool pose* to inform our understanding of young, Black, male athletes. Majors argues that some African American men, including athletes, have responded to systematic inequities by adopting a set of behaviors that allows for some degree of personal empowerment and self-expression. Hughes (2004) also argues that the National Basketball Association (NBA), for example, profits from the strategic appropriation of urban hip-hop aesthetic while silencing forms of self-expression it sees as too Black. In short, the intersection between cultural forms of expression and the psychology of performance have not been adequately addressed in sport psychology.

Our point here is not to suggest that sport psychology consultants are intentionally contributing to a larger corporate sport system that may not itself be in an athlete's best interest. Rather, we suggest that the entire applied field needs to carefully and honestly delve into questions of culture and power. Additionally, college athletes graduate in numbers just slightly above those of nonathletes, and African American athletes graduate at slightly higher rates than African Americans who are not athletes. Thus, the idea that corporate sport is wholly bankrupt of redeemable values and useful possibilities has little merit.

(RE)CONSTRUCTING SPORT PSYCHOLOGY

In conclusion, we argue that applied sport psychology is characterized by what Coakley (2007) called *functionalist approaches* to sport that overemphasize cooperation and unity while glossing over power, privilege, oppression, and identity politics. The authors of this chapter have written and presented on such issues for several years, but the largely uncritical ideological infrastructure of applied sport psychology has not changed substantially even as the global landscape following the September 11 terrorist attacks has transformed sport, U.S. society, and global relations in fundamental ways. If, as sport sociologists and

A cultural studies approach invites us to explore power in sport within and across races and ethnic groups.
© Jamie Squire/Getty Images Sport

HOW WE WOULD DESCRIBE THE IDEAL CSP

We began this chapter by asking, "What kind of sport psychology do we want?" In sum, it can best be described as CSP with the following emphases:

- A focus on athlete identities as multiple, fragmented, and dependent upon location rather than fixed or unchangeable
- A choice of academic methods and theories based on an intellectual sensibility revolving around a certain theoretical orientation or critical stance versus strict interdisciplinary boundaries
- An emphasis on seeing the developing athlete in a web of power dynamics and relationships that advantage some selves while disadvantaging others
- An interrogation of the institution of sport and how and when it has influenced athlete identities
- A critical examination of the politics of race and class and how they affect athletes and consultants
- An addressing of embedded politics and unacknowledged contributions in sport related to potentially exploitative relationships and damaging long-term consequences for health

We believe that there is no better time than the present to engage with these ideas in our field.

cultural studies scholars have long argued, sport is not, as Harry Edwards phrased it, "the toy department of human affairs" (HBO Home Video, 1995) but rather an important social institution and popular cultural phenomenon, a sport psychology that fails to address its embedded politics and unacknowledged contributions to potentially exploitative relationships and damaging long-term health concerns is highly problematic.

Following our discussion of AASP certification guidelines in the previous sections, we argue that the sport psychology consultants working in the corporatized Division I structure of U.S. intercollegiate athletics should critically assess their own contributions in ways that prompt them to take a stronger stance for justice and equity against coaches and administrators if necessary. We challenge ourselves and other sport psychology consultants to confront racist, sexist, and homophobic practices at all levels of organized sport, whether it involves the athletes with whom we work or the coaches and administrators for whom we work.

In the end, that is the question: For whom do we work, and what do we stand for in our work?

Applied sport psychology can be complicit in several troubling aspects of high-level sport and its institutional structures, or it can be a force of resistance where there is little resistance to speak of at present. Cultural studies at its best contains an activist component that frames cultural studies as far more than just engaging in the work of a traditional academic (see How We Would Describe the Ideal CSP). Though the notion of organic intellectualism or the idea that those within the academy (i.e., sport psychology) and elsewhere (e.g., writers, political activists, community organizers) has been the subject of some critique (Barker, 2003; Hall, 1992), we argue that sport psychology professionals are not only uniquely positioned to do critical work, but they are obligated to such endeavors if they subscribe to a cultural studies model of sport psychology. There is no time like the present to engage in these questions.

PART II

CONCEPTUAL REFLECTIONS

Part II comprises three chapters, which highlight a few of the conceptual issues that can be considered in reflexive cultural sport psychology (CSP). In chapter 4, the author identifies some commonly held assumptions of sport psychologists. The chapter elucidates how one might begin to integrate culture by first considering the status quo of the profession. The authors in chapter 5 extend the CSP discussion of multiculturalism to gender. The views of the authors are framed in relation to sport and activity in the United States. The chapter also features the multicultural guidelines of the American Psychological Association (APA) as part of the larger discussion. Of course, other multicultural guidelines are available when working with specific cultures; however, the guidelines featured in chapter 5 are helpful for informing general approaches to CSP. Finally, chapter 6 discusses several possible avenues for CSP research. Similar to many researchers, the authors of chapter 6 prefer postmodern methods in their work, although their preferences are not the only approach to gathering and making sense of research in multicultural exchanges.

Similar to part I, the authors in part II were asked to provide suggestions for the reader to consider in relation to the topic at hand. These final words are intended as hints that will need refining when working within specific multicultural contexts. As a whole, the chapters in part II offer possibilities for multicultural research and practice.

Understanding Your Role in Cultural Sport Psychology

Tatiana V. Ryba, PhD

The previous chapters introduced cultural sport psychology (CSP), which involves a variety of approaches that differ in philosophical underpinnings, terminology, political focuses, and priorities (see chapters 2 and 3). Cultural psychology attempts to elucidate the "cultural construction of the person including thoughts, emotions, motivation, development, [and] identity" (Kral, Burkhardt, & Kidd, 2002, p. 155) and how mainstream psychology privileges an ethnocentric (White, male, heterosexual, middle-class) way of knowing.

This chapter opened with a citation that highlights the underlying assumptions of my arguments. First and foremost, I believe that authoritative science is a social institution, and its practices cannot be divorced from sociohistorical and cultural contexts. Because sport psychology professionals work within the constraints of academic and business institutions, individual practices tend to reflect dominant social, cultural, and ideological norms.

My second assumption is that most sport psychology professionals are devoted to providing ethical, theoretically informed, and just services. Many of us wholeheartedly believe in doing good and doing well as practitioners of sport psychology, whether we are teachers, researchers, or consultants; hence, we tend to be uncomfortable with critical discourses, perhaps due to an uneasy feeling that the critique is directed at us. Critical discourses of sport psychology (e.g., feminist, queer, and cultural praxis[1]) critique the status quo, elucidating the role of power in the production and distribution of knowledge. Critical interroga-

tion into existing professional practices focuses on untangling structural power relations within a social discourse[2] and therefore does not target individuals; however, we have agency[3] to work against the grain of dominant, often taken-for-granted, sport and institutional systems.

> The discipline of psychology is moving beyond the myth of detached neutrality to discover virtue and to recognize politics as forces which determine ethical behavior . . . . The concept of personal individual ethics needs to be extended to the social and cultural environment, because the environment influences the ethical behaviour of psychologists and the quality of life of all citizens. (Pettifor, 1996, p. 1)

In this chapter, I offer several vantage points for critical self-reflection on the role of sport psychology professionals and our possible future in professional discourses that are regulated by the "tacit rules [of] what can and cannot be said, who can speak with the blessing of authority and who must listen, whose social constructions are valid and whose are erroneous and unimportant" (Kincheloe & McLaren, 2000, p. 284). I begin by outlining a cultural praxis version of sport psychology, which is an extension of my collaboration with Handel Kashope Wright on a theoretical articulation of applied sport psychology with cultural studies and is influenced by Donald Schön's (1983) reflection-in-action model. I then provide five strategies for acquiring the competencies that are necessary for effective and just delivery

---

[1]cultural praxis—An active and reflexive process that links theory, lived culture, and social action in a dialectical reciprocity. [2]discourse—A historically, socially, and institutionally specific regulated practice that accounts for a number of statements, categories, and beliefs. This usage stems from the work of Michel Foucault (1972, 1995). [3]agency—The human capacity to make and impose choices.

of sport psychology services to a culturally diverse clientele.

As a qualitative researcher, I have come to realize that there is always a tension between the scientific pressure to provide a certain answer and the fluid uncertainty of the human realm. Therefore, I find it problematic to offer the end product of cultural praxis, a prescriptive step-by-step manual of sorts. Instead, I offer a process, a hermeneutic[4] guideline that can change over time and across contexts.

SPORT PSYCHOLOGY AS CULTURAL PRAXIS

Sport psychology as cultural praxis is a critical discourse that emerged in response to the fragile and incomplete theory and practice in the field (Ryba & Wright, 2005). Much of the sport psychology knowledge base was developed from observations and practice involving collegiate, White, male athletes

and therefore was not particularly helpful to disenfranchised members of the sport community, such as women, athletes of color, and homosexuals. Building on the progressive and insightful work of Dorothy Harris (1972), Rainer Martens (1979, 1987), George Sage (1993, 1998), and Carolyn Sherif (1979, 1982), to name just a few, a cultural praxis version of sport psychology critiques the ethnocentric bias of mainstream sport psychology, which is often expressed in taking up the norms of Western culture as if they were universal laws of human nature. For example, an emphasis on the individual and the aggressive marketing of autonomy and self-determination as the key components of success create a powerful impetus for minority athletes to modify their own virtues (e.g., collaboration and communal welfare) and adapt to the expected behavior norms, often at great emotional cost.

Of course, everyone has to adjust when crossing into an unfamiliar cultural environment. Notions of double consciousness (DuBois, 1953), bifurcated

Winston Alexander Watt and Lascelles Oneil Brown of the Jamaican bobsleb team do not represent the White, male, heterosexual, middle-class athletic stereotype that remains dominant in Western culture today. Consider the effectiveness of a psychological intervention based only on that dominant culture for one of these athletes.
©AP Photo/Joe Cavaretta

---

[4]hermeneutics—The study of interpretation and understanding of texts.

consciousness (Smith, 1990), and nomadic consciousness (Braidotti, 1994) directly speak to the internal conflict between being African and American, female and employee, citizen of a nation state and migrant, and so on. They further reveal ambiguities, uncertainties, clashing values, and expectations that occur when awareness of self becomes permeated with awareness of how others perceive and, more significantly, represent us in scientific and popular discourses. The emphasis on power dynamics operating in the construction of a representative category expresses a concern that some groups have more power and resources than others in shaping normative systems beyond the individual level.

The ways in which disciplinary and professional knowledge is formed and purveyed are therefore saturated with cultural, historical, political, and economic influences and have an enormous effect on how athletes are constituted through discursive professional practices. As Ingham, Blissmer, and Davidson (1999) have observed, far from being ideologically neutral,

> the work of many applied sport psychologists unwittingly sustains the system of oppression and exploitation, and focuses on normalizing the individual's responses to such systems as if adjustment and accommodation are the only solutions to distress. (pp. 240-241)

I argue therefore that the cultural ineptness of psychology and subsequent mistrust of its practices by racial, ethnic, and other minority groups primarily stems from overdetermination of the individual and neglect of societal power disparities and injustice by mainstream sport psychology.

According to Schön (1983), for the last 300 years Western thought has been based on the rationality of positivism. Positivism is a philosophical stance that assumes the independent existence of an objective reality that can be revealed via careful and bias-free observation (Ponterotto, 2005; see also chapter 3). The conception in psychology that the individual as an autonomous, discrete, and unique phenomenon whose characteristics can be measured by means of rationality, modes of scientific thinking, and psychometric instruments is consistent with the philosophical underpinnings of logical positivism. Similarly, mainstream as well as cross-cultural sport psychology tends to treat culture as an external factor that is expressed as an independent variable in research designs. By specifying a particular culture as the independent variable (e.g., West African), we measure its influence on dependent measures (e.g., muscle twitch, aggression). Such objectification of culture as a fixed reality results in a scientific storehouse of

ultimate knowledge of a certain cultural group.

In the following section, I draw on Wright's (2007) ideas of the Western overdetermination of Africans and Schön's (1983) notion of problem setting in an effort to demonstrate how supposedly objective cultural knowledge presupposes the professional assessment of a problem and rules out alternative constructions.

EPISTEMOLOGY OF PRACTICE

Philosophy of science defines epistemology as theory about the nature of knowledge that presupposes the relationship between the knower and the known. Epistemological questions relate to how what exists may be known. Can we assume our knowledge to be a reflection of an objective reality, or is it a socially mediated phenomenon (Glesne, 2006; Ponterotto, 2005)?

Critiquing Western academic discourses for a false creation of Africa and Africans, Wright (2007) has asserted that before he was born in Freetown, Sierra Leone, he was already known to the West through a long history of colonial ethnographic depictions and representations. Wright offered the specific description of a Sierra Leonean ethnic group, the Temne, as provided in a colonial anthropological text by Frederick Migeod (1926): "The Temne is somewhat peevish . . . and once his anger is aroused it is difficult to talk him to reason" (p. 27). Texts such as this appeal to pseudoscientific knowledge of phrenology and social Darwinism in their description of details and aim at fitting preestablished so-called facts. Hardly any scholar today would write a description such as Migeod's; however, the popular myths of dangerous Black men are discursively linked to Migeod's text (and hundreds of thousands of others), producing real effects on how Black men are constituted and treated by Western legal and civic discourses.

For Schön (1983), epistemology of practice clarifies the relationship between the knowledge base of a profession and its practice. The taken-for-granted notion of practice is that it applies the systematic (i.e., specialized, tightly bounded, scientific, and standardized) knowledge base to concrete problems. This view perpetuates the hierarchical division of kinds of knowledge (i.e., basic and applied) and the institutional separation between researchers and practitioners, which Martens (1979, 1987) previously identified as problematic. Precisely, Martens indicated that in sport psychology, sometimes there is a disconnect between research inquiries and the applied needs in the field. He posited that research sometimes misses the mark because the focus is top-down and distanced from daily challenges as opposed to bottom-up and grounded in lived experience. In response, Martens suggested that sport psychologists step out of their laboratories and pursue their questions from the field in order to address relevant solutions to concrete problems. In addition, such a conception of practice suggests that problems are fixed and present themselves as givens. From the perspective of logical positivism, therefore, professional practice is a process of problem *solving*.

In the world of modern sport, which is complex, fast paced, uncertain, unique (both in terms of the context itself and also those within it), value laden, and permeated with role and commitment conflicts, professional problems do not emerge as clear givens. When the practice situation cannot be mapped onto a classic case or concrete category of applied theory, we do not yet have a problem to solve. According to Schön (1983), the emphasis on problem solving needs to be redirected to problem *setting*, the process by which

> we select what we will treat as the "things" of the situation . . . set the boundaries of our attention to it, and . . . impose upon it a coherence which allows us to say what is wrong and in what directions the situation needs to be changed. (p. 40)

In other words, practitioners need to construct problems from the fragmented situations that make no sense by naming the things that are perceived as relevant and setting them into the frame of a specific problem. When we consider how to motivate athletes, for instance, we usually deal with many factors at once (e.g., team culture, personal values, coaching style). Because achievement motivation is a multidimensional construct that includes psychological, social, cultural, and ideological concerns, we need to untangle and map particular features of the practice situation onto the categories of a certain theoretical model of motivation. By naming the features we find relevant, we "frame the context in which we will attend to them" (p. 40).

If we take Schön's assertion seriously, it becomes evident that our own psychosocial location in the world, cultural history, and disciplinary norms influence what information we consider important, what data we simply ignore, and what kind of attributions we make in our assessment of the problem. Without critical reflection on our problem-setting actions, we might be reducing professional assessment to mental shortcuts, tapping into the collective historical and commonsense Eurocentric knowledge (see figure 4.1).

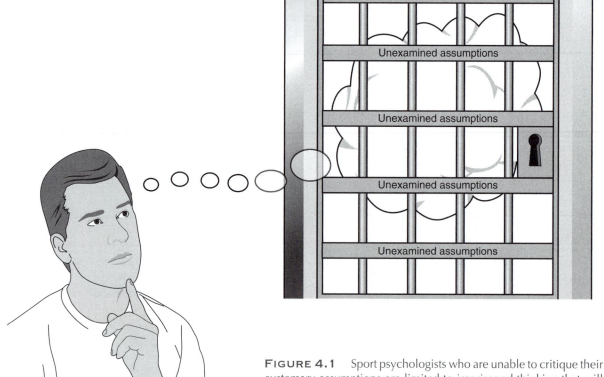

Unexamined assumptions

Unexamined assumptions

Unexamined assumptions

Unexamined assumptions

FIGURE 4.1 Sport psychologists who are unable to critique their customary assumptions are limited to imprisoned thinking that will severely affect their ability to deal effectively with clients from cultures different from those with which they are already comfortable.

As an example, the angry, Black, male basketball player who is sent by his coach to a sport psychology consultant might be immediately perceived as aggressive, irrational, and out of control. Because some people believe that men are more aggressive than women and Blacks are more aggressive than Whites, in their minds, aggression must be the issue. Using traditional psychometric tools that would validate this unrefined immediate assessment of the problem, such as the Aggression Questionnaire (Buss & Perry, 1992) or Spielberger's State-Trait Anger Expression Inventory (Spielberger, Reheiser, & Syderman, 1995), the problem can be quickly constructed and located within the athlete. The solution to the problem can then be found in any sport psychology handbook—behavior modification by means of cognitive reframing, relaxation, and other anger management techniques.

Although there is no doubt that some athletes can benefit from anger management, it is important to consider how we arrive at the decision to prescribe behavior modification. Critical approaches to sport psychology suggest focusing on sociocultural origins of distress instead of pathologizing clients. Could it be that the basketball player's anger stems from unjust treatment? Could it be that he does not get a fair share of playing time because he is gay? Could it be that he is frustrated with his team's double standards of perpetuating everyday racism despite a proclaimed culture of inclusiveness and open-mindedness? Or could it be that his overly aggressive behavior is an act aimed at concealing his homosexual identity?

An important aspect of a culturally reflexive and just practice of sport psychology is to examine the multiple ways in which athletes are positioned in and reconstructed by professional practice based on their sociocultural characteristics. Moreover, cultural praxis interventions attempt to transgress the individual–society dualism, helping athletes understand their identities and become aware of how they are situated within problematic sport subcultures, as well as creating possibilities for athlete empowerment and social transformation.

CAVEAT ON PERSONALITY

When most people think of psychology, the concept of personality often comes to mind. Although sport psychology investigations into personality to find a reliable link between successful performances and athletes' psychological profiles were abandoned in the 1970s due to limited predictive validity (Silva & Weinberg, 1984), we still seem to rely on numerous psychometric instruments and personality theories in professional practice. Perhaps the reason for reducing dialectical human experience to personality constructs lies in our search for causal relationships between external stimuli (e.g., culture) or internal stimuli (e.g., central processing mechanisms) and behavior outcomes and is grounded in unreflective use of research-based knowledge.

Personality theories vary widely regarding determinism, emphasis on nature or nurture, free will, and the degree to which personality changes over life span (cf., Freud, Jung, Adler, Fromm, Horney, Klein, Erikson, Allport, Skinner, Kelly, Maslow, Rogers, and May). Despite this divergence in approaches, major personality theories are Western creations and reflect a "historical form of individuality" (Seve, 1978). In their focus on individual growth and self-actualization, they tend to neglect the role of sociocultural contexts, ideology, and economic and social formations in shaping our concept of self (Sloan, 1997).

I have argued (Ryba, 2004, 2005) that sport psychology, as a discourse that "focuses on the individual" (Gill, 2000, p. 228), is intimately connected to how we understand the notion of personality. Specifically, the way the individual (or in poststructuralist[1] terms, the subject) is theorized is not merely central to the psychology of sport but in many ways determines the focus of its research and practice (in terms of pedagogy, methodology, research methods, and theoretical frame). Further, I have suggested a poststructuralist intervention that views subjectivity as fluid and fragmented due to our participation in the range of competing, contradictory, and overlapping discursive practices in and through which the concept of self is produced and reproduced (e.g., engaging critical issues in academic work; submitting for publication a position paper that critiques the status quo; negotiating what changes to make for the paper to be published).

In this view, personality is critically rearticulated as the product of historically specific, discursive sociocultural relations and moves from signifying an individual problem (e.g., physical inactivity) to signifying a social problem rooted in a particular discourse

---

[1]poststructuralist—This term does not have a singular fixed meaning but encompasses diverse theoretical positions developed from the work of Jacques Derrida, Michel Foucault, Julia Kristeva, Jacques Lacan, and others. Various forms of poststructuralism share certain assumptions about language, meaning, and subjectivity, asserting that meaning is unstable and constructed in the language of historically specific discourses (Weedon, 1997). Weedon further explains subjectivity as "the conscious and unconscious thoughts and emotions of the individual, her sense of herself and her ways of understanding her relation to the world" (p. 32).

(e.g., physical inactivity due to lack of economic, social, and learning resources) (see figure 4.2). In sum, I agree with Sloan (1997) that "my 'shyness' and your 'confidence' are manifestations of a complex intertwining of social class, ethnicity, socialization, life experience, identity development, and so forth. What we think of as 'individual' and 'social' are, in the final analysis, the same" (p. 100).

PRACTICING CSP

The starting point of the cultural praxis version of sport psychology proposed by Ryba and Wright (2005) is to work with the broad elements of theory, practice, and research, with an emphasis on critical forms of research that bridge the dichotomies between theory and practice, abstract text and lived culture. This understanding of sport psychology highlights the multidimensionality of practitioners who attempt to stay abreast of theoretical developments in the field to inform their practice while also reflecting on knowing-in-action, which is mostly tacit and revealed through the spontaneous behavior of

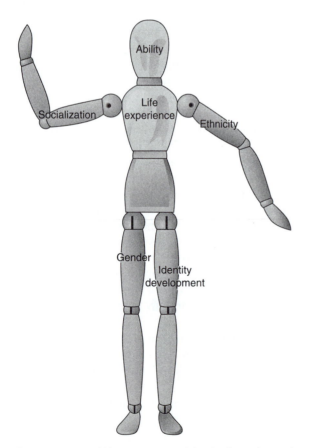

FIGURE 4.2 We construct our identity through a multiplicity of identifications with various discourses, such as gender, class, race and ethnicity, sexuality, and ability.

skillful practice. According to Schön (1983), "When someone reflects-in-action, he becomes a researcher in the practice context. He is not dependent on the categories of established theory and technique, but constructs a new theory of the unique case" (p. 68). Becoming a culturally reflexive practitioner is a process similar to that of an action-oriented qualitative inquiry and requires both time and effort. Whether you are a student or professional member of the sport psychology community, the following five strategies can help you develop the competencies necessary for effective and just delivery of sport psychology services to culturally diverse populations.

STRATEGY 1: LEARN ABOUT THE STATUS QUO

The first step in the direction of a culturally reflexive and just practice in sport psychology is to learn about the status quo of the field. Most introductory sport psychology and research methods texts are influenced by the tenets of logical positivism and rely upon scientific methods of inquiry, yet the philosophical assumptions underpinning positivist knowledge claims are rarely discussed, presuming no a priori logic. It is not surprising, then, that we tend to readily legitimize mainstream sport psychology theory and practice, which are grounded in hidden and seemingly indisputable premises of logical positivism.

Exploring the current prevailing paradigm and its conceptual premises, assumptions, and beliefs that guide our methodology and overall thinking about various psychological issues will help us to realize the uses and limits of the mainstream knowledge base. Once we realize that knowledge is always already from a certain perspective, we might be able to gain insight into the organizing purpose of the status quo. Highlighting Voltaire's point that "history is written by the victors," Vealey (2006) has elaborated on this idea. "Once a paradigm, or a box, is entrenched, there is a tendency to sit back and enjoy the bounty, to retreat to the security of established methods and questions within the box, and each day to rediscover the validity of hard-won but now well-worn principles" (p. 129). It is necessary, therefore, not only to learn the so-called facts of research-based knowledge but to understand the belief system from which these facts have emerged.

STRATEGY 2: SEEK ALTERNATIVE PERSPECTIVES

The second strategy encourages us to read outside the discipline of sport psychology. Despite increased calls advocating for an interdisciplinary approach to sport and exercise psychology, the field remains narrowly specialized and grounded in conceptual premises of logical positivism. Exploring competing perspectives inside and especially outside the discipline, such as those suggesting that "scientists construct an image of reality that reflects their own preferences and prejudices" (Schutt, 1999, p. 393), might help us to understand how sport psychology can disempower particular groups of the sport community.

A reflective analysis of the conceptual systems operating beneath the surface of the mainstream and other ways of knowing can further help us to clarify our own existential and epistemological positions. Just as the social sciences feature epistemological pluralism, there are conflicting paradigms of professional practice, "each of which entrains a distinctive approach to problem setting and solving" (Schön, 1983, p. 41). For example, in the positivist model of practice, rigorous professional knowledge is viewed as the effective application of research-based theory and technique to the problems of practice.

Many practitioners are bound by this epistemology of practice in the context of the Western performance ethic, which Coakley (2004) takes to mean that performance has increasingly become a "measured outcome and an indicator of the quality of the sport experience" (p. 133). If that is the case, we might be narrowly focusing on carving the disciplinary track of psychological dimensions of human behavior, overlooking the importance of the social and cultural context (Coakley, 1992; Conroy, 2006; Hardy, 2006). The excessive pressure to win at any cost and a subsequent single-minded focus on performance enhancement might lead to an objectification of the athlete insofar as the athlete's body is viewed as an instrument that needs to be worked to achieve a desired outcome. If we broaden our view of the rigorous professional knowledge to include intuitive and artistic ways of coping with uncertain situations of practice, we might realize that our way of framing the practitioner's role is also shifting.

Should we practice sport psychology rigorously in disciplining the athlete's mind and body to compete through pain and injury? Or should we forsake technical rigor to take account of critical social concerns that beset the world of sport today? The process of trying to position ourselves in highly contested belief systems that come with blurred boundaries and multiple ambiguities is longitudinal, ambivalent, and even anxiety provoking. The value of the effort, nonetheless, is that we emerge as reflective practitioners with a stronger sense of professional integrity and heightened awareness of diversity and richness of knowing.

STRATEGY 3: BECOME A RESEARCHER IN THE PRACTICE CONTEXT

The third strategy is to approach the real world as a researcher, shifting the focus from problem solving to problem setting. How do we assess a problem? Do we let the phenomenon speak for itself? Or do we see it as an effect of multiple discourses of gender, class, ethnicity, sexuality, ability, and so on? What professional discourses make our views intelligible? Do we tend to hold athletes responsible for their actions? Do we consider power relations in our assessment of the problem? And do we acknowledge the possibility of our contribution to the problem, predicated on largely unacknowledged privileges? When the practitioner asks these kinds of questions due to concern with the research process (i.e., problem setting) as much as with obtaining the findings (i.e., problem solving), the practitioner is engaging in reflexivity.

As defined by Schwandt (1997), reflexivity includes "examining one's personal and theoretical commitments to see how they serve as resources for generating particular data, for behaving in particular ways . . . and for developing particular interpretations" (p. 136). Reflexivity, both epistemological and personal, is a crucial piece in the process of efficient engagement and service delivery to populations outside the mainstream. Strategies 1 and 2 aim at mapping our beliefs and conceptual presuppositions to a particular epistemological paradigm. Enhanced by epistemological reflexivity, plunging into multiple layers of the self through personal reflexivity can help us to become more attuned to our ways of doing things, which are likely mediated through unearned privileges in addition to those gained from playing by the rules. In addition, this process might result in genuine realization that our cultural norms are not universal and that alternative normative systems exist that shape behavior and largely constitute cognition.

When we become researchers in our practice, we keep track of two simultaneous research projects: one into construction of a problem (What information warrants further exploration?) and the other into the self (What values and experiences shape your understanding and interpretation of the problem as well as your consequent decisions?). Such a model of knowing, though theoretically informed, is not bookish but constructed by reflecting on our intuitive knowing and capacity to cope with the unique, uncertain, and conflicted situations of practice.

Mastering the strategies described in this text will enable sport psychologists to deal more effectively with sport teams that are increasingly diverse.

© AP Photo/Mark Humphrey

STRATEGY 4: DEVELOP MEANINGFUL COMMUNICATION

The fourth strategy is to work toward achieving meaningful communication with clients. Even if we assume that culture can be learned, how can we familiarize ourselves with all variations within a culture, not to mention the dynamic hybridity of gender, class, race, ethnicity, sexuality, age, spirituality, education, geographical location, and so forth? In addition, growing global mobility produces intensified cultural contact between global culture and various local cultures and sometimes manifests in dramatic behavior transformations that cannot be attributed to any original culture. Basic understanding of alternative ways of knowing is certainly important, but the only way to attain an empathetic understanding of the worldview of the other seems to be through a meaningful dialogue.

Moghaddam and Studer (1997), for example, contended that the concept of meaningful dialogue is universal (i.e., there is enough similarity in a human society to create psychological universals that are present across cultures, such as having two persons for a dialogue to occur). However, they argued, "the norms of turn-taking [in verbal and nonverbal communication] are enormously various, expressing the widely different rights accorded to speakers and potential speakers in different cultures" (p. 198). For meaningful dialogue to occur, then, the two parties concerned have to operate at the same wavelength. This does not mean both speakers share the same cultural norms, but rather they are in the process of attaining a sharable language. Understanding is linguistically formed and always relational (Schwandt, 2000). As Schwandt has further explained, "In the act of understanding there are not two separate steps—first acquiring understanding; second, applying that understanding. Rather . . . understanding is 'lived' or existential" (pp. 195-196). Once again, our focus shifts from problem solving (i.e., resolving the problem of miscommunication) to problem setting (i.e., clarifying the conditions under which understanding takes place). Using this approach, our search for a sharable language transforms the information-gathering dialogue into shared experience.

I further assert that meaningful dialogue does not occur automatically. For the dialogue to break down the inherent power hierarchy between practitioners of sport psychology and minority (in terms of power) athletes, that breakdown has to be purposefully planned and actively pursued with a view to mitigating power imbalances. A good starting point would be letting go of Eurocentric exoticization of the other as bizarre or strange and resisting the "dual temptation of facilely assimilating what others are saying into our own categories and language without doing justice to what is genuinely different, or simply dismissing what the other is saying as incoherent nonsense" (Sparkes, 1998, p. 382).

STRATEGY 5:
ENGAGE IN CULTURAL PRAXIS

The fifth and final strategy advocates addressing social justice through coparticipatory and transformative professional practice. Cultural praxis fosters progressive social change by demystifying power relations and challenging assumed normative systems of the lived culture. According to Freire (1970, 1985), human reality is not static and a given destiny, but rather fluid and transformable. At the center of his understanding of praxis is education that serves as a catalyst for reflecting on the conditions of our lives and becoming agents of social transformation for ourselves and society as a whole.

Mastering performance-enhancement techniques such as concentration, for example, can be an incredibly empowering process for athletes. As they learn to recognize when they are losing their mental alertness and to refocus, they transform the way they are positioned in the competitive sport environment. These athletes are no longer blindly accepting or adjusting to the opponent's game, but they are creating the conditions in which seemingly effortless excellence is demonstrated. An intervention for performance enhancement can also be our pedagogical moment to help athletes to realize that they have agency in their dealings with oppressive and controlling sport structures. As Ryba and Wright (2005) pointed out, a cultural praxis version of sport psychology does not suggest that teaching techniques for performance enhancement is wrong. Rather, it calls for creating a space for both performance enhancement and individual empowerment with an aim of progressive social transformations.

From the perspective of cultural praxis, clients are the experts on their own experiences. By engaging in meaningful dialogue, they provide insight into the condition of their experience. Our role is to share our understandings and interpretations, deepening the dialogue and opening it to new possibilities of meaning. Our role shifts from being the expert who shapes minority athletes' responses to hegemonic[1]

SUMMARY OF POINTS FOR PRACTICE AND RESEARCH

If you are able to successfully discuss the following questions and issues, you have understood the major points of this chapter.

- Reflect on how your academic training has contributed to your understanding of the disciplinary norms in sport psychology and how it should be practiced.

- Discuss the ways in which your life experiences, embedded in particular cultural norms, largely predetermine how you treat research and applied problems.

- Consider how taken-for-granted normative practices of applied sport psychology may become the oppressive mechanisms of power, further marginalizing minority groups.

- Explain in your own words the cultural epistemology of practice.

- Provide an applied example of the process when practitioners shift their focus from problem solving to problem setting. What are the implications of this shift?

- Consider how disability (or other sociocultural characteristics) is constructed in our society. Explore the ways in which the commonsense knowledge of disability may differ from the first-hand knowledge.

- Discuss whether disability is a stable universal construct or might have different meanings and manifestations across cultures and subcultures.

normative systems in the name of athletic success to being a coparticipant in the collaborative process of learning, reflection, critical awareness, and intervention.

CONCLUSION

The goal of sport psychology professionals is to enhance personal development and well-being through participation in sport, exercise, and physical activity (Association for Applied Sport Psychology [AASP], 2006). Yet, critical scholarship outside the discipline has charged sport psychologists with dehumanizing athletes, viewing them as objects manipulated to achieve certain outcomes (Coakley, 1992; Hoberman, 1992; Ingham et al., 1999). The situation is exacerbated in our dealings with disenfranchised members of the sport community due to inherent ideological biases in mainstream psychology that "reflect the culture of the United States, particularly the main normative system of the culture, and more specifically the biases of the White males who have historically dominated the discipline" (Moghaddam & Studer, 1997, p. 200). It is important, therefore, to reflect critically on our role in professional discourses and understand whether our everyday practices create a space for the empowerment or the exploitation of athletes.

This chapter introduced a cultural praxis version of sport psychology that is interdisciplinary, fundamentally contextual, and culturally reflexive; focused on sociocultural difference and social justice; critically rearticulated personality as the product of historically specific, discursive sociocultural relations; and blended theoretical and practical work together in praxis. Culturally reflexive practice of sport psychology resists objectification of culture (as a fixed reality) and overdetermination of the minority athlete (as a cultural carrier)—an approach that often results in attempts to adjust the athlete's behavior to hegemonic normative systems in an effort to maintain the status quo.

This chapter further offered several points of reflection on our role in professional practice as well as the strategies for acquiring competencies that are necessary for effective and just delivery of sport psychology services to culturally diverse populations. It is my hope that by learning about the status quo of the field, seeking alternative perspectives inside and especially outside the discipline, approaching real-world problems as a reflexive researcher, working toward a sharable language with diverse cultural groups, and engaging in cultural praxis work, we will be better equipped to achieve a democratic, culturally reflexive, and just practice of sport psychology.

---

[1]hegemony—As proposed by Antonio Gramsci (1978), the term "describes the process whereby ideas, structures, and actions come to be seen by the majority of people as wholly natural, preordained, and working for their own good, when in fact they are constructed and transmitted by powerful minority interests to protect the *status quo* that serves those interests" (p. 15).

CULTURAL DIVERSITY IN APPLIED SPORT PSYCHOLOGY

Diane L. Gill, PhD, and Cindra S. Kamphoff, PhD

In this chapter, we take a North American, and more particularly, a U.S. perspective on cultural diversity in applied sport psychology. In keeping with the inclusive, multicultural perspective of this text, sport is interpreted broadly as including play, exercise, and all levels and forms of sport. The chapter begins with a multicultural framework drawn from the expanding multicultural scholarship in psychology and influenced by our feminist perspectives. Using that framework, the chapter examines the status of multicultural diversity in sport, society in the United States, and applied sport psychology research and professional practice. A more detailed presentation of related literature may be found in "Gender and Cultural Diversity" (Gill, 2007).

This chapter concludes with recommendations for advancing multicultural diversity and promoting cultural competence in applied sport psychology, which we call *sport for all*. Applied sport psychology research and practice can advance the public-interest mission of psychology by promoting safe, inclusive physical activity for the health and well-being of all and by highlighting cultural competence in professional practice.

MULTICULTURAL FRAMEWORK

The growing multicultural psychology scholarship, along with the feminist and sport studies literature, forms the multicultural framework for this chapter, emphasizing the following themes:

- *Multiple, intersecting cultural identities.* We all have gender, race and ethnicity, and many other cultural identities, with the mix varying across people, time, and context.

- *Power relations.* Gender and culture relations involve power and privilege. Who makes the rules? Who is excluded?

- *Action and advocacy.* Multicultural perspectives demand action for social justice. Culturally competent sport psychology professionals develop their own multicultural competencies and also promote sport psychology in the public interest.

Multicultural psychology is the "systematic study of behavior, cognition and affect in many cultures" (Mio, Barker-Hackett, & Tumambing, 2006, p. 3). Narrow definitions of culture emphasize ethnicity, but a broader definition refers to the shared values, beliefs, and practices of an identifiable group of people. Thus, both culture and multicultural psychology include race and ethnicity, language, spirituality, sexuality, and of particular relevance for applied sport psychology, physicality (including physical abilities and characteristics such as size and appearance).

Psychology, and particularly the American Psychological Association (APA), has moved beyond its decidedly nonmulticultural past, described in Robert Guthrie's (1998) aptly titled, *Even the Rat Was White.* Multicultural scholars have argued that we cannot fully understand the individual without considering the larger world. Trickett, Watts, and Birman (1994) advocated moving psychology from the dominant emphasis on biology, isolated basic processes, rigorous experimental designs, and a critical-realist philosophy of science to an emphasis on people in context.

Derald Wing Sue (2004), a leading scholar in multicultural psychology, noted that privileged people are often unaware of power relations and that color blindness often denies opportunity to others.

Sue argued that psychology must recognize White privilege and the culture-bound nature of scholarship and practice in order to advance the mission of psychology and enhance the health and well-being of all people.

Moving beyond cultural boundaries and traditional approaches is no easy task. Sport psychology is explicitly context dependent, and sport culture is unique in many ways. Applied sport psychologists must pay attention to power relations and social context in sport but also must retain concern for the person. The combined focus on the individual and cultural relations is the essence of a useful multicultural applied sport psychology that promotes inclusive and empowering sport for all. That practice is aligned with the cultural sport psychology (CSP) theme of this book.

CULTURAL DIVERSITY AND POWER IN SOCIETY AND SPORT

Sport participants are diverse in many ways, but they do not reflect the diversity of the broader population. In the early days of sport psychology, *athlete* meant male athlete, and those male athletes were hardly culturally diverse. School physical education and community youth programs are closer to reflecting community diversity, but elite sport programs reflect cultural restrictions. As our multicultural framework implies, it is important to go beyond overall participation numbers to consider power and privilege, or who makes the rules. Sue (2004) illustrated the power differential by noting that in the United States, although White males make up just 33% of the population, they hold 80% of tenured faculty positions and 92% of Forbes 400 CEO positions, make up 80% of the House of Representatives and 84% of the Senate, and make up 99% of professional athletic team owners.

COLLEGIATE SPORT

Richard Lapchick has been monitoring diversity in sport for several years, compiling data on participation rates as well as numbers of women and racial and ethnic minorities in leadership positions in U.S. collegiate and professional sport. The most recent *Racial and Gender Report Cards* (Lapchick, 2005, 2006) show clear racial and gender inequities and little progress. For example, for Division I intercollegiate athletics in 2004, African Americans were overrepresented at 24.6% of the male athletes and 14.8% of the female

athletes, but Latinos, Asian Americans, and Native Americans were vastly underrepresented; nonresident aliens (i.e., those in the United States temporarily on non-U.S. passports) made up a higher percentage (around 4.5%) than any racial or ethnic minority group other than African Americans.

When we consider positions of power, diversity is nonexistent. The 2004 racial report card reveals that White men dominate intercollegiate coaching, even of women's teams. African American men coach 7.2% of men's teams and 3.4% of women's teams, African American women coach only 1.6% of women's teams, and coaches of other racial and ethnic identities hardly can be counted. The 2005 report card shows that despite some improvement, administration remains solidly White male; people of color held 13% and women 7.8% of Division I athletic director positions.

Before Title IX of the Educational Amendments of 1972 banned sex discrimination in U.S. educational programs, over 90% of women's athletic teams were coached by women and had a female athletic director. Today fewer than half of women's teams are coached by women, and only 18.6% have a female director (Carpenter & Acosta, 2006). Kamphoff's (2006) dissertation research shows that female coaches in collegiate athletics experience marginalization, devaluation, and homophobia. The female coaches she surveyed and interviewed received fewer resources, lower salaries, more responsibilities, and less administrative support than their male counterparts. They had difficulty balancing work and family, and they reported that others saw them as distracted by motherhood if they had children. Furthermore, the women provided examples of rampant homophobia in U.S. collegiate coaching and reported feeling pressure to act in a heterosexual way to fit into the collegiate system.

PHYSICAL ACTIVITY AND EXERCISE

Greater diversity might be expected in exercise settings, but the typical exerciser in research and in the fitness club is a young, White, fit, middle-class male. Census data and public health reports indicate that physical activity is limited by gender, race, class, and especially by physical attributes. Physical activity decreases across the adult life span, with men more active than women, racial and ethnic minorities less active across all age groups, and young adult women (particularly African American women) one of the most inactive populations in the United States (Pratt, Macera, & Blanton, 1999; USDHHS, 2000). For example, Kimm and colleagues (2002) used a large national database to track girls' physical activity levels across adolescence. Physical activity declined dramatically—100% for Black girls and 64% for White girls—so that at ages 18 to 19, 56% of Black girls and 31% of White girls reported no regular physical activity.

Crespo, Ainsworth, Keteyian, Heath, and Smit (1999) looked at social class with a national database and found greater inactivity in less privileged social classes, with females more inactive in all classes. Crespo (2005) called for professionals to consider unique needs and cultural constraints when giving advice on exercise.

Sport Psychology Research on Cultural Diversity

Cultural influences are so pervasive that we seldom notice how cultural beliefs and contexts shape society and the world of sport. This section provides a brief overview of psychology and sport psychology schol-arship on cultural diversity. More detail on related research can be found in other sources (see Gill, 2002, 2007, for extended discussions). Here we highlight the scholarship on stereotypes and perceptions that influence participation and behavior in multicultural sport contexts.

Gender

Gender influence is obvious in society and particu-larly powerful in sport. Gender scholarship in psy-chology includes early and persistent research on sex differences, research on personality and gender roles, and more current scholarship on gender relations and social processes. In their classic review, Maccoby and Jacklin (1974) stated that few conclusions could be drawn from the literature on sex differences. Despite many claims to the contrary, continuing research con-firms that deduction. Hyde (2005) recently reviewed 46 meta-analyses of the extensive literature on sex differences and concluded that results support the gender similarities hypothesis; that is, males and females are more alike than different, and overstated

At its best, applied sport psychology research and practice promotes health and well-being for all.

claims of gender differences cause harm and limit opportunities.

Most psychologists look beyond the male–female and masculine–feminine dichotomies to developmental and social cognitive models, often taking a multicultural perspective. As Basow and Rubin (1999) explained, *gender* refers to the meaning attached to being female or male in a particular culture, and meanings vary with ethnicity, social class, and sexual orientation. For example, in the United States, dance is considered a feminine activity, but in many cultures, dance is part of masculine rituals. Psychological research confirms that how people think males and females differ is more important than how they actually differ. If children think that dance is for girls, boys will stand aside while girls dance. Gender stereotypes are pervasive, particularly in sport. Kane and Snyder (1989) confirmed gender stereotyping of sports and identified physicality—emphasis on physical muscularity, strength, and power—as the key feature. Stereotypes are a concern because we act on them, exaggerating minimal gender differences and restricting opportunities for everyone.

Fredericks and Eccles' (2004) review of the literature on parental influence and youth sport involvement revealed that parents held gender-stereotyped beliefs about athletics and were gender typed in their behaviors, providing more opportunities and encouragement to sons than to daughters. Fredericks and Eccles (2005) later confirmed that boys had higher perceived competence, value, and participation despite the absence of gender differences in motor proficiency.

RACE AND ETHNICITY

Duda and Allison (1990) first identified the lack of research on race and ethnicity in sport psychology, reporting that only 1 of 13 published theoretical papers and 7 of 186 empirical papers (less than 4%) considered race or ethnicity. In an update, Ram, Starek, and Johnson (2004) reviewed articles between 1987 and 2000 and found that only 20% of the articles made reference to race or ethnicity and 1.2% to sexual orientation. They concluded that there is no systematic attempt to include the experiences of marginalized groups.

Despite the persistent void in sport psychology research, the multicultural psychology scholarship on race and ethnicity is growing, and much of that work addresses well-documented health disparities (USDHHS, 2003). Contrada and colleagues (2000) summarized research indicating that racial and ethnic minorities face stress based on discrimination, stereotypes, and conformity pressures and that these stresses affect health and well-being. As Yali and Revenson (2004) suggested, socioeconomic disparities are likely to have an even greater effect in the near future, especially with the changing population demographics. That is, U.S. population trends indicate increasing numbers of persons who are older, are ethnic minorities, have disabilities, identify as sexual minorities, and are living in poverty; all those trends suggest greater social and cultural disparities. Health disparities are particularly relevant in that physical activity is a key health behavior and applied sport psychology professionals are in a position to promote sport and physical activity for health and well-being.

The extensive psychological research on stereotypes and stereotype threat—the influence of negative stereotypes on performance—indicates that stereotypes affect all of us (Steele, 1997; Steele, Spencer, & Aronson, 2002). That psychological research, primarily on gender and racial stereotypes in academic work, also indicates that the most devastating effects are on those minority-group members who have abilities and are motivated to succeed. On a more positive note, research suggests that even simple manipulations that take away the stereotype threat, such as telling people that test results have no relationship to gender, can help. Beilock and McConnell (2004) reviewed the related sport psychology literature, concluding that negative stereotypes are common in sport and lead to performance decrements.

Negative stereotypes for racial and ethnic minorities, particularly African American athletes, are well documented. Devine and Baker (1991) found the words *unintelligent* and *ostentatious* to be associated with *Black athlete*, and Krueger (1996) found that both Black and White participants perceived Black men to be more athletic than White men. Stone, Perry, and Darley (1997) had participants listen to a college basketball game and evaluate players they believed were Black or White. Both White and Black students rated Black players as more athletic and White players as having more basketball intelligence. Stone and colleagues (Stone, Lynch, Sjomeling, & Darley, 1999) later confirmed stereotype threat in a study where Black participants performed worse when told a golf task was a test of sport intelligence and White participants performed worse when told it was a test of natural ability. Both Harris (2000) and Sailes (2000) documented persistent stereotypes and reported that African American athletes are more likely than White athletes to see sport as a route to social mobility. These views may reflect stereotypes or barriers, but they certainly suggest cultural influences and power relations in sport.

SEXUAL ORIENTATION

Discrimination and prejudice on the basis of sexual orientation is often called *homophobia*. However, Herek (2000) noted that this term implies psychopathology and argued that the more appropriate term for negative attitudes is *sexual prejudice*. Psychological research confirms persistent sexual prejudice and hostile climates faced by lesbian, gay, and bisexual (LGB) people in society (e.g., Herek, 2000; Rivers & D'Augelli, 2001). Although scholarly research in sport psychology is limited, national reports from the National Gay and Lesbian Task Force Policy Institute (Rankin, 2003) and Human Rights Watch (2001), as well as observations and anecdotal evidence, suggest that organized sport is a particularly hostile environment.

In one of the few empirical studies, Morrow and Gill (2003) reported that both physical education teachers and students witnessed high levels of homophobic and heterosexist behaviors in public schools, but teachers failed to confront those behaviors. More than 75% of the teachers said that they want safe, inclusive physical education, but at the same time, more than 50% reported that they never confronted homophobia. In subsequent research, Gill, Morrow, Collins, Lucey, and Schultz (2006) examined attitudes toward racial and ethnic minorities, older adults, persons with disabilities, and sexual minorities. Overall, attitudes of preprofessional students were markedly more negative for both gay men and lesbians than for the other groups.

PHYSICALITY

Stereotypes and bias based on gender, race and ethnicity, and sexuality clearly affect perceptions and behaviors of participants and professionals in sport, and psychology research is beginning to address those issues. However, neither psychology nor sport psychology has addressed the more prominent role of physicality (e.g., physical abilities, size, appearance). Sport involves physical activity; hence, physical abilities and characteristics are prominent, and exclusion on the basis of physicality is nearly universal in sport and exercise. Opportunity is limited by physical abilities, skills, size, fitness, and appearance. Elite sport implies physically elite. Persons with disabilities are often left out in sport and exercise settings, but professionals seldom address physicality as an aspect of cultural diversity.

As part of the larger study on sexual prejudice cited earlier, Gill, Morrow, Collins, Lucey, and Schultz (2005) examined the climate for minority groups (racial and ethnic minorities, LGB people, older adults, and people with disabilities) in organized sport, exercise settings, and recreational settings. Notably, the climate was rated as most exclusionary for those with disabilities.

Physical diversity is more than ability or disability, and physicality is particularly relevant to applied sport psychology. Physical skill, strength, and fitness are key sources of restrictions and stereotyping. Physical appearance influences outcomes in subjectively judged sports such as gymnastics and figure skating. Physical size, particularly obesity, is a prominent source of social stigma and oppression in sport, and that is a particular concern for physical activity and health promotion programs.

CULTURAL DIVERSITY

As the preceding sections revealed, sport psychology research rarely addresses cultural diversity. Given that our focus is applied sport psychology, we can also look for signs of attention to multicultural competence in the other major professional areas—professional practice, education and training, and psychology in the public interest. Can we find evidence of cultural diversity in our educational programs (e.g., courses, resources, learning objectives)? Do sport psychology professionals demonstrate multicultural competence (e.g., use inclusive language or multicultural examples)? Do sport psychology professionals promote the health and well-being of all through sport (e.g., lobby for equal access to facilities)? Little direct evidence exists on professional activities, but observations and available evidence point to the answer to these questions: a resounding *no*.

Despite the diversity of participants and settings, professional practice focuses on elite sport, educational programs seldom incorporate multicultural competencies, and sport psychology does not truly serve the public interest. Perhaps the information in this book will help address this gap.

The clearest indication of the status of cultural diversity and multicultural issues in applied sport psychology may be found in AASP conference programs. Kamphoff and colleagues (Kamphoff, Araki, & Gill, 2004) surveyed the AASP conference programs from the first conference in 1986 to the 2003 conference and coded 240 AASP conference abstracts for diversity content. Abstracts were coded for diverse sample (e.g., nonmajority participants—females, non-Caucasians, youths under 18, adults over 50), diversity issue (e.g., gender differences, ethnic identity, stereotypes), and the first author's gender and country affiliation.

In general, the diversity of the first author's gender and country affiliation increased from 1986 to 2003. First authors of the abstracts in 1986 represented only 2 countries (the United States and Canada), whereas 16 countries were represented in 2003. When the gender of the first author was evident, 78.4% of the first authors were males and 19.6% were females in 1986. In 2003, however, the distribution was more equitable—50.1% of the first authors were males and 49.9% of the first authors were females. Inclusion of both diverse samples and diversity issues increased from 1986 to 1995, with little change from 1995 to 2003 (see figure 5.1). Diverse samples were mostly diverse by gender (including females), with some diverse by age (youth participants), but there were few other diverse samples. Diversity issues increased from 2 (4%) in 1986 to 54 (15.4%) in 2003. However, nearly all of the issues were comparisons of gender differences rather than more complex analyses of gender relations. AASP conference programs lacked discussion of race, social class, disability, older age, and LGB concerns, and they did not reflect any attention to specific multicultural issues. Although AASP conferences include international participants, the data are predominantly North American. It would be interesting to investigate the cultural diversity in conference programs of the European Federation of Sport Psychology (FEPSAC) and Asian South Pacific Association of Sport Psychology (ASPASP).

Under the leadership of Ruth Hall, the AASP diversity committee surveyed 192 attendees of the 2003 AASP conference about their experiences, attitudes, and skills in working with diverse clients. According to Hall's (2005) report, the majority of respondents believed that they included diverse groups of participants in their research and discussed implications of diversity in their work. Yet, according the research reviews cited previously (Duda & Allison, 1990; Kamphoff et al., 2004; Ram et al., 2004), culturally diverse samples are not easy to find in sport and exercise psychology research.

The majority of the AASP members who responded to the survey did not have specific coursework or training on diversity. Fewer than half of the respondents indicated they would seek diversity training if the AASP offered such training, and the majority did not seek consultation when working with groups who differed from themselves. Furthermore, the majority of the respondents did not live or socialize with diverse groups. Still, respondents felt there were no barriers to working with diverse populations. Notably, the majority of respondents were North American, able-bodied, heterosexual, White females. These results suggest that AASP members lack formal training in diversity concerns and may not understand how race, ethnicity, gender, age, class, nationality, sexual orientation, and disability influence behaviors and relationships in their work even if they feel comfortable working with diverse clients.

Overall, multicultural perspectives are missing and cultural diversity is marginalized in applied sport psychology research and practice. Sport settings and educational programs are culturally elite. In addition, professional practice focuses on the elite, increasingly so over the last 20 years. Our analysis of AASP programs and observations suggests that applied sport psychology is focused on athletes who are going for the gold in sport competitions, paying little attention to the broader public and diverse participants.

Educational programs appear to parallel that emphasis on the elite, perhaps driven by the enthusiasm of graduate students and future professionals for elite athletics. Student interests and preprofessional programs often focus on strategies for direct application and performance enhancement, placing little emphasis on the sociocultural scholarly base that might draw attention to cultural diversity. This elitist approach to professional practice is limiting in many ways. Certainly diverse, nonelite participants can benefit from sport psychology. Professionals who target youth development, senior sport, or rehabilitation programs may well find their services welcomed and effective. Moreover, those efforts could support social justice through the empowerment of marginalized groups.

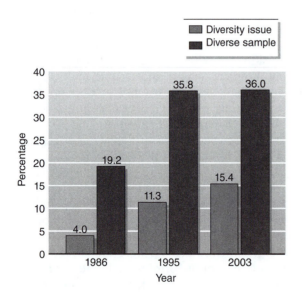

FIGURE 5.1 Percentages of abstracts with diversity content in AASP conference programs.

Data from Kamphoff, Arki and Gill 2004.

Applied sport psychology could advance multicultural diversity by promoting sport for all so that the health and well-being benefits are not limited to the elite. To do that, sport psychology must expand the research base on gender and cultural diversity, and it must adopt multicultural competencies for professional practice. Moreover, applied sport psychology could emphasize psychology in the public interest, the fourth major APA directorate (next section), just as we emphasize the research, practice, and education roles. Sport psychology could take the lead in advocating for inclusive sport programs and promoting multicultural competencies in sport professionals. But at present, public interest does not seem to be a factor in applied sport psychology.

APPLIED SPORT PSYCHOLOGY IN THE PUBLIC INTEREST

Multicultural competence takes cultural diversity directly into professional practice. Culturally competent professionals empower participants and challenge restrictive social structures. Multicultural competence, which is required in psychology and many health professions, refers to the ability to work effectively with people who are of a different culture. Multicultural competencies include three general areas (Mio et al., 2006):

- Awareness of one's own cultural values and biases
- Understanding of the client's worldviews (in all its multicultural complexity)
- Development of culturally appropriate intervention strategies

APA PUBLIC INTEREST DIRECTORATE

In addition to being organized into divisions by psychology content areas (e.g., Division 47–Exercise and Sport Psychology), the APA is organized into four directorates reflecting the major professional roles in psychology: science, practice, education, and public interest. As stated on the APA Web site (www.apa.org/pi), the APA Public Interest Directorate supports and promotes efforts to apply the science and profession of psychology to the advancement of human welfare. Public interest is of central importance to the field of psychology and to consumers of psychological services and the general public. According to the Web site, the major objectives of the APA Public Interest Directorate are to

- promote those aspects of psychology that involve solutions to the fundamental problems of human justice and equitable and fair treatment of all segments of society;
- encourage the use and dissemination of psychological knowledge to advance equal opportunity and to foster empowerment of those who do not share equitably in societal resources; and
- increase scientific understanding and training in regard to those aspects that pertain to, but are not limited to, culture, class, race and ethnicity, gender, sexual orientation, age, and discrimination, and to help improve educational training opportunities for all persons (www.apa.org/pi).

The APA has recognized the key role of multicultural competencies in fulfilling the mission of psychology to promote health and well-being, and its 2003 guidelines call for action for social justice. Sport psychology can move toward the goal of sport for the health and well-being of all by following those guidelines (see APA Multicultural Guidelines).

Not only does the APA specify and support multicultural scholarship and competencies, but APA Division 47 has adopted its own affirmation of diversity, which states the following:

Division 47 of the American Psychological Association strongly endorses the position of the APA respecting the fundamental rights, dignity, and worth of all people. Psychologists have an ethical responsibility to be aware of cultural, individual, and role differences, including those relating to age, gender, race, ethnicity, national origin, religion, sexual orientation, language, and socioeconomic status. The Division opposes participation in discrimination based on any of these factors, or the condoning of such discrimination. (Heyman, 1993)

PARHAM'S GUIDELINES

William Parham (2005), a leader in the multicultural efforts of the APA as well as an active sport psychology professional, offered useful guidelines based on his professional practice:

- Parham's first guiding premise—context is everything—is key when providing consultation services to diverse athletes. When working with diverse clients, history, economics, family, and social context are all relevant.

APA MULTICULTURAL GUIDELINES

The American Psychological Association has recognized the key role of multicultural competencies in fulfilling the mission of psychology to promote health and well-being. Following are the 2003 APA Multicultural Guidelines for practice and research. Sport psychology can move toward the goal of sport for the health and well-being of all by following those guidelines within sport and exercise psychology contexts.

- Guideline 1: Psychologists are encouraged to recognize that, as cultural beings, they may hold attitudes and beliefs that can detrimentally influence their perceptions of and interactions with people who are ethnically and racially different from themselves.
- Guideline 2: Psychologists are encouraged to recognize the importance of multicultural sensitivity, knowledge, and understanding about ethnically and racially different people.
- Guideline 3: As educators, psychologists are encouraged to employ the constructs of multiculturalism and diversity in psychological education.
- Guideline 4: Culturally sensitive psychological researchers are encouraged to recognize the importance of conducting cultural-centered and ethical psychological research among people from ethnic, linguistic, and racial minority backgrounds.
- Guideline 5: Psychologists strive to apply culturally appropriate skills in clinical and other applied psychological practices.
- Guideline 6: Psychologists are encouraged to use processes for organizational change to support culturally informed organizational (policy) development and practices.

- Parham's second premise—that culture, race, and ethnicity as separate indexes do little to inform us—reminds us that cultural groups are not homogenous, and every person has a unique cultural identity.

- Parham's third guiding premise underscores the importance of using paradigms that reflect differing worldviews. People from culturally diverse backgrounds often develop resiliency and strength in dealing with power relations. The Western worldview is culturally limited, typically emphasizing independence, competitiveness, and individual striving. Emphasis on connectedness rather than separation, mind–body interrelatedness rather than control, deference to higher power, and a sense of spirit-driven energy may be more prominent in someone else's worldview.

RECOMMENDATIONS FOR ADDRESSING CULTURAL DIVERSITY

Applied sport psychology must be inclusive of all people, and professionals must develop CSP skills in order to have effective and inclusive professional practice. All people can benefit from sport and physical activity programs that promote health and well-being, and those most likely to be excluded are often those who could most benefit.

As the previous sections indicate, scholarship addressing multicultural concerns is almost nonexistent and there has been no systematic attempt to include the marginalized groups in applied sport psychology research or practice. On the positive side, research and reports (e.g., Gill, Jamieson, & Kamphoff, 2005; Hall, 2005; Morrow & Gill, 2003) suggest that both sport psychology and the larger group of sport professionals want to serve diverse participants and would welcome resources and educational programs on multicultural competencies.

Given the status of current scholarship and practice, as well as the needs of professionals, participants, and the public, we offer several recommendations for addressing cultural diversity and multicultural competencies in applied sport psychology. These recommendations cover the full range of professional roles, paralleling the four APA directorates (science, practice, education, and public interest).

IN SCIENCE

First, although this chapter focuses on applied sport psychology, application in professional practice demands a sound scholarly base. Specifically, researchers must expand the limited multicultural scholarship in sport psychology. To adequately address the many cultural diversity issues in sport psychology, research must expand in terms of methodology as well as content. As Stanley Sue (1999) argued in a keynote address at the first APA multicultural summit, traditional psychological research models overemphasize internal validity and hinder research on ethnic minorities. To move forward, Sue advocated that all research studies address external validity and specify populations to which findings are applicable; that different research approaches, including qualitative and ethnographic methods, be appreciated; and that the psychological meaning of ethnicity or race be examined in ethnic comparison. Sport psychology researchers can advance our understanding of cultural diversity by following Sue's suggestions. Specifically, we offer the following recommendations:

- Address cultural diversity in applied sport psychology. Simple comparisons across cultural groups are not sufficient. Researchers might explore stereotypes, expectations, social relationships, or the influence of cultural context to get at relevant psychological processes and relationships. Research on the prominent role of physicality as a cultural phenomenon is particularly needed.

- Include diverse samples that reflect the wider population. As Sue argued, external validity is critical, and researchers must investigate applied sport psychology models, interventions, and programs across the range of populations. Extending this reach involves not only wider sampling in North American culture, but also more cross-cultural research that examines variations and adaptations across cultures. In doing so, cross-cultural researchers must consider the effectiveness of English-based tests in different cultures, the conversion of these tests to other languages, and the development of more culturally specific measures that evaluate sport psychology constructs (e.g., self-confidence) or psychological strategies (e.g., imagery).

IN PRACTICE

All sport psychology professionals must develop CSP skills. Cultural competence in the three general areas of awareness, understanding, and culturally appropriate interventions is essential in professional practice:

- **Awareness.** Becoming aware of our own limited worldviews, including culturally bound perspectives, stereotypes, and biases and how they influence our work in applied sport psychology, is a first step. In their discussion of work with LGB and transgendered people, Barber and Krane (2005) recommended first making a list of your perceptions and biases about diverse clients and then examining why you believe each perception and how the perception influences the client–consultant relationship.

- **Understanding.** Developing cultural competence is a continual process. We can all further develop our understanding of multiple cultures and intersecting influences. Further coursework or training in multicultural issues may be necessary for competent professional practice. At the very least, all sport psychologists must be familiar with and follow the APA multicultural guidelines. We could all benefit from further understanding of multicultural issues, and continued education benefits both our clients and ourselves.

- **Interventions.** If working with a client who is culturally different from you raises uncertainties, seek supervision or consultation with a colleague who is more knowledgeable or experienced with similar situations. If you do not have adequate skills and knowledge to work with someone, refer that client to another professional.

IN EDUCATION

Scholarship on cultural diversity and the development of multicultural competency must be part of educational programs in order to address cultural diversity in applied sport psychology. Moreover, multicultural competencies and CSP are relevant not only for applied sport psychology but for all sport and physical activity professional settings. Sport psychology specialists can play an important role in helping all sport professionals develop cultural competence.

The need for sport psychologists to accept this role in the professional community has been brought home to us by a project we have been working on with the long-term goal of developing inclusive, empowering programs for culturally diverse youth (Gill, Jamieson, & Kamphoff, 2005). As a first step, we used surveys and focus groups to investigate the climate and cultural competencies of professionals in physical activity settings.

As in our earlier research (Gill, Morrow, et al., 2005), both professionals and participants rated the climate as inclusive, particularly for African

American youths. Young people with physical or mental disabilities were most often excluded, followed by LGB youths. Responses from adolescent girls, however, suggested that the programs catered to boys and the physically skilled. Professionals reported that they were confident about their multicultural competencies, rated their ability to deal with students of other cultural backgrounds as good, and recognized the importance of cultural competence. However, they recognized exclusion in physical activity settings, seldom took any proactive steps to promote inclusion, and noted a lack of training and resources. These preliminary results suggest that although professionals and participants see the need for resources for cultural competence, the work has barely begun.

Graduate sport psychology programs are the logical focus for the CSP approach, but sport psychologists can also extend educational programs to other sport professionals (e.g., coaches, teachers, trainers), future professionals, and the wider public. Here are several suggestions for sport psychology that can extend to other sport professionals:

•   Sport psychology professionals are in position to advocate and educate other sport professionals (e.g., teachers, coaches, athletic trainers, fitness instructors) about diversity. For example, coach or teacher education workshops might incorporate multicultural competencies through role-playing that involves gender stereotypes.

•   Faculty in sport psychology programs can ensure that courses and practical experiences adequately address multicultural concerns. Programs might offer a specific course on diversity in sport psychology. If no specific course exists, they can ensure that cultural diversity is covered in other sport psychology courses and that multicultural competencies are addressed in internship and practicum experiences.

•   Regardless of whether specific courses cover diversity issues, all courses must provide real-world examples that reflect the diversity of the population and the range of cultural variations. Similarly, texts and resources should reflect the true diversity of sport. If current texts are not adequate, seek other resources and call on authors and publishers to address multicultural diversity. Offices of multicultural affairs, community programs, organizations, and online resources that specifically address cultural competence and diversity are especially helpful.

Applied sport psychologists can go beyond typical athletic programs to promote inclusive sport for all.
© China Photos/Getty Images Sport

IN THE PUBLIC INTEREST

To become competent practitioners of CSP, applied sport psychologists must go beyond traditional institutions and consulting practices and advocate for inclusive, empowering sport for all. Sport psychologists can be advocates for diverse and underrepresented groups in their communities and in the larger sport world. They can extend services to a wider population, help other sport professionals develop multicultural competencies, and advocate for public policies and programs that ensure that sport programs promote health and well-being for all.

- Applied sport psychologists can expand their consulting services beyond elite athletes. Consultants in the United States typically seek contacts with university teams, Olympic training programs, and professional sport. Youth programs, public schools, and community programs offer sport to a more diverse population, and those participants (including the coaches and instructors) can benefit from applied sport psychology. Students looking for internships, as well as their faculty supervisors, might look to the YMCA and YWCA, Boys and Girls clubs, and community agencies as potential sites.

- Sport psychology professionals can work with other sport professionals, particularly coaches and program administrators, to help address discrimination and diversity and promote fair treatment for all. Sport psychology consultants can assist athletic departments and community sport programs in developing or revising policies to better serve diverse populations. For example, sport and exercise psychology professionals could suggest policies related to the recruitment and retention of minority or female coaches.

KEY POINTS FOR ADDRESSING CULTURAL DIVERSITY

The multicultural and sport psychology literature reviewed in this chapter highlights several themes and directions. Following are key points for advancing a sport psychology that affirms cultural diversity.

- The multicultural framework that guides this chapter emphasizes the following themes:
  - We all have multiple cultural identities that vary across individuals, time, and context.
  - Gender and culture relations involve power and privilege.
  - Multicultural perspectives demand action for social justice.
- Sport does not reflect the cultural diversity of the larger population. White males are overrepresented in sport, especially in power positions such as coaching and administration. Physical activity decreases across the adult life span, with men more active than women and racial and ethnic minorities less active across all age groups.
- The extensive literature on sex differences supports the gender similarities hypothesis (i.e., males and females are more alike than different). However, gender stereotypes, perceptions, and social context are powerful influences on sport and exercise behavior.
- Stereotypes and bias based on gender, race and ethnicity, and sexuality affect perceptions and behaviors in sport. Exclusion based on physicality (i.e., physical abilities, size, appearance) is seldom discussed but is nearly universal in sport and physical activity programs.
- Recommendations for addressing cultural diversity cover science, practice, education, and public interest:
  - Researchers must expand the multicultural scholarship and methodologies.
  - Practicing professionals must develop multicultural competencies in the areas of awareness, understanding, and culturally appropriate interventions.
  - Multicultural scholarship and competencies must be part of graduate programs, and sport psychologists can extend educational programs to other sport professionals.
  - To truly demonstrate multicultural competence, sport psychologists can extend services to a wider population, help other sport professionals, and advocate for public policies and programs that ensure sport for all.

- Sport psychology professionals must understand and adhere to the APA multicultural guidelines. Within our own professional organizations—the AASP and the International Society of Sport Psychology (ISSP)—members can advocate for addressing diversity in organizational programs, policies, and publications. As Kamphoff and colleagues (2004) demonstrated, cultural diversity is rarely addressed at AASP conferences. Organizations can offer continuing-education workshops and demand that certified consultants demonstrate multicultural competencies and practice CSP.

- Sport psychology professionals can also advocate for sport for all at the societal level. As professionals, we can call on elected officials and governmental agencies to support policies and programs that are inclusive and beneficial to the wider population. We can advocate for public policies and programs that provide open access and availability of sport and physical activity in our communities.

These recommendations are a starting point. Sport psychology professionals can find many ways to promote sport for all so that the benefits are not limited to the elite and mainstream clients. To do that, sport psychology must expand the scholarly base on cultural diversity, adopt multicultural competencies for professional practice, ensure that educational programs include multicultural diversity, and advocate for inclusive, empowering sport programs that contribute to the health and well-being of all.

Strategies for Reflective Cultural Sport Psychology Research

Kerry R. McGannon, PhD, and Christina R. Johnson, PhD

In the sport psychology literature, the term *cultural sport psychology* (CSP) is broad. Thus, CSP research can be carried out in a variety of ways. It can focus on marginalized cultures and ethnicities using quantitative research tools (Duda & Allison, 1990; Duda & Hayashi, 1998; Ram, Starek, & Johnson, 2004) or qualitative research tools (Hanrahan, 2004; Schinke et al., 2006). Culturally sensitive strategies can also be employed in applied settings, with workshops and specialized courses developed for service providers who work with marginalized athletes (Hanrahan, 2004; Martens, Mobley, & Zizzi, 2000).

CSP research can further include exploring the experiences of athletes, consultants, and coaches using a critical cultural studies approach that focuses on social difference, distribution of power, and social justice as interrelated concerns (Butryn, 2002; Fisher, Butryn, & Roper, 2003, 2005; Roper, 2001; Roper, Fisher, & Wrisberg, 2005; Ryba & Wright, 2005). Examples of topics in this genre include exploring how sport psychology training privileges a particular gender, race, and social class or how particular narratives on sport identity categories (e.g., minority athlete, female athlete, lesbian athlete, disabled athlete) have implications for psychological experiences. Additionally, categories such as race, ethnicity, and gender may be explored in terms of how they create social justice issues between consultant and sport institution, consultant and athlete, coach and athlete, athlete and athlete, or researcher and research participant. Endorsing a single method is the antithesis of a cultural studies approach (King, 2005). Given that critical cultural studies assumes people's personal experiences are produced by complex contexts (e.g.,

political, economic, gendered, racial), qualitative approaches that capture this complexity of experience and context tend to be highlighted (King, 2005; Silk, Andrews, & Mason, 2005). In choosing to carry out research in this manner, the researcher faces a conundrum: Which qualitative approaches capture an intricate analysis of context, culture, and personal experience? How can we decide if we have chosen an approach that allows for critical analysis in a cultural studies framework?

To begin answering these questions, we first explore what it might mean to do reflective sport psychology research. Following from this, we examine a more specific form of reflective sport psychology research—reflexivity—from a critical cultural studies perspective. The implications of reflexive research that takes a critical cultural studies perspective will be discussed in the context of self and identity, a topic at the forefront of reflective and reflexive CSP research. We begin by defining the term *reflective* in the context of CSP and then delineating the term from a critical cultural studies perspective, including researcher reflexivity. The implications of carrying out reflexive research for the self, identity, and the research process will then be discussed.

Next, we outline how CSP research traditionally conceptualizes self and identity in ways that are reflective, but not reflexive, in the context of critical cultural studies. We then take a look at creative analytical practice (CAP) ethnography (Richardson, 2000a, 2000b; Richardson & St. Pierre, 2005) as a means of exploring the details of carrying out reflexive research from a cultural studies perspective as it relates to the self and identity of the researcher. Finally, we present two examples of writing stories (Richardson, 1995; 2000a; Richardson & St. Pierre, 2005; Sparkes, 1996) to illustrate reflexive sport psychology research from a critical cultural studies perspective. By structuring the chapter in this way, we illuminate potential questions and suggest some ways those questions might begin to be answered—that is, we offer techniques for reflectively and critically exploring how the researcher's self and identity might affect both the techniques and the conclusions of sport psychology research (Smith & Sparkes, 2005).

TERMINOLOGY CLARIFICATIONS

It might be useful to clarify some terminology before proceeding. The terms *positivism*, *postpositivism*, *postmodernism*, and *poststructuralism* are used frequently to talk about research, and often they are used to mean different things. Here we provide a brief definition of how each term will be used in this chapter.

Positivism has previously been defined as a philosophical stance that assumes the independent existence of objective reality that can be revealed through careful and bias-free observation (Ponterotto, 2005; see also chapters 3 and 4). Positivism suggests that things have meaning before and independent of any scientific awareness of them. With this in mind, the positivist researcher sets out to discover reality while trying to maintain a value-free, objective stance.

Postpositivism diverges from positivism while still embracing some of the same basic views. Whereas a positivist research stance might hold that reality can be revealed with certainty through sound research techniques, a postpositivist stance is more moderate. Postpositivism differs from positivism in that it "talks of probability rather than certainty, claims a certain level of objectivity rather than absolute objectivity and seeks to approximate the truth rather than aspiring to grasp it in its totality or essence" (Crotty, 1998, p. 29).

> If lives, stories, bodies, identities, and selves in sport and physical activity are multidimensional, constructed, complex, and changing in time and with context, then researchers might seek forms of analysis that are sensitive to, and respectful of, this complexity and multiplicity. (Smith & Sparkes, 2005, p. 214)

Postmodernism questions the notion that any one particular method, theory, discourse, or worldview is the right way to know about people. Truth and knowledge claims about people serve particular interests that

are located in local, cultural, and political struggles. Although researchers can claim to know something about people, that knowledge is partial, local, historical, and fragmented (Richardson, 2000b).

Poststructuralism is a form of postmodernism that gives primacy to the process and outcome of language, as opposed to the content, and how language is tied to discursive and social practices. Understanding language as competing discourses and competing ways of giving meaning to the world makes language a site of exploration and struggle. Because people are subject to competing discourses to make sense of who they are, their sense of self is shifting and contradictory. Researchers are therefore invited to explore ways of knowing to understand themselves reflexively as people writing from particular positions within discourses (Richardson, 2000b).

The terms *postmodernism* and *poststructuralism* are complex, contested, and used in multiple ways (Crotty, 1998; Grenz, 1996; Weedon, 1997). Thus, our explanation of postmodernism and poststructuralism should not be viewed as *the* way to make sense of their meaning. Our intention in choosing these particular views is in keeping with our focus on researcher reflexivity with a critical cultural studies sensibility (page 59). These definitions were largely drawn from Richardson (2000a, 2000b), whose work has informed research in the cultural studies realm of sport and physical activity.

REFLECTIVE CSP RESEARCH

The notion of reflective practice has been applied widely in teacher education (Cruickshank, 1985; Dewey, 1910; Hatton & Smith, 1994; Kane, Sandretto, & Heath, 2004) and coaching (Gilbert & Trudel, 2001; Schinke & Tabakman, 2001). In a classic sense, reflection is an "[a]ctive, persistent, and careful consideration of any belief or supposed form of knowledge in light of the grounds that support it, and the further conclusions to which it tends" (Dewey, 1910, p. 6). More recently, Osterman (1990) defined reflective practice as "challenging, focused, and critical assessment of one's own behavior as a means toward developing one's own craft" (p. 134). Hatton and Smith (1994) expanded the definition to include critical reflection as "making judgments about whether professional activity is equitable, just, and respectful of persons or not . . . critical reflection locates any analysis of personal action within wider socio-historical and politico-cultural contexts" (p. 35). Reflective CSP research can use positivist, postpositivist, postmodern, and poststructural perspectives. It also involves careful consideration of two key items: how knowledge is created and the cultural and social implications of research.

REFLEXIVITY

From a critical cultural studies perspective, the term reflective is tied to notions of reflexivity, whereby issues relating to the self and identity of the researcher and the research process come to the fore. Reflexivity raises questions such as, "How do my identity and social position bring me to ask particular questions and interpret phenomena in particular ways?" and "How do my own identity and social position privilege particular choices in the research process while also marginalizing particular choices?" Such questions shape the research process in politically, socially, and culturally specific ways (Sparkes, 2002). These questions have further implications for how marginalized cultures and identities are researched, portrayed, and ultimately written about in sport psychology. Asking these questions may also result in the researcher producing narratives that challenge, produce, or perpetuate power structures that empower or disempower coaches, consultants, or athletes.

Being reflexive also means questioning the possibility of collecting and evaluating data with complete detachment and objectivity. Thus reflexive researchers actively acknowledge and view their own experiences in the field by exploring how such interpretations come about, asking themselves, "What do I know, why do I know, and how do I know it?" (Hertz, 1997). For example, a Caucasian sport psychology consultant working with minority athletes might ask the following: In what ways do my social class and social position produce particular power hierarchies? Toward what end do those power hierarchies structure my interactions with, and interpretations of, the athletes? How do these same issues structure how the athletes respond in the consulting context? A researcher who seeks to interview minority athletes or gay or lesbian athletes to understand their experiences in a particular sport might ask similar questions.

Examining such questions in the context of power dynamics between consultant and athlete or researcher and athlete would also require attention to the larger institutions (e.g., cultural capitalism in sport contexts) and social norms (e.g., normative heterosexuality) that create spoken and unspoken power differentials. Asking questions in relation to power goes beyond conducting a bracketing interview (Denzin & Lincoln, 1994) in which the researcher explores how biases facilitate or limit data collection, analysis, and interpretation, though such acknowledgment is important. From a critical cultural studies perspective, in order to be reflexive,

researchers need to reflect on the political dimensions of fieldwork, the webs of power that circulate in the research process, and how these shape the manner in which knowledge is constructed. Likewise, they need to consider how issues of gender, nationality, race, ethnicity, social class, age, religion, sexual identity, disability, and able-bodiedness shape knowledge construction. (Sparkes, 2002, p. 17)

Thus, researchers not only acknowledge their own biases and the social categories to which they belong, but they also explore how these biases and categories position research participants in relation to the social categories to which participants belong. (As the term is used here, *research participant* refers to people whom the researcher is interviewing and trying to glean experiences from. The term *coparticipant* is sometimes used when referring to the research process to minimize inherent power dynamics between researcher and researched.) Further, exploring how such positioning of researcher and coparticipant shapes what is reported and (re)presented is also an important step in being reflexive (Richardson, 1998, 2000a, 2000b). This exploration of how the researcher and coparticipant shape representation in the research process is in contrast to research reports that situate research participants in cultural and historical locations and then (re)present their experiences (Sparkes, 2002). In those reports, the researcher is absent from most segments of the finished text with only the words, actions, and thoughts of the participants written as research; in other words, the researcher disappears behind a descriptive narrative (see figure 6.1).

IMPLICATIONS FOR RESEARCH

These ideas have profound implications for representation in qualitative research because they challenge the notion of the researcher as an impersonal, invisible narrator. By being reflexive, researchers dispel the notion that they are speaking from a neutral voice and speaking for research participants. This acknowledgment of the researcher's voice influencing the research process further highlights power relationships in field research in the form of authorship issues (Gergen & Gergen, 2000). How might researchers treat their own voice? Should the researcher's voice be one among many or should it have special privileges? Which voice speaks in the research and why? What voices are suppressed and how might these voices be heard and represented? These questions become even more salient when exploring marginalized cultures and identities in sport because of the power and social

FIGURE 6.1 As CSP researchers, we must recognize that our perceptions of ourselves and our research participants are highly subjective, even for people of shared cultural backgrounds.

CSP researcher

Research participant

structures that often hold particular norms, values, and ideas as natural, and therefore unquestionable, truths. Acknowledging power relationships by exploring multiple viewpoints and values can begin to empower marginalized cultures and identities to speak for themselves.

In his edited volume, *Telling Tales in Sport and Physical Activity: A Qualitative Journey,* Sparkes (2002) outlined how the expanding landscape in qualitative research in a postmodern age has placed qualitative researchers in the difficult position of confronting representation, reflexivity, and voice. There are no easy solutions to these dilemmas. Similar to Sparkes (who advocated Tierney's [1997] approach), however, we see researcher reflexivity as an opportunity to confront confusion and discomfort during the research process. More specifically, reflexivity may present the researcher with dilemmas about how to express one's social position and identity without marginalizing other cultures and identities. Such dilemmas provide researchers with the opportunity "to confront the issues of identity and representation and consider how we might develop texts that highlight the problematic worlds we study, our relationships to such worlds, and how we translate them" (Tierney, 1997, p. 34).

Before exploring ways in which this opportunity might be realized, we will outline how traditional approaches to self and identity contribute toward understanding culture in sport psychology. We will also highlight differences between the goals of traditional research and those of research emphasizing reflexivity from a critical cultural studies perspective. Bringing these differences into focus will allow us

to illuminate what a reflexive approach to self and identity entails and the potential contributions of such an approach to sport psychology research.

EXPLORING SELF AND IDENTITY WITH POSITIVIST AND POSTPOSITIVIST PARADIGMS

We have shown that reflexive CSP research from a critical cultural studies perspective involves self-conscious choices on the part of the researcher regarding research questions, methodology, and writing styles, all of which stem from a particular paradigmatic and epistemological standpoint. These choices are quite different from those made by the majority of CSP researchers on self and identity.

PARADIGMS

A good place to begin to understand the differences in perspectives and their implications for self and identity research is to outline the concept of paradigms. A paradigm is a set of assumptions, concepts, values, and practices that defines reality for the communities that share it (Denzin & Lincoln, 2005; Guba, 1990). A paradigm encompasses a researcher's worldview on epistemology, methodology, ethics, and ontology (Denzin & Lincoln, 2005). Epistemology is how we explain how we know what we know (Crotty, 1998; Denzin & Lincoln, 2005). For example, a researcher may believe that social or cultural realities are orderly, predictable, and describable. That epistemology will influence the researcher's methodology for acquiring—and constructing or perpetuating—knowledge about the world or a given phenomenon (Crotty, 1998; Denzin & Lincoln, 2005).

For example, the researcher who subscribes to an epistemological starting point that the world is orderly and predictable is likely to choose methodologies that aid in prediction or description, such as the use of survey data to construct descriptive or predictive statistical tests. Methodological choices—as well as analytic and rhetorical choices—are tied to underlying epistemological and theoretical perspectives (Crotty, 1998; Denzin & Lincoln, 2000, 2005; Saukko, 2003). In this sense, methodology reflects a "wider package of both tools and a philosophical and political commitment that come with a particular research 'approach'" (Saukko, 2003, p. 8).

Let's continue the example of research that begins with the paradigm of the social world as orderly and predictable. In an insightful paper, Weinberg and colleagues (Weinberg et al., 2000) first sought to describe and "compare motives for participation of youth in competitive sport versus physical activity" (p. 325) and to "examine the relationship between culture and participation" (p. 326). In other words, a postpositivist epistemological approach was adopted whereby the research was geared toward the characterization of reality as a research goal. Weinberg and colleagues sought to "compare" and "examine" what they measured as the realities of motives for sport and physical activity participation.

The methodologies chosen for this paradigm often involve experimental treatments or comparisons among groups. These methods quantify social worlds so as to facilitate order, explanation, and prediction (Guba & Lincoln, 2005; Heron & Reason, 1997). Weinberg and colleagues used a postpositivist perspective to guide the questions asked in the research process, the data gathered, and the analysis created. They used various questionnaires to quantify participation motives. Further, belonging to a certain gender or culture—the researchers compared samples from the United States, Australia, and New Zealand—were treated as variables. This is important for two reasons. First, each of the cultures represents a centrally Westernized and industrialized lifestyle. Second, by treating both gender and culture as categorical variables, the complex diversity that exists in genders and cultures is somewhat masked.

Psychology and sport psychology have tended to subscribe to postpositivist assumptions that characterize the individual as a fixed or given entity, separate from culture, history, or situation. The features of the self are thus regarded as predictable from a small number of identity categories such as gender, race, religion, ability, and age (e.g., uses of self throughout Fox, 1997). CSP research that begins in a postpositivist perspective, such as the example cited above, allows for the belief that identity differs across various cultures. This research may assume that the variability in groups or cultures is minimal, thus simplifying potentially large and rich sources of diversity. Weinberg and colleagues dealt with this in the analysis by suggesting that the "amount of variance not accounted for . . . may be indicative of such cultural variation" (2000, p. 341).

A number of scholars in sport psychology have begun to call for culturally sensitive research (e.g., Butryn, 2002; Ryba & Wright, 2005; Weinberg et al., 2000). Currently, the notion that the truth of self and identity is singular and knowable through sound scientific techniques characterizes a great deal of research in CSP (see Culver, Gilbert, & Trudel, 2003, and Krane, Anderson, & Strean, 1997, for useful reviews of the state of sport psychology research). Rigorous CSP research such as that of Weinberg and colleagues is reflective as defined previously. This work is well thought out, is contemplative, and offers useful examination of broad differences between cultures. This type of work is not reflexive in the critical cultural studies sense of the term, but it offers useful generalizations regarding cultural differences. However, it may miss the richness of detail that alternative ways of writing and knowing could offer.

APPLYING POSTPOSITIVIST EPISTEMOLOGY

Using a postpositivist epistemology to carry out reflective CSP research (what Sparkes [2002] characterizes as scientific or realist tales), authors may use their own relative position of power, authority, and objectivity to "obscure and apparently distance the disembodied author from the data" (Sparkes, 2002, p. 44). The self and identity of the researcher remain absent to maintain so-called objectivity. Further, identities (e.g., race, gender, nationality, age) of the researcher and research participants are regarded as biological givens residing in the individual. Self and identity from a postpositivist perspective, then, are conceptualized as structures or processes in the mind, or as social properties of culture that later become internalized into the mind (Cerulo, 1997); that is, the thing we call *self* is stable, exists concretely somewhere in the person's mind, and is formed only in part via cultural categories of identity such as race, gender, nationality, and age.

In a small body of CSP literature, authors have examined various identity categories (e.g., race, ethnicity, gender) and their relationship to sport participation from this perspective. These studies include quantitative work (Brandl-Bredenbeck & Brettschneider, 1997; Caglar & Asci, 2006; Curry & Weiss, 1989; Gano-Overway & Duda, 2001; Weinberg et al., 2000). This research is particularly compelling because it offers concrete, quantifiable evidence that culture matters. Cultural background makes a difference in how people see themselves and the world. With one interesting exception (Gano-Overway & Duda, 2001), quantitative work relied on cross-cultural comparisons to examine differences between groups. Specifically, racial or ethnic groups were categorized and then were compared using univariate or multivariate analyses of variance techniques (see table 6.1). Because analyses of variance are strengthened by the assumption that within-group variance is minimized and between-group variance is maximized (Bernard, 2000), this technique cannot account for the many complexities in identity categories.

Gano-Overway and Duda (2001) partially circumvent this issue through the use of hierarchical regression techniques. In examining the goal orientations of American athletes, these authors dichotomized race (African American or White American) but captured ethnic identity on a continuous scale using Phinney's (1992) Multigroup Ethnic Identity Measure (MEIM). The primary purpose of this study was "to examine the main and interaction effects of race/ethnicity, ethnic identification, and gender on goal orientations" (Gano-Overway & Duda, 2001, p. 347), which again seeks to find differences among groups and assumes similarity in groups. This approach is particularly useful when the research goal is to compare broad cultural generalizations across various groups. Research of this type can provide the basic framework to begin considering some of the deeper complexities among as well as within cultures.

Three qualitative studies provide examples of delineating similarities and differences among groups in regard to various identity categories (Dagkas & Benn, 2006; Lally, 2007; McGinley, Kremer, Trew, & Ogle, 1998). Using structured, semistructured, or in-depth interview techniques, the authors of these studies also considered identity inherent with group membership (e.g., religious groups, active versus retired athlete groups; see table 6.2). Krane (1996, 2001; Krane, Barber, & McClung, 2002) took a different angle by acknowledging a number of social forces and powers through which identities, specifically sexual identities, are formed and claimed. Krane and colleagues describe the effortful, social process of establishing a stable or predictable identity as "individuals organize and attach meaning to their social environment . . . and define their place in society" (2002, p. 28). Similar to postpositivist quantitative research, postpositivist qualitative research provides useful descriptions of variations among groups. Moreover, this type of qualitative work gives voice to silenced identities (e.g., lesbian identities), adds richness in identity description, and acknowledges the variability in groups.

Regardless of their methodological approach (quantitative or qualitative), these postpositivist studies are reflective but perhaps not reflexive in a critical cultural studies sense. Postpositivist, reflective CSP research contributes greatly to the field by highlighting the importance of studying culture in the first place as well as providing the starting point for acknowledging the existence of multiple viewpoints in sport psychology. These postpositivist, reflective studies also offer important insights in the realm of self, identity, and CSP. Further, sport psychology has been slow to consider culture as a variable (Duda & Allison, 1990; Duda & Hayashi, 1998), and although projects that consider culture as a singular variable may risk overlooking the diversity within cultural or identity groups, they provide a place in which diversity can be considered (see figure 6.2).

Additionally, these works are the beginning of a body of literature that reminds sport psychology researchers and practitioners that multiple viewpoints exist. Postpositivist approaches committed to exploring cross-cultural differences are the beginning of an acknowledgment that celebrating a diversity of cultures "can occur only when researchers and consultants focus on the inclusion of subjects from outside the mainstream and conduct their work with an openness and flexibility to variation" (Duda & Hayashi, 1998, p. 481). Again, considering our original definition of reflective as thoughtful or contemplative, numerous existing studies (e.g., Brandl-Bredenbeck & Brettschneider, 1997; Calgar & Asci, 2006; Curry & Weiss, 1989; Dagkas & Benn, 2006; Gano-Overway & Duda, 2001; Lally, 2007; McGinley et al., 1998; Weinberg et al., 2000) provide excellent reflective postpositivist methodological examples.

In light of the underlying assumption of postpositivist research—that a truth can exist in the abstract, separate from culture or discourse—the ways in which gender, race, ethnicity, and social class shape knowledge in politically, socially, and culturally specific ways may go unacknowledged. By acknowledging the political forces surrounding knowledge and self and by writing ourselves into our research, we can also begin to reflexively understand

TABLE 6.1 SELF AND IDENTITY: QUANTITATIVE METHODS IN CSP USING POSTPOSITIVIST POSITIONING

	Brandl-Bredenbeck & Brettschneider (1997)	Caglar & Asci (2006)	Curry & Weiss (1989)	Gano-Overway & Duda (2001)	Weinberg et al. (2000)
Theoretical perspective	Self-concept (Shavelson, Hubner, & Stanton, 1976)	Self-concept (Fox & Corbin, 1989; Shavelson et al., 1976)	Symbolic interactionist (Mills, 1940) Sport socialization (Donnelly & Young, 1988)	Goal perspective theory	Competence motivation theory (Harter, 1981) Goal orientation theory (Nicholls, 1984) Self-determination theory (Deci & Ryan, 1985)
Operationalizing self/identity	Nationality Gender Age Hierarchical/ multidimensional self-concept	Gender National identity in collective vs. individualist cultures (Hofstede, 1991)	Gender Country of residence	Gender Race Ethnic identity (continuous variable)	Gender Nationality
Population	Former West German adolescents (n = 1,106) Former East German adolescents (n =1,018) New York adolescents (n = 551)	Turkish university students (female: n = 419; male: n = 466)	Austrian student sport club members (female: n = 142; male: n = 159) American student athletes (female: n = 178; male: n = 219)	White American (N = 161; female: n = 65; male: n = 51) and African American track and field athletes (N = 55; female: n = 23; male: n = 32)	Males (n = 822) and females (n = 650) from United States (n = 474), Australia (n = 577), New Zealand (n = 421)
Data collection	Self-Description Questionnaire-II (SDQ-II) (Marsh, 1990)	Physical Self-Perception Profile (PSPP) (Fox & Corbin, 1989) Physical Activity Assessment Questionnaire (PAAQ)	Modified Sports Identity Index (SII), including Self-Role Scale (involvement of self in sport) and RP Scale (reasons for participating)	Multigroup Ethnic Identity Measure (MEIM) Task and Ego Orientation in Sport Questionnaire (TEOSQ) Beliefs About the Causes of Sport Success Questionnaire (BACSS)	Questionnaires: Peer comparisons of physical activity participation (Kimiecik et al., 1996) Reasons for participation in sport or physical activity (Gould et al., 1985)
Analytic strategy	Quantitative, ANOVA, ANCOVA	Quantitative, 2 × 2 (female/male × low-high physical activity group) MANOVA	Quantitative, 2-way ANOVA	Quantitative, hierarchical regression analysis	Between-group multivariate analyses of variance
Interpret/present	Cross-cultural comparison Scientific tale	Comparison with extant data on Western cultures Scientific tale	Cross-national comparison Scientific tale	Cross-racial comparison Scientific tale	Cross-national comparison Scientific tale

TABLE 6.2   SELF AND IDENTITY: QUALITATIVE METHODS IN CSP USING POSTPOSITIVIST POSITIONING

	Dagkas & Benn (2006)	Krane (1996)	Krane, Barber, & McClung (2002)	Lally (2007)	McGinley, Kremer, Trew, & Ogle (1998)
Theoretical perspective	Interpretive/ comparative	Conceptual model for studying lesbians in sport	Social identity theory	Self-schemata (Markus, 1977)	None
Operationalizing of self/identity	Religion Gender Nationality	Sexual identity	Sexual identity	Athletic vs. retired identity	Religion and community membership
Population	Greek Muslim females, aged 13-15 (*n* =24) British Muslim females, aged 18-21 (*n* = 20)	None	Female athletes (*n* = 123)	Canadian student-athletes (female: *n* = 3; male: *n* = 3)	Male and female adults from Northern Ireland (*n* = 1007)
Data collection	Semi-structured interviews	Consolidation of previous literature into a conceptual framework	Gay Games V participation survey	In-depth, unstructured interviews	Structured interview
Analytic strategy	Qualitative, thematic analysis	Review of literature	Qualitative, inductive content analysis	Qualitative, longitudinal, inductive content analysis	Qualitative
Interpretation/ presentation	Thematic Greek vs. British experiences Realist tale	Positioning for model Realist tale	Thematic Realist tale	Thematic Realist tale	Comparison by community Scientific tale

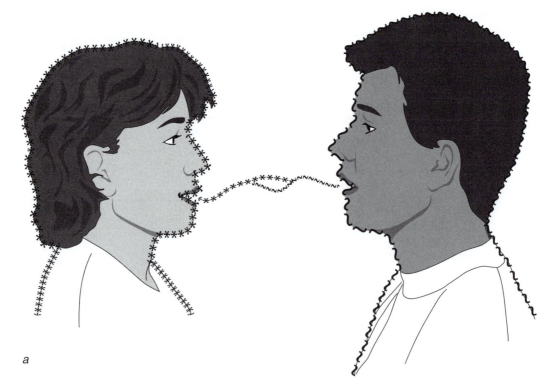

a

FIGURE 6.2   Are we ever able to fully (a) understand or (b) represent other people and their experiences?

how the innumerable, divergent, and competing social, political, and historical processes surrounding the construction of knowledge shape our research, our writing, and our work. With this in mind, we turn next to how a reflexive understanding can begin to be realized using a methodological tool (i.e., CAP ethnography) grounded in a paradigm different from that of postpositivism: postmodernism.

POSTMODERNIST IMPLICATIONS FOR SELF, IDENTITY, AND RESEARCH

In contrast to how self and identity are conceptualized in postpositivism, critical cultural studies researchers subscribe to a postmodernist paradigm that eschews notions of self and identity residing solely in the mind or tied solely to biology (McGannon & Mauws, 2000, 2002). Postmodernist perspectives also avoid privileging any one theory, discourse, or view of truth when it comes to conceptualizing the self and identity (Richardson, 2000a). No one particular method, theory, or discourse is claimed as the best for understanding the self and identity in sport psychology. Instead, all truth claims serve interests that can be located in personal, cultural, and political struggles—including those of the researcher (Richardson, 2000a; Richardson & St. Pierre, 2005).

POSTMODERNISM, POSTPOSITIVISM, AND POSTSTRUCTURALISM

A postmodern view of self and identity need not negate postpositivist methods and research. Rather, methods grounded in postpositivism can exist alongside postmodernist methods as part of several potential choices and research tools that can contribute toward multiple ways of knowing about the self and identity (Richardson & St. Pierre, 2005). For example, a researcher may take a postpositivist perspective to quantitatively explore how two cultures perceive competition in a sport context. Once similarities and differences are noted, the researcher may then use a postmodern sensibility to explore multiple explanations from the athletes' perspectives as to why such similarities and differences exist, how those similarities and differences are reproduced, and toward what end the experiences are empowering or disempowering for the athletes. The resulting insights could also be explored in the broader social and political context in order to ground the athletes' subjectivities and identities in socially and culturally specific ways.

A related form of postmodernist thinking that sheds further light on the conceptualization of self and identity is poststructuralism (McGannon & Mauws, 2002; Weedon, 1997). The contribution of poststructuralism to conceptualizing self and identity, which in turn has

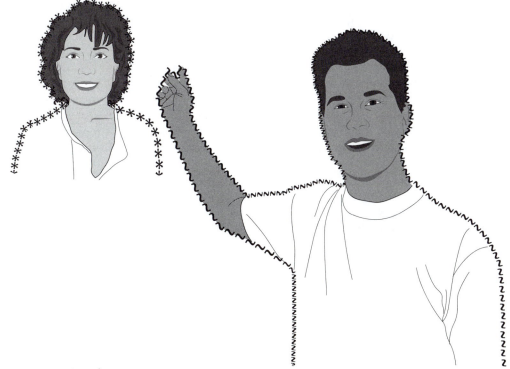

b

FIGURE 6.2 *(continued)*

implications for research exploring self and identity, is its focus on language as constructing, rather than reflecting, self-related views. This means that language is not the result of the self; instead, self and identity are a discursive accomplishment that is simultaneously local, social, cultural, and political (Richardson, 2000a; Richardson & St. Pierre, 2005).

Knowledge and conceptualizations of self and identity are further contextualized in social practice and webs of power (Weedon, 1997), making language the means by which "social organization and power are defined and contested and the place where one's sense of self—one's subjectivity—is constructed" (Richardson & St. Pierre, 2005, p. 961). Language and taken-for-granted social and biological identity categories (e.g., race, ethnicity, gender, sexuality) are understood as competing discourses that offer competing meanings and ways of thinking, feeling, and behaving in relation to the self. The interest is in how language is used in particular ways and in particular contexts to construct particular views of the self. In turn, the social, political, and behavioral effects connected to particular self-constructions are also of interest.

INSTRUCTIVE EXAMPLES

Poststructuralism has implications for how people make sense of themselves depending on the discourses available. If people make sense of their identity by drawing on limited discourses, they will have limited possibilities for thinking, feeling, and behaving. For example, a female athlete may find herself positioned in discourse that assumes women's bodies in sport are less feminine if they are muscular. In this discourse, female athletes must be a particular size and shape (e.g., smaller and less muscular) if they are to retain femininity. A female athlete who draws upon this limited discourse to make sense of her physical self may conclude that she is too big and too muscular, experiencing dissonance and disempowerment in relation to her athletic body.

In turn, since particular behaviors are connected to this discourse, the athlete may begin to police her dietary practices in unhealthy ways and undertake unhealthy exercise regimes to attain the body that this discourse naturalizes as feminine. Changing this way of thinking, feeling, and behaving when relating to her body may be difficult because broader sociocultural structures circulate these female body discourses as assumed truth. In this regard, the media reproduce limited views of athletic females by sexualizing them and reinforces these views by circulating stereotypes of female bodies that deviate from the socially con-

structed norms of femininity, such as the idea that muscular women are lesbians or masculine.

Additionally, other female athletes may construct their bodies in this same limited discourse, saying and doing similar things in relation to their own bodies that normalize what is said and done in this sport context. Finally, the athletes' coaches may say and do things that reinforce the so-called normal female body as a particular size and shape. Together, these social, cultural, and discursive practices reify (i.e., make concrete as a real and fixed truth) a particular view of the female body in athletics that is tied to various webs of power (e.g., the diet and fitness industry, patriarchal capitalism in sport, heteronormative values).

According to a poststructuralist perspective, people's subjectivity and sense of self are competing discourses, so it is also possible for female athletes to resist the views outlined previously and have empowering experiences in sport by drawing upon alternative discourses to make sense of their athletic identities. In this regard, a female athlete may draw upon a discourse of muscularity and performance in which muscle and size are viewed as resources for performance, strength, and empowerment. Female athletes who draw upon this discourse reject the notion that they cannot be feminine if they are muscular or that their sport and performance are tied to femininity in the first place.

Coaches who draw upon alternative discourses may interact with athletes using nongendered terms when constructing training sessions, emphasizing performance and skill rather than aesthetics and femininity. At the broader cultural level, in the media female athletes may speak out and serve as role models by drawing upon this alternative discourse. Together, these social, cultural, and discursive practices have the potential to construct alternative possibilities that enable women in athletics to experience their physical selves as empowering.

Note that because the discourse that muscularity is not feminine tends to be ubiquitous, female athletes drawing upon resistance discourses will find themselves simultaneously positioned in competing and contradictory discourses. This makes the female athlete's identity both a site for and subject of discursive, political, and power struggles, making power at times contested and at other times reproduced. Moreover, in light of these competing discourses, this final point reinforces that identity and subjectivity is shifting, contradictory, and complex, as opposed to stable and fixed (Richardson & St. Pierre, 2005).

What these examples reveal is that because poststructuralism focuses on power and discourse in the construction of self and identity (McGannon & Mauws, 2002; Weedon, 1997), it can be a useful theoretical tool for realizing researcher reflexivity. Specifically, for those interested in conducting and writing qualitative research from a poststructuralist perspective, this notion of self and identity as a historical, local, discursive accomplishment that is contradictory and complex suggests that researchers also need to be aware that they too are writing from particular positions in discourses at specific times (Richardson & St. Pierre, 2005).

As alluded to in our earlier discussion of reflexivity from a critical cultural studies perspective, although research participants are constructing their own identities in various power-infused discourses, so too are researchers. This has profound implications for what research questions are asked, how data are analyzed, and ultimately how results and voices are (re)presented. Acknowledging and embracing complexity of self and identity thus urges the researcher to be reflexive to further illuminate such understanding.

CONDUCTING CAP ETHNOGRAPHIC RESEARCH

Not surprisingly, an awareness of the constructed self as multifaceted and fluid raises the previously discussed conundrum facing researchers who employ a postmodernist sensibility: With genres of research and writing blurred and enlarged for multiple audiences, and with the researcher's own voice also the subject of research and inquiry, how might such work be carried out? In her work on alternative genres in qualitative writing, Richardson (1995, 1998, 2000a, 2000b) advocated forms of ethnographies that can challenge the assumptions of postpositivist approaches but are in-line with postmodernist assumptions, including any work "wherever the author has moved outside conventional social scientific writing" (Richardson & St. Pierre, 2005, p. 962).

CAP ethnography assumes that its product (i.e., research results) is inseparable from those who produced it (i.e., the researcher and research participants) and how it was produced (i.e., the methodology and methods), and that the research will be conducted in a postmodernist climate (Richardson, 2000a, 2000b; Richardson & St. Pierre, 2005). In light of this commitment to postmodernist assumptions, CAP ethnography thus holds promise for capturing the self and identity with a reflexive sensibility in sport psychology.

In her writings on CAP ethnography, Richardson pointed out that although it appears contradictory

to outline rigid standards for CAP writing practices, it is possible to be cognizant of particular questions when conducting research in this genre (Richardson, 2000a, 2000b; Richardson & St. Pierre, 2005, pp. 974-975). Because postmodernist perspectives emphasize that self and identity are discursively, socially, and politically constructed and are therefore complex, the overriding question now becomes, how might this complexity be captured? We suggest the following questions as a starting point for exploring CSP research using CAP ethnography:

- Are the authors cognizant of postmodernism?
- How did the authors come to write this text?
- How was the information gathered?
- How have the authors' subjectivities been both producers and products of this text?
- Do the authors hold themselves accountable to the standards of knowing and telling of the people they studied? (Richardson, 2000a)

TWO WRITING STORIES

In the examples that follow, we attempt to explore some of these details of researcher reflexivity (see table 6.3) via the construction of two related writing stories, or stories about the process of writing research (Holt, 2003; Richardson, 1995; Richardson & St. Pierre, 2005). In the first story, "Torn," Christina Johnson writes about her discomfort in the research process from field notes, interviews, and current self-reflections in relation to her experiences interviewing a coparticipant in her dissertation research. The goal of this writing story is to show how Christina's socially and discursively constructed identities affected the research process on many levels—her sense of identity led her to interact with research participants and to interpret her data in particular ways. By creating this writing story, Christina explores how those identity dilemmas in the research process led her to create a different narrative than she would have without the reflexive process.

"Torn" reflects a cross-cultural exchange between Christina Johnson and a participant in her dissertation research. Inspired by Jegatheesan's (2006) auto-ethnography of lived experience, it explores the complexity of author positioning in the research process and demonstrates how field work is complicated by the social positions from which researchers construct themselves in relation to research participants. This story further illustrates that researchers' identities are multiple, layered, and infused with ethical and power issues that require personal examination in light of their implications for writing about others (i.e., research participants). These records of thoughts, emotions, and conversations are one way of exploring the intricate and difficult aspects of considering one's own position—being reflexive—while doing cross-cultural research.

The second writing story, "Why Me? Exploring the Value of PMS," is based on a recorded conversation between authors Kerry McGannon and Christina Johnson about whether "Torn" accomplished its goal, and if so, how and for whose benefit. This piece was inspired by Ellis and Bochner's (2006) conversational story in which the merits of another researcher's work were analyzed, as well as Holt's autoethnographical (2003) story of recreated conversations about a manuscript he tried to publish.

This writing story is intended to reveal central tensions that both authors experienced (e.g., issues of power and representation in expressing a postmodernist voice without suppressing a postpositivist voice) when creating each writing story. These central tensions between power and representation are (re)produced in light of the authors' identities (e.g., feminist researcher, nontenured professor, Caucasian, middle class, female), all of which are constructed

TABLE 6.3   CREATIVE ANALYTICAL WRITING PRACTICES: THE *HOWS* OF REFLEXIVE RESEARCH

What it is	What it does	How to do it	How we did it
Create writing stories.	These are reflexive accounts of how you came to write the piece that allow you to situate your work in context. Writing stories remind us that the self and social science are culturally constructed and coconstructed.	Write about politics, family, sport/athletic experiences, and other personal biographies. Write historically and in the present.	Contrasted "Torn" with preceding text and tables. Conducted, recorded, and transcribed an interview about "Torn." Constructed a story called "Why Me? Exploring the Value of PMS," which is about the process of writing "Torn" and the current chapter.
Consider a field-work setting.	Allows you to consider various identities and subject positions you have or have had within the field.	Articulate your identities and social categories and note if, and, or how they change as the context changes (e.g., am I a feminist? A woman? Coach? Athlete? White?). Write about the event from these positions. What do you know from these different positions? Let the positions be in dialogue with one another. What is discovered? Are there inequalities?	["Torn": See especially the 2nd-5th journal entries and intervening notes; see also the 11th-13th entries and notes.] "Why Me?" weaves Kerry's and Christi's identities of researcher and academic into the text. Power issues are represented throughout the text.
Write a layered text.	Puts self into text and text into literatures and traditions of social science.	Begin with self story. Look at the narrative from your disciplinary perspective. Insert relevant analytical statements or references into narrative. Layering can be theoretical and include different speakers or ways of speaking.	["Torn": See notes throughout, especially 7th-10th journal entries and thoughts on tradition while reviewing the text of Maia.] "Why Me?" has academic talk, and the quoting of research is woven into the story. Both titles are metaphorical and rhetorical attempts to communicate multiple and different identities that both authors hold.

in the context of academic politics (e.g., wider social conventions for tenure-track professors). With both narratives, we hope to reveal that "rather than hiding struggle, concealing the very human labor that creates the text, writing stories would reveal emotional, social, physical, and political bases of the labor" (Richardson, 1995, p. 191).

TORN

December 07, 2007: Some notes for my readers: This has not been an easy project to write. Nor, I suspect, is it an easy thing to read. My intention, as I found the comments on the dated entries emerging as a narrative, was to create a text that was layered and complex. Within the following paragraphs, I hope the reader will encounter a layering of ideas, identities, and social and research issues. The dated journal entries that are interspersed throughout the narrative provide temporal and stylistic layering to the text. Readers may note that the journal entries are not in chronological order but instead represent a certain messy logic as I try to offer the reader a glimpse of my reflexive process and the careful consideration that goes into reflexive research. I encourage readers to consider their own identities as they read this text and to explore the different meanings that might emerge for them.

Let me tell you about torn. It isn't the sort of torn that happens when you take a bad step, feel the ligaments of your knee stretching and then snapping, although the visceral sensation is the same: a void where there once was substance. A structure is strained, pulled, and then broken. Something you once trusted as solid or stable becomes thin, pulled to the extent of its laxity. Torn is messy. Torn leaves jagged edges, messy, untidy bits that seem to have held together at one time but now are falling apart. Torn is that fleshy ripping sound that you feel more than hear, sense more than see, experience more than touch.

November 03, 2007: *Thoughts on writing a CSP chapter while jogging* Why tearing? It is a forcible and often unwilling process of separation. It is painful but can lead to rehabilitation, creating new strengths and new interpretations of meaning. Torn is a metaphor for challenging dominant paradigms—a physical sensation that refers to a less concrete process. Can we relate on different levels? Tearing away from something important to you? Tearing away from something you once trusted? Tearing away from what you thought

you knew was right? Tearing like this damn MCL (medial collateral ligament). What I trusted has failed me and now I have to cope.

It is with this sensation, this feeling of torn, that I would like to tell you about Maia. I would like to say that I know Maia and I can capture her here in words that will then tell her, become her, represent here. After all, Maia was, is a participant in my research, a subject in my study. Or was she, is she, a coparticipant in a writing project to create or construct knowledge? A cocreator in a creative project that I may have initiated but now share ownership of with the others who lend their stories to my writing?

June 02, 2006: *Notes on subject selection* Maia will provide an interesting perspective on physical activity and martial arts. She wears her headcovering during workouts and is respectful of me as a higher-ranking martial artist, but we seem to be peers as grad students. Good rapport, but we each have something to say to one another. She's Egyptian, and should be good contrast to Jamie from Senegal and Gretchen from American suburbia.

Maia and I are a world apart, yet I may presume to tell her story. Or, perhaps I am only telling my own. Maia tells me, so that I can recount, her story of her childhood in Kuwait, her adolescence in Egypt. Maia tells me about the ways she makes meaning out of the scarf she wears to cover her head, about how she feels naked if the slightest bit of her wrists or ankles are exposed in mixed company, about her pride in her sexual naiveté. She tells me about her experience of her body as a participant in a coed martial arts class. And I am torn because Maia's perspective is very different from my own in terms of how women should present in public.

June 28, 2006: *Field notes before interview* I'm at the House of Aromas and worried. I have an interview with Maia today and I'm nervous. Not sure why. Previous interviews have gone well. Am I threatened by Maia? She has strong opinions, and I am not sure what she thinks of me.

Our conversation happened in the summer, and I recall from my field notes consciously choosing to interview her in a coffee shop where we often encountered one another. It seemed a comfortable place, neither invading her private space nor using my crowded, noisy office as a place where my authority as interviewer would be foregrounded.

So, in the coffee shop, I sipped my three shots of espresso with a touch of sweetened milk and she sipped her water. It was hot that day as the late June sun was beginning to spur Iowa cornfields to life and turn my farm-girl complexion from pink to bronze. I had long since shed my winter jeans and long sleeves for summer shorts and T-shirts. As Maia talked about covering her body as part of her religious beliefs and cultural practices of femininity, she did not judge me. I judged myself as perhaps overly liberal in my dress.

February 12, 2007: *Reflections on field notes of Maia* Why does Maia make me question *me?* What have I learned from her and what have I learned about myself? I am a rural Midwesterner: privileged, pretty (I think), and with a promising future. I recall being forgetful one time; I asked my partner specifically what WASP stood for. The reply was quick, "It's you, dear." When I said, "No, really, I thought it had something to do with income," the reply was again quick: "Yes, it's you, dear." When I frowned and asked, "OK, what am I?" the picture became clear: White, Anglo-Saxon, Protestant, of middling socioeconomic status, heterosexual, and in the middle years of my life.

Maia offered insight into her culture without attempting to use my own as a standard of comparison. She talked about internalizing the values that were outwardly marked with her head scarf. She talked about being feminine without advertising her sexuality. She talked about her discomfort at having to occasionally "touch a boy" in the martial arts practices that we shared, how mortified she was that it was a "co-class" (coed). She echoed again, "It's a co-class. I just couldn't. But I did. But it was a co-class."

February 12, 2007: *Notes on writing about Maia* I am a feminist scholar, trained in the shadow of great women. Why did I not challenge her traditional beliefs?

June 28, 2006: *Field notes during interview* What's wrong with too much closeness in a co-class? If a male brushes your hand or touches your knee? I should physically push him back.

At a later point, when Maia launched into something resembling a tirade about the "college Barbies" who "sell themselves" and their sexuality on Friday nights at the bars, she talked about how they had missed the point of college. Maia was adamant about the ways in which sexuality becomes a marker for the physical presentation of college women.

June 28, 2006: *Field notes during interview* Does she buy into her own oppression? Is she oppressed? Also, is she blaming women for not coming halfway to end their own oppression? The Barbie girls, do they carry the blame for maintaining the power structure? Because she has not been Barbie (has she?), can she critique what they do?

I am torn about how to claim a position to "write up" Maia. She has told me of intimate moments, her experiences of her body, the cultures she has claimed as her own, the influences that were meaningful for her as she constructed a value system, a relationship with her physical self, or a sense of self at all. I am torn about how to "tell" Maia in research language.

June 29, 2006: *Notes following interview* Wish I had pointed out the irony of how her critique of other college women contrasted with her own internalized views on sexuality. Wish I had pointed out that the ways she marked her sexuality might be construed as oppressive, in her case covering from head to wrist to ankle to literally shroud any feminine markers from view, much in the ways she read the Barbies' presentation choices as oppressive. At the same time, I feel exposed, not wearing enough clothes to challenge her here. Do we have enough in common for me to challenge her?

Maia was part of my dissertation research. I was lucky enough to have a supportive, if not sometimes downright enthusiastic, adviser and a multidisciplinary committee that trusted my judgments and my arguments at nearly every turn, offering only respectful hints such as, "In my field we might examine . . ." Any drama was entirely of my own making and stemmed largely from a process of questioning the assumptions that I had extracted and internalized and claimed as my own from the rules of engagement of sport psychology. It was a certain tearing away from traditional assumptions and toward a riskier way of presenting myself.

March 10, 2007: *Thoughts on tradition while reviewing the text of Maia* From a traditional perspective, my opinions, my views, my emotions as author did not matter or even exist. I was to disappear in my text so as to allow that text to speak for itself, offering a clear and unambiguous portrait of reality. I was to offer insights into Maia's inner world, so different from my own, and give examples of the ways she voiced her realities. I was to create a text that was unequivocal. From the Latin, *unequivocal* translates roughly to "not of single voice." And I was to do this by claiming Maia's voice and blending it with or comparing it with the voices of others who had shared stories with me. I was to create a blend of Maia and the other research cocreators. But just not me—I was to disappear in my own text.

May 27, 2007: *Thoughts on constructing a CSP chapter* Reviewer's comments read, " 'Not of single voice' is confusing as *unequivocal* means 'unambiguous' or having only one possible meaning or interpretation." Although I do not mean to confuse my readers, the complexity I strive to capture is this: To be unambiguous or unequivocal in a research sense necessarily involves the blending of many voices ("not of single voice") into a homologous reproduction of what those voices might sound like if speaking together. To be unequivocal in a research sense means to create a single voice while risking silencing the singing of many voices. To be unequivocal in a research sense is to disregard the complexities inherent in recognizing that diverse research participants are "not of single voice." Yet the very meaning of the term *unequivocal* demands us to recognize that all research participants speak in different voices.

Torn. Maia and I are so alike but at once so different. We are both young professionals, students at the time of our research, both women challenged by our competitive choice of professional field, both actively participating in a martial art. But we are so different in cultural heritage, in upbringing, in attitudes, in values, in the ways we negotiate our own self-stories. And Maia differs radically from the other participants, with whom I could compare her story, reduce her richness of presentation to a simple statement of "Maia differs from Gretchen or Jamie or Vaughn or William in this way. . ." As Maia exposes and composes her stories for the benefit of my tape recorder and me, I know my vested interest is to turn those stories into a research piece and use them to my own advantage.

This is not a forum to tell Maia's story or even to examine the ways in which her story overlaps or challenges my own, but I will say one thing: The process of communicating with Maia across a cultural and political ocean and through the filter of differing uses of the English language was taxing, and I found myself questioning my own views of culture, art, and physical activity. At one point, Maia shook the loose end of her head scarf at me. In telling her story of talking with a man at the gym, she recounted, "You can't know me by the markers of my culture." When we wondered together if we could ever know each other, she said, "Yes, you can ask questions and learn." Then, she argued the point when I said, "No, you can't know me because my story shifts with every new circumstance."

This is a forum for me to communicate one key idea. The key idea is this: It is easy and comforting to internalize the ideals of the mainstream or dominant paradigm. I can internalize dominant values in regard to my understanding of people from diverse cultural or social groups and hence participate in the maintenance of cultural hierarchies.

June, 29, 2006: *Notes following interview* I am so aware of my Whiteness with Maia. Perhaps this is why she was threatening, why I had nerves before our interview. My arms and legs hang long from my shorts and short sleeves, and they are so pale next to her darker features and covered skin. My ignorance of world politics is highlighted next to her knowledge and passion for world affairs. I speak and write of being a feminist, desiring to make changes in the world that fit the principles that I hold dear. While Maia does make changes and fervently chooses to live out her values, I push for physical activity and sports for girls and women. I feel shallow, living in my privileged sphere, not knowing the hardships faced more globally.

In the same way, I can internalize the values and practices of dominant research and writing customs and hence write comfortably in a space where my voice tacitly puts forward scientific facts and findings. It is easy to exist, socially or professionally, in a dominant paradigm in which certain ways of being or knowing are privileged, particularly if we can choose to be, or know, or look a certain way.

May 11, 2007: *Notes on writing a CSP chapter* It would be so easy now to walk away, to leave the work behind. It pains me to write formulaically, and it pains me more to push the paradigm. There is safety in hiding behind "the way we've always done it." And there's nothing but hardship in doing it a new way. It would be such a privilege right now to disappear in my text, and the irony is this: I could! But instead, I will don my shorts and short sleeves. I feel naked next to Maia.

And so I am torn by competing interests and the process is no less painful than unlacing the ligaments of my arthritic knee. I have a vested interest in constructing scholarship that will allow me to keep my job and write and publish useful pieces of work. At the same time, it is meaningful to me to communicate the story that research cocreators such as Maia share with me in an ethical and sensitive way. As she tells her story of identity as a physically active person, a recreational athlete, and a member of a particular culture, I feel responsible to not consume that identity in my own. All the while, I am motivated and afraid as I develop this new facet of myself as an author.

To be reflective or reflexive is to expose oneself. To be reflective is to understand the joys and privileges and powers inherent in the job of psychology: meeting new people, gaining an understanding of how they negotiate themselves, and communicating this diversity publicly. To be reflective is also to understand the fear, embarrassment, or uncomfortable motives behind our work: that the status quo protects those who do not challenge the boundaries. And I am torn.

WHY ME? EXPLORING THE VALUE OF PMS

"**Does** 'Torn' deliver?" I begin. "That's what I was wondering—how do you feel about it and the goals that you set out to accomplish?"

Christi responds, "I think it got better with the insertion of my field notes and reflections, which was kind of a struggle because as I was writing I knew what was going through my head, right? And scribbling down on paper I knew what I was thinking in trying to communicate that, but making it concrete is a hard thing, remembering how much you have to guide the reader's hand so that your readers can get it."

"**You** know, one of the things I thought was funny—as I'm looking at the story—I notice that the phrase *postmodern story* acronyms to PMS!"

Christi laughs, "On so many levels!"

I echo the sentiment, "Yes, I know it's PMS on so many levels. Yet you've used realist words. You have one insert, where you talk from your field notes, and you have written, 'Notes on subject selection'—you're calling her a subject in postpositivist research terms?"

She nods. "Yeah, that was a conscious choice, calling it *subject selection*, because the whole notion of trying to figure out who would be useful participants in this study felt to me like selecting subjects. Because once selected, they seemed to understand themselves as subjects with a preloaded set of

assumptions about what it meant to be part of my dissertation research. They followed the rules, waited for me to ask questions, then answered. So I was actually going through a kind of a schizoid consciousness, like a double consciousness."

"**Christi**, I'm kind of worried. Are people going to get this? Will they see value in being self-reflexive or simply dismiss it as nonscientific, narcissistic navel gazing?"

She responds, "Do you think 'Torn' accomplishes the purposes we set out?"

I have to think for a moment before I answer, because the truth is, I have been wrestling with this since Christi gave me "Torn." I tell her my reservations: "Yes, but then again I understand postmodernism. Still, writing evocatively is not easy. I remember the first time I read Sparkes' autoethnography, *The Fatal Flaw* (1996). He sent it to me when I was getting ready to defend my dissertation, in 2001. As my external examiner, he was concerned. His comments on my dissertation were, 'You're absent from your own text,' and 'Have you thought about those kinds of things and the implications?' And I was like, 'Well, no I haven't, thanks!' So when I read *The Fatal Flaw* and reflect on it and what others say about it, they're very moved by it because it *is* evocative on so many levels. It draws you in, it makes you think, it makes you feel what he might be feeling. It's what makes his story valid, I guess, in terms of applying scholarly criteria when judging this genre of research as worthy and scholarly. But I don't know if people realize how difficult it is to write such a piece or what that process was."

Christi agrees. "Sparkes makes it look effortless because he's a clear writer and his form of layering is different from mine and different from Jegatheesen's. His style makes it look like, 'Oh these are just thoughts I dashed down on paper,' and yet the writing is so deeply contextualized. There are surface layers and deeper layers with that *Fatal Flaw* piece. I'm not sure I have that kind of talent—holy shit, he's good!"

"**I** feel the same way about my own writing in the CAP writing genre, but we're writing a different kind of reflexive story than Sparkes," I say defensively, "and we don't get to see what his process was in writing *The Fatal Flaw*—though I know he's published other pieces about criteria used to judge that piece as worthy scholarship. *The Fatal Flaw* is an autoethnography of his embodied self and not a writing story per se. Both are forms of evocative writing, though, in the sense that they do draw you in, and you can relate to it because you can share the various emotional aspects of the story, just accomplishing different purposes."

ON NARCISSISM: FOR WHOM AND FOR WHAT?

"**You** know, as I was writing "Torn," I was thinking about the few published writing stories—Richardson, Ellis and Bochner, and Holt as well. And I was thinking, 'When do we hit the saturation point of people talking about the writing process?' When does it get boring to hear about the writing process? Or does it?"

I recoil, "You've just triggered another one of my fears, that people read this chapter and they think, 'Useless navel gazing! Me looking at myself—so what? Who gives a rat's ass?'"

Christi nods, "Yeah, narcissism . . . but Richardson (1995, 2000a) talks about writing stories not as forums for self-indulgence and as replacements of other forms of ethnographic writing but instead regards them as a way to 'demystify students in the writing as research process. Reconfirm our relationships with humanities. Valorize reflexivity through the research process and . . . if we have access to other qualitative researcher's writing stories, our readings of their work would deepen and expand' (1995, p. 191). Which is what we said about Sparkes—we don't know what his process was, and if we did, that would be another phenomenal layer to show how difficult or easy evocative writing is. But then again, we're throwing around names like Richardson, Sparkes, Ellis and Bochner, Denzin and Lincoln—big players who are tenured and established in their careers. It's legit for them to take risks, whereas I feel we might not be afforded the same luxury if we take such a risk."

Knee deep in the tenure process, I relate particularly to her last statement. "I think just that idea of taking a risk and exploring one's own self and identity is important when exploring power issues and then articulating them. I mean, who can challenge in that context? Someone—whether researcher, student, coach, or athlete—might read this and say, 'This is all well and good, but you know I can't have that voice because there are things that won't allow it.' But I think the point of being self-reflexive is not to self-indulge but to

create a space where people can acknowledge these kinds of power issues.

"I know this is true of me. I don't always realize who I am silencing so at times it goes unspoken or unrealized. When you talk about race or you talk about ethnicity or gender and gendered categories—this idea of 'We're all just going to live in harmony and we're going to give equal voice to all these pieces' might then erase the fact that there are power issues that need to be acknowledged. Power issues like the social position of the researcher who is afforded more status and control in the research process than research participants are. Power issues that Roper (2001) talked about in relation to sport psychology consultants, and researchers who want to embrace feminist perspectives but face struggles and stereotypes because feminism is marginalized in the field. Or gay or lesbian athletes who feel silenced in particular sport contexts in light of the history and culture in that sport that silence their voices. Or power issues around White privilege when one is interviewing athletes of different races and ethnicities, like what Ted Butryn talked about in his 2002 paper where he explored his own White privilege as a researcher and a consultant in relation to an African American graduate student. So I hope reflexive work provides a space for those issues to be explored or further explored as well."

Christi responded, "Something that I tried to get out at the end of "Torn" is that there are power issues that you choose to be a part of and there are power issues that are written on you, you know, like when someone just by virtue of being able to see that you are a woman or a different race—you are visibly marked by power issues because of the meanings that people attribute to particular gendered or racial categories. So people can really see you and what's taken for granted is written on you. There are power issues surrounding race and gender, age, and socioeconomic status and people write them on you, on sight. I think there are power systems that we play into in silent, tacit ways and those are the power systems that we can choose to belong to. I think the power issues in academia are power issues that we choose to maintain and social structure is no less profound . . . but . . . it's still present and there is a certain element of choice that goes into it. And I think that you could probably say the same thing with the coach–athlete relationship, or relationships among coaches, or relationships among athletes, and so on."

REVISITING THE WRITING PROCESS AND GOALS

With this, I come full circle back to my original question to Christi, "Does 'Torn' deliver, and what can be learned about self and identity from this kind of writing?"

She answers, "For me, it was learning about how I write because part of the struggle was staring at this and being under the gun and a deadline and saying, 'Oh my god, I can't do this.' And that was part of the thinking about calling it 'Torn.' I tossed around the idea of starting out with 'Let me tell you about angry,' because that's one of the emotions I've gone through. From excited to pissed off, to confused to . . . to really torn about the exposure that comes with writing this way."

"But then how do you feel about your exposure with writing about your participants? I mean, you talk about White privilege?" I ask.

On this answer there is no hesitation from Christi. "That's another level of exposure that's equally scary and it's something that I feel writing this piece helped me get a handle on, why Maia was so threatening to me. I see that coming through loud and clear. I remember walking up to the coffee shop to meet her and my hands kind of shaking. I knew that she was going to have expectations of me. And she is also a sharp person. She's finishing her PhD in journalism and concerned about world affairs and there are power markers between us. You know me—White blondish farm girl and her of Middle Eastern origin, with head covered, accented speech, and liberal views on world politics and conservative views on gender and sex. Counterbalance that with my liberal views on gender, sex, and sexuality and my . . . not exactly apathy about world politics, but my concern about the world in a different sphere than how the United States is engaged in the Middle East right now. I think it's a big deal, but I think there are other things to worry about here at home. Which is a form of arrogance, ethnocentrism, and egocentrism in and of itself and then to say, 'I think it's important that little girls and women participate in sport and physical activity.' And that's what my career is about and that somehow seems petty when I contrast it with what Maia does. And then in my head I have to remind myself why the work I do is important."

With that, Christi smiles and looks at me, "Same question right back at you: What do you take from the construction of this project?"

I pause and then respond, "I guess I see it as the looking-glass self where I don't know what to take from it until I'm told by others what to take. It's like that piece about losing weight (Austin, 1999) where the woman says something like, 'I don't know how to feel until I look at the numbers on the scale—they tell me what to feel.' So I feel like I'm not going to know until I have feedback. On a purely self-indulgent level it's been fun. I made this joke to my graduate student and said, 'I laughed! I cried! I spat at the screen!' Writing autobiographically has been around for a long time, yet autobiographical experiences are usually in the margins of research. It doesn't become *the* subject of the piece as we've done here. Will others think it's useful when carrying out their own CSP projects? I don't know. But my intent was not that people come away with the need to go out and construct writing stories; self-reflexivity is not solely about writing stories. In the bigger picture, it is about looking at yourself and the implications of that, offering the possibility of reframing how we know what we know and ultimately, how we tell it."

SUMMARY

CSP research is broad and can be carried out from multiple standpoints such as cultural studies and cultural psychology perspectives. Regardless of perspective, reflective CSP research means questioning carefully how we as researchers know the things we know and how we present that knowledge. The research goals and the methodological tools employed by CSP researchers differ across perspectives, but all research that strives to highlight the importance of studying culture and diverse viewpoints can be part of a reflective CSP project. We conclude our chapter by summarizing two broad goals and three key points for reflective CSP researchers to consider (see CSP Goals and Key Points to Consider). These ideas cut across paradigmatic standpoints—from postpositivist to postmodernist—and stem from our earlier delineation of reflective CSP research.

As highlighted in this chapter, reflexivity from a cultural studies perspective via the use of writing stories is but one way to explore the researcher in relation to power processes. However, other CSP researchers have used postpositivist approaches to empower previously marginalized people. For example, Schinke and colleagues have positioned Canadian aboriginals as coparticipants who actively partake in the research process by designing research questions and (re)presenting research results. The end product is research that benefits and is given back

CSP GOALS AND KEY POINTS TO CONSIDER

Reflective CSP research can be directed toward two broad goals:

- Attending to how knowledge is created about people and ideas
- Understanding the cultural and social implications of the research being produced about people and ideas

Within these broad goals, we suggest three specific points for reflective CSP researchers to consider: acknowledging how our own background and perspective affects the production of knowledge, recognizing viewpoints other than our own, and confronting power issues by celebrating multiple viewpoints in the research process.

- The first of these three points is that by acknowledging our own backgrounds (e.g., education, ethnicity, gender, and sexuality), we take note of the ways in which our views influence the research process and participants in socially and culturally specific ways. Researchers may self-reflect in different ways depending on the research goals and methods employed. For example, researchers using a more postmodernist CSP perspective may make themselves the subjects of the research by engaging in reflexive research methods, as we explored in our writing stories. Alternatively, researchers using a more postpositivist CSP perspective may choose to reflect on their involvement by conducting a bracketing interview and using field notes to explore how their own backgrounds influence access and gaining of trust in the research field. The bracketing interview and field notes can be used to further contextualize data analysis but would not be the subject of the analysis per se. Each example stems from a different perspective and has different research goals and outcomes, but both allow the researchers to reflect on how their backgrounds affect the research process.

- The second point is that in addition to critically examining our own background, we can acknowledge the existence and value of viewpoints outside our own. Further, by conducting reflective CSP research, we can examine the ways in which social, structural, and cultural forces marginalize the many viewpoints of people from diverse cultural and social backgrounds. That is, by acknowledging both our own viewpoints and the views of others, reflective CSP researchers can begin to unpack the complex power relationships that exist in the research process.

- Third, reflective CSP research not only acknowledges the power issues inherent in the research process and sport context, but also seeks to change the conditions through which certain diverse voices are marginalized in the research process. Researcher reflexivity and power are often associated with postmodernist approaches, but it is possible to challenge oppressive power relationships from any standpoint or paradigm. For example, by including viewpoints that are typically marginalized or left out of research, we allow previously silenced voices to be heard. This is one way of acknowledging and dealing with power issues in CSP research. Such work need not be unique to one research paradigm or methodology, but instead may be carried out by all reflective CSP researchers.

to a formerly marginalized community (Schinke et al., in press).

How researchers carry out these reflective practices will vary greatly with the specific research goals, the social and cultural context of the research, and the paradigm from which the research stems. Researchers working from various perspectives—from postpositivist to postmodernist and everything in between—can commit to reflective research and practice by being self-reflective, by exploring cross-cultural differences, and by valuing cultures outside the mainstream. These three suggestions for researchers support the two central

goals of reflective CSP research: to attend to how knowledge is produced, and to take on the cultural and social implications of that knowledge. The strength of reflective CSP research lies in its potential to explore power issues in the research process to ultimately empower previously disempowered cultures and communities. These goals can be realized in all research paradigms as reflective CSP researchers maintain an openness and flexibility to variation—variation of self, variation of culture, variation of experience of research participants, and the variation of how data are collected, written up, and ultimately (re)presented.

PART III

APPLIED PRACTICE

Part III features 12 applied chapters written by authors who were identified through publications, conferences, and existing collaborations. Those selected to author the applied chapters have presented information about athletes within a specific context, taking a national perspective (e.g., Brazil, Ghana, Japan, Nigeria, Russia, Sweden) or a focus on religion (e.g., Kuwait). Some speak about several cultural communities within a country and how to practice effectively in relation to each (e.g., Israel, Singapore). Others focus on information about cultural communities outside the mainstream in a country (e.g., specific minority groups in the United States, indigenous peoples in Canada and Australia). Adding to the richness of part III, the contributors authored their chapters based on firsthand experience as practitioners. Some of the contributors are members of the highlighted cultural community, whereas others share their experiences of working in a culture other than their own. In each chapter, the contributors provide anecdotes framed as case studies, as well as final suggestions based on their experiences. This section of the book places the focus squarely on applied practice and how one might engage in multicultural exchanges.

This book is the first cultural sport psychology (CSP) compilation available and does not pretend to cover all of the cultures in the international arena of sport. For those engaged in multicultural work with cultures that are not specifically addressed within this volume, many suggestions in this book can be considered as a starting point in any culture (e.g., the consideration of time, space, eye contact, and language use). Because cultures are dynamic and practices change over time, there can never be a definitive guide to any culture. In addition, because each person is unique, it would not be appropriate to assume that the general characteristics of a culture apply equally to all members of that culture. The onus is on practitioners to modify or create strategies that suit themselves and their clients in relation to the culture and the context.

Strategies for Reflective Cultural Sport Psychology Practice

Peter C. Terry, PhD

In their work as applied practitioners, sport psychologists face a challenging yet rewarding task in trying to help athletes or teams fulfill their athletic potential. For any athlete, a wide range of internal and external forces can influence performance and psychological well-being. The list of factors that impinge on individual performance grows considerably once the complexities of group dynamics are added, and when working with teams our professional skills are likely to be severely tested at times. Take this complex challenge and put it into a completely new cultural context, and the complexity grows still further; the ground may even appear to shift beneath your feet. This chapter has been written to provide guidance for sport psychology practitioners who work cross-culturally and who recognize that cultural differences may necessitate significant changes to their normal way of operating.

Such changes may extend beyond merely adopting a flexible approach to interactions and encompass a more fundamental reevaluation of how to *do* sport psychology. According to Kontos and Breland-Noble (2002), applied sport psychology "has traditionally been practiced from an ethnocentric, white male perspective" (p. 297), and only recently have we begun to more fully explore multicultural dimensions of sport psychology practice (see Martens, Mobley, & Zizzi, 2000). The traditional dominance of North American and European cultural perspectives in the field has characterized sport psychology practice in a way that may be of limited relevance to most cultural contexts throughout the world. This chapter draws on my experiences over the past 25 years working as an applied practitioner with athletes and coaches of many cultures. These experiences include living and

working as a sport psychologist in Australia, Brunei, Canada, and the United Kingdom, plus working with individuals and teams from countries as varied as China, Germany, India, Indonesia, Ireland, Japan, Kazakhstan, South Korea, Malaysia, New Zealand, Russia, Singapore, South Africa, Ukraine, and the United States.

By definition, culture pervades all aspects of human functioning and refers to patterns of language, thoughts, actions, customs, beliefs, courtesies, rituals, manners, interactions, roles, expected behaviors, and values associated with race, ethnicity, and religion (Ford, 2003). The terms *culture* and *multiculturalism* can also be used in reference to sexual orientation and disability (e.g., Pope, 1995), but for the purposes of this chapter, *culture* will be used primarily with reference to distinct racial, ethnic, or religious groups.

The weight of evidence is overwhelmingly in support of cross-cultural differences across a wide range of variables that sport psychologists typically see as salient when dealing with athletes. Researchers have identified cultural influences on processes as diverse as athlete identity (Hale, James, & Stambulova, 1999), attributions for success and failure (Hallahan, Lee, & Herzog, 1997; Si, Rethorst, & Willimczik, 1995), coping style (Hoedaya & Anshel, 2003), goal orientations (Isogai, Brewer, Cornelius, Etnier, & Tokunaga, 2003; Papaioannou, 2006), participation motives (Kolt et al., 1999), preferred coaching behavior (Bolkiah & Terry, 2001; Chelladurai, Inamura, Yamaguchi, Oinuma, & Miyauchi, 1988; Terry, 1984), regulation of emotions (Mesquita & Frijda, 1992), responses to athletic retirement (Stambulova, Stephan, & Jäphag, 2007), and social physique anxiety (Isogai, Brewer, Cornelius, Komiya, Tokunaga, &

Tokushima, 2001). In short, cultural influences and psychological responses are closely linked.

Given these cross-cultural differences, it is hardly surprising that athletes from various cultures would respond differently to sport psychology. Martin, Lavallee, and Kellmann (2004) demonstrated that differing attitudes toward sport psychology consulting are associated with different cultures, even after controlling for previous experience with sport psychology. A cultural dimension has also been identified in terms of the psychological skills that athletes typically learn. For example, Xinyi, Smith, and Adegbola (2004) showed significant cross-cultural variations across a range of mental toughness dimensions among professional athletes from China, North America, Nigeria, and Singapore. Similarly, Cox and Liu (1993) showed cross-cultural differences in self-reported psychological skills among athletes from China and the United States.

Athletes from different cultures have also been shown to vary significantly in the extent to which they use various psychological techniques (e.g., Heishman & Bunker, 1989), and Anshel, Williams, and Hodge (1997) showed that cultural differences accounted for 95% of the variance in how athletes coped with stressful events in sport. Given that helping athletes cope with the stress of competition is generally a central focus for applied sport psychology, this finding is particularly germane for those who face new cultural contexts and points to the need for practitioners to gain understanding of the cultural influences on the athletes with whom they are working.

This chapter first provides a theoretical framework for reflective practice by sport psychologists working in different cultural contexts. It then addresses a range of issues that may be encountered when working in diverse cultural settings, exploring such topics as gaining entry into a new world; facing a new set of values, attitudes, priorities, behavioral norms, and linguistic challenges; and finding ways to adapt existing professional practices to new cultural contexts. After discussing these cross-cultural differences, general strategies will be provided to assist sport psychologists who are working cross-culturally. Throughout the chapter, examples of cross-cultural issues and recommended strategies will be drawn from my practitioner experience at four Olympic Summer Games (in Barcelona, Atlanta, Sydney, and Athens), three Olympic Winter Games (in Albertville, Lillehammer, and Nagano), three South East Asian (SEA) Games (in Brunei, Vietnam, and Thailand), the 2006 Asian Games in Qatar, and more than 50 other international sporting events.

MODEL OF REFLECTIVE PRACTICE

Sport psychology professionals have shown an increasing interest in processes that promote effective practice, whereas previous emphasis was on the content of psychological interventions (see Andersen, 2000). The ability of sport psychologists to build therapeutic alliances with athletes is often cited as essential to effectiveness, and it has been suggested that a willingness on the part of the practitioner to embrace a reflective approach plays a major role in determining the success of this process. Anderson,

Peter Terry (far right) with the Brunei tennis team at the 1999 SEA Games.

Photo courtesy of Peter Terry.

Knowles, and Gilbourne (2004) have produced a thorough and insightful overview of this area, in which they defined reflective practice as "an approach to training and practice that can help practitioners explore their decisions and experiences in order to increase their understanding of and manage themselves and their practice" (p. 189).

Clearly, an expanding literature promotes the role of reflection among professional groups allied to physical activity and sport. Reflective practice is generally advocated for all professionals who have a critical need to understand and interact effectively with those they are trying to support. Such groups include coaches (see Cushion, Armour, & Jones, 2003; Knowles, Gilbourne, Borrie, & Nevill, 2001; Nelson & Cushion, 2006) and teachers (see Gibbs, 1998), as well as sport psychologists (see Anderson et al., 2004; Holt & Strean, 2001).

Several principles underpin a reflective approach to practicing sport psychology. The first involves recognition that the personal characteristics of psychologists exert a powerful influence on their effectiveness (see Andersen, 2000). Psychologists are people first and practitioners second; therefore the cultural and personal values they bring to a working alliance with an athlete or coach will inevitably influence the effectiveness of that relationship. For example, a sport psychologist might espouse a model of equal expertise for interacting with athletes and coaches (see Terry, 1997). Such a model, which emphasizes the value of the unique expertise that all parties bring to a working alliance, might fit well into a democratic cultural context, such as in Scandinavia, but it might be challenged in more hierarchical structures found in many parts of the world, where the views of athletes are given less prominence (see chapter 11 for a comparison of Swedish and Russian contexts).

A second principle promotes the benefits of seeking self-knowledge regarding how practitioners might be perceived by those athletes and coaches they seek to help. Scottish poet Robert Burns once wrote, "O wad some Power the giftie gie us, to see oursels as ithers see us!", which, roughly translated, means "It would be wonderful to have the gift to see ourselves as others see us!" Continuing the equal expertise example, if the psychologist didn't reflect on interactions with athletes and coaches or seek relevant feedback, she might remain completely unaware that her approach is perceived as inappropriate in a new cultural context. An inherent advantage of a reflective approach to analyzing the effectiveness of consultations is progressive awareness of how we are perceived by others.

A third principle of reflective practice was elaborated by Martindale and Collins (2005), who made the point that the nature and extent of the direction provided tend to reflect the practitioner's own theoretical orientation and professional philosophy. For example, practitioners whose approach has cognitive-behavioral roots are probably more directive and provide more psychoeducation or mental skills training than those with a humanistic perspective. However, experienced practitioners are likely able to adopt different perspectives for different scenarios, perhaps being directive with less experienced athletes and more person-centered with athletes who have a greater range of life and competition experiences.

A model to guide the process of reflective practice is presented in figure 7.1. This six-stage model, developed by Gibbs (1998), is useful both for providing a framework for practitioners to reflect on

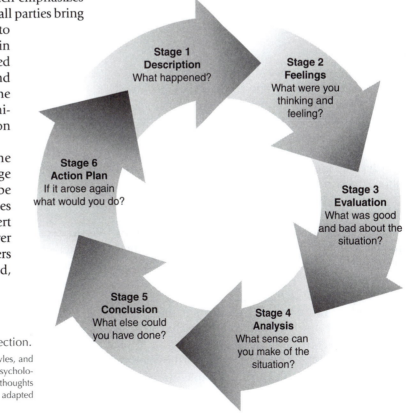

FIGURE 7.1 Six-stage model of reflection.

Adapted, by permission, from A. Anderson, Z. Knowles, and D. Gilbourne, 2004, "Reflective practice for sport psychologists: Concepts, models, practical implications, and thoughts on dissemination," *Sport Psychologist* 18, 188-203; adapted from Gibbs 1988.

USING THE SIX-STAGE MODEL OF REFLECTION

Some years ago I was appointed to work with the national football team of an Asian country. The team was coached by a former professional player from the English leagues who was highly directive in his approach and emotional in his treatment of players. Despite his passionate and often critical manner, or perhaps because of it, he managed to convey genuine concern and affection for his players that motivated them to greater effort and contributed to successful results.

One of my first sessions with the players involved a group meeting to discuss a forthcoming game against a prominent rival. Such sessions are usually highly interactive and good humored, with lots of suggestions coming from the players themselves. On this occasion, however, the opposite was true. My questions about the strengths and weaknesses of the opposition team and how they might be countered or exploited (see Munroe, Terry, & Carron, 2002) were greeted with a deathly hush and refusal to make eye contact. When this happened (stage 1), my thoughts (stage 2) were that the athletes were bored or unimpressed and, in consequence, I felt ineffective and incompetent.

To evaluate (stage 3) and analyze (stage 4) what had happened during this session, I turned to the head coach and his local assistant coach for feedback. They were both grinning broadly as we discussed what had happened. "They didn't seem to respond very well," I ventured. "That's because no one's ever asked them what they think before," the coach replied. Most of the players were poorly educated and were used to following instructions to the letter rather than being asked for suggestions. Their silence and lowered heads reflected shyness and respect rather than boredom.

I concluded (stage 5) that I should have done more preparatory work with the players, notably getting to know them and winning their trust, before I asked them for their opinions in front of their coaches. My action plan (stage 6) for the immediate future focused on identifying ways to break down the inherent power differential between me and the players. I decided to do this by spending considerable time with them in environments in which they were comfortable, such as on the football field, over lunch, or around the pool table.

A forthcoming overseas trip with the team provided ample opportunity for such interactions, and gradually the power differential was bridged and players began to accept me as a part of the coaching team. This led to greater willingness by the players to speak up in group meetings in response to my questions.

the effectiveness of consultations with athletes, as proposed by Anderson and colleagues (2004), and for providing a framework for athletes to learn competition skills by reflecting on their athletic performances. The six stages of the model are description (What happened?), feelings (What were you thinking and feeling?), evaluation (What was good and bad about the situation?), analysis (What sense can you make of the situation?), conclusion (What else could you have done?), and action plan (If it arose again, what would you do?). An illustration of using this model to reflect on applied practice in a cross-cultural context is described in Using the Six-Stage Model of Reflection.

The benefits of reflective practice are particularly relevant for practitioners operating in an unfamiliar cultural context, who often find themselves unsure of the best way to address concerns that arise. Typically, sport psychology training in North America, Europe, and Australia encourages practitioners to

function as systematic problem solvers who identify evidence-based solutions and then apply clearly defined techniques underpinned by well-established theories derived from the scientific process. Unfortunately, as Schön (1987) pointed out, practitioners frequently face situations in which a broad array of forces impinges on the choice of an intervention intended to preserve performance and protect the psychological well-being of the people involved. In consequence, it is often far from clear which intervention is the most appropriate. Selecting an effective intervention can be seen as the crossroads where art meets science, and successful melding of the two is critical to a practitioner's involvement with a particular team or client.

As Anderson and colleagues (2004) have suggested, the ability to take what we know about sport psychology and apply it to meet current challenges is the essence of our craft. Many experienced practitioners use a reflective practice model to develop their professional skills as much as possible from interactions with clients. They use this valuable strategy either consciously or instinctively to help gain a better understanding of how to apply their craft. Further, in some instances what we have learned during our training in sport psychology simply does not apply to a new cultural context. A reflective approach to consulting may help to bring such instances into sharper focus.

COMMON CROSS-CULTURAL ISSUES

The range of issues that sport psychologists might face is almost as extensive as the variety of cross-cultural contexts in which they might work. I have presented examples from my own experience to provide a glimpse of the challenges that cross-cultural practice presents. Issues range from the sport psychologist's performance anxiety—which can occur whatever the cultural context but may be intensified in an unfamiliar culture—to cultural-specific issues relating to language, religion, and previously unencountered belief systems and behavioral norms.

PRACTITIONER-CENTERED ISSUES

Sport psychologists in unfamiliar cultural settings might face many internal issues. Four such challenges include performance anxiety, finding an appropriate communication style, working authentically with the culture while not losing your professional identity, and avoiding sensitive stereotyping.

PERFORMANCE ANXIETY

The reality of working as an applied practitioner in any sphere, especially in a competition environment and even more so in a new cultural context, may be different from the textbooks you are familiar with or the formal training you might have received:

1. In the cauldron of intense competition, there may be an acute time pressure to identify and implement immediate solutions to pressing concerns, often along the lines of "OK, psychology specialist, this is where you earn your money. Please provide an effective intervention *now*." Naturally, we do everything possible to provide the best intervention for the prevailing circumstances, but what we deliver in such circumstances is essentially our best guess, albeit a highly educated one.

2. Presenting issues are often complex and do not fit readily into the context of examples found in the literature, thereby generating the feeling of flying without a compass.

3. Sport psychologists often operate from a base of personal insecurity because they have either no contract at all or one of limited duration.

Any of these situations can create the acute feeling that our worth is constantly being judged, which may result in either a conservative approach where we say little for fear of doing the wrong thing (effectively crossing our fingers and hoping for the best) or abandoning our training and going for the grand intervention in the hope of cementing our reputation. Either way, it's an uncomfortable feeling that often triggers performance anxiety in the practitioner. We fear that we may not be as smart as our position implies—a dissonance between self-image and external reality known as *impostor syndrome* (see Buchanan, 2006). These forces can create an uneasy feeling at the best of times, but in an unfamiliar cultural context their effects may intensify considerably.

COMMUNICATION STYLE

Sometimes the issue can be as simple as an incompatibility in communication styles, a factor with a strong cultural influence. For example, Schinke (2005) reflected on his career as a coach struggling to communicate with athletes from Asia, by whom he was perceived as "blunt, overly direct and insensitive" (p. 1), as well as with athletes from South America, who saw him as too reserved. His self-reflections coincide with my own experiences of working as an applied practitioner in many parts of the world and finding that my typical approach was greeted with surprise and confusion in some cultural contexts. Several interpretations of the same behavior are possible when we work with athletes of different cultures.

PROFESSIONAL IDENTITY

My Western orientation, based in a tradition of self-determination and individual responsibility for athletic performance even in a team setting, has on occasions been perceived as a novel, perhaps self-indulgent, strategy in a collectivist environment where athletes were told what to think, feel, and do, as is found in many Asian cultures, or in an Islamic environment where athletes believed they would win if God willed it, seeing themselves as relatively powerless to influence the outcome. The dilemma I have often felt is whether to become a cultural chameleon and embrace the values and behavioral norms of the culture in which I am operating at the time or to remain true to my cultural heritage and leave the athletes with the challenge of adjusting to my way of doing things. The resolution has usually been to find the middle ground where I can act in a culturally sensitive manner without feeling that I have abandoned my roots. This has rarely been easy, requiring me to ask a great many questions of others regarding the best way to do things, as well as a huge amount of self-reflection on my part to find the answers.

Sensitive Stereotyping

In the quest for greater cultural sensitivity, there is an inherent danger of giving broad cultural generalizations precedence over individual differences. Sport psychologists working cross-culturally must maintain a delicate balance between becoming familiar with the beliefs, practices, and behavioral norms of an athlete's cultural heritage while at the same time avoiding the pitfall of what Andersen (1993) referred to as *sensitive stereotyping*, whereby this knowledge of cultural differences brings about a stereotypical interpretation of the athlete's behavior. For example, while working with the Brunei women's lawn bowls team, the athletes decided to compete wearing their traditional head scarves, known as *tudongs*, even though they were granted special dispensation by religious leaders to wear alternative headgear, even baseball caps, more suited to performing in the oppressive heat. My initial, stereotypical, interpretation of their decision was that it was based purely on religious devotion. However, the players explained that it was principally a matter of practicality because they found the tudongs more comfortable and slightly cooler, and it also involved a degree of team bonding because one athlete was reluctant to forsake her tudong for religious reasons.

In a 2005 overview of consulting with Latin American athletes, Kontos and Arguello expanded on the concept of sensitive stereotyping, pointing out the perils of assuming that different countries in the same geographical area share the same cultural values. Given the great diversity of adjoining nations in Europe, for example, European values and culture include diverse worldviews (see chapter 11). This is also true of Africa (see chapters 14 and 15) and Asia (see chapters 17 and 18). Additionally, every country on earth includes different cultural groups with whom a sport psychology might have cause to work. Ultimately, the only legitimate strategy is to forego cultural assumptions in favor of learning to understand the worldview of the client group and the individuals therein. Of course, this does not discount the value of increasing personal knowledge about different cultures; such knowledge is an important starting point for the more detailed investigation that is essential in specific cultural settings.

Quantitative Assessment

Standardized tests in a cross-cultural context is another area filled with potential problems. Assessment tests typically used by sport psychologists have an inherent cultural bias toward the environment in which they were developed, often North America or Europe. Direct translation of scales into the first language of clients appears to rectify some of the problems, but it may not address the underlying cultural bias and may create factorial instability for the measure.

At the very least, it could be expected that measures used cross-culturally would demand culturally appropriate norms as a reference point, although preferably a full revalidation process would be conducted. In the absence of such a process, it is wise to remember the significant limitations of cross-cultural use of standardized tests beyond their more general limitations as diagnostic or predictive tools. A further consideration in some cultures, notably that of Canadian aboriginals (see chapter 8), is that quantitative assessments are simply not well received, meaning that alternative assessment methods are required. On the other hand, some cultures, such as those in Southeast Asia, may overestimate the value of data from standardized tests, unrealistically expecting tests to identify champion athletes. In such circumstances, it becomes a considerable challenge to educate all concerned about the uses and limitations of quantitative assessments.

Client-Centered Issues

Belief systems have a profound effect on how people relate to both one another and themselves. Issues commonly associated with belief systems are a reluctance to disclose personal information; fatalism; and nonscientific explanations for troublesome phenomena.

Unwillingness to Disclose

Collectivist cultures, notably those in Asia, tend to place great importance on being a valuable member of a group, be it family, community, or team, rather than on the individualistic pursuit of self-actualization. One effect of this orientation is that collectivist cultures often do not promote open discussion about anxieties or individual weaknesses, some of the very concerns that sport psychologists are trained to address. A practitioner trying to support Asian athletes will often encounter reluctance to discuss performance anxieties or possible limitations, and this reluctance may prevail until complete trust is built. The reasons why probing questions may be greeted with complete silence are often complex. For example, a taciturn response from male athletes of Chinese heritage may be attributed to the perceived potential shame of losing face in front of a respected outsider (i.e., the sport psychologist) and bringing dishonor on their broader cultural group.

FATALISTIC ATTITUDES

In 1999, I spent 8 months living and working in the Sultanate of Brunei on the island of Borneo as part of a team from the Australian Institute of Sport (AIS). The AIS was contracted to prepare the national teams of Brunei for their participation in the SEA Games, which was hosted in the capital, Bandar Seri Begawan. After the first of a planned series of psycho-educational lectures to introduce key performance skills to national team athletes, I was approached by some of the national coaches, many of whom were Australian or American. The essence of the conversation was, "We really like this sport psychology stuff, but if you could just get them to turn up for practice, that would be a great start."

Coming from a background where sport had high standing in society and where athletes typically showed a strong work ethic, this comment came as a surprise. It quickly became apparent that the strong Islamic influences in the country did not wholly approve of sport as an appropriate object for devotion, especially for females. Further, the traditional condition placed on any future plans—*inshallah* (translated as "God willing")—seemed to endow all goal-setting exercises with the fatalistic attitude that if God wills it, then it will happen, apparently downplaying the role of the athlete in determining the outcome. Perhaps as a result of these twin influences, many Bruneian athletes had a relaxed attitude toward putting in the necessary effort to make things happen. I decided to address this matter during my next group lecture. A Learning Experience recounts what happened.

BELIEF SYSTEMS

In Brunei, I encountered some belief systems fundamentally different from those with which I was previously familiar. For example, the culturally appropriate way to build relationships as a precursor to conducting any sort of business, including providing psychological support, was to sit down with a drink and a snack and chat about family, friends, and life. I quickly realized that winning hearts and minds in this cultural context involved a much less businesslike approach and a much greater relationship orientation than the one I had typically implemented in my own culture.

However, some of my experiences in this tiny but wealthy country, with a population of only 300,000 people, shook my understanding of what is normal. An experience in the athletes' village during the SEA Games, for example, lay completely outside my previous range of consulting experiences. A Difficult Spirit describes this encounter.

A Difficult Spirit

> One morning a small group of female hockey players approached my office and gently pushed one of their teammates, a goalie whom I'll call Sharil, in to see me. "Go see Dr. Peter," they urged.
>
> "Come in, Sharil, take a seat. How can I help you today?" I asked.

NEGOTIATING PERFORMANCE WITH ATHLETES FROM AN UNFAMILIAR CULTURE

With about 200 athletes and coaches in attendance and His Royal Highness Prince Sufri, the sultan's brother and an accomplished clay target shooter, sitting in the front row, I commenced a talk that owed much to Dr. Martin Luther King's famous address. "I have a dream," I offered, "that one day all Bruneian athletes will win a SEA Games medal" (spontaneous polite applause) "Inshallah" (more polite applause). "Inshallah is an interesting concept," I ventured, "God willing" (much nodding of heads). "In my belief system," I went on, "God helps those who help themselves." The room fell silent and all eyes settled on Prince Sufri, waiting for a lead on the appropriate response to my controversial comment. "I could be on the next plane out of here," I thought to myself. To my great relief, the prince considered my suggestion and slowly nodded in agreement, which set off a wave of similarly nodding heads. It was a significant cultural breakthrough followed by suggestions of how the athletes could help themselves, such as turning up for practice, working hard to improve, and following the advice of their expert support staff.

"I feel very bad, Dr. Peter. Something's wrong," Sharil offered.

"Tell me about it," I suggested.

"A spirit has come inside my body," Sharil went on. "It makes me feel very upset, very angry. I cannot play good."

At this point I was intrigued. Sharil was a well-educated woman with a university degree, a high school teacher, who had traveled extensively. What exactly was she telling me?

"This spirit," I ventured. "Where has it come from?"

"My room in the athletes' village is on the edge of the jungle. The spirit came from the jungle last night," she explained.

"Has this ever happened before?" I inquired.

"Yes, many times, Dr. Peter. Many times every year," she told me.

"And when was the first time, Sharil?"

"First time was when I was maybe 14 or 15."

"How often does the spirit come into your body, and how long does it stay?" I continued, starting to understand things a little better.

"The spirit comes many times every year and stays maybe a week each time, then goes away," Sharil explained.

"I think I know about this spirit, Sharil, and I think you're going to be fine," I reassured her, reminding myself that the mood-disturbing effects often associated with the menstrual cycle know no cultural boundaries. I concluded from this incident that I had only begun to scratch the surface of the belief system with which I was now interacting, and I had so much more to learn.

BEHAVIORAL NORMS

Behavioral norms are another potent source of misunderstandings. Reluctance to disclose personal information was discussed as a function of belief systems, but, as explained next, it can also stem from behavioral norms. Other issues associated with behavioral norms include customs regarding eye contact, punctuality, acceptable and unacceptable dress, and physical contact.

A reluctance to disclose personal information can sometimes be explained by factors that simply lie outside a practitioner's previous sphere of experience. For example, female athletes from a traditional culture in India may be unwilling to discuss personal information for fear of revealing a character weakness that

could harm their marriage prospects. Such a concern may be irrational, but in some cases it may be well founded. It is not unknown for a potential husband's family to make extensive background checks, and revelations of regular sessions with a psychologist may raise questions over a woman's suitability as a wife and mother.

Factors such as language, socioeconomic status, awareness of customs and values, and gender in particular can have a significant moderating effect on how cultural differences are expressed in behavioral terms. As a simple example, in some cultures it is considered rude to make eye contact with someone of a higher status or inappropriate for a married female to make eye contact with a male other than her husband, whereas in other cultures it is considered rude or inappropriate *not* to make eye contact in business or social contexts. However, individual differences in extroversion or shyness on the part of the people concerned may override such cultural norms, illustrating how cultural stereotyping is fraught with inconsistencies.

Punctuality is a typical example of how differing behavioral norms can generate confusion and frustration for sport psychologists working in an unfamiliar culture. Hanrahan, for instance, recalled her experiences while working to enhance self-worth and life satisfaction among adolescent Mexican orphans, including the problems associated with persistent lateness on the part of the adolescents involved (see Hanrahan, 2005).

I have also encountered this characteristic in my work with athletes from India, who considered it normal to arrive 30 minutes or more beyond the agreed time for an appointment. Initially, I interpreted such behavior as insulting, but I soon realized that the athletes assumed that I would arrive even later than they did because of what they perceived as my superior status. With a little negotiation, we quickly reached a common understanding that when it was crucial for all concerned to be punctual, the appointed hour would be designated as Swiss time rather than Indian time.

A behavioral norm of great cultural sensitivity concerns acceptable dress. In liberal Western cultures, such as Australia, prescriptive approaches to sport psychologists about what to wear are unusual. My preference when working with athletes is to dress like an athlete, typically in a polo shirt and shorts. However, when working in Islamic and some Asian countries, I have been reminded to dress modestly, including wearing long pants, in all environments except the playing field itself. Similarly, with the issue of physical contact, it is considered taboo in many countries for a man to touch a woman, even to shake hands. For male practitioners who are naturally tactile and used to making innocent physical contact, this can require restraint.

RECOMMENDED STRATEGIES

Many widely different strategies are proposed in the literature. Some are formal and others informal, but all are designed to enhance cultural sensitivity as part of a reflective approach to sport psychology practice.

FORMAL STRATEGIES

Baruth and Manning (1999) provided a series of experiential exercises aimed at developing greater cultural sensitivity via examining your feelings, attitudes, and behaviors toward various cultural groups. These experiences included watching movies oriented toward specific cultures and attending meetings devoted to diversity concerns.

Fisher, Butryn, and Roper (2003) went further, advocating formal training in cultural studies as an appropriate way to enhance the effectiveness of sport psychology practitioners. In preparation for participation in the 1998 Olympic Winter Games in Nagano, the British Olympic Association provided the entire contingent of athletes, coaches, and support staff with a series of workshops on Japanese culture meant to enhance the effectiveness of interactions with local administrators, officials, and volunteers during the Games. As a member of the team at the time, I found that training experience to be extremely valuable, and it has stood me in good stead ever since.

INFORMAL STRATEGIES

Looking beyond formal training to more informal strategies, I have found that one of the most effective approaches is to spend considerable time interacting with athletes in a variety of contexts, building the rapport that underpins a successful therapeutic alliance, and gradually learning to understand their world. First, however, it is essential to leave your expectations at the door. Cultural stereotypes should be recognized for what they are—generalizations that will help explain some observed behaviors but will be hopelessly wide of the mark for others.

Throughout my career as an applied practitioner, I have spent endless hours at training camps and on tour with teams. During these times, I have often joined many of the scheduled physical activities, such as training in the gym, joining social games of golf or tennis, and helping out at skills practice (even

if that entails no more than retrieving errant balls). Such occasions provide a valuable glimpse into the athletes' world, helping me to appreciate the nuances that influence their responses to the world around them and encouraging them to see me as a person committed to learning whatever I can to help me be able to help them.

Occasionally, such involvement has extended further. For example, many years ago when I began work in bobsledding, a winter sport about which I knew little, the athletes arranged for me to compete in the four-person event of the national championships to help me understand what it was all about. The insights I gained into the finer points of the sport and subcultural norms through being intimately involved in sled preparation, transportation, testing, and competition proved invaluable to my future involvement as national team psychologist over the next 10 years.

I find it particularly useful to just hang out with athletes wherever and whenever the opportunity presents itself (although not, I would emphasize, with women's teams in a Muslim culture.) While doing so, I have many times heard criticisms of coaches

Peter Terry, on the left, pushing a four-man bobsled as part of his initiation into the sport.

Photo courtesy of Peter Terry.

or fellow support staff and have witnessed indiscretions by individual athletes. I have always taken this willingness on the part of athletes to talk frankly and behave naturally in front of me as a sign that I have, at least in part, won their trust and that they believe in the confidentiality of our working relationship. I have often found that by fostering relationships that encourage open disclosure of concerns, I have been well placed to help athletes reinterpret, for example, coaching behaviors of which they were previously critical, and on other occasions, I have been able to represent athlete concerns to the coaching team in an impartial manner without betraying any confidences. However, in some cultures, such as Japan, coach–athlete relationships operate according to a formal hierarchy that is not easily challenged. Hence,

it is important to learn the structures of a culture and how to operate successfully in it.

Finally, throughout my experiences of cross-cultural practice, I have always made an effort to learn a few words of the first language of athletes or to gain some appreciation of the subcultural linguistic norms of the athletic group, not to enable me to talk like them but rather to avoid having to repeatedly ask for explanations. I see this as part of a broader process of building effective communication between sport psychologist and athlete, enhancing the therapeutic alliance by bridging the cultural divide.

In summary, at least two things are clear about cross-cultural delivery of sport psychology. First, a broad array of cultural influences can affect the delivery of sport psychology services for good or ill.

ISSUES AND STRATEGIES TO CONSIDER WHEN WORKING IN A DIFFERENT CULTURE

Based upon my experiences consulting outside of my home country, I have several suggestions for applied consultants working in multicultural sport contexts. The suggestions below are intended as a starting point to inform CSP general practice.

- Recognize that other cultures have a different view of the world.
- Accept the complexities of cross-cultural practice and resolve to address them.
- Adopt a reflective approach.
- Be prepared to reevaluate your own values, attitudes, and behavior.
- Emphasize processes that promote effective practice rather than issues of content.
- Find ways to adapt familiar professional practices to new cultural contexts.
- Accept that methods that work well in some cultural contexts are simply unsuited to others.
- Modify your communication style to suit the prevailing cultural context.
- Be especially sensitive to religious and gender concerns.
- Leave your expectations at the door when meeting athletes and coaches from new cultures.
- Understand the behavioral norms of the culture, especially those that denote respect or are taboo.
- Learn at least a few words of any new language.
- Recognize the linguistic norms of the subculture, even if the clients speak English.
- Watch movies or listen to the music of the culture in which you are working.
- Undertake formal training in specific cultures if appropriate.
- Spend time interacting with athletes and coaches in a variety of contexts.
- Get to know athletes and coaches in their environment—on the playing field, over lunch, and so on.
- Join in physical and social activities if appropriate.
- Accept that different cultures have different hierarchical structures.
- Remember that individual differences often exert greater influence than cultural factors.

Second, adopting a reflective approach to applied work, especially in an unfamiliar cultural context, can pay rich dividends. Hopefully, this chapter provides a useful framework for such an approach.

Finally, the pitfalls of cultural generalizations must be reemphasized. Although in international competition one might see brash, confident Americans; inscrutable Chinese; dour, machinelike Russians; quiet, achieving Australians; and so on, underneath these cultural stereotypes lies a great deal of commonality. All athletes have personal lives, relation-ships, hopes, and fears. Getting to know athletes as individuals is the only legitimate way to understand what makes them tick. In the words of Kontos and Breland-Noble (2002), "Although some athletes may act in accordance with one or more of these ethnic and racial generalizations, each athlete represents a unique ethnic and racial worldview" (p. 298). Gaining insight into the unique worldview of individual athletes from whatever culture they originate is a cornerstone of becoming an effective psychologist in the world of sport.

ENTERING THE COMMUNITY OF CANADIAN INDIGENOUS ATHLETES

Robert Schinke, EdD; Amy Blodgett, MA candidate; Stephen Ritchie, MA; Patricia Pickard, PhD; Ginette Michel, MA; Duke Peltier; Chris Pheasant, BEd; Mary Jo Wabano; Clifton Wassangeso George, BPHE; and Lawrence Enosse, BA

In many chapters of this book, the authors have considered athletes from mainstream cultures in a geographic region. The present chapter addresses another cultural consideration: athletes who come from a minority or marginalized population in a region or country. (See also chapters 9 and 16.) The chapter begins with an overview of the relevance of sport among the aboriginal peoples. Afterward, an overview of aboriginal history and practices frames discussions pertaining to applied practice when working with this population. Our chapter concludes with recommendations for sport psychology practitioners based upon Rob's work and Duke's confirmation regarding how to proceed when entering into a community of Canadian indigenous athletes.

SETTING THE CONTEXT

Marginalized populations in North America are often represented in elite sport in disproportionately higher numbers (Kontos & Breland-Noble, 2002). Discussions have addressed the relevance of sport among, for example, African American athletes focused on professional sport and the attraction of a lucrative career (Hill, 1993). Though financial gains do provide an opportunity for minority athletes to climb the socioeconomic ladder, they are also attracted to sport and pursue it to the elite levels for other considerations that have not been fully considered in the literature. For the applied practitioner interested in working with athletes from minority populations, it is worthwhile to gain a better understanding of who

these athletes are, why they have chosen to pursue sport, and how to engage in effective multicultural practice with them.

Among the Canadian aboriginal population, interest in sport is a cultural phenomenon best explained as a means to teach life skills, including courage, camaraderie, and persistence (www.aboriginalsportcircle. ca). However, these skills only tease at the importance of sport and what it signifies among the Canadian aboriginal community. Sport represents more than just athletic prowess, it also provides "a means to combat some of the negative factors affecting Aboriginal communities, in particular those affecting their youth" (Winther, Nazer-Bloom, & Petch, 1995, p. 2). The direct benefits of sport involvement include fitness and lifestyle habits among a group of people at risk for both types of diabetes (Aboriginal Diabetes Initiative, 2004), increased rates of incarceration (approximately 5-7 times higher than the national average), and trends in substance abuse well above the national average (see Adrian, Payne, & Williams, 1991; Scott, 1995).

Indirect benefits include adaptive cultural representation inside and outside the cultural community (Danielson, Schinke, Peltier, & Dube, 2006). Inside the cultures, successful athletes offer stories and examples (pathways) of what is possible to aspiring athletes from the same cultures despite historic and current challenges. An indirect external benefit of successful athletics is that they promote the values, customs, and capacities of the marginalized population among the mainstream. Additionally, extracultural promotion creates an awareness of perspectives pertaining to sport practice that extend beyond a monocultural approach (Ryba & Wright, 2005). All these benefits are over and above the athletic accomplishments experienced by the athletes themselves.

If you were to visit the Web site that represents the mission and parameters of the Canadian Aboriginal Sport Circle (www.aboriginalsportcircle.ca), you would begin to notice the depth of emerging sport organizations created by aboriginal Canadians nationally, extending beyond local community initiatives. Role-model systems are available for aspiring aboriginal athletes (www.aboriginalsportcircle.ca), specialized educational modules that address aboriginal athlete management are available to all coaches (www.aboriginalsportcircle.ca), and national (e.g., the National Aboriginal Ice Hockey Championships) and continental sport competitions and cultural celebrations (e.g., the North American Indigenous Games) are heavily attended. Embedded in these initiatives is an implicit understanding of the benefits that Canadian aboriginal athletes gain from sport.

Despite momentum in the development of culture-specific sport initiatives, there are still strong indications that sport science has not fully met the needs of athletes from the aboriginal cultures. At the 2002 North American Indigenous Games, an elite aboriginal athlete said it best when she indicated that what she wanted from sport psychology was "a sport psychologist that will understand you, coming from that community, coming from your reality . . . that would be my dream" (Brant et al., 2002, p. 67). Her view was based upon experiences before and during international competitions in which sport psychology providers were lacking in contextual knowledge and cultural sensitivity. The present chapter is intended as one step toward relevant sport practice when working with athletes from the Canadian aboriginal community. We presuppose the value of cultural community involvement, and following logically, community coauthorship and postpublication integration. It is only through such strategies that we support professional advancement and empowerment among minority and marginalized populations.

This chapter, which is based on earlier work (e.g., Schinke, Hanrahan, et al., 2007), proposes that those who work with Canadian aboriginal athletes require relevant cultural sport psychology (CSP) skills beyond the mainstream tactics available from typical service providers, including those found in the Canadian Sport Centres. In this chapter, academic authors from the Canadian mainstream (i.e., White, European descended, Judeo-Christian) have partnered with members from an aboriginal community, the Wikwemikong Unceded First Nation Reserve.

Together, the authors discussed which cultural topics were most important to include, bearing in mind the intended audience, and it was decided that

Left to right, authors Robert Schinke, Duke Peltier, Patricia Pickard, and Stephen Ritchie standing in front of native artwork on the grand stage at a Wikwemikong Pow Wow in August, 2006.

Photo courtesy of Stephen Ritchie.

the chapter would comprise four sections. In the first section, we overview Canadian aboriginal history and how historical events have contributed to the present-day aboriginal client. The second section is a brief overview of community structure in which we consider the extensive community involvement experienced by many Canadian aboriginal athletes. In addition, the role of reciprocal role models and reciprocity are discussed, primarily because aboriginal athletes are raised in gift cultures whereby wisdom is gifted from the talented athletes of one generation to the next. Third, we consider an aboriginal cultural nuance that underpins cross-cultural communication: listening and feeling before speaking. In the fourth section, we present suggestions based on what we have learned from a sample of elite amateur and professional Canadian aboriginal athletes who were identified by the Wikwemikong from those known to them.

The first author (Rob) has spent more than a decade working with elite Canadian amateur and professional boxers, encountering many Canadian aboriginal athletes, coaches, families, and communities as clients. The authors in this chapter also have had extensive experience working with elite aboriginal athletes in ice hockey, shooting, lacrosse, cross country running, soccer, and wrestling. The community lead author (Duke) is a former varsity ice-hockey athlete with extensive experience performing in his own cultural community as well as in the mainstream sport community. Beyond his identity as an athlete, Duke also has had 15 years of coaching and administrative work with Canadian aboriginal athletes from his community as they competed provincially, nationally, and internationally.

CULTURAL TERMINOLOGY AND HISTORY

In this section we overview the working terminology and history of Canadian aboriginal people. We believe that both aspects provide a useful starting point from which sport psychologists can begin to understand this population, especially its history of marginalization. It is our experience that by taking the preemptive step of learning more about working terminology and history, consultants can gain a better appreciation of their athletes' perspectives while also affirming an interest in the athletes' cultural identity. Next, our working terms are considered in a brief summary of aboriginal history. In the discussion of history, we draw particular attention to sources of initial distrust when one begins working with aboriginal athletes.

WORKING TERMINOLOGY

Government Web sites are available in many countries that provide information about their minority cultures. In Canada, the national government has designated a Web site to represent the mandate of Indian and Northern Affairs (www.ainc-inac.gc.ca). The site includes sections on salient terms, history, art, language, and treaties. This Web site was suggested to Rob S. by Duke Peltier when they began working together. Here we have defined key terms that are important to understand when approaching the aboriginal cultures. The mainstream authors became acquainted with these terms and concepts before their relationship with the Wikwemikong community partners began.

- **aboriginal people**—Three groups of aboriginal people in Canada make up 3.3% of the national population: Métis (1%), Inuit (0.2%), and Indians (2.1%) (www.statcan.ca). The Metis reflect mixed aboriginal and French ancestry, and the Inuit and Canadian Indians are entirely of aboriginal bloodlines. Distinctions beyond lineage are found in language, cultural practices, diet, and spiritual beliefs. Eleven general dialects dependent on community of origin (www.ainc-inac.gc.ca) are used in aboriginal communities. When Rob began his first research project with Wikwemikong, the participants self-identified as either Metis or Indian, and considerable pride was associated with being part of the specific aboriginal subsets. Among the dialects, Cree, Ojibway, and Inuktitut are the largest. The original territories where each cultural community settled are also distinct. Inuit most often reside above the permafrost (60° north) whereas the Metis and Indians are traditionally from across Canada. Canadian Indians are the most salient group in relation to this chapter primarily because most of what is known to the authors about Canadian aboriginal athletes reflects experiences in the 10 Canadian provinces and not from above the permafrost line. The targeted populations refer to themselves as aboriginal or First Nations people with the inclusion of their language family (e.g., Ojibway, Cree, Salish) and not Indian because of the unrepresentative national connotation with India.

- **oral history**—Among the aboriginal people, knowledge is typically passed from one generation to the next through spoken word. In Canada, oral histories often pertain to historical events, including land claims. The intent of oral histories is to communicate cultural aspects or to validate claims pertaining to history. Those who receive the oral history are meant to draw their own conclusions in relation to their present social context. During a consulting meeting with a national team boxer, the athlete revealed to one of the authors how bravery is an inherent part of his cultures. The athlete learned about bravery through a story from a community elder that he now passes on to younger athletes. The story was about a young warrior who stood his ground (literally) in a battle where he was greatly outnumbered by tying himself to a stake. By remembering that story before important bouts, the athlete maintained a positive perspective, primarily because the odds of standing his ground in the boxing ring were better than those of the warrior. At least two levels of importance are associated with oral histories. On one level, oral histories support the merit of qualitative approaches (storytelling, talking circles) when working in a culturally sensitive way with aboriginal respondents (see Running Wolf & Rickard, 2003). Consequently, the centrality of oral histories in the cultures suggests that qualitative approaches (storytelling, talking circles) rather than data collection forms or interviews based on narrowly specific questions are more appropriate when working in a culturally sensitive way with aboriginal respondents. Second, stories passed from one generation to the next are used to motivate traditional athletes (Schinke, Hanrahan, et al., 2007).

- **reserve or community**—A reserve is a tract of land set aside by the federal government through treaties upon which a community of Canadian aboriginal people live. Each reserve (614 in total) has a governing body comprising one chief and several councillors. Community members typically choose the chief and council by election or traditional appointment. In relation to sport, many communities, including the Wikwemikong, have sport and recreation programs that train, launch, and subsequently support aspiring aboriginal athletes. Some aboriginal people refer to their home communities, or First Nations (when they are born in cultural communities outside of urban centers), as *reserves*, whereas others refer to them as *communities*.

- **self-governance**—Historically, the First Nations negotiated self-governance under the Canadian constitution. When working with aboriginal populations as a clinician or researcher, it is important to respect this arrangement. The sport psychology professional is responsible for leaving knowledge and sustainable outcomes with the community, as well as sharing decision making about what is investigated or delivered, how information is gained, and who owns rights to what has been learned (Schnarch, 2004). Among our earlier applied research project, the knowledge was published in peer-reviewed journals, and only copies of what was learned were provided to participants and the Wikwemikong. More recently, however, the Wikwemikong have suggested a community-based research project with educational training modules developed with and eventually relinquished to community members. In addition, our present data collection strategy is talking circles that are developed and led by community members. Self-governance is meant to extend beyond mechanistic strategies to longer-term empowerment and capacity building within the cultures.

- **on and off reserve**—Many aboriginal people have Indian status, but this does not necessarily mean that they are currently living on reserve. Those who were born on reserve are more likely to speak an aboriginal tongue as their first language, especially in remote communities. Among the elite aboriginal athletes we have met, equal numbers are from reserves and off-reserve locations. Regardless of where they are born and where their families reside, many elite aboriginal athletes in Canada live away from their cultural community in order to pursue sport at the elite level. That being said, aboriginal clients often regard themselves as band members belonging to a community. The practitioner must understand which community and language family (if any) clients belong to in order to better understand their customs, degrees of traditionalism, and beliefs.

HISTORY OF THE CULTURES

Archaeologists in the West have different views regarding how long aboriginal people have lived on Canadian lands. Some support the migration theory, which holds that some 12,000 to 14,000 years ago, during the last Ice Age, people migrated from Asia, crossing a now-submerged land bridge connecting Siberia to Alaska (see Dickason, 2006; Nelles, 2004). However, in a discussion with an aboriginal community member from Wikwemikong, Rob was informed of a diverging perspective regarding cultural origins, one that Dickason also recognized as the view of aboriginal people across Canada. According to our authors from Wikwemikong, aboriginal people have always inhabited North American land and did not migrate from Asia. All of the authors in this chapter support this historical perspective of the Wikwemikong and believe that what has been proposed by the mainstream has little bearing when the intent is to understand others from their own viewpoint.

FIRST EUROPEAN CONTACTS

Encounters between aboriginal and nonaboriginal people began to increase in the 1500s as Europeans started settling in Canada. Over time, cross-cultural relations developed from mutual curiosity to an emphasis on sharing and cooperation. Both parties engaged in the exchanging of goods, bartering, and trade deals (land was often exchanged by First Nations people for alcohol, glassware, and so on) through trade alliances. Cooperative efforts resulted in friendships among the cultures that lasted until the 19th century. The aboriginal and nonaboriginal people viewed one another as independent populations in charge of their own affairs. Early discussions regarding cultural autonomy continue to be important for aboriginal people during cross-cultural exchanges today.

Cooperative efforts between the aboriginal and nonaboriginal people were formalized through the development of treaties written by European negotiators and honored by aboriginal nations (communities) in oral and visual records. The idea behind treaties was to offer peace, respect, equality, jurisdiction, and protection to both parties. However, over time the treaty process became a confusing series of agreements and interpretations among diverging cultures. From an aboriginal standpoint, the purpose of treaties was to work out ways of sharing lands and resources with settlers without any loss of access to the lands for hunting and fishing. The Europeans, on the other hand, regarded treaties as private claims to desirable land. Diverging cultural views regarding proprietary ownership, in addition to broken promises to the aboriginal population, have contributed to present-day distrust and resentment of European ways. At present more than 100 treaties are under dispute by Canadian aboriginal people.

ASSIMILATION EFFORTS

In the 1800s, as the number of European settlers increased, their cultures became the mainstream cultures. As opposed to the earlier observance of partnerships and cultural autonomy, aboriginal people were now expected to abandon their cultural identity and assimilate into settler (mainstream) society. One of the most evident and damaging efforts of assimilation by the federal government was the residential school system. The federal government played a role in the development and administration of schooling as early as 1874. The intent was to provide a mainstream education to aboriginal people. Education was viewed as a means of establishing a unitary culture, and the vision included three subgoals: a justification for removing children from their communities and families; a specific strategy for resocializing children; and a system for integrating graduates into mainstream Canadian society. Religious and government

Some tension between aboriginal and nonaboriginal cultures is beginning to lessen and celebrations like this can be enjoyed by many.

© AP Photo/CP, Andrew Vaughan

leaders of the time believed that mandatory residential schooling would solve the so-called problem of aboriginal independence (self-governance) from the mainstream. It is estimated that approximately 100,000 aboriginal children attended residential schools from 1874 to the mid-20th century.

It was not until April 1, 1969, that the federal government reconsidered the initiative, and by 1975 the program was abolished for the most part. The years of socialization through the residential schools resulted in many aboriginal people becoming ashamed of their cultural heritage and reinforced long-standing skepticism of mainstream policies, values, and education. Because sport psychology was created from European values, elite aboriginal athletes have begun to wonder to what extent the discipline aligns with aboriginal ways (see Schinke, Hanrahan, et al., 2007).

PRESENT DAY

Attempts are now being made to enhance relations among aboriginal and nonaboriginal people. One aspect of the large integrative effort involves treaty resolutions. For most First Nation communities, the historical treaties are sacred, lying at the heart of how original inhabitants and settlers wanted to coexist. Despite the possibility for positive cross-cultural relationships, distrust and skepticism remain part of the aboriginal athlete's mindset. At present there are 720,000 accounted-for aboriginal people living in Canada, and projected growth is estimated at 1 million people by 2016 (www.ainc-inac.ca). The steady growth of Canadian aboriginal populations gives ample reason for the development of culturally relevant practice. It is in the present societal backdrop that the authors of this chapter eventually found each other and now work together to enhance sport initiatives among Canadian aboriginal sport enthusiasts, starting at the community level.

COMMUNITY AND ITS ROLE IN SPORT

Chapter 1 proposed that cultures vary in how they value the individual in relation to the collective. It is apparent that even in sport, aboriginal people value their community and its resources from the collective rather than the individualistic point of view. Even the ways in which people track and support their athletes epitomize community support and pride.

PARTICIPATORY DECISION MAKING AND GROUP PROCESSES

When the nonaboriginal authors began their partnership with Wikwemikong, one of us was asked to meet at the reserve's council chambers (a formal room where chief and council decide policies by which the reserve is governed) and propose research objectives to Duke and a few invited guests. I (Rob) arrived on schedule and walked into a room filled with at least 16 people representing the community. The group members were already seated in a circle, with the chief and his advisers seated at the farthest point from the presenter and the younger members seated outward from that point. I had created a PowerPoint® presentation to help explain the rationale for the study and its relevance to the aboriginal people. The group listened in silence while I spoke. There were a few polite questions and extensive group discussion, and then lunch was served. During lunch, the chief and one of the community elders introduced me to a few of the invited members. From that moment, the project was assigned community-appointed contact people (Duke, Chris Pheasant, and Laurence Enosse) to ensure that the community and cultures were represented with integrity, and also that their representatives had the power to influence the initiative from the planning stages to completion.

Decisions including those relating to athlete sponsorship and providing sport psychology are often made through community consensus. By the time sport psychologists are brought in to work with an aboriginal athlete, the community often will have already decided what service is needed, especially among band and council and sport and recreation staff tracking the athlete's progress. When personal exchanges with the aboriginal athlete begin, the athlete will typically expect that the community (including the athlete) will continue to be involved in any decisions the psychologists wish to make regarding the athlete. Contrasted with the athlete's desire for consensus decision making is the top-down strategy that some coaches and practitioners employ in mainstream sport (Schinke, Ryba, et al., 2007). When conflicts arise between athlete and coach, it is often the result of two colliding paradigms regarding who is to make the decision: the leader (hierarchical) or group members (circular). The importance of athlete and community involvement in decisions supports the emphasis of the collective over the individual while also ensuring the integration of respect.

POSITIVE INVOLVEMENT OF COMMUNITY

In earlier published work, Schinke, Eys, and colleagues (2006) indicated that in Canadian aboriginal cultures, elite athletes experience significant community support. See Community Involvement for a story pertaining to the community involvement experienced by one elite national team boxer while attending an international competition in his own country.

Some aboriginal athletes clearly have a close relationship with their community. The relationship between Jim and his community motivated the athlete while also reaffirming the community in its own eyes, as well as among the mainstream spectators. From that experience with Jim, I now ask all aboriginal athletes to what extent they are affiliated with an aboriginal community. For those who either come from reserves directly or indirectly through extended family, discussions pertaining to motivation always return to pride of being a community member and of the expansive cultural resources that support the athletes in their pursuit of excellence.

RECIPROCITY WITH THE COMMUNITY

Earlier we mentioned that Canadian aboriginal athletes are raised in gift cultures. It is of little surprise, then, that the White authors of this chapter have

COMMUNITY INVOLVEMENT

Twelve Canadian national team boxers were participating in the Pan American Championships. Jim (fictional name) was a traditional enculturated Canadian aboriginal athlete. While the other Canadian boxing team athletes of European, African, and Latin descent went about their final preparation for the tournament in ways that were typical in the mainstream (e.g., technical sparring, short jogs, tapering, listening to mainstream music), Jim kept to himself. Because the coaching staff regarded Jim as less engaged than his teammates, they were not all that interested in him. They were accustomed to expressive athletes, or at least athletes they viewed as easier to get to know and therefore to work with.

I (Rob) approached the athlete in the same way I approached every athlete and asked whether it would be acceptable if we sat down together for a coffee. In hindsight I now can only imagine what Jim might have thought or felt given that sport psychologists (Schinke, Hanrahan, et al., 2007), and the domain of psychology in general (Thomason, 1991), are not typical social-support resources in his culture. Often, assistance that closely resembles sport psychology is provided in traditional Canadian aboriginal communities by medicine men, elders, and family members. In addition, I represented the mainstream culture to an athlete who most likely did not regard my culture as sensitive or trustworthy (see also Peltier, Danielson, Schinke, Michel, & Dube, 2006).

Once we began our discussion, I realized that Jim was quite approachable and even glad to have someone to talk with from the team even though he hadn't made the first move. One of the first indications of his traditional orientation came when he proudly showed me an eagle feather given to him by the chief and council of his reserve. He explained that each eagle feather awarded to a community member represents an act of bravery. For Jim, the act of bravery was representing his community as a boxer internationally in mainstream sport. The traditional keepsake also signified community support and appreciation, aspects that would resurface a few days later when he competed.

Jim's first bout was scheduled on the fourth evening of the tournament. Before that, audience attendance was fewer than 500 people at any given time in a stadium that seats several thousand. Parking lots were consistently near empty, and athletes went about their performances with most of their cheering sections comprising teammates and coaching staff. When the team arrived at the venue by bus on the fourth evening, however, the ambience was different. Where the driver typically parked, there were at least 20 school buses and countless other vehicles. As our team walked into the stadium, we saw that most of the seats were taken by spectators, especially children, from Jim's cultural community. Though Jim was not the most accomplished athlete on the team, the support he received from his local reserve exceeded that of all the other athletes combined.

That evening, the audience was electric. Jim was scheduled to fight against an internationally acclaimed athlete who had stopped his earlier opponent in the first minute of the first round. In keeping with being awarded an eagle feather for bravery, when Jim performed that evening he became the only opponent to last all four rounds with his adversary. During the bout, he danced around and celebrated the moment in a way that was visibly different from his teammates. Jim wasn't desperate or fearful; instead, he was brave and daring. Many years later, Jim still recounts that experience as one of many similar stories of community support. According to Jim, these experiences are an integral part of where he and others from his cultural community draw their inspiration—they are members of a larger group, not just self-determined athletes.

received gifts from the local aboriginal community, including talking sticks, clothing, artwork, and most important, time and wisdom. Also forming the basis of our experiences has been an awareness that when one takes something from the community, be it knowledge, sport expertise, or material possessions, what is taken must be counterbalanced with material items or skills that are gifted back to the community. During the recent 2006 North American Indigenous

Games educational symposium, a few of us described an intriguing motivational resource that also illustrates the importance of reciprocity in aboriginal cultures: role models (see Danielson et al., 2006).

As mentioned earlier, the Canadian Aboriginal Sport Circle has a role-model program designed for elite athletes to share their stories with aboriginal groups across the country. We realized when interviewing elite athletes that all had stories about their youth and the role models from their local and national cultural community who inspired them. Later, as the athletes considered their own elite sport experiences, all indicated that they regularly contributed to at least one aboriginal community, either as a coach or a spokesperson sharing motivational strategies and life skills with the next generation of aspiring athletes. Being a role model is an example of reciprocating what was first learned from the cultural community. It is also a reminder to practitioners interested in gaining knowledge from an aboriginal community that in addition to sharing results or lessons learned through written reports, those interested in building long-standing collaborations are also expected to assist with the integration of findings to the point of sustainability.

EFFECTIVE CROSS-CULTURAL COMMUNICATION

Psychology (Thomason, 1991) and sport psychology (Hanrahan, 2004) literature have approached the subject of effective communication when White and aboriginal populations collaborate. Other chapters discuss aspects of communication such space, time, eye contact, and the accompaniment of another to meetings (see chapters 7 and 16). In this chapter we emphasize speaking and listening.

In the earlier discussions on history and consensus building, the importance of understanding the aboriginal people of Canada was implicit. But how is that understanding built? How does multicultural understanding (and also misunderstanding) happen when Canadian mainstream and aboriginal people meet? When one of the authors of this chapter was invited to attend 5 days of cultural sensitivity training (Our Way Native Awareness Training) a few years ago, at least part of the complex answer to that question became a little clearer. About a dozen White participants were invited to learn from aboriginal presenters representing First Nation communities from across Canada. The first lesson was listening before feeling and feeling before speaking. Many of the White participants struggled with that chain of communication proposed by the aboriginal leaders, primarily because we were taught from childhood to be outspoken.

Most readers have probably found themselves in situations where they have spoken before fully understanding what was said by the other person. The nonaboriginal authors have often found themselves filling in silences and responding prematurely to what was said by their aboriginal community partners

while visiting Wikwemikong. Now it is becoming common to have bouts of silence in dialogue when our multicultural team meets. The skill of listening to what has been said, feeling the meaning of the other's message, and only then responding with clarity achieves the spirit of effective cross-cultural practice. Ross (1985) cited an anonymous source that encapsulated what we think is meant by the difference in cultural communication strategies, an adage he learned as a White person visiting a community in the same general region (Northern Ontario) as the authors of this chapter: "I believe you understand what you think I said, but I'm not sure you realize that what you heard is not what I meant" (p. 6). When a White sport psychologist assumes that silence on the part of the athlete equates with being uninterested, the aboriginal athlete might regard the overactive engagement of the practitioner as ill informed and self-indulgent (see Feeling Before Listening, Listening Before Speaking).

The exchange I had with Karen during my infancy as a sport psychology consultant epitomizes many of the critical errors that tend to happen when client and service provider are enculturated with different communication strategies. Effective cross-cultural communication typically happens when people are aware of their own as well as each other's culturally bound communication practices. I was comfortable with eye contact and believed that people who averted their eyes were dismissive, dishonest, or painfully shy. In retrospect, my inability to accurately gauge what Karen wanted was a matter of cultural insensitivity.

Karen was born and raised on a reserve, and her cultural community, unlike Jim's (page 97), reflected quite a few assimilated behaviors. For example, she did not speak her native language, she did not employ traditional medicines, and she did not have any community elders or community members as resources. Though one might assume that Karen's behaviors were entirely assimilated, this was not the case. For example, I learned later that she responded to everyone, including her personal coach, friends, and family, in the same way—with few words. Her coach informed me afterward that Karen is a good listener and rarely fills silence with unnecessary discussion. Rather, she prefers to hear what others are saying, think about their words, and then respond succinctly. In addition, it also became clear that Karen regards eye contact as a sign of disrespect and invasiveness. Finally, when I met with Karen, my goal was to discuss her identity as an athlete and quickly move on to a conventional sport psychology strategy (her competition plan). What I had in mind was not even remotely close to

FEELING BEFORE LISTENING, LISTENING BEFORE SPEAKING

As indicated in Community Involvement (page 97), I (Rob) have worked for several years with Canadian elite boxers. During my tenure, I consulted almost every year with at least one—and often several—aboriginal athletes on the Canadian National Boxing Team. During one of those experiences I was asked to meet with a talented female aboriginal boxer. The athlete was in the midst of the team selection trials, and previously, she was ranked among the best in the world in her weight division. I met first with the athlete's coach to better understand the athlete's background, including her sport-related experiences and her personal background (e.g., family, employment). Karen (fictional name) was quiet as I attempted to introduce myself and engage her in dialogue. For every question I asked, Karen replied with succinct answers, typically no more than three to five words. It was my tendency in such instances (when I thought that clients weren't forthcoming) to pepper them with ongoing questions and fill the silence. After about 15 minutes of a stilted conversation, I concluded that the athlete was not committed to the process, and I wasn't sure why we were meeting at all. Beyond her concise responses to my questions, Karen was also avoiding eye contact, and she sat farther away from me than most athletes I had encountered to that point. In short, I thought that something wasn't working, but I didn't suspect that it had anything to do with me.

A few hours after the discussion, Karen's coach thanked me for supporting her. What I initially thought of as a failed discussion was actually effective in Karen's eyes—she wanted to discuss her family ties to establish some perspective before the competition that evening. The athlete was employing her competition plan, which was to reinforce her sense of community through a discussion of family relations. Though I did not realize it at the time, strengthening that sense of community was a far more effective competition plan than solely discussing what she needed to implement in the upcoming performance. Her competition plan included familial relations and her sense of community.

what Karen wanted to discuss with me. Instead, she talked about her personal relationships.

CROSS-CULTURAL EXCHANGES AND PERFORMANCE ENHANCEMENT

In 2004, the authors of this chapter embarked on a collaborative relationship with the Canadian aboriginal community thanks to funding by the Social Sciences and Humanities Research Council of Canada (SSHRC). Following are four strategies for assisting aboriginal athlete adaptation that were shared with us in semistructured interviews with 23 elite Canadian aboriginal athletes.

STRATEGY 1: IDENTIFY WHETHER THE CLIENT IS TRADITIONAL OR ASSIMILATED

We have encountered traditional and assimilated athletes in almost every region of Canada, but regional trends need to be considered before meeting with an athlete. From our experience, athletes from Western Canada are more likely to be traditional in terms of

customs and values. The reason for this trend is a longer history of residential schools in Eastern and Central Canada, primarily because the general educational policy migrated westward. Among traditionalist practices are using sacred medicines (strategy 3), eating traditional foods, integrating elders for spiritual guidance and motivational advice, speaking a native dialect as first language, praying to the Creator, and participating in sweat lodges, drumming ceremonies, and sun dances. Though most aboriginal clients will be familiar with these aspects of their cultures, traditionalists integrate cultural practices into daily life, including training and competitions, whereas others do not (Schinke, Hanrahan, et al., 2007).

In contrast, some aboriginal athletes are Christian by religion and assimilated in their daily living. Assimilated athletes speak primarily in English, eat mainstream diets, listen to modern music, and socialize in a culturally mixed peer group. Assimilated athletes often come from acculturated reserves or have been born in large urban centers. It is believed that much of the loss in cultural heritage among acculturated athletes resulted from residential schools. The consequences of this loss may manifest in assimilated athletes as uncertainty or embarrassment regarding personal identity.

Therefore, upon learning that you will be working with aboriginal athletes or coaches, it is worth investigating to what extent their community integrates traditional and assimilated practices. Once you have taken this initial step, it is also worthwhile to learn from the clients about their families. For example, you might ask whether the family continues to hunt and fish, what their favorite foods are, and what their relationship is to extended family and community. In learning about the athletes' preferences and social networks, you will indicate a genuine interest in the athletes, including their cultural identity.

STRATEGY 2: UNDERSTAND CROSS-CULTURAL ADAPTATION

In an earlier research project, we learned that aboriginal athletes often experience challenges of cross-cultural adaptation when pursuing sport in the mainstream (see Schinke, Michel, et al., 2006). Especially among athletes raised on reserves, adjustment to mainstream sport practices and mainstream communities can be challenging. The contextual challenges identified to us include the mainstream priority of beating one's competitor as opposed to celebrating the competition process, technical instruction in lieu of playing, confrontational strategies by coaches and team captains in front of the larger group, and an emphasis on the individual over the team. The more general adaptation challenges for those relocating to mainstream communities with unfamiliar customs include physical distance from family and friends, a lack of cultural appreciation by mainstream coaches and athletes, and limited access to traditional foods.

Effective adaptation strategies have been proposed for aspiring aboriginal athletes. Some of these strategies are meant to be managed by the athletes, including the use of sacred medicines and integration of cultural community support. Cultural resources need to be maintained in the community of origin (e.g., family, community peers, elders), and they can be developed with cultural resources from a nearby community (e.g., local reserve contacts, cultural centers, sport circles). Indirect strategies can also contribute to effective adaptation. These include promoting cultural appreciation on the part of coaches and teammates and expressing an interest in the athlete's development of friendships in the new team and community.

STRATEGY 3: LEARN ABOUT RELEVANT CULTURAL PRACTICES

Aboriginal athletes have integrated a variety of cultural practices in daily training and competition.

For example, there are four sacred medicines: cedar, tobacco, sweetgrass, and sage (Bordon & Coyote, 2006). Cedar helps people acclimate to heat. When one of us struggled with heat during a sweat lodge ceremony, an elder offered a piece of cedar to chew on. Extract of cedar is also used in cedar baths as part of a physical, mental, and spiritual healing ritual. Tobacco can be offered to elders in exchange for wisdom and spiritual advice. In addition, tobacco and sweetgrass can be smoked in a pipe at the beginning and end of a ceremony and to seal a binding formal agreement. Sage can be burned in a shell or seven strands of sweetgrass can be burned at the beginning and end of each day to thank the Creator for the events of the day. The sacred medicines can also be burned at competitions to pray for bravery and health, both one's own as well as the opponent's. These medicines are part of larger bundles that sometimes include eagle feathers and bear teeth, among other keepsakes. Additionally, nonmaterial cultural practices include the importance of listening before speaking and respecting elders and the community over one's own interests.

Note that each First Nation and each region is distinct in terms of relevant cultural practices. For example, some in the larger cultural community enter circles clockwise before moving to their assigned place among the group during gatherings (e.g., Ojibway), whereas others enter counterclockwise (e.g., Mohawk). Though all of the mainstream authors have struggled with learning how to be respectful when working in partnership with Wikwemikong, we have also learned that the indigenous people of Canada are patient. Doing what is correct is important, and correctness is something we all continue to strive for. More important than correctness, however, is interest in learning. Because European cultures have become the mainstream cultures in Canada (i.e., French Canadians, English Canadians), those in the aboriginal cultures have learned about mainstream cultures and values. That understanding needs to be reciprocated so that the marginalized cultures can gain equal privilege and voice.

STRATEGY 4: INTEGRATE CULTURAL HUMAN RESOURCES

Many providers of cultural and social support are available to the aspiring aboriginal athlete. Recently, Schinke, Eys, and colleagues (2006) learned that cultural resources include family, elders, chief and council, the home community, the national cultural community, and cultural resources in educational institutions. For example, elders can offer motivation and wisdom through stories and spiritual guidance.

ISSUES AND STRATEGIES TO CONSIDER WHEN WORKING WITH CANADIAN ABORIGINAL ATHLETES

Based on the discussion thus far, readers should consider the cultural features listed here as possibly affecting their interactions with Canadian Aboriginal athletes. The suggestions that follow are based upon experiences with a limited pool of elite athletes, and thus should be considered closely in relation to each athlete's Aboriginal community of origin.

- There are as many differences as similarities among the aboriginal practices of potential clients. Nuances worth considering include province of origin, whether athletes have been raised on a reserve or in mainstream society, and whether they have retained traditional practices.
- At the very least during initial meetings, it is thoughtful to ask clients whether they would like to be accompanied by either a family member or peer. The athletes might be more comfortable sharing their perspectives when the meetings involve triads as opposed to one-on-one discussions.
- Among enculturated aboriginal athletes, meeting times might be regarded loosely. In keeping with event-based time, meetings might begin several minutes after the scheduled time.
- Though consultants sometimes book their athlete meetings for set amounts of times (e.g., 30 minutes, 1 hour), meetings with aboriginal clients should be scheduled with some extra time to account for the possibility of lengthier discussions. Given the oral tradition of aboriginal people, the athletes might relay their experiences within larger stories. Sometimes stories consume more time than scheduled.
- Adjust eye contact in relation to the athlete's eye contact. In the aboriginal cultures, especially among those who are enculturated, consistent eye contact is sometimes regarded as a form of aggression.
- Sometimes there will be gaps of silence in discussions. Wait for the athlete to continue instead of filling pauses with words. The consequence of filling silence prematurely is that one may be regarded as a poor and impatient listener.
- Aboriginal athletes might vary in regard to motivation. Some might be inspired by the support of their cultural community, and others might be self-determined in their motivation.

The chief and council may provide financial support, leading to training and competition opportunities that would be unavailable otherwise. The home community can attend important Canadian competitions and also offset loneliness while encouraging athletes from afar through letters, telephone calls, and e-mail. It is important for sport practitioners supporting aboriginal athletes to solicit cultural and social support on their athletes' behalf beyond the support that mainstream resources tend to offer.

CONCLUDING REMARKS

When considering the aboriginal client, it is clear why mainstream sport practices can miss the mark. Canadian aboriginal athletes must overcome historical challenges and social marginalization. Some of the athletes considered in this chapter come from communities that are economically disadvantaged,

displaced, or both. In addition, many carry cultural stories of betrayal that their ancestors experienced at the hands of mainstream Canadian cultures. The aforementioned hardships can manifest in distrust of mainstream cultural values—values that are inherent in sport psychology as it is usually practiced today. However, there is a place for sport psychology among the aboriginal people of Canada. As with most clients, it is for the aboriginal athletes to determine what they would like to integrate from mainstream sport psychology. Traditional mainstream sport psychology skills can contribute to a solid cross-cultural relationship if they are offered in respect for the athlete's cultures and the incorporation of First Nation cultural practices and beliefs are appropriate for each athlete's level of acculturation.

It is imperative to gain a cultural appreciation of Canadian aboriginal clients for many reasons. Primarily, though, an interest in clients in relation to their cultures provides a strong basis upon which mutual respect and understanding can be achieved. When working with those who have been marginalized, an awareness of who they are and how we can support the inclusion of their voices in mainstream sport practices can culminate in reflective practice, mutual respect, and enhanced trust. Ideally, sport psychologists can be trained from within the aboriginal cultures, and these professionals will be able to provide in-culture support for athletes from their national community while also suggesting effective CSP strategies for mainstream sport psychologists who want to tailor their strategies in a meaningful way for the aspiring aboriginal athlete.

Multicultural Sport Psychology in the United States

Anthony P. Kontos, PhD

In 2000, approximately 282 million people resided in the United States, including 70 million people (25%) who represented one or more racial or ethnic minority groups (U.S. Census Bureau, 2001). In addition, more than 31 million Americans (11%) are foreign born and 212 million (75%) identify with a specific cultural group (e.g., Irish American, Italian American, Greek American). The mosaic of cultures in the United States presents unique challenges and opportunities for the sport psychology professional, including cultural assumptions and awareness, worldview integration, and athlete acculturation. These challenges are complicated by the geography and cultural colloquialisms of a country that is nearly 9.6 million square kilometers in area. Moreover, nearly 400 years of slavery, institutionalized racism, and poor treatment of its indigenous population and minority groups have adversely affected cross-cultural relations.

In this chapter I will explore the multicultural challenges facing applied sport psychology professionals in the United States, beginning with a brief overview of racial and ethnic diversity trends in the United States in general and in sport. Second, I will provide an overview of the four major and one emerging racial and ethnic groups that compose the bulk of the U.S. racial and ethnic minority population. Third, I will consider the interaction of socioeconomic status with multicultural issues. Fourth, I will discuss the challenge of acculturation in understanding race and ethnicity. Fifth, I will discuss the cross-cultural nature of sport psychology work and propose a model for multicultural competencies for sport psychology professionals. Finally, I will consider challenges facing sport psychology in the United States.

Before exploring current trends in race and ethnicity in the United States, it is important to define the terms that will be used in this chapter. *Race* has both biological and social distinctions; however, in the United States the term is often reduced to one overarching concept that is essentially a proxy for skin color or physical appearance. *Ethnicity* is similarly misconstrued and is often used to infer physically or culturally distinct features. Ethnicity does not represent biologic uniqueness and therefore should not be used interchangeably with race. Instead, ethnicity indicates a unique set of cultural and social characteristics, including nationality, language, religion, and other customs (Sue et al., 1998). Ethnicity is largely a product of where one is born rather than one's physical appearance. For the purposes of this chapter and to simplify the discussion, the combined term *race and ethnicity* will be used.

> *We have become not a melting pot, but a beautiful mosaic. Different people, different beliefs, different yearnings, different hopes, different dreams.*
>
> Jimmy Carter, former president of the United States

The use of terms such as *African American, Latino,* or *Hispanic* to represent ethnic groups is equally confusing and mired in semantic and political debate. The best approach to race and ethnicity, which is advocated by the APA (2001), is to refer to specific subgroups such as Mexican American and Chinese American, but even these can be further distilled into regional and other subgroups. Although the preceding approach is best for understanding broad within-group (i.e., Asian American) differences and working with individual athletes, for the purposes of the discussion here, the following terms will be used: *African American, American Indian, Arab American, Asian American, Latino,* and *White.* These terms, which are based on the Centers for Disease Control and Prevention (CDC) Office of Minority Health and U.S. Census Bureau (2001) terminology, are admittedly general, and delineations among subgroups are made wherever possible.

DEMOGRAPHIC TRENDS IN RACE AND ETHNICITY

To reflect on race and ethnicity in U.S. sport, one needs to consider both general demographic trends as well as racial and ethnic representation in sport. Both of these aspects are covered next.

GENERAL POPULATION

In general, there are two overarching demographic trends within the U.S. population: the continued expansion of the Latino population, and the large number of people reporting multiracial or ethnic affiliation. According to the U.S. Census Bureau (2001), 12.5% (35.3 million) of the U.S. population is Latino or Hispanic (both terms were used in the survey). This number represents an increase of nearly 40% from the 1990 U.S. Census. The majority of Latinos (59%, or 20.6 million) identified themselves as Mexican American.

In the 2000 U.S. Census, nearly 2.5% (6.5 million) of the population represented two or more racial or ethnic groups. This was the first time U.S. residents could select a multiracial or ethnic delineation; therefore, comparative data are unavailable. The representative population growth among African Americans and Asian Americans was nominal from 1990 to 2000, although both groups increased in overall numbers. The greatest percentage growth occurred among American Indians, who doubled in number during the same 10 years. This growth can be attributed to two trends: the change in the 2000 U.S. Census categories to include American Indian in combination with other racial and ethnic affiliations (U.S. Census Bureau, 2001) and greater self-identification with American Indian heritage. It remains to be seen if the increase in cultural identification will continue. In contrast, the White population in the United States actually declined in overall representation by 6.5% (from 80.3% to 75.1%) from 1990 to 2000.

These trends are affected by regional geographic location and population density. For example, much of the Latino population in the United States is concentrated in the Southeast, Southwest, and West Coast. In contrast, the African American population, which represents 12.9% (36.4 million) of the population, is high in urban areas (e.g., Detroit, Chicago, Los Angeles) and in the Southeast. Asian American populations tend to be highest in the Pacific Northwest in areas such as Seattle and San Francisco. Consequently, regional geography must be considered when examining racial and ethnic trends in the U.S. population.

SPORT IN THE UNITED STATES

Population trends in sport in the United States do not mirror the overall population trends. Among professional and collegiate athletes, African Americans have higher representation in sports such as basketball, American football, and track. This trend is evident in the racial and ethnic diversity data reported by the NCAA (2003). Specifically, African Americans represented 41% of men's and 27% of women's basketball, 31% of American football, and 21% of both male and female track athletes in the NCAA.

The representation of African Americans is particularly related to competitive level, with significantly higher representation at Division I and II institutions (20%-25% of total) compared with Division III (<10% of the total). In professional sport, the representation of minority groups, especially African Americans, is even greater than in the collegiate sport population. For example, in 2004 nearly 78% of NBA athletes were minority athletes (mostly African American), 67% of athletes in the Women's National Basketball Association (WNBA) were African American, and 69% of athletes in the NFL were African American (Lapchick, 2004). The highest concentrations of Latino athletes were found in Major League Baseball (MLB), where 37% of players were Latino, and Major League Soccer (MLS), where 14% of players were Latino (Lapchick, 2004).

Because sport psychology professionals working with athletes at highly competitive levels in the United States are more likely to work with African American or Latino athletes than athletes from other racial and ethnic minority groups, sport psychology professionals in the United States would benefit from cultural awareness and sensitivity training that focuses on African American and Latino culture.

The relatively high representation of certain racial and ethnic minorities in some sports together with the high number of White sport psychology professionals and coaches creates many multicultural situations.
© Icon SMI

However, as mentioned, the client population will also vary with geographic location.

CAUTIONARY WORDS

As sport psychology professionals, we should be aware of the dangers of stereotyping our clients. Thus, before proceeding to the particulars of cultural generalizations it is important to consider the tendency to indulge in sensitive stereotyping, the challenges of acculturation, and the temptation to equate a single socioeconomic status with a specific race or ethnicity.

SENSITIVE STEREOTYPING

As Parham (2005) suggested, sport psychology professionals are often oblivious to their own simplified and often caricatured beliefs about athletes from different racial and ethnic groups. Typically,

the sport psychology professional's beliefs are based on a Eurocentric cultural viewpoint. Moreover, multicultural training and cultural knowledge in sport psychology is limited (Martens, Mobley, & Zizzi, 2000). The resulting one-size-fits-all approach to sport psychology is wrought with pitfalls such as sensitive stereotyping (Andersen, 1993), or perpetuating and generalizing stereotypes to all athletes from a particular racial or ethnic group without acknowledging individual differences.

A better approach is to be aware of cultural differences but to apply them to each athlete on an individual basis (Kontos & Breland-Noble, 2002). Therefore, the following review of racial and ethnic minority groups is designed to create awareness of the largest minority groups in the United States and potentially shared characteristics of each group. Awareness, in turn, should provide context for the sport psychology professional who works with athletes from these cultural groups.

Variation within any racial or ethnic group is large (Lloyd, 1987). Thus, sport psychology professionals should incorporate cultural context into their work with individual athletes rather than trying to fit athletes into a culturally stereotyped and ethnocentric box. The following generalizations should never be automatically applied to any individual athlete, but they can serve as possible clues to understanding that person's culture in the context of background information, conversation, and other interactions.

CHALLENGES OF ACCULTURATION

Athletes experience their culture differently; therefore, sport psychology professionals must consider the acculturation and enculturation of both themselves and the athletes with whom they work (Kontos & Breland-Noble, 2002). Acculturation is the process of cultural change toward the dominant societal group (Marín, 1992), and enculturation is the process of adopting and practicing the cultural qualities and skills of one's own racial or ethnic group (Berry, 1993). Athletes who acculturate to the dominant culture risk selling out their own racial or ethnic group or sacrificing their own identity, causing acculturative stress (see the American Indian section on page 110 for more information), which can manifest as depression or hostility. In contrast, athletes who maintain high enculturation might have trouble crossing over to nontraditional sport and fitting into roles in sport (Coakley, 2004). See Stress of Acculturation for an example of how acculturation and regional geography might affect an athlete.

Similar to many phenomena, such as arousal or confidence, acculturation and enculturation occur on a continuum. Moreover, an athlete may maintain different levels of acculturation or enculturation for different cultural characteristics. For example, an athlete may be acculturated to the dominant culture in appearance and language but remain enculturated with regard to religion, food, and other cultural customs. Therefore, the sport psychology professional should not assume that an athlete has a single overarching level of acculturation or enculturation that applies to everything.

SOCIOECONOMIC STATUS, RACE, AND ETHNICITY

Race, ethnicity, and socioeconomic status are typically conceptualized as mutually exclusive entities. (This chapter uses *class* interchangeably with *socioeconomic status*.) They are more accurately viewed as simultaneous identities that interact to form one's overall identity (Robinson & Howard-Hamilton, 2000). At

no time in U.S. history was this interaction of identities more evident than in the aftermath of Hurricane Katrina in New Orleans.

What was depicted in the media as a largely racial and ethnic problem was actually an intersection of socioeconomic status and race and ethnicity in New Orleans. As someone who resided in that city for 6 years (before, during, and after Hurricane Katrina) and experienced firsthand the interaction of class, race, and ethnicity on a daily basis, this did not surprise me. The city of New Orleans, as are many seemingly integrated cities in the United States, is segregated by both race and ethnicity and class. Many African Americans who were unable to evacuate the city before the arrival of Hurricane Katrina were unable to do so because of their low socioeconomic status, yet they were subsequently depicted largely by their racial and ethnic minority status. Only later was their low socioeconomic status considered. At the same time, the large numbers of middle- to upper-class African American families who live in the suburban-like area of New Orleans East (which also flooded extensively) and reflect a growing middle class of African Americans were rarely depicted by the media. Based on media coverage of New Orleans following Hurricane Katrina, one might have assumed, as often occurs in the United States (Ford, 1997), that all African Americans in New Orleans were poor.

Unfortunately, the intersection of socioeconomic status, race, and ethnicity has received no attention in sport psychology. Even the counseling and psychology literature has provided limited attention to socioeconomic status, race, and ethnicity (Robinson & Howard-Hamilton, 2000). Moreover, the discussion of many racial and ethnic groups in the United States is fraught with generalized assumptions that these groups tend to be poor (Ford, 1997), but much of what is assumed to be culturally relevant to racial and ethnic groups may only be relevant to people who are also of low socioeconomic status.

Specific concerns that may affect racial and ethnic minorities in the United States who are of moderate to high socioeconomic status include double standards, isolation, token status, and identity conflict or acculturative stress. Some minorities assume that to succeed in a White-dominated environment they must do considerably more than the norm to be accepted by the dominant group (Ford, 1995). Yet if they succeed, they risk rejection by their own group as sellouts as well as rejection by the dominant group (i.e., Whites), who might feel threatened by their success. This conundrum is particularly relevant to athletes who are trying to excel in a crossover sport,

STRESS OF ACCULTURATION

José, a 19-year-old baseball player from the Dominican Republic who recently immigrated to the United States to play professional Minor League Baseball, was referred to a White, female sport psychology professional for what his manager described as motivational issues. According to the coaching staff, since his arrival with the team, José had not practiced with much effort or enthusiasm and as a result had yet to be inserted into a game. He was in jeopardy of being sent to a team in a lower division if things did not improve.

At his first session, which was also attended by a Mexican American assistant coach who doubled as the Spanish interpreter for the team, the sport psychology consultant learned that José spoke mostly Spanish. José indicated that he felt burned out and that the travel and constant practices decreased his motivation. Moreover, his responses seemed guarded and lacked emotional content. He seemed to be basing his responses on the interpreter's reactions. As a result, the sport psychology consultant asked the team to provide a new interpreter who was not affiliated with the team.

In subsequent sessions, José was much more animated and forthcoming. He indicated that he initially played for a team in Florida, but only for a month before being traded to his current team, which was located in the Midwest. Before coming to the United States, José was a standout pitcher in the Dominican Republic semiprofessional league, where he impressed a talent scout from the United States. José had played professionally since completing high school and had never traveled outside the Dominican Republic until arriving in the United States. José indicated that during his time in Florida with his first team he had attended a local Catholic church on a regular basis, shared an apartment and most meals with two teammates who were also from the Dominican Republic, and been visited by extended family who lived in a nearby city. After only a month with his first team, José learned that as a result of his excellent play, he was going to be traded to a Midwestern team in a higher division.

José stood up and gestured angrily while describing how upset he was about being traded, and said that he had not felt like playing baseball since that had happened. He felt alienated from his new team, which included only one Latino player from Venezuela with whom he had little in common. However, due to their assumption that all Latinos are similar, his coaches believed that he and the athlete from Venezuela had much in common, which further isolated him. He lived alone in an apartment and called his family in the Dominican Republic at least twice a day. José also indicated that he did not like the weather or food in the new location.

Based on his sudden change in performance and the report of the coaching staff, it had seemed logical to infer that motivation or burnout were at the core of his problems. However, after a few sessions and with the new interpreter, it became apparent that José's problems were largely related to acculturation and associated feelings of isolation. As part of the intervention for José, the practitioner worked with him to develop social engineering methods for maintaining his cultural affiliation and practices. For example, during road trips, the team arranged for José to engage in Dominican cultural opportunities when they were available. The manager made some minor changes to the training schedule to allow José (and several other teammates, as it turned out) to attend church services either Saturday night or Sunday morning. In addition, they discussed how José could influence his situation by focusing his energy on playing to improve the likelihood that he would soon play at the next level, possibly in a city with more Dominican cultural opportunities. Finally, the sport psychology professional and José worked together to employ the Internet and Web cameras to allow him to communicate more effectively with family and friends in the Dominican Republic and to connect him with cultural events in the United States. José ended up having a successful season, and the next season he moved to an MLB team that was located nearer to the Gulf South, where he was able to connect with a strong Dominican community.

such as Venus and Serena Williams in professional tennis or Tiger Woods in professional golf.

In the United States, the sport industry exhibits a tendency to give specific racial and ethnic minorities token positions in which their power is significantly restricted (Coakley, 2004). This situation can frustrate athletes and lead them to fulfill sport roles that are accepted by the dominant culture. This so-called race logic (Hoberman, 1997) can pervade a minority group to the extent that it limits perceived opportunities for success in certain sports (e.g., African Americans in ice hockey). For example, an African American male growing up in an urban area might be directed by his family and peers toward basketball and American football because perceptions of success are high in those sports. In contrast, a Latino growing up in the same environment may gravitate toward football (soccer) or baseball because perceptions of success are higher in those sports.

Among minorities of higher socioeconomic status, pressures may come not from their own group but from the dominant White culture that they have entered, which is trying to reconcile their minority status with a stereotyped sport or position. Each of the previous issues resulting from the interaction of class, race, and ethnicity creates challenges regarding identity conflict and acculturative stress, which must be considered when working with minority athletes of moderate to high socioeconomic status.

RACIAL AND ETHNIC GROUPS AND CULTURAL BELIEFS

A brief overview of the past oppression of the most prominent minority groups in the United States is presented next to provide a framework for understanding their varying cultural characteristics. This overview is followed by a more detailed discussion of each group.

HISTORICAL OPPRESSION OF MINORITY GROUPS

People from each of the racial and ethnic groups discussed here have been influenced to varying degrees by the historical context of their exploitation (e.g., Latinos), displacement (e.g., American Indians), subjugation (e.g., African Americans), and persecution (e.g., Arab and Asian Americans). For example, a historical context of oppression might result in cultural distrust and lead to hostility toward the dominant group who oppressed the minority groups (Vontress & Epp, 1997). A sport psychology professional working in such a cross-cultural situation might find it difficult to develop the trust of an athlete that is necessary for a successful working relationship, which is particularly salient given the large number of White sport psychology professionals working with athletes from other cultures in the United States (Kontos & Breland-Noble, 2002).

For nearly 400 years, the practice of slavery brought Africans (primarily, West Africans) against their will to the United States. Current prejudices and stereotypes toward African Americans can be directly attributed to their marginalized and oppressed status in U.S. society as slaves throughout much of their history.

The United States has an equally negative history of systematic displacement and attempted cultural eradication of its indigenous American Indian population (Deloria, 1983). The resulting geographic relocation and stripping of cultural and tangible resources (Red Horse, 1982) have contributed to American Indians having one of the highest poverty and lowest health rates among minority groups.

Asians have been discriminated against since the arrival of Chinese immigrants as cheap labor for the mining and railroad industries during the mid-1800s. At no time was their persecution more overt than during World War II when thousands of mostly Japanese Americans were stripped of their property and possessions, separated from family and friends, and placed in internment camps. There they were subject to appalling living conditions, extreme deprivation, and often outright brutality. Since the 1970s, many Southeast Asian (e.g., Vietnamese, Laotian, Cambodian) immigrants were involuntarily forced to seek refuge in the United States due to politics or warfare (Chung, Bemak, & Okazaki, 1997). Forced relocation left them with limited resources, higher poverty rates, and tremendous personal and psychological adjustment challenges (Bemak & Greenberg, 1994). For example, many Southeast Asian immigrants report feelings of guilt associated with leaving family and friends behind, as well as stress-related trauma associated with premigration events (Chung et al., 1997).

In general, Latino history in the United States has been exploitative, largely revolving around the dominant stereotype that all Latinos are in the United States illegally or as migrant workers. This fairly recent stereotype (Latino immigration to the United States began in earnest in the 1950s) has contributed to the educational, social, and economic marginalization of Latinos in the United States. Even more recently, the terrorist attacks of September 11, 2001, have resulted in a culturally and politically hostile climate for Arab Americans. This climate and unfamiliarity with Arabic culture have cast Arab Americans and their cultural beliefs and practices in a negative light in the United States (Jackson, 1997); thus, Arab Americans have begun to attract some of the collective U.S. cultural disdain away from the other racial and ethnic groups discussed in this chapter.

GENERAL CHARACTERISTICS OF SPECIFIC MINORITY GROUPS

The following sections provide a brief introduction to five racial and ethnic minority groups in the United States, including African Americans, Asian Americans, Latinos, American Indians, and Arab Americans. The use of general cross-cultural knowledge is important for working with racial and ethnic minority groups. This information, however, must be applied in a flexible approach wherein the focus is on the individual rather than the group.

AFRICAN AMERICANS

African Americans face evolving cultural challenges and environments (Cross, 1995). Age and gender affect African American cultural identity in the United States, particularly in urban areas. Young, urban, African American males tend to feel alienated and face numerous psychosocial stressors (Evans & Evans, 1995; Patton, 1995). Their feelings can be attributed, in part, to constant encounters with violence and limited educational and employment opportunities (Lee & Bailey, 1997). Not surprisingly, many African American males view sport, especially basketball and American football, as a means to escape this cycle. These athletes carry with them the skepticism, survival skills, and coping strategies that helped them succeed in a challenging environment outside sport (Lee & Bailey, 1997). Some of their views and strategies can subsequently be incorporated into positive sport psychology skills (e.g., approaches to adversity and challenge; see Brooks, Haskins, & Kehe, 2004).

In general, African American culture values kinship, commitment, and spirituality. Family values and a sense of commitment are instilled in young African Americans via strong female role models because direct male role models are limited (Lee & Bailey, 1997). As a result, some African American males may seek a fatherlike relationship with a male sport psychology professional. The incorporation of religion and spirituality into sport psychology work with African American athletes may further enhance resiliency.

As with each of the groups discussed in this chapter, regional differences and rural or urban location play key roles in the expression of African American culture. Regional racial and ethnic subgroups of African Americans such as Creole Blacks (of West African and French ancestry) and Caribbean Blacks have created unique regional variations in African American culture and identity (Watkins-Duncan, 1992). For example, Creole and Caribbean Blacks might speak patois (a language that incorporates English and African words), practice religion that combines Christianity with West African spiritual beliefs, and eat foods that include French, Spanish, and African influences.

LATINOS

Latinos comprise numerous racial and ethnic subgroups (e.g., Mexican Americans, Puerto Ricans, Cuban Americans) from the Americas, and differences among the groups must be considered in any sport psychology work. From a geographical perspective, Mexican Americans tend to be concentrated in California and Texas, Puerto Ricans in the Northeast, and Cuban Americans in Florida. (See Kontos and Arguello [2005] for a review of cultural differences related to sport psychology services for Latin American athletes and a caveat for generalizing across specific subgroups.) Among the shared cultural characteristics for Latinos are *familismo* (i.e., family), *machismo* (i.e., masculinity), *personalimso* (i.e., personal interactions), and *simpatia* (i.e., being easygoing).

Familismo is the dominant cultural theme among Latinos and can extend into a general sense of community (Marín & Marín, 1991). Central to this concept are honor, cooperation, and affiliation, which lead to a strong support system for Latino athletes. However, if Latino athletes are geographically isolated from this extended support system, they may encounter adjustment and coping problems.

Machismo affects the expectations for behavior and pride among Latino males and females (Casas & Pytluk, 1995). These expectations can manifest in sport and must be considered as an explanation for masculine behaviors such as aggression. Similarly, as a result of *hembrismo* (i.e., femaleness), Latinas may exhibit behaviors such as withdrawal from sport to fulfill roles at home (Comas-Díaz, 1989). In both cases, the sport psychology professional must be careful not to stereotype the client's behaviors.

Personalimso and *simpatia* are interrelated and reflect the importance of establishing personal relationships using an easygoing and likable manner (Gloria, Ruiz, & Castillo, 2004). These characteristics may result in an athlete wanting to develop a personal relationship with a sport psychology professional through invitations to personal or family events. Regardless of whether practitioners agree to such an invitation, it is important to respect the offer so as not to offend the athlete.

ASIAN AMERICANS

In contrast to the prevalent stereotypes of other racial and ethnic minority groups in the United States, Asian Americans are often viewed as successful, hardworking, disciplined, and educated (Morrissey, 1997). Their perceived social, economic, and educational success has led to the misconception that Asian Americans are accepted by dominant White culture and not discriminated against (Sue & Sue, 1999). The depiction of Asian Americans as the model minority in the United States has led other minority groups to chastise them because they believe that Asian Americans are advantaged (Sue & Sue, 1999).

Much of Asian American culture is centered on family and religion. The importance of family may open the door to a family systems approach to sport psychology. Religion in Asian culture, which ranges from animism to Zen Buddhism, is diverse and cannot be properly summarized in this chapter. Nonetheless, religion plays a significant role in the cultural beliefs and practices of many Asian Americans, and it may also play a role in performance enhancement (Chung et al., 1997).

A unique, though not universal, aspect of Asian American culture is neurasthenia, or the reporting of somatic manifestations (i.e., symptoms) of psychological distress (Chung & Kagawa-Singer, 1996). For example, a self-referred Vietnamese American golfer with whom I worked presented with complaints about frequent illnesses and body pains with no apparent medical cause. During the intake session, it became apparent that his symptoms were somatic manifestations of anxiety associated with qualifying for a competition. The athlete at first denied the connection, but after some challenging, he indicated that being physically sick was more acceptable in his family and culture than having psychological problems. In cases such as this one, there is a concomitant expectation for quick resolution of these somatic symptoms (Chung et al., 1997), which may lead to greater acceptance of cognitive-behavioral sport psychology techniques such as progressive muscle relaxation, deep breathing, biofeedback, and imagery. However, this expectation may also lead to frustration in the absence of symptom resolution or progress. For instance, the Vietnamese American golfer was receptive to cognitive restructuring, relaxation, and breathing techniques, but he expected them to fix his situation immediately. I focused on immediate changes such as the athlete feeling better and less nervous, and I indicated that just as with physical

practice, mental strategies require practice and consistency to have the greatest effect on performance.

AMERICAN INDIANS

Key cultural issues for American Indians include Indianess, tribal affiliation, location, and acculturative stress (Kontos & Breland-Noble, 2002). Indianess is represented in external displays of tribal beliefs and practices (Red Horse, 1982). Tribal affiliation and location (urban or rural) affect one's Indianess. For example, the Indianess of Cherokee Indians living in the reservation in Tahlequah, Oklahoma, may be more overt than among those living in Oklahoma City. American Indians who live in urban environments away from the reservation are susceptible to acculturative stress resulting from the constant identity clash between their Indian culture and the dominant White culture (Kontos & Breland-Noble, 2002). The recent explosion of tribal casinos in the United States has resulted in further debate and confusion regarding Indianess across tribal groups (tribal groups use blood quanta ranging from 1/16 to 1/2 as minimum requirements for tribal registration).

Tribal cultural differences are vast and generalizations across tribes should be avoided. The practitioner should instead focus on specific tribal awareness or regional similarities (e.g., Southwest Indians, such as Navaho, Hopi, and Apache). In spite of regional and tribal differences, American Indians tend to share underlying cultural values, including a holistic approach to health, emphasis on cooperation over individual success, and respect for family and elders (Sage, 1997). Cultural beliefs and practices vary considerably among the 542 recognized American Indian tribal groups in the United States (U.S. Census Bureau, 2001). Consequently, American Indian athletes' approaches to sport psychology will vary based on regional geography, intergenerational issues, urban and reservation locations, cultural understanding of health, and other challenges (Sage, 1997).

ARAB AMERICANS

Although Arab Americans represent a fairly small ethnic group in the United States at 1.2 million or .42% of the population, (U.S. Census Bureau, 2001), they are among the fastest growing groups in the United States at an increase of 40% in 10 years. Arab Americans include a heterogeneous group of people who speak Arabic and have ethnic origins primarily in North Africa and the Middle East.

Family and religion are foremost among the cultural influences of Arab Americans that sport psychology professionals should consider. Traditionally, family unity with a strong chronological patriarchal

Arab Americans represent a growing minority group in the United States with whom sport psychology professionals may work.
© Karim Sahib/AFP/Getty Images

hierarchy forms the foundation of Arab American culture (Jackson, 1997). The other pillar in Arab American culture is religion, whether it is Islam or Christianity. Arab Americans who are Christian tend to acculturate more easily than those who are Muslim (Jackson, 1997). The practice of Islam among Arab Americans is tied to family loyalty and piety (i.e., religious devotion and spirituality) (Nydell, 1987).

Unfortunately, the unfamiliarity with and vilification of Islamic culture and Arab Americans in general following September 11, 2001, has resulted in widespread intolerance in the United States (Erickson & Al-Timimi, 2004). This general hostility may lead Arab American athletes to be suspicious of mainstream sport psychology professionals and take a guarded approach to sport psychology (see Cultural Awareness).

STRATEGIES FOR INCREASING MULTICULTURAL COMPETENCY

The following section explores several strategies for expanding sport psychology professionals' multicultural competencies. The section begins with a review of underlying multicultural competencies, including self-awareness, worldview integration

and sensitivity, and multicultural skills for effective practice. A new model from which sport psychology professionals can develop their multicultural competencies is then explored.

AWARENESS OF SELF AND OTHERS

The core of every multicultural competency is self-awareness. Sport psychology professionals can begin their journey to multicultural competence with an introspective look at their own cultural selves. This introspection must start with an examination of one's racial and ethnic assumptions, including stereotypes, generalizations, and negative emotions. To accomplish this, practitioners must ask themselves questions such as the following: What do I believe about athletes from different cultures? How does my own worldview affect my perceptions of athletes from different cultures, and how do I interact in cross-cultural relationships? What aspects of my cultural, communication, and counseling competencies can I improve? How do my assumptions and worldview affect my conceptualization of sport psychology? Part of this journey to multicultural awareness and competency should also include an examination of one's multicultural self-efficacy—that is, one's confidence working with people from different cultures (Constantine & Ladany, 2001).

CULTURAL AWARENESS

Asad, a 17-year-old cross country runner at a high school in the metropolitan Detroit area, was referred by his coach to me, a White, male sport psychology professional. Asad was the reigning champion in the 1500-meter distance. Recently, he had missed several training sessions and a competition, and his coach was concerned that he would not qualify for the state championship. His coach could not understand why this was happening because Asad had been a dedicated runner until then.

Asad, the oldest of four children, was born in the United States, resided with his extended family, and was Muslim. He missed his initial scheduled session with me. I had worked with Arab American athletes in the past and was aware of the potential importance of both family and religion in Asad's life. I called Asad to reschedule, making sure to schedule our session at a time that did not conflict with his family or prayer schedule. At our first meeting Asad was polite, attentive, and proud of his competitive accomplishments. However, he became defensive when asked about missing training sessions and the competition.

Asad told me that his father had become ill a month ago and could no longer work. As the oldest son, it was Asad's responsibility to work at the family business, and thus he had missed a couple of practices. He felt he was letting his family down by missing the practices, yet he would also be letting them down if he ignored his obligation to support them. Because he was too embarrassed to tell the coach about his situation, he had decided it would be best if he simply stopped running altogether. However, he didn't want to tell his father that he was no longer competing because it was something of which his father was proud.

I worked with Asad to develop a plan to deal with his communication and time conflicts and encouraged him to discuss the situation with his father. As a result, Asad's younger brother started helping at the store so that Asad could attend training sessions and competitions. In the process, Asad was able to qualify for the state championship while also maintaining his important family role. After Asad's father discussed the case and its positive resolution with the high school athletic director, I was invited to conduct a cultural awareness session for the coaching staff at the high school. My awareness of Arab American culture was the key to the outcome of this case.

I think self-awareness is the most important thing to becoming a champion.

Billy Jean King, former professional tennis player

All sport psychology professionals incorporate their own biases, values, and beliefs into their work with athletes. These concepts form the foundation from which one interprets and makes sense of the world, and this foundation is referred to as a *worldview* (Kehe & Smith, 2004). The underlying component to a person's worldview is racial and ethnic identity development (see Sue et al., 1998). As mentioned earlier, most sport psychology professionals in the United States are White. The majority of professionals in the field develop a worldview that is largely a product of the cultural conditioning and socialization that comes with being members of the dominant cultural group (Sue et al., 1998). Hence, the core of any multicultural competency for sport psychology professionals is based first on becoming aware of and understanding their own worldview, which represents the influence of their experience, perceptions, and interactions with others. For example, a personal encounter (positive or negative) with an American Indian athlete will influence one's understanding of other American Indians. Only by becoming aware of this fact and the effects of such interactions on perceptions can one's worldview expand and benefit from that earlier encounter.

Every head is a world.

Cuban proverb

A multiculturally competent sport psychology professional must also attempt to understand the athlete's worldview. In doing so, it is important for the practitioner to avoid negative judgments about the athlete's worldview (Sue et al, 1998). A key component to this sensitivity is developing an understanding of specific racial and ethnic groups. Another component of being culturally sensitive to an athlete's worldview is to be aware of one's own emotional reactions toward other racial and ethnic groups (Robinson & Howard-Hamilton, 2000).

SKILLS FOR EFFECTIVE INTERVENTIONS

The APA (1993) and Pope-Davis and Coleman (1997) recommend the following guidelines for effective sport psychology interventions:

- After developing self-awareness and a strong worldview integration and sensitivity, sport psychology professionals should turn their attention to the development of specific multicultural skills.

- Goals and techniques for sport psychology should be aligned with each athlete's cultural values and worldview (Sue & Sue, 1999). In essence, traditional approaches to sport psychology may not work with certain groups. For example, client-centered or passive approaches, such as Rogerian talk-focused strategies, might be too indirect or slow for use with Asian American athletes because of neurasthenia and the desire for quick results that were discussed earlier. A direct, cognitive-behavioral approach might be more appropriate in such cases. In another example, the use of self-disclosure (a common technique in sport psychology) by White sport psychology professionals may be incongruent with an American Indian athlete's worldview, which might include historical distrust of the dominant White culture. These examples highlight the need for flexibility and a wide range of skills in multicultural sport psychology.

- Avoid becoming entrenched in a method or approach that is used with nearly all of the athletes with whom you work. This homogenized approach leaves little room to develop the skills necessary for multicultural competency.

- Break from your comfort zones and explore new approaches and interventions.

- Become aware of your multicultural limitations in working with athletes from different cultures. For example, a sport psychology professional may be comfortable working with Latino athletes but have limited experience with Asian American culture and athletes. Moreover, self-awareness of lingering prejudices or other worldview-related issues may inhibit a practitioner from working with an athlete from a specific racial or ethnic group. Hence, multicultural referrals should be used whenever a sport psychology professional lacks the training, awareness, comfort, or skills to work with a specific athlete. However, professionals should also embrace this

limitation as a challenge for expanding their multicultural awareness.

INTEGRATED MODEL FOR MULTICULTURAL COMPETENCY

As indicated previously, sport psychology professionals must become multiculturally competent. To achieve this, they must acquire the necessary multicultural knowledge and skills proposed by Pope-Davis and Coleman (1997), including

- awareness of self and others,

- knowledge of and sensitivity to each athlete's culture and situation, and

- competent counseling and interpersonal skills.

The proposed integrated model of multicultural competency in sport psychology combines all three aspects of multicultural competency for sport psychology professionals (see figure 9.1). Specifically, the model illustrates that practitioners should develop a strong sense of cultural self, including self-awareness and worldview, from which they can form the basis of their multicultural work with athletes.

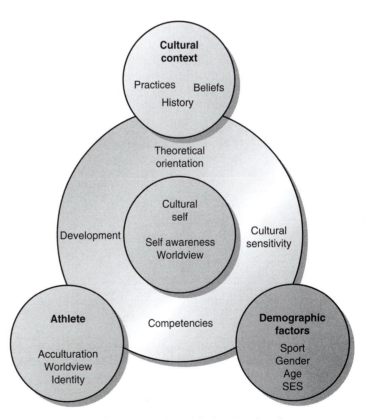

FIGURE 9.1 The integrated model of multicultural competency provides sport psychology professionals with a framework from which to work with culturally different athletes.

The cultural self influences the sport psychology professional's cultural sensitivity (e.g., awareness of stereotypes, racial and ethnic beliefs and practices), theoretical orientation (e.g., cognitive-behavioral orientation), competencies (e.g., communication skills), and development. These four components (depicted in the largest circle) represent the internal aspect of the sport psychology professional's multicultural competency.

The relevant external aspects (depicted by the three circles outside of but in contact with the large circle) represent understanding of three key domains:

- The athlete, including acculturation, worldview, and racial and ethnic identity
- The cultural context from which the athlete comes, including practices, beliefs, and history
- Demographic factors, including socioeconomic status, sport, gender, and age, that interact with race and ethnicity

The proposed model is the foundation for the example in A Multicultural Approach.

A MULTICULTURAL APPROACH TO A LONG-DISTANCE RUNNER

Janeese, a 24-year-old African American runner who was trying to qualify for the U.S. Olympic team at the 5K distance, self-referred to me, a White male sport psychology professional, to improve her mental skills for running. During the first session, it became apparent that Janeese did not employ many psychological strategies in training or competition. She had performed well thus far but was excited about developing a consistent preperformance routine as well as working on imagery and concentration skills.

At first, this case seemed straightforward, and my cognitive-behavioral orientation (i.e., theoretical approach) appeared to be a good fit. I had participated in several workshops about racial identity and was aware of my assumptions and worldview, as well as my place of privilege in working with an African American athlete (i.e., awareness, sensitivity). I was also aware of the potential importance of historical context, religion, and family and its support among many African American athletes (i.e., competencies, demographics). As it turned out, one of the key concerns for Janeese was erosion in family social support, which coincided with her long training sessions with her coaches away from her family and friends. During such times, she felt burned out and isolated.

I thought her isolation might be compounded by the crossover nature of Janeese's event, the 5K: She was one of only two African American distance runners on the women's team, and she was constantly stereotyped as a sprinter (i.e., cultural context). However, Janeese had been running the 5K distance her entire career, she grew up in an integrated suburban, middle-class neighborhood, and she was fairly acculturated through her life experiences to being "the only black girl running more than a lap," as she called it (i.e., athlete acculturation). Thus, her feelings were not related to crossing over at all.

I believed that part of the strategy for Janeese should involve connecting her to a social support network because it was not practical for her family to relocate or for her to train at home. Hence, I took on the role of consultant, as discussed in the multicultural workshops I had attended, and engaged members of Janeese's family, track team, and community to develop a network of social support for her during her training away from home. This engagement involved connecting and facilitating social interactions between Janeese and these familiar groups. In addition, Janeese continued to meet with me to work on cognitive-behavioral techniques to enhance her performance. Janeese's performance continued to improve and she posted several personal best times during the season.

I learned from my work with Janeese that socioeconomic status, acculturation, and worldview are key factors to understanding such cases. I also extended my multicultural skill set to include a consultant role and in the process made valuable cultural and social connections in the African American community that would enable me to expand this role in the future. These experiences, in turn, changed my worldview and further developed my multicultural competency.

FUTURE DIRECTIONS

Despite repeated calls for increased consideration and inclusion of racial and ethnic minority groups in sport psychology research (Duda & Allison, 1990; Ram, Starek, & Johnson, 2004), applied work (Kontos & Arguello, 2005; Kontos & Breland-Noble, 2002), and training (Martens et al., 2000), sport psychology in the United States remains a predominately White domain. In contrast, as discussed earlier, many sports in the United States have high representations of minority groups. This juxtaposition has resulted in a proliferation of cross-cultural sport psychology relationships in which the sport psychology professional is typically White and the athlete is from a minority group. There are certainly times when the athlete may be White and the sport psychology professional African American or Latino and thus there are no issues of White privilege (Butryn, 2002); often, however, racial or ethnic incongruity exists, which can lead to hesitancy or suspicion among athletes seeking services from sport psychology professionals (Martin, Wrisberg, Beitel, & Lounsbury, 1997; Wrisberg & Martin, 1994). Unfortunately, this incongruity can exacerbate the stigma that athletes associate with sport psychology services and may result in even fewer minority athletes working with sport psychology professionals (Martin et al., 1997).

In 2002, Breland-Noble and I advocated for increased representation of racial and ethnic minorities in the field of sport psychology. Since then, only minor changes have taken place. The AASP Diversity Committee has provided recommendations to AASP leadership regarding racial and ethnic diversity in membership, programming, and training. Also, recent conference programming at AASP has included diversity workshops. Unfortunately, there are no published data on the representation of racial and ethnic minorities in professional organizations such as the AASP or APA Division 47 to determine if representation among these groups has changed.

Regardless, sport psychology has a long way to go regarding multicultural inclusion; hence, I will repeat our previous call for increased racial and ethnic diversity in sport psychology. Specifically, master's and doctoral sport psychology programs in the United States must increase their numbers of minority students and graduates. However, this recruitment must start at the undergraduate level. Undergraduate minorities should be actively mentored and recruited into graduate sport psychology programs. Racial and ethnic minority scholarships for study in sport psychology must be added to existing student funding schemes. Recruitment should be followed by professional opportunities. To further stimulate racial and ethnic minority involvement in sport psychology, professional organizations such as the AASP, APA Division 47, and the North American Society for the Psychology of Sport and Physical Activity (NASPSPA) need to institute funding opportunities to involve minorities in conferences, leadership, research, and other experiences. Journals such as the *Sport Psychologist, Journal of Applied Sport Psychology,* and *Journal of Sport and Exercise Psychology* should include more minorities on their editorial boards and dedicate special issues to multicultural sport psychology.

Regardless of the future expansion of racial and ethnic minority representation in the field of sport psychology, multicultural training in the field must be expanded (Cox, 2002). Martens and colleagues (2000) provided an excellent review of multicultural training suggestions that focused on a universal training model. This model addressed four domains: awareness and sensitivity, cultural knowledge, simulated cultural sport psychology (CSP) experiences, and direct, supervised experience working with culturally different athletes. However, at this point, AASP Certified Consultant requirements do not even mandate a multicultural training course. It is merely optional to include such a course toward the requirement for social bases of behavior. Few graduate programs in sport psychology include multicultural sport psychology courses. Moreover, many professionals already in the field did not benefit from such courses in the past. Hence, the AASP and other organizations should continue to provide culture-based training through workshops. Hopefully, this trend will continue to expand and multicultural classroom training will become a required component in sport psychology graduate programs.

Classroom and textbook training are important, but they should be viewed as preparation for the next step in training: immersion. Immersion allows sport psychology professionals to gain firsthand understanding of working with a minority athlete via supervised practicum and internship experiences, and it is crucial to extending classroom learning to practical application. Supervised immersion, such as that proposed by Martens and colleagues (2000), allows sport psychology professionals to develop their multicultural competencies, including awareness of a particular racial or ethnic group, their own worldview and assumptions, and which sport psychology strategies are most effective under specific cultural contexts. Immersion training opportunities can also be provided as part of AASP and APA Division 47 diversity workshops and count toward professional development.

ISSUES AND STRATEGIES TO CONSIDER WHEN WORKING WITH U.S. MINORITIES

Following are a few suggestions for consultants who are interested in working with U.S. minority athletes. My recommendations are intended as an entry point to tailored strategies that address cultural nuances.

- Awareness of self and racial and ethnic groups
- Stereotyping
- Factors that influence racial and ethnic groups (e.g., historical context, socioeconomic status)
- Worldviews of athletes and sport psychology professionals
- Acculturation and enculturation level of athletes
- Multicultural competencies (model of multicultural competency)

SUMMARY

The U.S. population is becoming increasingly diverse. Certain minority groups, such as African Americans, are represented in significantly higher numbers than in the overall population in sports such as basketball, American football, and track. Awareness of the historical context and cultural beliefs and practices of minority groups is important to developing multicultural competency in sport psychology. However, sport psychology professionals must be aware of the tremendous variation within each racial and ethnic group, which can be affected by athletes' level of acculturation and worldview. Socio-economic status is another factor that can influence the effects of race and ethnicity and stereotypes of minority athletes. The majority of sport psychology professionals in the United States are White, which creates cross-cultural challenges. Sport psychology professionals must integrate their own worldviews with athletes' worldviews. They must also develop the necessary multicultural skills for effective sport psychology interventions with athletes from different cultures. A new model for multicultural competency in sport psychology should help to frame the development of multicultural skills in the field. Concurrently, efforts to recruit and mentor racial and ethnic minorities in sport psychology must be supported and expanded.

WORKING WITH BRAZILIAN ATHLETES

Luis Carlos Moraes, PhD, and John H. Salmela, PhD

Organized Brazilian sport is a relatively new phenomenon and is intimately tied to a variety of factors in Brazilian life. Although football (soccer) enjoys exceptional training facilities and an enthusiastic fan base, Brazil—a developing country—lacks both training facilities and widespread support for sport. Sport is subsidized by the government, but in general there is a lack of financial resources. However, the role of families, the national predisposition to rhythm and dance, and powerful religious forces all contribute to the unique nature of sport in Brazil.

OVERVIEW OF BRAZIL

Portuguese explorers entered Brazil in 1500, and the present population is more than 189 million (Ministério do Planejamento, 2007), with a great deal of intermarriage among the Portuguese, indigenous Indians, Arabs, and former Black slaves from West Africa. Brazil is an immense country that covers 8,514,877 square kilometers (http://en.wikipedia.org/wiki/Brazil). Given the nation's diversity of races and cultures, every state has a variety of foods, customs, and celebrations that influence Brazilian sport.

The climate is strongly affected by the Atlantic Ocean and includes both tropical and more temperate areas. Indoor and beach football, track and field, and beach volleyball are popular in Northern Brazil, and swimming, basketball, and artistic gymnastics are practiced in Southern Brazil. In addition, all of Brazil plays football and volleyball, the two most popular sports. The climate provides appropriate weather to practice outdoor physical activities for almost the entire year, especially along the coast. Access to beaches has significantly contributed to the development of active sports such as beach football and volleyball, which are practiced by Brazilians of all ages. Some of this passion and success comes directly from the notion that Brazilians have a natural gift for football, perhaps in the same way that Canadians believe their cold weather develops their winter sport expertise, which is crucial to ice hockey (Salmela, Marques, & Machado, 2004).

BRAZILIAN HERITAGE AND THE SPORT CONTEXT

Many factors affect the practice of sport in Brazil. They include access to training and cultural support for sport participation, the family, a national love of rhythm and dance, and religious diversity.

NATIONAL ACCESS TO TRAINING AND SUPPORT

Some researchers emphasize the importance of genetics, or natural talent, in athletes' success (MacArthur & North, 2005; Zanoteli et al., 2003). Others have stressed the influence of environmental factors, such as training conditions, family support, coaching, and personal effort (Janelle & Hillman, 2003; Salmela & Moraes, 2003). In Brazil, as everywhere, both of these influences are instrumental in the selection and success of athletes. However, personal determination is perhaps even more necessary for Brazilians for a number of reasons:

• With the exception of a few sports such as volleyball, swimming, and professional football, there is often a lack of organization, human resources, and financial support (Salmela et al., 2004). This means that many Brazilian athletes have to acquire on their own the approximately 10,000 hours of deliberate practice that Ericsson, Krampe, and Tesch-Römer (1993) have stated are required for the development of highly skilled performance. In many cases, these athletes have managed to reach the highest levels of expertise without the specialized instruction and feedback provided by coaches (Salmela, Marques, Machado, & Durand-Bush, 2006).

- The absence of a strong sport culture manifests in a lack of support for athletes. For example, a female cyclist complained to me (L.C.) about training difficulties caused by automobile drivers in her city of residence. Some drivers would cut cyclists off for no apparent reason, and others would yell insulting comments at female cyclists.

- Through an overemphasis on football and underreporting of almost all other sports, the media contribute to this lack of a general sporting culture. Rarely more than four articles on sports other than football appear in a six-page sport section in a typical Brazilian newspaper. For example, we recently analyzed the sport section of the *Estado de Minas*, a reputable newspaper in Belo Horizonte, over a full week. On average, each day there were 6.3 articles on various sports and 15.3 on football. When the length of the coverage for each article was measured in centimeters, the other sports measured 2.19 meters and the football articles totaled 6.17 meters. Although volleyball, swimming, and gymnastics receive some media attention, athletes from football usually take up 29 of every 30 minutes of televised sport.

FAMILY

Because of the unreliable availability of formal sport training and support in many communities, the family often becomes the locus of sport resources for Brazilian athletes. In Brazil, as is the case in the majority of Latin American countries, the patriarchal system is the basis of the family structure. In part related to Catholicism, the patriarchal system positions the father as the head of the family. One female athlete related that most of the decisions in her family ended with the final word from her father. She believed that this type of decision making was a behavioral pattern learned from her family background and reinforced by her father's financial responsibilities. Although the father is usually the primary breadwinner and the mother takes care of the family, the patriarchal relationship in the family is changing as women are slowly becoming more independent. In modern society, they can be mothers taking care of their children and also have part-time jobs. In some circumstances, the mother controls the finances and consequently becomes the informal leader of the family.

Sport in Brazil is understood to be a vehicle for social mobility, so parents of low economic status often encourage their children to invest great effort in practicing many sports, especially football. A number of successful amateur athletes, such as gymnast Daiane dos Santos and several beach volleyball athletes, earn six-figure annual salaries from endorsements. Other athletes are passionately attracted to football and the million-dollar contracts that it can bring. Expectations of footballers solving their families' financial problems are greater than expectations in other sports. In general, athletes who come from low-income families attempt to gain lucrative contracts and realize their dream to buy a beautiful house for their parents. Even though some parents do not support their children financially in sport, they often are a source of inspiration for their children to succeed (Moraes, Rabelo, & Salmela, 2004).

Middle-class parents also have great expectations for the success of their children in sports such as volleyball, football, swimming, tennis, and gymnastics (Moraes, Salmela, Rabelo, & Vianna, 2004). These parents have behavioral profiles similar to those of parents from Canada and the United States. Parents often sacrifice their own livelihoods to help their children reach high levels of performance, especially in amateur sports such as swimming and tennis (Moraes, Salmela, et al., 2004).

RHYTHM AND DANCE

Carnival, samba, and capoeira (a mixture of Brazilian martial arts and dance) reflect Brazilians' love of rhythm and dance. Samba and capoeira are relevant to Brazilian self-expression in various segments of the culture and can spill over into sport. This sense of rhythm translates into *ginga*, a type of rhythmical activity that includes creative dance movements, which many athletes in Brazil, especially football players, have integrated into their tactics to deceive their opponents. People who are familiar with samba and capoeira can observe these rhythmical elements in Brazilian football matches. This folkloric legacy originated from African influences during the Portuguese colonization and has become an important aspect of Brazilian culture.

RELIGION

With a population of more than 180 million, Brazil is the largest Catholic country in the world. Evangelical Christian churches are also well organized and growing rapidly. In addition, there is a traditional Afro-Brazilian influence in both daily life and in football practices (Salmela & Marques, 2004).

It is not uncommon for Catholic religious practices to be used in Brazilian football. For example, the Athletes of Christ movement began in Brazil more than 20 years ago and is common among football players. Members of this group stamp the

The joyful movements of Brazilian dance are an expression of a national exuberance that sport psychologists must accept if they are to be successful working with most Brazilian athletes.
© Angelo Cavalli/age fotostock

figure of Christ inside their shirts, and immediately after scoring a goal they pull up their shirts and run around the field showing this image to the spectators. The Brazilian sport psychology consultant from the Athens Olympics has stated that Athletes of Christ are an important subculture that practitioners need to be aware of to do their job effectively. During the Athens Games, the Brazilian Olympic Committee hired a priest to work with national teams (athletes, coaches, and management). He reportedly assisted approximately 20% of the Brazilian contingent.

Many athletes also employ traditional religious superstitions and practices in their sport. For example, some wear necklaces with Christ on the cross for personal protection against *azarão*, or bad luck in sport. Others use African voodoo rituals, called *mandinga* and *macumba*, during ritual practices called *candonblé* and *ubanda*. These indigenous strategies are popular among Brazilian athletes from African backgrounds, especially in football. In Northern Brazil, a chicken was once buried under the football field to give bad luck to the opposing team. The targeted team later dug up the entire football field to remove it. Coaches have also integrated superstition into their practices. For example, coaches have been known to wear the same uniforms, shirts, or other apparel during the sport season to give them luck against their opponents. They also sometimes use amulets or rituals to help them in competitions.

Sport psychology consultants need to think twice when working with athletes or coaches to ensure that their interventions do not contradict or belittle religious influences that are common in Brazil. Religion is central to Brazilian culture, and many athletes attribute their successes first to God and then to other causes such as training (Salmela & Marques, 2004). One point of interest is that in São Paulo alone, there are more than 2,000 registered religious sects. Many Brazilians believe that participating in numerous religious denominations increases their chances of practicing the right one. It is not uncommon for Brazilians to be devout Catholics yet in times of stress, such as in sport competitions or illness, to revert to spiritualism or black magic practices.

INTERACTING WITH BRAZILIAN ATHLETES

In addition to becoming familiar with and developing respect for Brazilian culture, sport psychologists should be aware of specific strategies that will be helpful when working with Brazilian athletes. Following are some examples.

USE COMMON SENSE

Some strategies may seem so obvious as to be matters of common sense. However, our experience with non-Brazilian sport psychologists has demonstrated that not all such situations are obvious, especially if a language or cultural barrier exists.

One concern is that sport psychology consultants should be careful not to interfere with the work of the coaching staff. For example, D.M. Samulski (personal communication, November 13, 2006) found that cheering the players to motivate them to try harder isn't always a good idea. He learned this when he was at an international tournament and the head coach asked him to stop cheering the athletes on. After the game, the coach explained that he had told his players to hold back, changing the tactics of the game for defensive purposes. Thus, it was not helpful to have two coaching staff voices present at that moment. After this experience, Samulski reflected that he sometimes encouraged the athletes too much instead of just supporting them and there are instances when it is better to remain silent than to become a cheerleader. In Brazil, the role of the sport psychologist in the heat of competition can be motivational, but only as specified by the head coach.

In addition, when working with athletes of a different culture, consultants must take extra care to make sure they have communicated clearly. One athlete told me (L.C.) that his foreign coach told him only 2 minutes before an international taekwondo competition that he was going to use nonverbal signs regarding technical performance. The signals would indicate that the athlete should advance, retreat, move, or turn to the left or right. The athlete, however, did not have adequate time to clarify the coach's instructions, so he did not understand the gestures during the bout. The athlete felt that the misunderstanding was caused by communication differences. In a sport such as taekwondo where speed is critical, poor communication can be detrimental to performance, and this small break in attention could have cost the athlete a medal.

TELL THE TRUTH

Though in many cultures being candid is the obvious thing to do, in others people use indirect and culturally mediated ways of expressing the truth. Brazil is one of the former cultures. Maurício Marques, a Brazilian futsal (indoor football) coach who holds a master's degree in sport psychology, has significant experience with Brazilian athletes and also coached the 2004 Australian national futsal team. He pointed out that the key to positive communication with his Brazilian athletes is telling them the truth (personal communication, February 22, 2007).

It is crucial for consultants in Brazil as well as in most cultures to tell the truth about commitments one has made, such as when athletes open up about personal affairs. One national team athlete stressed her negative experiences dealing with a sport psychology consultant during her participation with the national team. According to the athlete, the staff lacked discretion when she shared concerns with them. Here is some of what she had to say to L.C.:

> One thing that I needed to emphasize concerned the indiscretion of the professionals with whom I confided. More than once, I opened up to a coach, assistant coach, or psychologist and told them about my fears and concerns, only to hear at the next day's practice my words spelled out to the group by the confidant himself or by another member of the coaching staff. The psychologist repeated that he wouldn't reveal our secrets to the coaches. He said he would simply inform them of our general discontentment, and through training and mental training techniques, help us work out whatever problems we had with the coaching staff, smooth the communication processes and the relationships between both parties. To our great disappointment, however, we realized from the head coach's attitudes and lecturing the next day that every single word that had been uttered during our meeting with the sport psychologist had been reported to the head coach.

This athlete went on to suggest that every consultant should participate in training sessions about ethical practice before working with any athlete. She noted that it was difficult to open up to people if she did not trust them and therefore sport psychologists should develop proper rapport and trust before consultations.

Take a Positive Approach

From working as mental training consultants for Brazilian athletes, we have learned that a positive approach helps improve athletes' performances. For example, when one of us interviewed a world-class athlete, she confided that a negative approach during training or performance contributes to a non-trusting relationship with the coach or consultant. She believed that negative communication with a Brazilian athlete indicates that the sport psychology consultant or coach doubts the athlete's capacity. On the other hand, building trust over the long run is an effective strategy with Brazilian athletes.

Realizing that the athletes' life experiences have probably been different from their own may help coaches and sport psychologists develop rapport and therefore trust. In Brazil, aside from in middle- and upper-class sports (e.g., equestrian, shooting), coaching staff and athletes often come from different origins. Whereas the practitioners might be from a middle-class background and have a formal college or university education, the athletes in sports such as football often come from more modest beginnings and have limited education, making it challenging to develop trust. Consequently, coaches must delve into family histories, religious beliefs, and the economic status of their athletes to determine how best to intervene.

The more critical style of training often used by foreign coaches can result in negative emotional states for the athletes. Even when the athletes respect the coach, some still won't understand that the critical approach is intended to be constructive and motivat-ing. This is just one example of what can happen if a coach or consultant fails to take Brazilian culture into account.

Appeal to Emotions

D.M. Samulski (personal communication, November 13, 2006), a German sport psychologist who has worked with athletes in Brazil, has commented that Brazilian culture is complex, with many regional differences that seem inexplicable to foreigners. When he first came to Brazil, he was surprised by how intensely the volleyball teams celebrate when they win, becoming euphoric or almost hysterical while dramatizing the victory. He also learned that these transparent emotional states, which are reflected in behaviors such as kissing the Brazilian flag, represent the athletes' positive side. On the other hand, Samulski noted that when athletes lose, it is not uncharacteristic for them to cry nonstop. In view of these experiences, he suggested that foreign practitioners in Brazil adapt their approach to suit the passionate nature of the culture.

Maurício Marques (personal communication, February 22, 2007) observed, "I used to express my feelings of anger, anxiety, frustration, joy, and happiness during training or competition." He also mentioned that Brazilians use nonverbal communication mixed with gestures and guttural sounds in sport contexts. He affirmed that because Brazilians are sentimental and emotional, they are open to sharing their personal problems, talking with the coach, and discussing their families' well-being, among other personal concerns.

Winning Through Encouragement

An example of positive Brazilian coach–athlete communication came from an international martial arts athlete who told me (L.C.) about a time he was competing abroad in a close fight. During a time-out, the coach approached the athlete, who anticipated criticism. Instead the coach reassured him that there was no problem and then explained what to do. The athlete returned to the fight and won. The athlete added that the worst thing is when the coach points out mistakes and then makes disparaging remarks, such as "I've told you this so many times."

Although there may be a time for criticism from coaches or sport psychologists, emotional encouragement is usually more appropriate when working with Brazilian athletes. Time-outs in taekwondo are usually short, so coaches need to develop the ability to communicate quickly using a positive approach. In this case, the coach realized that telling the athlete that what had just happened was not a problem would enable the athlete to let go of worry about it so he could relax and concentrate on the coach's suggestions for winning the fight.

BONDING THROUGH CHALLENGING

When sport psychology practitioners understand the sensitive nature of Brazilians, they are better able to help the athletes succeed in sport. But if they are truly skillful, they will know that sometimes negative emotions can be a more powerful motivator than positive ones, and they will be able to recognize situations when this is true. This is illustrated by the following example from M. Marques (personal communication, February 22, 2007) about a Brazilian national futsal coach.

At the prematch briefing, the coach said to the players: "I will tell you the truth. This team is much better than ours and I can't see you beating them. You are good and young, but they have more experience. It is hard to say that, but I do not want you to be disappointed after the match. I understand your limitations. Go out there and try to do something." The coach then left the dressing room and asked the assistant coach to go and listen to what they had to say. When the assistant coach got into the dressing room the players were fired up, abusing the coach, saying that the he was old and worthless and that they would prove their value on the court. They did and they won!

Another example of how the Brazilian athlete can be challenged occurred during the final match of the national Brazilian football championships in 2003. Before the game, Vanderlei Luxemburgo, the coach of one of the finalists, brought a box into the locker room for each team member, including the assistant coach and physical trainer. Inside this box was the championship emblem. However, one defensive player who was 17 years old received a box with the emblem and a diaper. The coach told him to decide which one to wear, the emblem or the diaper. Of course, the player complained and threw away the diaper. This player proved himself to be one of the best in the game and his team was the winner of a sensational final. Today he is a great player in Europe (Luxemburgo, 2004, p.16).

OBSERVE UNIQUE ASPECTS OF BRAZILIAN CULTURE

If foreigners who work with Brazilian athletes do not understand certain aspects of Brazilian culture, they can give or receive the wrong messages. For example, one female athlete observed that Brazilians, especially females, are affectionate: "They hug, kiss you on the face, and talk while touching you with their hands, but they are not flirting with you!" Marques also recalled that in some countries, drinking is a social habit; for example, athletes from rugby and cricket often celebrate with a beer after the game. In Brazil, however, drinking is directly related to partying, and therefore one should be careful about drinking when working as a consultant (M.P. Marques, personal communication, February 22, 2007).

In the Latin American world, yelling at someone is usually an invitation to fight. Some athletes, especially younger ones, are not used to coaches yelling at them during training or competition. Thus, there is more to mutual understanding than clear communication when working with Brazilian athletes. A female Brazilian cyclist with international experience confided that she responds more positively when her coach talks to her instead of yelling. One exception is during competition because of the demands of her sport. If her coach needs to communicate in the middle of a competition, he has to yell because of the speed of the race.

In general, Brazilians have a great sense of humor. They tend to face mistakes and financial, political, and other problems with a humor that indicates that somehow the problem will be solved. Every problem they face is followed by a joke or some black humor. Jokes regarding misfortune are one of the approaches to challenges. For example, if someone misses a kick, making the ball go backward, a teammate might comment "Are you developing a new kick?" The phrase *dar um jeitinho*, meaning "somehow this can be solved," is often used to express this optimism. Because of this attitude, Brazilians can appear to be unconcerned during pressure situations. For example, Brazilian coaches generally bring a positive feeling to the sport environment and often laugh in adverse situations. Although someone from outside the culture may interpret this behavior as inattentive or negative, it does not indicate disrespect or lack of concern. When practitioners learn about Brazilian culture-bound behaviors, misinterpretations among sport psychology consultants, coaches, and athletes can be circumvented.

Another unique aspect of Brazilian culture is that the athletes from the *favelas*, or slums, require special attention. In general, *favelados* (children from favelas) are highly agitated and impatient because of the

A Special Case: Favelados

J.R.P. Couto, a Brazilian psychology consultant working with various sports, has pointed out that it is important to consider the sociocultural level of the group with which one is working (personal communication, January 20, 2007). For example, athletes from favelas are more susceptible to critical feedback than upper-middle-class athletes. He suggested that perhaps the favelados feel more repressed than and socially inferior to athletes from the upper middle class, who are more independent, self-confident, and protected by their parents and therefore are more resistant to criticism and flexible when given special attention. However, Couto added that although there are differences between the two groups, athletes from both groups trust him when he explains his point of view in a clear manner and gives convincing examples.

context in which they live. They talk loudly because they are never taught to talk more quietly. Usually, they have poor motor experiences in sport since they have had no physical education. However, they are motivated to learn and eager to try anything. They are willing to negotiate deals, but they will not follow a specific rule if was not previously discussed; thus,

it is necessary to discuss the deal first or otherwise it will not work.

Unfortunately, many favelados will not reach personal freedom for many reasons. Some will die from violence, some will not continue in school, and some will turn to drugs. Therefore, palliative support will not work; they need be involved in a committed governmental program to deal with these challenges. In addition, it is our experience that effective coaching staff (sport psychologists included) can offer positive social support to these athletes providing they are able to gain trust by using the positive strategies outlined earlier (e.g., gleaning information about family history, religious beliefs, and socioeconomic status).

FUTURE OF BRAZILIAN SPORT PSYCHOLOGY

Not many sport psychology consultants work with elite athletes in Brazil. During the campaign for the 2004 Athens Olympics, the Brazilian Olympic Committee created a sector for sport psychology consulting led by Samulski. According to his knowledge (D.M. Samulski, personal communication, November 13, 2006), of the 27 Brazilian sport federations, only 9 had applied sport psychology consultants working with elite athletes. Sport psychology consultants were only working with men and women in football, taekwondo, judo, gymnastics, boxing, handball, diving, and tennis. It is possible that there was a lack of sport psychology information or interest among the neglected sports, suggesting a need for education in Brazil regarding the benefits of sport psychology.

The attitude and behaviors of the sport psychologist discussed previously who betrayed the confidence of his athletes reflected the low level of professionalism at that moment in Brazilian sport psychology. His actions represented a lack of knowledge about

Favelados will have had different experiences than upper-middle-class athletes, potentially resulting in different responses to organized sport, coaches, and sport psychologists.

© AP Photo/Silvia Izquierdo

ISSUES AND STRATEGIES TO CONSIDER WHEN WORKING WITH BRAZILIAN ATHLETES

Practitioners working with Brazilian athletes may find it useful to keep in mind the following points:

- Brazilians are a touchy-feely people, and aside from an introductory handshake, warm greetings, hugging, and light face kissing are common, even among men. If you do not participate, you will be considered *sem graça,* or dull and boring.
- Brazilians can be verbose, and they require time to express their feelings. Patience may be required during interventions.
- Given the religious divide in the Brazilian population, care must be taken when making both positive and negative attributions after games as to whether the results were due to effort, skill, luck, or divine interventions.
- Social class barriers exist because sport psychologists are university trained and most athletes are not. You have to demonstrate that despite your degrees, you are a regular person just like them.

athletes' rights and about the roles of coaches and consultants in dealing with sensitive concerns. More than one athlete has expressed the same concerns pertaining to confidentiality. These ethical issues should be discussed by sport psychology professionals in Brazil. In North America, Australia, and Europe, a professional code of ethics in sport psychology exists, but in Brazil, a code has yet to be established.

Another factor that influences the viability of sport psychology in Brazil is the education level of the athletes. It is our impression that a stigma is attached to sport psychology services, especially among less-educated athletes and coaches. Educated athletes are open to the benefits of psychological skills training, whereas others believe that sport psychologists only work with athletes experiencing deep psychological problems. During the Athens Olympic Games, some athletes preferred to talk to the sport psychologist only late at night instead of during the day to avoid being seen with the psychologist.

Another problem with sport psychology services in Brazil is that some consultants in the country do not have a sport science background, knowledge of

any particular sport, or sport psychology knowledge in general. This lack of credentials has contributed to misunderstandings and skepticism about this sport science. Thus, non-Brazilian sport psychologists working with Brazilian athletes may need to put extra effort into winning their clients' trust.

CONCLUSIONS

Brazil is a complex society that has the potential to develop great athletes due to the cultural context and extremely high enthusiasm within and outside of sport. However, the field of sport psychology is in its infancy and will have to progress through the predictable stages of professional development with increased education of sport psychology consultants, coaches, and athletes. Throughout the ongoing evolution of sport development in Brazil, there will be cross-cultural relationships among sport scientists and athletes. This chapter has provided the reader with a few considerations of how to effectively proceed when working with Brazilian athletes.

Sport Psychology Consulting in Russia and Sweden

Natalia Stambulova, PhD; Urban Johnson, PhD; and Alexander Stambulov, PhD

Modern sport is characterized by its double nature. On the one hand, it is a cultural phenomenon; hence, athletes are embedded in specific sociocultural and historical contexts that influence all aspects of their development, including their athletic careers. On the other hand, sport has become an international phenomenon. The international culture of sport involves some basic values (e.g., fair play and doping-free training and performance), laws (e.g., doping control, a list of Olympic sports), and traditions (e.g., sports for a more peaceful world), and each sport has its own international subculture. Athletes have to learn and accept both national and international sport cultures as a part of their athletic success. Another trend is an increase in mobility. Athletes and coaches not only travel internationally but often move to other countries to compete, and they sometimes experience difficulties adapting to a new country. To summarize, sport has become an arena not only for competitions but also for international and intercultural exchange. In response, sport psychology consultants have to develop multicultural competencies (Gill, 2007) so that they can not only help athletes and coaches within their own cultures but also help them adjust to new cultures.

Paradigms Used in This Chapter

The two main paradigms for analyzing the effects of culture on psychological processes, behavior, and human development are cultural psychology and cross-cultural psychology. Cultural psychology (e.g., Greenfield & Keller, 2004) claims that a cultural context creates special meaning; thus, human behavior is context specific and should be studied within culture, not comparatively. Cross-cultural psychology (e.g., Berry & Triandis, 2004), on the other hand, has a comparative emphasis. This chapter combines both paradigms in the discussion of applied psychological work with athletes in Russia and Sweden, which was inspired by ideas of two developmental psychologists, Lev Vygotsky (1896-1934), with his sociocultural theory, and Urie Bronfenbrenner (1917-2005), with his ecological model of human development.

Vygotsky grew up and lived his entire life in Russia. He organized research in different parts of the country to show how local sociocultural environments influenced children's strategies for solving everyday problems (Leontiev, 1990). In his sociocultural theory, Vygotsky (1983, 1984) emphasized two interrelated lines in human development: natural (i.e., biological maturation of brain and body) and cultural (i.e., learning beliefs, values, and tools of intellectual adaptation accepted in a culture). According to Vygotsky, the learning process is socially mediated and culturally specific (i.e., adults teach children what to think and how to think to help them adjust to the particular society).

Bronfenbrenner was born in Russia but moved with his parents to the United States when he was 6 years old; he went through the process of adapting to a new culture, and those experiences made him sensitive to sociocultural issues (Woo, 2005). In

Acknowledgment

The authors thank Professor Yuri Hanin (KIHU, Finland), who gave constructive comments on an early draft of the chapter.

his ecological theory, Bronfenbrenner (1979) also emphasized the importance of the sociocultural context in human development. But in contrast to Vygotsky, he focused not only on one-to-one social interactions but on the multilayered interaction of the various social systems in which a child is embedded directly (e.g., family, school, peers) or indirectly (e.g., families of peers, parents' coworkers). According to Bronfenbrenner, the wider culture (e.g., laws, values, traditions, policies, religion) of a particular society has powerful direct and indirect influences on the development of people in that society.

Both Vygotsky and Bronfenbrenner attracted attention to contextual factors and person–environment interaction. The aforementioned changes in today's sport affect athletes and create new problems for them, such as language barriers and misunderstandings with coaches from other cultures. Sport psychology consultants frequently play the role of mediator, helping athletes deal with such problems. One author of this chapter was born in Sweden and has worked as a sport psychology consultant in Sweden (U.J.), and the other two were born in Russia and have worked as practitioners in Russia and Sweden (N.S. and A.S.). In the sections that follow, we present brief overviews of historical and cultural contexts in Russia and Sweden. We proceed with Russian and Swedish cases, emphasizing a cultural approach. Then we share our experiences of working together in Sweden with a Swedish athlete and a Russian coach, emphasizing a cross-cultural approach and teamwork. After the description of every case you will find our reflections on our experiences in sport psychology consulting. Last but not least, we summarize the lessons learned in our consulting experiences in Russia and Sweden in reference to Vygotsky's and Bronfenbrenner's theoretical frameworks, followed by recommendations for consultants to consider when working with Russian or Swedish athletes.

Introduction to Russia

Modern Russia is rooted in the Soviet regime but also in the thousand-year history of the Russian state. Ethnically, Russians are East Slavs. Currently Russia covers a huge territory in both Europe and Asia with a population of around 143 million (Rosenberg, 2006). Following is a brief overview of Russian history, culture, sport, and applied sport psychology.

History and Culture

Ancient Russia, the Tsardom of Russia, the Russian Empire, the Soviet Union, and the Russian Federation are main milestones in the history of Russia. During the 20th century, Russia experienced cardinal changes in its political system in 1917 (socialist revolution), which marked the start of the Soviet era, and in 1991 (disintegration of the Soviet Union and formation of the Russian Federation), which marked the beginning of modern Russia.

The Russian Federation is a multicultural country, but Russians and Russian language dominate. Church and state are officially separated. Religion is represented by many denominations, with the Russian Orthodox Church playing a leading role after gradually regaining power following its waning during the Soviet era.

Russian political traditions historically have been formed under conditions of military conflict inside and outside Russia. As a way to survive, Russia became a centralized and autocratic state. Militarization and a centrally administered economy, bureaucracy and corruption, and a cult of ideology and propaganda have characterized Russian society. The enemy image both inside and outside the country has been actively exploited by state propaganda as a force to consolidate the nation. Russian politicians have always advocated that Russia define its own way. As described in Russian poetry, it is impossible to understand Russia rationally or to measure it by common criteria; the only possible way is to believe in Russia. This may be one of the reasons why Russia has difficulties fully integrating into the world community. Despite some liberalization in the political system after the collapse of the Soviet Union, Russia maintains its aforementioned political traditions.

The Russian economy can be described as a combination of Soviet-style centralized administration and a free market. Capitalization involved much criminality, and as a result Russian society is currently divided into two unequal groups: a small group of rich people, and the vast majority of the population, which has rather low living standards. This socioeconomic situation is associated with the Russian demographic crisis (Rosenberg, 2006), a high death rate combined with a low birthrate and low average life expectancy (e.g., 59 years for men). Families typically have a maximum of one or two children, and both fathers and mothers work. Often two generations live together, and grandparents are engaged in the children's upbringing. Females contribute actively to the society but males dominate among upper-level decision makers.

Russian culture is collectivistic in the sense that it denies people's privacy and supports communal living and sharing among people. On the other hand, it stimulates competition among people, and it also maintains a competitive spirit with regard to other countries. Interests of the state have always been positioned over interests of individuals. Working hard and suffering today for the sake of a better future, finding happiness in struggling with life circumstances, and working for the interests of the motherland are among the main values propagated by the state. Adherence to the state ideals and being a good executor at work, readiness to give all, and winning at all costs are also appreciated by the Russian state. When it comes to solving everyday problems (e.g., lack of money, corruption, criminality), Russians have to be inventive to survive. People do not feel protected by the state, and instead of trusting the state they trust family and friends. All of this might help to explain the so-called enigmatic Russian soul with its equal readiness to be a winner and a victim based on a combination of passion and compassion, aggressiveness, and sacrificing oneself for others.

SPORT SYSTEM

The state organization and political traditions are mirrored in the centralized Russian sport system with a power vertical. It consists of the Federal Sport Governing Body and the Russian Olympic Committee at the top of the system and national sport federations, regional sport committees, and voluntary sport societies at the lower levels. State financing has dominated but currently lottery and sponsorship money are also involved.

Russian sport has earned a good international reputation. After the first and successful participation of the Soviet team in the Olympic Games (1952), the Communist Soviet government decided to use sport as a trump card in the ideological struggle with the capitalist world to demonstrate the advantages of the socialist way of life. As a result, serious financial investments were made in sport facilities, professional coaching education, and sport sciences. A network of specialized sport schools for children was created. The schools were staffed by professional coaches who worked with young athletes from the first steps of their athletic careers. A system of sport talent selection was successful because of the huge size of Russia and the scientific basis behind the

Nadyezda Olizarenko (281) sprints to win the gold medal for the women's 800 meter and set a new world record at the 1980 Olympic Games in Moscow. The Soviet Union regarded the Games as an opportunity to showcase the superiority of the socialist system.
© PA Photos/S&G

system. For many young people in the country, sport was (and still is) the only opportunity to see the world and to make a lifelong career.

When Moscow won the bid to host the 1980 Olympic Games, the Soviet state intensified both its demands concerning and its support of sport. The main focus was on elite sport and developing reserves for the national teams. The most talented young athletes from all over the country were selected to attend sport boarding schools in Moscow and Leningrad, where they lived, studied, and trained under the guidance of the best coaches. In addition, the senior national teams were provided with scientific support groups consisting of representatives from various sport sciences. Since the beginning of the 1990s, radical changes in Russian society have influenced the sport system, mainly negatively, especially in terms of state financing. Today, Russia tries to keep its best traditions in sport, but due to a lack of financing it has lost many professional coaches and sport scientists who have left the field or emigrated.

APPLIED SPORT PSYCHOLOGY

Applied psychological work with athletes and teams began in the Soviet Union in the early 1970s and intensified before the 1980 Olympic Games in Moscow. Sport psychologists were involved in the scientific support groups, where they cooperated with sport medicine, physiology, and biomechanics professionals. The main task of these groups was to assist athletes and coaches in improving the effectiveness of their training, especially for competitions at the elite level. Applied sport psychologists worked as full- or part-time employees and could collaborate with athletes and coaches on a long-term basis. Centralized organization of the athletes' preparation facilitated the psychological work because athletes were obliged to cooperate with sport psychologists. However, sport psychologists were dependent on head coaches and also on special persons responsible for ideological work in the teams. The focus was on performance enhancement, and in team sports, also on team building and communication.

Because the international exchange of sport psychology ideas was limited, Soviet practitioners had to develop and test their own theoretical frameworks and approaches to work with athletes and teams. The psychological preparation for the competition model (Puni, 1969, 1973; see also Ryba, Stambulova, & Wrisberg, 2005; Stambulova, Wrisberg, & Ryba, 2006), the psychological control frameworks (e.g., Hanin, 1980, Iliin, Kiselev, & Safonov, 1989), and the psychological support of elite athletes model (Gorbunov, 1986) are examples of the most popular

frameworks. Applied work involved a combination of multilevel assessment, counseling, mental training, and working on routines, attitudes, motivation, and relationships (e.g., Alexeev, 1978; Rodionov, 1983; Viatkin, 1981; Zagainov, 1984), with sport results as the main criterion for effectiveness. Currently, Russian applied sport psychologists work both as state employees and as private consultants. They keep the traditions developed during the Soviet era but are also becoming open to frameworks and approaches developed in other countries.

INTRODUCTION TO SWEDEN

Sweden is situated in Northern Europe. As will be highlighted in the following sections, it has retained its political stability and positive economic tendencies during the last hundred years. Following is a brief overview of Swedish history, culture, sport, and applied sport psychology.

HISTORY AND CULTURE

The history of Sweden dates back several thousand years. Among the first documented descriptions are those from the Viking age, around the 9th to 12th centuries. During the course of its history, Sweden has received many important influences from abroad. Most prominent was probably the German influence during the Middle Ages, when the Hanseatic League dominated trade in Northern Europe. French culture was adopted at court and among the upper class in the 18th century, and German cultural influence had a revival in the 19th century. Due to poverty during the 19th century, about a quarter of the nation (1 million people) left the country, many ending up in America. Since the beginning of the 19th century, Sweden has not been involved in any major wars, including the first and second World Wars. Swedish foreign politics can be characterized as neutral throughout the 20th century. More recently, Sweden took a step toward internationalism in 1994, when the Swedish people decided in a referendum to join the European Union. General living standards in Sweden today are among the highest in the world.

The four major Scandinavian languages—Danish, Swedish, Norwegian, and Icelandic—are closely related. Finnish, on the other hand, is not a Germanic language, and is completely different from the other four. The languages have played an important role in creating and preserving national identity and culture. One of the ties that link all the Scandinavian countries (including Finland) is a common Lutheran religion.

In terms of cultural traditions, Swedes highly value being together with family and good friends, especially around Christmas and midsummer. The people of Sweden are sometimes stereotyped as reserved, introverted, and even a bit boring, especially in comparison to southern Europeans. Most of the time this stereotypic description falls flat when observing Swedes interacting at various social events, such as midsummer celebrations or spectator sports. On these occasions extroversion, joy, and general outspokenness are highly visible.

One other prominent feature of Swedish culture and society is the drive for equal justice and democracy for inhabitants regardless of political value and economic status. This striving for equality in general also reflects the struggle for equality in gender representation in government, community, and sport. Another characteristic is that you are not supposed to behave as though you are better than your neighbor (Sandemose, 1934). The Jante law directs people to behave in a modest way, avoiding any demonstration of superiority in front of other people. People who violate this law may experience relationship problems with Swedes.

Sport System

Few things in Swedish society interest people as much as sport. Sport clubs and associations are the backbone of Swedish sport. Almost half of the 9 million Swedish residents between the ages of 7 and 70 are members of sport clubs (Swedish Sport Federation, 2002). About two million are active sportsmen and women. Around 650,000 are involved in competitive sport at various levels. Sport plays an even more prominent role among young people. In the age group of 7 to 15, more than two-thirds of boys and half of girls belong to a sport club (Swedish Sport Federation, 2002). The Swedish sport system encourages physical activity for youth, and currently no clear organization for talent selection exists. However, the Swedish Olympic Committee strongly advocates elite sport and financially supports potential Olympic candidates (e.g., through scholarships and traveling grants).

The widespread activity of clubs and associations is specific to Nordic countries. Nowhere in the world are there more clubs per capita (Swedish Sport Federation, 2002). The Swedish Sports Confederation accepts only nonprofit associations as members. Nonprofit associations are steered by laws that demand democracy in the form of annual meetings, a board of directors, a nominating committee, a time frame for submitting motions, and so forth. At a time when the membership of virtually all organizations except those in sport is declining, the contribution of sport to schooling in democracy becomes increasingly important. The role of sport in social economics is receiving increasing attention at the national and European Union levels. Sport has multiple benefits, partly in monetary terms but mainly in the form of greater well-being, better health, social contact, entertainment, joy, and meaningful activities for millions of Swedish residents.

Applied Sport Psychology

Sport psychology has a relatively short history in Sweden. The same is true for applied sport psychology. Historically, few internationally recognized theoretical frameworks for applied sport psychology have been founded by Swedes. Two exceptions are Gunnar Borg, who developed the well-known Borg scale (Borg, 1998), and Lars-Erik Unestähl, who promoted the concept of integrated mental training (Unestähl, 2001).

Traditionally, applied sport psychology in Sweden has focused on competitive sport, but today the most politically correct focus is on exercise and health psychology (Forsberg, 2005). Most sport psychologists work for private athletes (e.g., competitive golfers) or teams (e.g., ice hockey). Unfortunately, not all applied sport psychologists have proper academic qualifications, a situation that has led to ethical problems such a lack of confidentiality and informed consent from athletes and teams (Johnson & Fallby, 2004). Since 2002, advanced courses in applied sport psychology are taught at Halmstad University (Johnson & Stambulova, 2006). Interest in these courses is growing among students from all over Sweden and even from other Scandinavian countries. At the moment no certification system is accepted throughout the country; hopefully this will change in the near future (Johnson, 2006).

Russian Case

In this section we present a Russian case, the first of three (Russian, Swedish, and Swedish–Russian). After the presentation, each of us will reflect on the case, emphasizing cultural and cross-cultural issues.

Background

This case presents the experience of Alexander Stambulov from his work as a full-time applied sport psychologist with the Soviet Union national diving team in the 1970s and 1980s. It shows how applied sport psychologists worked in the former Soviet Union and what formed the sociocultural context for that work.

Nikolay Karpol is a Russian coach famous for his competence in volleyball but also for his autocratic style of management. Not all Russian coaches are like Karpol, but he demonstrates a common pattern for many Russian coaches: feeling that they own their athletes.
© Adam Davy/EMPICS Sport/PA Photos

The case is still relevant because many features of the sport system (e.g., vertical power, autocratic decision making) remain the same in Russia today.

The case can be categorized as a relationship crisis dealing with an athlete–coach relationship and conflict. Precursors for the conflict situation had arisen at the national team camp 2 weeks before the European diving championship. It was usual procedure that not only main candidates for the championship were invited but also reserve athletes so that they could replace the main participants if necessary (e.g., due to injury or illness). In addition to the rigors of twice-a-day training routines, athletes experienced the stress of uncertainty. The choice of main candidates was only preliminary, and the final decision was expected to be made by a head coach during the camp. The divers' personal coaches, the head coach, and members of the scientific support group, including the sport psychologist, formed a coaching board. Although the board members could offer suggestions

and arguments to the head coach, they were not the decision makers, so both athletes and coaches were under the stress of uncertainty.

Another factor was related to the psychological atmosphere of the team, which was typical for national teams in individual sports. On the one hand, athletes and coaches were members of the same team and were supposed to support each other. On the other hand, they all were rivals for selection for the championship. All the athletes were at the elite level, and differences between their technical competencies were slight. At the same time, the social and financial consequences of being selected (i.e., the opportunity to win medals, which was realistic considering the high reputation of the Soviet divers) were great. Thus, athletes and coaches experienced high levels of competitive stress in their everyday practice, which affected athlete–coach, athlete–athlete, and coach–coach relationships. Both athletes and coaches competed for selection and its related privileges, honorary titles, money, travel abroad, and high public recognition. Those who did not succeed were soon replaced in the team by new athletes.

INTRODUCTION AND CASE

A 16-year-old female athlete and her rather young coach were participants in the camp. They had already experienced success working together at the elite junior level, but they were both new to the senior level of competition. Based on the results of previous competitions during the season, the diver was among the main candidates to be selected for the European championship. It was a great opportunity for the athlete and the coach.

The first half of the camp went well. The athlete demonstrated quality dives, and the coach showed the others that he fully controlled the athlete's preparation for the championship. Nevertheless, the psychosocial context of the training sessions was competitive, and it reached its peak shortly before the head coach was expected to make his final decision. The personal coach increased pressure on the diver in practices. On one occasion, the coach told her off publicly when she made an unsuccessful dive, and the latent mutual tension turned into an open conflict. The athlete left the pool in the middle of the practice and later declared that she refused to work with her coach. The athlete's behavior attracted attention and generated talk among the team.

The next day the coaching board discussed the incident. Coaches who trained rivals of the diver insisted on her immediate deselection. They argued that because the coach could not manage the athlete in training sessions there were doubts that the two

RUSSIAN INTERVENTION AND RESOLUTION

The only immediate request I made of the coaching board was for a moratorium on any discussion of the conflict to prevent it from developing further (e.g., through reproaches, complaints, or accusations). This first step in the intervention was aimed at limiting the number of people involved, or freezing the conflict situation. The second step involved talks with the diver and the coach separately. The purposes of those talks were twofold. First, they both were asked not to discuss the conflict with anybody on the team. In addition, I wanted to find out what behavior and attitude on the part of the coach would be acceptable to the athlete, and correspondingly, what expectations the coach had in terms of the athlete's behavior and attitude.

It appeared that the diver wanted the coach to show her more respect and not perceive her as a small performing robot but as a grown-up athlete and person. The coach wanted her to follow the training program and to be tolerant of his emotional reactions. Based on those conversations, I formulated norms for their behavior when they needed to work together. Control of both verbal and nonverbal communication was a central part of the norms. The third step was to persuade each side to accept the norms and to follow them.

It was easy to arrange things with the coach, who was motivated to solve the conflict as soon as possible. To better control his emotional reactions, the coach wanted to reduce verbal communication with the athlete, at least initially. I came up with the idea of using the experience of an older and famous coach in the team who used active nonverbal communication with his athletes (e.g., gestures, whistles, finger snapping), especially under high-pressure conditions such as competitive practices and competitions. This symbolic language was familiar to both the coach and the athlete, who could observe how it was used by that famous coach, and it was realistic to incorporate it fairly quickly into training routines.

The coach had planned his first meeting with the diver after the conflict situation. His strategy was to apologize to the athlete and then to introduce the idea of using the symbolic language. The coach felt ready to reestablish the working relationship. However, the athlete perceived me to be on the side of the coach, so I arranged for one of the team leaders to talk to her. He was an experienced male athlete who was about the same age as the diver's coach and was well liked and respected by the team. He explained to the diver that conflicts could often happen in high-pressure situations, and in conflicts people often said things they did not mean. Advocating for continuation with her coach, the leader drew the diver's attention to the fact that her personal coach knew her best and her success was the only thing he wanted. The athlete seemed persuaded.

The fourth step in the conflict resolution was monitoring the athlete–coach communication during several training sessions. The head coach and I attended each session and showed support and trust in the athlete and the coach. During the first practice they both were polite but still tense. They also had some difficulties with the symbolic language. But after 3 days their working relationship was reestablished to a point where they could continue preparation for the championship.

The conflict was solved and the working athlete–coach relationship and interactions were restored. The athlete was selected and then won a silver medal in the European championship. The athlete and the coach continued to work together after the championship.

could work together successfully during the championship. The coach reacted with indignation and annoyance but had to assume that the situation was out of his hands. The head coach assigned me the task of solving the conflict within a few days. Because I had attended all the practices, was aware of the atmosphere in the team, and knew both the coach and the athlete, I accepted the task.

REFLECTIONS ON THE CASE

Following you will find our reflections on the case. Alexander Stambulov starts with his self-reflections, Natalia Stambulova adds her thoughts based on knowing the Russian sport and culture, and then Urban Johnson reflects on the case from the perspective of the Swedish culture.

ALEXANDER STAMBULOV'S REFLECTIONS

It is interesting for me to reflect on this case from the viewpoint of my current life and work experiences. Many things that at the time were perceived as natural and even inevitable on the elite sport level now seem questionable. Forcing athletes and coaches to endure the stress of heavy competition within the team, basing athletes' selection on the autocratic decision of the head coach, planning medals, providing external motivation through a system of privileges for winners and punishments for losers, ethical problems—all of these created a ground for manipulative relationships among the team members.

The head coach supported that kind of climate. He was a nonaggressive, rational, and experienced person, but he was also a man of the system and followed its rules and demands from the upper level. Gold medals justified all means. The careers of athletes and coaches were not taken into account and their interests were easily sacrificed for the sake of the team results. It is worthwhile to add that interpersonal relationships in the team were also complicated because athletes and coaches represented different Soviet republics (e.g., Ukraine, Belarus, Georgia, Armenia) and correspondingly different cultures; athletes were also of different ages (between 14 and 30 years old). In such conditions, I think it could be impossible to solve the conflict in such a short time without constantly being with the team and knowing the whole situation (not only the athlete's and coach's views) from the inside.

NATALIA STAMBULOVA'S REFLECTIONS

From my viewpoint, the case demonstrates several peculiarities of the Russian culture, mentality, and sport system. First of all, it showed how autocratic leadership of the head coach influenced the psychological climate of the team. Stimulating high levels of competition among the candidates and keeping athletes and their personal coaches dependent upon his final word were among the ways in which the head coach demonstrated his power. The psychologist was helpless to change that situation because it was an essential part of the preparation of elite athletes. The head coach's decision to give the athlete and the coach a chance to solve the relationship problem and his support of the solution suggested by the psychologist were among the decisive conditions for solving the problem. In such a competitive team atmosphere, the initial step in the psychological intervention (i.e., freezing the conflict situation) was justified. It is also important to mention that the freezing strategy worked well because both athletes and coaches were

used to complying with the norms approved by the coaching board.

Analyzing potential reasons for the conflict between the athlete and the coach, I have to admit that high situational stress was not the only factor. The other reason can be found in the nature of the athlete–coach relationship typical of Russian sport culture. Traditionally, in individual sport, especially in sports with early specialization such as diving, coaches who started to work with athletes from their first steps in the sport quickly became parent figures for young athletes, taking care of them and controlling them both inside and outside the sport. Furthermore, many Russian coaches felt that they owned their athletes because they had invested a lot in them over many years; hence, it was not important for them to show respect to athletes or to control themselves properly in stressful situations. Athletes were often perceived as material the coaches used to make champions. All of these can be seen as negative aspects of involving professional coaches from the beginning of young athletes' careers in sport. At 16 years old, the diver protested against her coach taking such a position and emphasized in her talk with the psychologist that she wanted more respect from the coach. There is an obvious parallel between the coach–athlete relationship in this case and a typical parent–child relationship in teenage years.

One more cultural issue in the case relates to Russian mentality. As mentioned, Russians are equally ready to be winners and victims; they also easily move from one position to another. Before the conflict, the athlete and the coach felt they were among winners (i.e., main candidates to participate at the championship), but the conflict turned both of them into victims. The coach's victim position was clear and that is why he was so motivated to correct the situation. The athlete's position was more complicated. She was ready to risk losing her participation in the championship (to be a victim), but only because by means of this she could demonstrate that she had the coach in her power (to be a winner). The psychological intervention provided a win–win outcome by refocusing both participants from competition and fighting with each other to cooperative concentration on the task at hand.

URBAN JOHNSON'S REFLECTIONS

One striking observation about the Russian case is the rather harsh psychological climate that existed among the national diving team. Not only the athletes competed against each other; the coaches also seemed to compete against each other to gain a leading position. Compared with the competitive context

I have dealt with in Sweden, such strong competition in a group leading to conflicts is uncommon. These differences in a team climate might reflect the differences in Russian and Swedish cultures and sport systems (e.g., autocratic versus democratic traditions in management and coaching). A conflict inside a Russian sport team may emanate from a collective culture that stimulates competitive attitudes, whereas conflicts among Swedish athletes sometimes paradoxically originate from a collective culture where too much respect and privacy leads to alienation among the players and thus insecurity about following the collective plan.

Another issue to consider is that Sweden is much smaller than Russia and therefore the selection of talent and competent coaches is narrower, probably leading to a more homogenous group of athletes and coaches. This in turn leads to a situation where athletes consider themselves more as friends than competitors. I appreciate the freezing approach as the first step to resolving the conflict between the athlete and the coach. But more important is the second step involving talks with the athlete and the coach separately, listening to the different stories and then forming an agenda or norm for further action. I also find the use of nonverbal communication between the athlete and the coach under high-pressure conditions to be a good idea.

SWEDISH CASE

In this section we present the second of the three cases—the Swedish case. As before, after the presentation, each of us will reflect on the case, emphasizing cultural and cross-cultural issues.

INTRODUCTION AND CASE

In the following case, Urban Johnson presents his experience as an applied sport psychologist working with a football (soccer) player in a professional football club in Sweden. What makes this case especially interesting is that although the player was born in former Yugoslavia, he moved to Sweden with his parents as a preschooler, he grew up and was socialized in Sweden, and Swedish was his primary language. Thus, he exhibited both Yugoslav and Swedish characteristics and was working with a native Swedish coaching staff, leading to cultural learning experiences in the applied work.

During the autumn of 2005 I was called by the head coach and the physiotherapist of the club and asked if it was possible to give psychological support to a talented football player in the club who seemed to be experiencing psychologically related pain in his legs, especially when playing important games. Moreover, it was reported that the player had some attitude problems related to his low acceptance of his playing position on the team, raising a potential problem for the head coach (and team). Before the first meeting with the player, I gathered information from the head coach and the physiotherapist. Based on this information, I organized a series of five meetings with the player with the primary aim of exploring a potential relationship between the experience of pain and the attitudinal concerns related to the player's role in the team.

REFLECTIONS ON THE CASE

In the discussion of the Swedish case, it is natural to start with Urban Johnson's reflections. Alexander Stambulov's and Natalia Stambulova's discussions will follow.

URBAN JOHNSON'S REFLECTIONS

This case illustrates several interesting cultural issues. The initially prioritized problem of pain was not the primary working issue; instead it turned out that different perspectives on playing in a team were the focus, leading to role conflict. This conflict was partly due to different cultural perspectives and different perspectives on being a member of a sport team. It is not unlikely that the Jante law influenced the situation. However, it was important for me not to judge or be biased by potential cultural differences, but instead try to find win–win solutions for the role conflict. In this case, the mental key words and material served as a mediated link between the player's and the coaching staff's points of view. In the first meeting the player seemed suspicious of talking to a psychologist with a different cultural background. However, the open and unbiased atmosphere in the consulting process probably led to a positive trust between the player and me. Maybe this democratic structure in the meetings helped to place the focus on what was important.

ALEXANDER STAMBULOV'S REFLECTIONS

Discussing potential reasons of the athlete's attitudinal problem, I would like to emphasize two traditions in understanding roles and interactions in a team that appeared obvious in this case. The talented young player from the immigrant family demonstrated egocentric behaviors that came into conflict with Swedish traditions of collectivism, discipline, and status leveling. It is important in team sport to find a proper balance between team tactics (executing tactical combinations trained in advance) and players'

SWEDISH INTERVENTION AND RESOLUTION

During the first meeting with the player, the head coach and the physiotherapist were present. The focus in this initial meeting was to learn more about the player's pain problem; thus, he was told to express his problems in relation to playing a game, worries about physical and psychological pain when running, and worries about not taking a permanent place in the starting lineup. Thus, the player was encouraged to express his feelings and concerns, and the psychologist and the coaching staff would seek a strategy to help the player. In essence, this was a cognitive reconstruction strategy of replacing negative thoughts and feelings associated with pain (e.g., expecting the pain and being afraid of it) with positive ones (e.g., affirmations and images placing pain out of the body).

During the second and third meetings, I identified one issue as the most important—the player's role in the team and thus his behavior toward other players. Before the second meeting, the head coach once again expressed concerns about the player's egocentric and sometimes immature behavior in relation to other players on the team, especially considering the Jante law (see page 129). In a highly performance-related structure such as a professional football club, this rule is somewhat dampened but is still visible. Since the player had not been raised in the context of the Swedish Jante law and at the same time exhibited a high opinion of his own competence while the coaching staff did not share this conviction, a conflict was inevitable. At this point, much time was spent discussing the importance of accepting whatever role the coach assigned for the good of the team. In addition, to be accepted as a full member of a hard-working team, it is vital to accept the same rules that the other players in the group accept. On an intellectual level, the player understood the rationale of this discussion but was not fully able to behave in the way we discussed. This led to elevated tension, especially between the player and the head coach.

The goal for the last two meetings was to follow up in more detail on the player's behavior in team situations, since it was a priority of the coaching staff to solve this problem. The pain problem was also discussed. My idea was to consider the pain syndrome as related to the attitudinal problem—the player felt insecure in the team and that feeling could contribute to the psychosomatic pain. Just before the fourth meeting, the player and the club were about to go for a 2-week training camp abroad to prepare for the start of the league. Consequently, much time was spent constructing mental key words and materials that the player could bring to the training camp to perform at his best. In particular, having an elite attitude, including acceptance of whatever role was delegated by the coaching staff, and developing SMART (specific, measurable, action-oriented, realistic, and time-based) goals (Moran, 1996) for the upcoming camp were outlined. The player was also asked to identify game situations that could lead to feelings of insecurity, anxiety, and pain. Hence, we continued to work with the cognitive reconstruction strategy appreciated by the player.

The role conflict was partly solved in the sense that both the player and the coaches more thoroughly understood each other's standpoint, and the athlete seemed to accept his role in the team. However, later in the season he decided to leave the club, and he is currently playing for a professional team in Europe.

improvisations based on their individual mastery and understanding of the game. In some cultures (African teams are good examples), coaches support improvisation. But in Swedish sport culture, coaches tend to require that players follow the tactical plans. It was not easy for the young athlete to understand the coaching staff's criteria for a good player. The athlete focused on demonstrating his individual mastery, but the coaches most appreciated the players who could effectively contribute to execution of their tactical plans and the team mastery. That is why the player had such unrealistic expectations in terms of his role in the team. Balancing mutual expectations of the athlete and the coaches and helping the athlete understand the importance of following the established traditions were key in this intervention and they helped to solve the problem, at least temporarily.

NATALIA STAMBULOVA'S REFLECTIONS

Discussing this case, I would first like to acknowledge Urban's flexibility and ability to prioritize working issues. Being called on to deal with pain syndrome, he had to change the main focus and deal with cultural issues. As mentioned, Sweden is becoming a country of immigrants. Some immigrant families are trying to understand and to accept the new culture, but some families continue to live abroad as if they are in their country of origin. Values and rules that come from family are difficult to change. The strong point of the intervention was that the consultant worked with both the player and the coaching staff, helping them to understand each other's positions. Perhaps meeting with the player's parents would also have been useful. It appears that his family was not fully embedded in Swedish culture, which influenced the athlete immensely. Maybe this is a reason why the player left the team to play in a professional team outside Sweden.

One more reflection relates to a difference between Russian and Swedish traditions in administering sport psychology services. Briefly, the Swedish system is more formal and more structured as a sequence of preliminary scheduled meetings with particular goals for each. Therefore, it is easy to report about the case by describing meeting 1, meeting 2, and so on. The Russian system is less formal and even a bit vague in terms of how much time the consultant should spend with the athlete. It is not typically planned from the beginning how many meetings will be needed. In addition, some meetings can be long and the others quite short. For example, I never mentally structure my interventions as a sequence of meetings but more in terms of the issues to be solved, the content of the work, and the outcomes we want to achieve.

Swedish–Russian Case

All the authors of this chapter have worked together in Sweden. The case presented here deals with an elite Swedish male gymnast and his Russian coach, and all three authors eventually worked together to assist these men in their work. The collaboration started in late autumn 2001 and lasted until August 2003.

Introduction and Case

The male gymnast was in his mid-20s when the collaboration started. For several years he had been one of the leading stars in Sweden. The Swedish Olympic Committee believed that the gymnast had a good chance to make it to the 2004 Olympic Games in Athens. His goal was to be among the first 36 gymnasts at the selection tournament in August 2003. Thus, the primary purpose of the applied work was to prepare the gymnast psychologically for the Olympic

qualification tournament. To be optimally ready for the tournament, several psychological issues had to be addressed in the daily training routines and preparatory competitions.

In his younger years, the coach had been a fairly high-level gymnast, and he already had more than 10 years of coaching experience when he came to work in Sweden. During the first several months he experienced adaptation difficulties. He could not communicate effectively and had a lot of unanswered questions about his status and life in Sweden. He also felt alone. He shared that he was anxious and experienced homesickness and sleep disturbances. In his working situation there were some good things and some obvious difficulties. On the one hand, he had a motivated athlete, good conditions for training, and organizational support from the local club. On the other hand, due to the language barrier, his communication with the athlete was mainly nonverbal (e.g., demonstration). In verbal communication they used a mixed language with international gymnastic terms and some basic words from Swedish, English, and Russian. The gymnast's chances to be selected for the Olympic tournament were presented favorably in the media, and people developed high expectations for the athlete. The coach was not fully comfortable with the media presentation because he perceived it as additional pressure on him to provide the athlete's success. He concluded that it was possible to reach the goal but felt that more time was needed because the athlete had to improve the basic techniques and also make his competitive combinations more complex in order to be at the level of the best gymnasts in the world. Therefore, a deficit of time was one more source of stress for the coach.

The Swedish Olympic Committee hired the Russian coach and invited Urban Johnson to serve as a psychologist for the athlete. Because this was the Russian coach's first contract abroad and at the beginning he could only speak Russian, Johnson invited Natalia Stambulova and Alexander Stambulov to help build an optimal relationship between the athlete and the coach. After the first contacts, we realized that the coach needed psychological assistance in adapting to Sweden, and he also became a client. We agreed to work as a team, with Johnson focusing on direct work with the gymnast and Stambulova and Stambulov focusing on the coach and influencing the athlete mainly through the coach. We met several times and observed the practices, discussing them afterward. We also held some separate meetings with the gymnast and the coach, and we observed competitions in Sweden.

SWEDISH–RUSSIAN INTERVENTION AND RESOLUTION

A working model was constructed for the athlete based on a previous meeting with him, visits to the daily practice arena, and our discussions with the coach and senior gymnast. The model was then modified when we observed competitions. In short, we based the model on four mental techniques and approaches to improve the gymnast's mental status, listed here in order of priority:

1. The most important issue for the athlete was to help him understand the role of self-confidence and its relation to quality performance, especially with regard to events that the gymnast had had problems with in the past, such as the pommel.

2. Related to this, and also considered important in the drive for excellence, was teaching the athlete to physically and mentally relax between training sessions and at competitions. The gymnast was particularly attentive to mental relaxation. This basic psychological technique turned out to be especially important to recover mentally and physically between the sets of hard training and repetition of new and demanding drills.

3. The third technique was to help the gymnast extend his social network, for instance by taking classes at the university, with the purpose of meeting people other than those encountered at daily training sessions.

4. The final technique, equal in importance to the third, was to use previous successful competitions as models to help the athlete focus and concentrate on difficult moves and skills connected to training and competition.

During the intervention we held several meetings, and the athlete demonstrated promising results, especially at the national championships. The results at international meetings were more modest but still encouraging.

At daily practice the athlete sometimes complained about the heavy physical training load that the Russian coach was demanding in contrast to his former Swedish coaches. In response, we spent an hour discussing how to behave and what to think about to prevent the occurrence of injuries, such as avoiding training hard when faced with many prior stressors and being mentally prepared for especially tough training sessions. However, the athlete generally felt that the training and at least the new technical drills were positive and had a favorable effect on the overall training and competitive development, which were also confirmed by the coach. During the last 6 months of preparation, the athlete experienced high levels of motivation and self-efficacy for the upcoming competition. He wanted to learn more about performance behavior, including acting confident and looking contented and relaxed. In the final meeting before the competition, the athlete was focused and was looking forward to the qualification, and the communication between the athlete and the coach was friendly, goal oriented, and positive.

According to the coach, the athlete had an old-fashioned technique and needed to add all-around fitness training to his regular training regime in order to renew his technical skills. The athlete did this but often complained that it was too hard for him. In such conditions—where training was somewhat forced—we decided to help both the athlete and the coach to pay more attention to injury prevention and effective recovery.

In addition to emphasizing the importance of well-balanced physical loads and recovery, work with the coach was focused on reducing his stress, improving his communication and mutual understanding with the athlete, and helping him to cope with adjustment to the new country. The focus was increasing the coach's confidence in his ability to work successfully in Sweden.

We had several meetings discussing differences between Swedish and Russian sport and culture, including analyses of disagreements that appeared from time to time between the coach and the athlete. For example, the coach wanted to follow the Russian coaching tradition to keep the athlete's training and all related factors under his control, but the athlete was not always ready for this. Talking about sport nutrition, the coach strongly recommended that the athlete take vitamin pills every day, arguing that, without vitamins, a gymnast cannot cope with the necessary training load. But the athlete argued that food in Sweden is much better than in Russia and that Russian athletes may need vitamins but there is no such tradition among Swedish athletes, and he refused to comply. The coach accepted this refusal but recommended that the athlete check his diet with a nutrition specialist. So, a compromise was found for the sake of maintaining a good relationship.

Often the coach reported that his Russian stereotypes did not work in Sweden. Once, after an unsuccessful competition performance, the coach and the athlete were supposed to meet representatives of the national federation. Based on his Russian experiences, the coach expected negative feedback on the last performance and tried to prepare the athlete for it. But the athlete said, "Don't worry! They won't tell me off. They will embrace me and say some supportive words that next time they expect me to win." The athlete's expectations were realized, which was a relief for the coach, who did not get negative comments on his work as he had expected.

Other factors were helpful to the coach in dealing with his adjustment difficulties. For example, he was persuaded to take language courses. He was also helped in his negotiations with the club director about his status and living conditions, which reduced his stress level. After several months, his wife and daughter arrived in Sweden. As a result of those developments, he started to feel more confident both socially and psychologically.

The outcome of our collaboration was positive. The coach learned to communicate with the athlete more effectively and gained a sense of control over his life in Sweden. The athlete went through the preparation without serious injuries. Although he was not selected for the Olympic Games, at the selection tournament he demonstrated one of his best performances at international-level competitions. After that, he decided to retire from sport, and his coach took another coaching position in Sweden.

REFLECTIONS ON THE CASE

In the discussion of this case you will find a mixture of self-reflections and reflections about the clients and our teamwork. Urban Johnson takes the first word (because he worked with the athlete), and then Natalia Stambulova and Alexander Stambulov share thoughts and impressions about this cross-cultural experience.

URBAN JOHNSON'S REFLECTIONS

The case illustrates many different cross-cultural dimensions and applications of several applied sport psychology techniques in the pursuit of excellence. Combining the best of the Swedish and Russian applied sport psychology for not just the athlete but also for the coach, jointly as well as separately, is probably unique. My first impression of the coach was that he felt uncomfortable in the situation as a head coach for a foreign sport club. This was partly due to his new living conditions abroad without close friends and family and not being able to speak either Swedish or English. But my foremost impression was that the coach had a leadership style that was not in congruence with traditional Swedish coaching, which is more democratic than the Russian coach was used to. The coach felt this incongruence, and he was therefore unable to employ all his competence and energy.

In a situation where an athlete sometimes doubts his own capacity and also exhibits low self-confidence in regard to different drills and events, it is important for coaches to behave confidently and with trust. This was not initially the situation; however, as time passed and the social situation got better, the coach seemed to adapt to the new conditions and thus acted with greater security in relation to the athlete. This was manifested in many ways, for example through more distinct body language and a more relaxed attitude toward the surroundings. The athlete also confirmed that the chemistry had improved and gradually a trust had built up between the athlete and the coach. Working together with two other experts in the field and dividing the responsibility was a positive learning experience. The input I got from my Russian colleagues about not only the psychological status and well-being of the Russian coach but also about the Swedish athlete (e.g., body language) strongly enhanced my ability to provide professional support and to see the working alliance between the coach and athlete from a broader cultural perspective.

NATALIA STAMBULOVA'S REFLECTIONS

I agree that it was a unique professional experience for all of us to work with two clients representing different cultures as a team of three consultants representing the same cultures. Mutual cultural exchange and learning were at the core of our collaboration, helping all of us to understand what happened to the athlete, what happened to the coach, and how their relationship and trust were gradually developed. Without this exchange of cultural experiences, it might have been impossible to deal effectively with issues such as the language barrier, the athlete's and coach's differences in understanding the preparation of elite gymnasts, mutual adjustment, searching for compromise, and so forth. Taking into account Urban Johnson's particular expertise in athletic injury rehabilitation and prevention (see Johnson, 2000), it was easier for us to coordinate the athlete's work on relaxation and optimal recovery and for the coach to find optimal physical loads for the athlete. Russian coaches are often pushy and tend to overload athletes. Therefore, it was important to continually draw the coach's attention to the athlete's health and well-being. As a result, even though the athlete worked on improving his technical skills and making his competitive routines more complicated, which is associated with a high injury risk in gymnastics, he went through the entire preparation process without serious injuries.

ALEXANDER STAMBULOV'S REFLECTIONS

It was especially interesting for me to deal with the coach's internal conflict between his well-established style of coaching behavior, rooted in Russian general and sport culture, and the new environment. It is possible to say that the coach was a representative of the old Soviet system of sport coaching and management. This system was maintained in gymnastics due to a head coach of the national federation who executed this role for 20 years. This head coach was famous for his autocratic style of decision making and militaristic discipline in the national team, and the other coaches were used to simply complying with his decisions. When the coach arrived in Sweden as a high-level gymnastics expert, he had to sustain this level of expectations. The freedom he had in making decisions about all the aspects of preparation of the athlete was largely new to him. He experienced a lot of hesitation and doubt about different things. Even the support the coach received from the athlete, the other gymnasts, and the club director was sometimes a source of stress because he linked it to the others' high expectations. He also worried about his future and did not know if he would stay in Sweden. These worries and doubts acted as barriers to learning the Swedish language and accepting Swedish culture. However, he had some internal resources, such as self-discipline and carefulness in work and communication with people around him, that helped him to adapt.

LESSONS LEARNED AND CONCLUSIONS

Analyzing our sport psychology consulting experiences from the cultural and cross-cultural viewpoint, we all agree on several lessons learned:

- First, we admit that cultural contexts exist that can be a resource or a barrier for a client depending on the situation.

- Second, we agree that a holistic view of athletes, which typically refers to considering them both in sport and other spheres of life, should be expanded to viewing the athlete in the broader cultural context.

- Third, we emphasize that in spite of shared cultural features, each athlete and coach is unique. Therefore, we would like to encourage practitioners who work with athletes of different cultural backgrounds to listen to the clients carefully and to respect diversity.

To briefly summarize, if something is different from what you think is right, it is not necessarily wrong.

The cultural and cross-cultural experiences presented in this chapter show that historical and sociocultural contexts influence all the participants of psychological services (i.e., athletes, coaches, and sport psychology consultants). Both micro- and macrosociocultural aspects are involved in these environmental contexts, as was emphasized by Vygotsky and Brofenbrenner.

Working inside one culture facilitates mutual understanding because consultants and their clients share basic cultural values, norms, traditions, and understanding of sport and life. Using Vygotsky's terminology, consultants educate athletes and coaches about adjusting effectively in their own sport system and developing culturally specific strategies for adaptation. They may not be fully aware of these cultural influences, simply accepting them as a natural part of their lives (the Russian case illustrates this well).

But when athletes or coaches move to another culture, they often experience a dissonance in the new culture. For example, the Swedish case demonstrates how a lack of interaction and overlap between the Swedish club microsystem and the immigrant family microsystem (Bronfenbrenner, 1979) created a problem between the player and the coaching staff. In the Swedish–Russian case, the coach often experienced dissonance, and many of his Russian stereotypes appeared to be barriers to adjusting in Sweden.

ISSUES AND STRATEGIES TO CONSIDER WHEN WORKING WITH RUSSIAN AND SWEDISH ATHLETES

We have divided the following issues and strategies into two groups. Russian athletes have different characteristics from Swedish athletes, and it's important to take these characteristics into consideration.

Russian Athletes

Here are several issues that we recommend non-Russian sport psychology consultants keep in mind when working with Russian athletes.

• Russian athletes, especially those from provincial places, are highly motivated to achieve in sport, considering it as a way to move to big cities, such as Moscow or St. Petersburg, or to move abroad, where living standards are perceived to be higher than in Russia. Thus Russian athletes who work with sport psychologists from other countries will usually be motivated to work with the consultant to adjust to their new life.

• Consultants with a non-Russian background can expect difficulties in establishing a trust relationship with Russian athletes. The athletes may be afraid that a consultant will share private information with sport authorities in power. When starting your work with Russian athletes, you need to clearly state the ethical norms, especially confidentiality. Be ready for athletes who may test you on how you follow the norms. If you manage to establish trust, Russians can be sharing, open, and cooperative.

• Russian athletes are used to hard work and struggle. Coaches teach them to give 100%. They have grown up in a society where a highly competitive spirit directs athletes to win at all costs. They are often ready to put their health at risk, perceiving this as heroic behavior. Thus, a sport psychology consultant has to pay special attention to the athletes' health, emphasizing prevention of injuries, overtraining, and drug use.

• Russian athletes are sensitive to the reactions of authorities. In Russia, a winner can easily become a victim in the political games of sport. Athletes usually do not complain or create public scandals; they try instead to present themselves well under all circumstances. In difficult situations, Russians rely mainly on their friends and family and avoid addressing state organizations or authorities. When abroad, they may be even more suspicious of unknown people and afraid to make mistakes. These tendencies mean that consultants should explain to Russian athletes how the system in their new country works and what people and organizations can be resources for them. Happily, the athletes' trust in a consultant can become a basis for trusting other people working with them.

Swedish Athletes

Following are issues that a non-Swedish sport psychology consultant should take into account when working with Swedish athletes.

• Keep in mind the Swedish democracy and collectivistic system, and be aware of how the general democratic tradition influences Swedish sport and athletes' mentality. Swedish athletes tend to appreciate a sport psychologist who helps them to discuss issues related to their individual development or team progress. It is important to be an authority but not an autocratic leader.

• Many Swedish athletes exhibit independent behavior compared with athletes from other countries. This is probably because Swedish children learn how to stand on their own. Many who are 15 to 17 years old are used to traveling abroad, where they also learn how to be independent. Therefore, consultants working with Swedish athletes are expected to provide advice and support but not make decisions for them.

• Many Swedish athletes are modest in response to personal success. This is typically not due to low self-efficacy but rather to the cultural tradition described previously (the Jante law). Swedish athletes generally prefer not to show off and instead acknowledge the contributions of other people to their success. Thus, a wise strategy for sport psychology consultants is to avoid pushing athletes to public appearances if they feel they are not ready for them.

• Swedish culture has a long tradition of gender equality with many women in professional and technical jobs and leadership positions. This tradition is also mirrored in Swedish sport with many female coaches and leaders. Therefore, consultants should avoid stereotyped views of gender roles.

The same is true of sport psychology consultants who move to a new country. For example, two authors of this chapter went through this process and know that it takes time and effort to learn how sport is organized in the new country, how athletes and coaches think and prioritize, and what athletes and coaches expect from psychological services. It is important to be open-minded and motivated to learn. Additionally, consultants' cross-cultural experiences are useful for helping them understand not only the new culture but also their own. What was invisible from inside becomes salient from the outside (i.e., from the perspective of the new culture). As Russian poet Sergei Esenin wrote, "Face to face you cannot see the face. Big things are visible at a distance."

Cultural sport psychology (CSP) as a trend in applied work dealing with cultural and cross-cultural experiences should be developed further, such as through international networks of sport psychology consultants, forums for exchange of cultural and cross-cultural experiences between consultants from different countries (e.g., European Forum of Applied Sport Psychologists), and greater attention to cultural issues in applied sport psychology education (e.g., preparing consultants to work with athletes from different cultures). Bringing cultures closer to each other in politics, economics, or sport is a long-term, complicated process that requires understanding of cultural diversity, respect for other cultures, searching for basic universal ethical principles, and excluding any violent methods in this process. Many conflicts have their roots in a lack of empathy and understanding between people representing different cultures. International sport plays an important role in helping people from all over the world understand each other, and sport psychology consultants with multicultural competencies can also contribute to this mission.

WORKING WITH ELITE ATHLETES IN ISRAEL

Ronnie Lidor, PhD, and Boris Blumenstein, PhD

In this chapter, we will discuss how sport psychology services can help elite athletes in Israel to overcome some of the regional and professional challenges they must face. More specifically, the purposes of this chapter are

- to outline several of the regional challenges that athletes in Israel must confront with the help of sport psychology consultants, and

- to provide concrete psychological solutions so the athletes will be able to cope effectively with these challenges.

The chapter is composed of four parts. The first part presents a short historical overview of the development and status of elite sport in Israel, and the second discusses the professional status and services of sport psychology in Israel. The third part presents the authors' approach to practicing psychology with elite athletes. Both authors have worked with novice and elite athletes in Israel and have applied similar principles of consultation. (See Lidor, Blumenstein, and Tenenbaum, [2007a], for detailed information on the psychological program for elite athletes in Israel.) However, the current chapter focuses mainly on the psychological services provided by the second author (B.B.) to elite football (soccer) players and rhythmic gymnasts.

More specifically, the third part outlines five regional challenges that the sport consultant had to consider while planning a psychological program for the athletes. The psychological framework and the interventions used to help the athletes cope with these challenges are discussed. In addition, the relevant background of the sport consultant is described. The fourth part provides psychological reflections and practical tips for sport consultants who work in a country with challenges similar to those faced by Israel. It focuses on providing psychological services to elite athletes, using familiar psychological techniques, and encouraging athletes to consult the sport psychologist at any time during political upheaval.

ISRAELI CONTEXT

The State of Israel was established in 1948. Located in the Middle East and surrounded by Arab countries—Egypt to the south, Jordan to the east, and Lebanon and Syria to the north—Israel is a multicultural society composed of about 7 million residents, among them 5.3 million Jewish citizens, 1.4 million Arab citizens, and 300,000 immigrants, mostly from East European countries, who have not yet registered as Israeli citizens ("Statistical aspects of Israel," 2006). The Jews, Arabs, and other members of the population live side by side, scattered among small and large cities, as well as in rural areas.

Throughout its 60-year history, Israel has faced external threats due to unstable relationships with neighboring Arab countries, most recently Lebanon and Syria. Since peace agreements were signed with Egypt and Jordan, the relationships with these countries have been stable and to some extent even friendly. In addition, Israel has to face another almost daily threat emerging from the long-term historical and political conflict with the Palestinian Arab population that lives mainly in the Gaza and the East Bank areas. The battle between the Israelis and the Palestinians over land has required not only national and international political negotiations but also the use of military force from both sides. For many years the Middle East has been perceived as an unstable and unpredictable region. The numerous armed conflicts that have occurred in this region in the past 60 years have affected both the international and national affairs of most countries in the Middle East.

Inevitably, the regional battles in the Middle East have influenced the economical, political, and social status of Israel. Since its establishment, the country has struggled to protect its residents from military or terror attacks from both outside and within its borders. For example, in 2001 about 1,800 terror attacks occurred in Israel and in 2002 about 1,780 occurred (Police Report, 2002). Between 2000 and 2005, during which time the tension between the Palestinian Arab and the Jewish population sharply accelerated, about 20,000 terror attacks took place ("Terror Attacks," 2007). At the same time, the government has tried to enable Israeli residents to maintain a normal way of life, to continue their personal development, and to attain a high level of achievement in fields of interest such as art, education, industry, science, and sport. It is common for people in Israel to live under a military or terrorist threat and simultaneously strive to maintain a normal life from personal, family, community, and professional perspectives.

One of the domains that best illustrates the way of life in Israel under such regional circumstances is sport, and particularly elite sport. Elite athletes in Israel—Jewish, Arab, and foreign—must cope not only with the regional challenges that every resident faces but also with the usual physical and psychological obstacles that are part of sport. Jewish, Arab, and foreign athletes are a microcosm of the multicultural phenomenon existing in the population at large in Israel.

OVERVIEW OF ISRAELI SPORT

Traditionally, sport and physical education have been separate domains in Israel (Lidor & Bar-Eli, 1998; Simri, Tenenbaum, & Bar-Eli, 1996a, 1996b). In 1939, the General Council of the Jews in Palestine—the prestate Jewish government—established a physical training department to address all aspects of physical education except competitive sport. In 1948, when the country of Israel was established, the physical training department was placed under the framework of the Ministry of Education and Culture. In 1960, the department was replaced by the newly created Sport and Physical Education Authority, whose task was to supervise both competitive sport and physical education (Lidor & Bar-Eli, 1998).

Dealing with domestic terrorism is an unavoidable reality of being an athlete in Israel.
© DAVID FURST/AFP/Getty Images

Since 1948, sport in Israel has been free from direct government control; however, it has been closely linked to the various political parties (Reshef & Paltiel, 1989). In the beginning years of the state, the government, headed by the Labor Party, indirectly controlled competitive sport through its substantial political majority in the various sport bodies. About 740,000 immigrants, most of them from European countries, arrived in Israel between 1948 and 1954 (Ben-Porat, 1993). During these years and the following decade, an effort was made to fulfill the needs of these new immigrants, including employment, housing, education, and health services.

It was a difficult mission to help the immigrants establish themselves in their new country—they did not speak Hebrew, their educational backgrounds varied considerably, and few jobs were available to them. The leaders had to rapidly establish governmental bodies (e.g., education, employment, international affairs) to create an effective system to govern the new state. These governmental bodies and their structures contributed to the development of the sport structure as well. As a result, sport became a popular activity among both the native population and immigrants not only as a recreational activity but also as a competitive one. After a political upheaval in 1977, the government, headed by the Likud Party, made a substantial effort to become more directly involved in sport.

One result of these developments was the decision of the Ministry of Education, Sport, and Culture and the Israeli Olympic Committee to establish the Elite Sport Department in 1984. The main objective of the department was to provide the optimal preparatory conditions—from both physical and psychological perspectives—to the elite athletes whose aim was to participate in major international sport events, such as the Olympic Games, world championships, and European championships. Since its establishment, the Elite Sport Department has provided assistance not only to the athletes but also to the professionals who work with them, such as coaches, athletic trainers, sport physicians, and sport psychologists. The assistance is mainly given to those involved in individual sports such as judo, kayaking, wrestling, swimming, and rhythmic gymnastics.

Elite sport in Israel has also been developed in the private sector, particularly in professional clubs that are owned or managed by affluent individuals or big businesses that decided to invest money in sport development. Typically, the televised ball games—basketball, football, team handball, and volleyball—are played by professional male (in basketball and football) or semiprofessional female and male (in basketball, team handball, and volleyball) athletes. At the elite level in Israel, there are approximately 670 professional male athletes, 735 semiprofessional male athletes, and 700 semiprofessional female athletes. Professional players in basketball and football are paid well by their clubs and therefore can focus solely on their sport. The semiprofessional players are also paid to play for their clubs; however, their salaries are low compared with those of professional players and therefore most of them have another job. The professional and semiprofessional players play for clubs in professional or semiprofessional national leagues and participate in European championships for professional clubs.

SPORT PSYCHOLOGY IN ISRAEL

The development of sport in Israel has also influenced the development of sport sciences. More and more athletes, coaches, sport administrators, and sport policy makers have become aware of the contribution of sport sciences, such as sport medicine, biomechanics, sport nutrition, exercise physiology, and sport and exercise psychology, to sport performance enhancement. The use of empirical and applied knowledge emerging from sport sciences has increased by sport professionals who work with elite athletes. The Elite Sport Department as well as several professional sport clubs hire professionals such as sport physicians, biomechanists, conditioning and strength coaches, and sport psychologists to build a coherent team and provide the coaching staff with updated scientific and applied knowledge. Coaches can use this information to plan better training programs and consequently facilitate the achievements of the athletes.

RECENT DEVELOPMENTS

Sport and exercise psychology, one of the major theoretical and practical domains in the sport sciences, has gained a position of influence in elite sport in Israel during the last 30 years (Bar-Eli & Lidor, 2000; Lidor & Bar-Eli, 2001). Sport psychology interventions have been provided to both female and male elite athletes on a regular basis in training programs for team sport (e.g., basketball; see Lidor, Blumenstein, & Tenenbaum, 2007b), individual sport (e.g., judo; see Blumenstein, Lidor, & Tenenbaum, 2005), kayaking (Blumenstein & Lidor, 2004), and swimming (Bar-Eli & Blumenstein, 2004). Many of these interventions have been provided by sport consultants from the Elite Sport Department, which is supported both ideologically and financially by the Israeli Olympic Committee. In essence, sport psychologists are assigned to work with elite athletes and are part of the professional staff that prepares the athletes for upcoming sporting events. This means that the sport psychologists attend practice sessions, team meetings, and competitions.

Professional sport clubs also hire sport psychology consultants to provide interventional consultations to athletes and coaches; however, only a few work as part of the professional staff. For example, there are 12 professional football clubs in Division 1 in Israel, but only 3 of these clubs have a sport psychology consultant working full-time as an integral part of the coaching staff. In 4 other clubs, consultants provide psychological services on only a few occasions during the season, mainly upon the request of the coaching staff. The situation is similar in elite basketball. There are 12 professional basketball clubs in Division 1, but in only 2 of these clubs is the sport psychology consultant part of the professional staff. In the other 10 clubs, the head coaches may consult sport psychologists on various occasions throughout the season. Typically, the majority of the consultants who work in the private sector provide psychological services only when the team loses a series of games and the head coaches want to obtain relevant information that can help them put their teams back on the winning track.

DIVERSITY AMONG ELITE ATHLETES

Elite athletes in Israel represent different cultures and religions. To illustrate, there are about 22 football players in each professional club in Israel. Among the players, the majority (about 15 players) will be Jews who were born in Israel. In addition, there will probably be 2 or 3 Arab players who were born in Israel and 3 or 4 foreign players who were born mainly in European countries. Most of the Arab players are Muslims and most of the foreign players are Christians. All have to adjust to the Israeli mentality (i.e., being able to maintain a normal life while living under a military or terrorist threat) to achieve their best in daily practices and weekly competitions. This multicultural phenomenon is one of the critical issues with which sport psychologists have to contend (figure 12.1). Among the multicultural challenges are the language barrier, differences in discipline, and differences in dealing with terror and military attacks.

The main objective of the psychological program we offer to elite athletes in Israel is to help the individual athlete or the team to be cognitively and emotionally prepared for the upcoming season. For the purposes of this chapter, we will stress the psychological interventions that helped the athletes overcome the challenges they faced while practicing and competing in Israel.

CHALLENGES FOR ELITE ATHLETES

The psychological interventions presented in this chapter were created and managed by Boris Blumenstein, a sport psychology consultant, while working

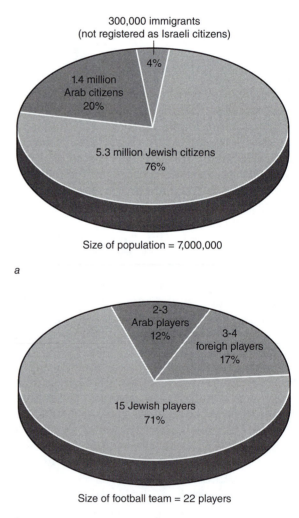

FIGURE 12.1   The ethnic diversity of Israel is reflected in the makeup of a typical team, as seen in these two graphs: (a) the distribution of ethnic and religious groups in the nation of Israel, (b) the distribution of ethnic and religious groups in a typical professional football club.

with professional football players and elite rhythmic gymnasts. Thus the remainder of the chapter will be written from his point of view—a male with 30 years of experience working with elite athletes, 15 years in his native Russia and 15 years in Israel.

I identified five regional challenges during my work with elite athletes in Israel: language, personal cultural preferences, fans' expectations, different levels of discipline, and terror and military attacks. The first four can be discussed as cultural differences.

CULTURAL DIFFERENCES

Given the enormous variety of ethnicities in the Israeli population, as well as the high number of foreign elite athletes in the country, it is not surprising that cultural differences abound in the Israeli sport world. These include language barriers, ethnic standards and tastes in dress and music, Israeli fans' expectations of athletes, and differing levels of discipline characteristic of different cultures.

LANGUAGE BARRIER

The official language in Israel, Hebrew, was not spoken by every athlete. Hebrew was spoken by the Jewish and Arab football players but not by the foreign players, who spoke their native language and English. The Jewish and Arab football players could also communicate in English. The native language of the team staff was Hebrew, but all could speak English as well.

A similar observation can be made for the rhythmic gymnasts. The Israeli-born rhythmic gymnasts spoke Hebrew, but not all the gymnasts who had immigrated to Israel were able to speak or understand the language. However, all the gymnasts spoke English. The native language of the coach as well as a few of the leading gymnasts was Russian, and some of the Israeli-born gymnasts had difficulty communicating with the coach in Hebrew. Therefore, in both sports—football and rhythmic gymnastics—English was the official language when the entire team gathered. However, during practices and games the coaching staff and the athletes developed a mixed language for communication, speaking a combination of Hebrew and English.

Not all of the athletes felt comfortable participating in a sport psychology consultation; some were not open to sharing their thoughts, feelings, and preferences on issues related to the team and the coaching staff. If players feel that they will not be understood by the sport consultant or their teammates due to a language barrier, they will probably demonstrate an even greater hesitation to participate in a sport psychology consultation. This is the main reason why I attempted to overcome language barriers. I wanted to facilitate a positive climate during consultation sessions, particularly during the individual sessions, and give the athletes the feeling that language should not be an obstacle for effective communication.

DIFFERING PERSONAL PREFERENCES

The Jewish, Arab, and foreign football players, as well as most of the gymnasts, had grown up in different cultures. As a result, a variety of dress codes, nonsport activities such as listening to music and going out after practices or competitions, and other personal preferences were observed among the athletes. For example, the Jewish and the Arab football players preferred to dress informally before and after practices and games, whereas the foreign players were more formal in their dress code. A similar observation can be made about the gymnasts: Those who immigrated to Israel were more formal in their dress code than those born in Israel.

Music preferences also could be distinguished among the players in terms of cultural perspectives. The Jewish and Arab players listened to Mediterranean-style music most of the time, usually songs in Hebrew. The foreign players listened to soft music and songs in their native language. Different music preferences sometimes created conflicts when the team was traveling to play a game on the road and the players would ask the bus driver to turn on the radio. Too often there was disagreement among the players with respect to the type of music to be played.

Although the dress code and the music issues did not greatly influence the cross-cultural relations on the team, they were symbols of subteams within the team, a challenge that I had to cope with (see A Unique Difficulty). In addition, the football players practiced different religions and observed religious holidays, which took place at different times.

LEVELS OF DISCIPLINE

Not all of the athletes demonstrated the same level of discipline. The foreign football players and the gymnasts who were born in Eastern European countries seemed to be more committed to their profession than the native Israelis; in the early stages of their sport development, they developed their skills in sport clubs that stressed hard work, a high level of discipline on and off the court or field, and total commitment to their sport. They accepted the coach as their professional leader without questioning the coach's authority, coaching philosophy, or interactions with the athletes. The football players

A Unique Difficulty: A National Anthem That Does Not Represent the Entire Nation

The Israeli anthem, *"Hatikva,"* was first published by the Jewish poet Naftali Hertz-Imbar in 1886. It was originally written as a poem, but over the years the Jewish population turned it into a song that became the official anthem. The song focuses on the hope of the Jewish people to be free and live in the land of Israel. Since the song focuses only on the will of the Jewish people, the Israeli Arab population claims that the anthem does not represent them, which is why the Arab population does not join the Jewish population in singing the anthem. At the current time, there have been more and more initiatives to replace the anthem with a new one representing all subgroups of the Israeli population, particularly its Arab citizens, but for now the playing of the national anthem at Israeli sporting events presents a special problem for some fans and athletes. This difficulty will be discussed in the context of the case examples.

and gymnasts who were born in Israel, on the other hand, were not as disciplined or committed as their teammates from other countries. They worked hard during practices but did not maintain a high level of consistency and commitment during the entire season. The football players often complained about the heavy training load and lack of playing time, and the gymnasts complained as well about the high level of intensity during practices.

The divergence in the players' level of discipline influenced team relations. The foreign football players expected the Jewish and Arab players to elevate their discipline to a level that would contribute more to the team effort and therefore improve its performance. They argued that the Jewish and Arab players should make a greater effort during the daily practices. The gymnasts who immigrated to Israel had similar demands; they wanted the Israeli-born gymnasts to be more disciplined and to work harder during practices. One of my objectives was to decrease the tension among these athletes.

Fans' Expectations

An additional issue for non-Israeli players is the expectations of fans. Due to the constant stress with which people in Israel have to cope, sport is perceived as a release. Sport is a popular activity to watch and fans like to be close to their heroes, particularly in football, the most popular sport. The players are stopped on the street, engaged in light conversation, asked for autographs, and given the feeling that everyone is their friend. Some foreign football players complain that they do not have a private life. For most of them, this behavior is a cultural shock. In contrast, the Jewish and Arab football players feel comfortable with their popularity and even seek out opportunities to meet with their fans. Furthermore,

they feel unappreciated if their fans ignore them. One of my immediate goals was to prevent player dropout during the season, and therefore the players, particularly the foreign ones, were informed of this common fan behavior.

Terror and Military Attacks

Israel is probably one of the few countries that must cope with terror attacks and military threats on a regular basis and at the same time attempt to maintain a normal way of life, including participation in national and international sport activities. The foreign football players and rhythmic gymnasts who immigrated to Israel were already familiar with the existing relationship between Israel and its Arab neighbors and the Palestinians. At the beginning of the season, they were apprehensive about the political situation in the country and the possibility of terror attacks. They showed a greater sensitivity to the existing situation than the football players and gymnasts who were born in Israel. When a terror attack did occur, the foreign football players were in a panic whereas their Israeli teammates managed themselves effectively and performed as usual. In addition, the occurrence of a terror attack elevated the number of discussions among the players on issues such as Israeli politics, military actions that the Israeli army should or should not take, and the complex relationship between Jewish and Arab citizens.

It was not an easy task to help the foreign players put aside the terror attacks and concentrate on playing football. I spent a considerable amount of time discussing the uncertain situation with these players, and I managed to convince them to focus their attention on the daily practice sessions as well as on other team activities, such as team meetings with the coaching staff and watching videos of upcoming opponents. Although I attempted to use conventional sport psychology strategies to help the foreign players to cope with the occurrence of terror attacks (see Group Interventions on page 148), I often found myself reassuring them that the situation was not so bad. The immigrated athletes eventually became accustomed to terror attacks and learned that they could perform well while under terrorist threats. The ability of the Jewish and the Arab players to ignore the situation also helped the foreign players to adapt.

Case Examples

The psychological program presented in the following case examples was provided to football players and rhythmic gymnasts by the same sport psychology consultant. The case studies for football and rhythmic gymnastics are presented separately and describe the major regional challenges encountered.

Interventions in a Football Team

The team consisted of 22 male athletes (mean age = 27.3 years) who played for one professional club located in a large city in the north of the country. The club was part of Division 1, which was the highest professional football division in Israel. The team practiced 5 days per week, and on some days two practice sessions were scheduled. The team also played one game per week in the national league. The team played about 30 games during the season. Among the players, 16 were Jewish and were born and raised in Israel. The Jewish players came from all over the country; however, they resided in cities and villages in the north of the country while playing for the club. Four players were born and raised in Eastern European countries. (According to the regulations of the Israeli Soccer Federation, each team could draft four foreign players who were not Israeli citizens.) Finally, two players were Muslims who were born and raised in medium-size Arab cities located in the north of the country. These Arab players were Israeli citizens as well.

I used three frameworks for presenting psychological interventions to the athletes: individual sessions, group sessions, and home assignments.

Individual Sessions

The objective of the individual sessions was twofold: to develop a psychological profile for each player that reflected his characteristics and needs and to provide each athlete with specific psychological interventions. The individual sessions were typically conducted before practice or at the end of the practice. Each individual meeting lasted about 45 minutes.

In an individual session, mental techniques such as attention focusing (Moran, 2005), relaxation accompanied by music (Blumenstein, 1992), imagery (Hall, 2001), goal setting (Weinberg & Butt, 2005), and self-talk (Henschen, 2005) were addressed. These techniques were also used for coping with the regional challenges. In general, since one of the regional barriers among the foreign players was language, it was more convenient to work one on one. The foreign players then spoke without the fear of being misunderstood by their teammates, and they were comfortable enough to speak freely with me even though they were aware of their poor language skills.

Individual Interventions

To overcome the language and multicultural barriers, I used a goal-setting technique. Short-term goals, such as "I will learn more about the personal background of my teammates" or "I will pick up some common words in the language of my teammates that will help me communicate with them not only during practices and games but also off the field," were set in individual sessions early in the season. Long-term goals were set as well, such as, "We have to be one team no matter what our background, culture, or religion is" or "I should treat my teammates equally on and off the field."

The goals I proposed were not fully accepted by the coaching staff and the players in the early phases of the season. Both the coaches (the head coach and his assistant) and the players were somewhat suspicious; they wanted to understand where I was trying to lead them. At the end of the meetings, the players would ask questions such as, "Are you sure that it's going to work out for us?" or "Are these really goals or just slogans?" These questions stopped after five or six sessions, when the coaches and players understood the purposes of the specific psychological techniques as well as the objectives of the entire psychological program. Both coaches and players needed some time to digest these techniques.

Another regional issue that was handled in the individual sessions was the matter of discipline, particularly with the Jewish and Arab players. Once again, I used a goal-setting technique. I used the high level of self-discipline demonstrated by the foreign players during practices as an example to motivate the Jewish and Arab players. We discussed the concept of good discipline in sport and why most of the foreign players on the team were viewed by the coaching staff as having a high level of discipline. My approach was, "Let's learn from those who are good at . . ." and "Let's share with the others what we are good at." This approach helped promote cross-cultural understanding among the athletes.

The foreign players were the highest-paid players on the team. The Jewish and Arab players occasionally complained that the foreign players received such high salaries only because they came from Europe and that they were paid much more than they deserved. In the initial consultation sessions, the Jewish and Arab players criticized me for exclusively using the foreign players as examples of desirable behavior. However, I did not give in because I believed that the foreign players did demonstrate a high level of discipline. I did not touch on the financial contracts of the foreign players with the Jewish and Arab players, and I tried to convince them to expend more effort. In this matter, I received some help from the coaches, since they also stressed the high level of commitment and discipline demonstrated by the foreign players during practices and games.

GROUP SESSIONS

The group sessions were conducted in two forms—sessions with the entire team and sessions with three to five players. Reasons for the players' selection to the smaller group sessions included the following:

- Players had similar roles on the team (e.g., goalkeepers, defensive players, strikers).
- Players shared a similar psychological state (e.g., low self-confidence, low motivation).
- The coaching staff made a request or I decided it would be helpful (e.g., preparing the foreign players to cope with terror attacks, preparing the Arab players to cope with hostile fans of the opponent).

The purpose of the group sessions was to facilitate team building and to help the players cope with external distractions that were not related directly to their performance on the field. As in the individual sessions, the group sessions were held before or after practices. The group gathered in a well-equipped meeting room, and I used PowerPoint® and video presentations that I prepared specifically for each session. Group sessions lasted 60 minutes.

According to my philosophy of consultation and because of language barriers, small-group sessions were the preferred framework. I wanted to achieve good communication between myself and the players, and an effective way to achieve this communication was by meeting with one or a few players at a time. Only when required did I meet with the entire team. There were two limitations to group sessions with the entire team. First, in football there are typically 22 players on the roster, which is a big group to work with at one time. Second, the players had different ability levels for mastering the psychological skills, and it was more convenient to work with only a few players who were at the same level of mastering the psychological skills (e.g., focusing attention).

The group sessions were more likely to succeed if the leading players on the team expressed interest in what I did. The other players would carefully listen to me and cooperate because the best players did so and thus led the way.

GROUP INTERVENTIONS

Similar to the individual sessions, at the beginning of a typical group session I asked the players to share their feelings with me about their professional and social involvement in the team, satisfaction or dissatisfaction with their professional and social status on the team, and special requests they had for me. Among the topics discussed in the meetings with the entire team were the professional goals of the team. To stress the importance of cohesion among the Jewish, Arab, and foreign players, I used an interpersonal relations approach (Estabrooks & Dennis, 2003; Lidor et al., 2007b). I emphasized that to achieve the goals set by the coaching staff, the team must perform as one unit regardless of the players' different backgrounds or roles on the team. I prepared video presentations that showed effective performances of the team that led to victories, as well as weaker performances that contributed to losing games. I also used a goal-setting approach in these meetings. In addition, the players applied imagery to visualize good and poor team performance. While imagining themselves performing defensive or offensive maneuvers, the players were asked to stress the necessity of cooperative work.

Another topic that was discussed in the group sessions was how to cope with external distractions, such as the hostility of the crowd toward a few players on the team, particularly the Arab players. When the team played an away game, the Jewish fans of the host team demonstrated negative verbal behavior toward the two Arab players. This behavior was against the policy of the league, and in many cases host teams were fined for their fans' behavior. The Arab players who played for clubs in Division 1 served as targets for hostile behavior. I asked the other players on the team to stand behind the Arab players when racial slurs occurred and also to try imagining themselves in such a situation. Then we held an open discussion in which the players suggested how they would support the Arab players during spectator abuse. I summarized the suggestions (e.g., being physically close to them during the act, hugging them while the event occurred, or speaking out against the phenomenon in the press) and encouraged the players to use them when the situation actually occurred.

One more issue that was discussed in the sessions with the entire team was how to cope with military threats and terror attacks. It was important to deal with this regional issue since a few terror attacks had taken place during the time I had worked for the football club. First, in early stages of the season, I met with the foreign players and explained the political situation between the Israelis and the Palestinians and what can happen during a terror attack. In the group sessions held after the occurrence of the attacks, I used relaxation techniques accompanied by music to allow the players to relax and get rid of negative thoughts. I also emphasized the need of the team to stick together because all the players were professional athletes who had to do their job.

Military threats and terror attacks were also dealt with in the smaller group sessions. For example, I gathered the foreign players after such attacks and practiced relaxation and attention-focusing techniques with them. We worked on how to focus attention on the defensive and offensive drills practiced during the time when the terror attacks occurred. It was not an easy task to provide consultation during those difficult days due to the emotional reactions of the Israelis after such events. However, I maintained an attitude that most of the events were under control and that both the players and the coaching staff should stay on target and fulfill their mission. This attitude helped me convince the foreign players to routinely practice psychological techniques. At first, it was difficult for them to understand why they had to practice sport psychology techniques aimed at coping with events not related to their sport. Only after a series of meetings did they begin to realize that the techniques could help with relaxation off the field as well.

I also used the sessions with selected players to overcome cultural barriers within the team. For example, I met with the Arab and foreign players and discussed some symbols of Israeli culture with them, such as the national anthem. It is true that most of the Arab players were aware of the prominent symbols of the Israeli culture. However, I wanted to make sure that the meaning of these symbols was clear

to them. For example, the Israeli anthem is played before the football games. I stressed to the Arab and foreign players that they were not expected to sing the anthem, but I asked them to respect the event. At the session, I instructed the players to imagine themselves standing with the entire team before the game while the anthem was being played. I asked them to stand erectly and listen to the song, waiting patiently until it ended. The Arab players did not make an issue of this request. After the discussion, they understood that playing the anthem was part of the official ceremony before the game.

HOME ASSIGNMENTS

I asked the players to practice psychological techniques at home in a quiet and relaxed atmosphere. The objective of the home assignments was to increase awareness of appropriate use of the psychological interventions (e.g., attention focusing and imagery) they had learned during the individual and group consultation sessions. Although the ecological validity of the home assignments might be low due to the sterile settings in which the players performed the psychological techniques, I believed that it would help them assume personal responsibility for mastering the relevant techniques.

HOME ASSIGNMENT INTERVENTIONS

The effectiveness of the home assignments could not be assessed. One of the goals of a sport psychology consultant is to develop the athletes' responsibility for practicing psychological techniques at home, and I considered the players to be professionals who strived to achieve their best. I did not regularly check to see if the players practiced the psychological techniques at home; I only occasionally asked them if they spent some time doing the psychological training.

INTERVENTIONS IN RHYTHMIC GYMNASTICS

The gymnasts (8 females; mean age = 18.2 years) were members of the Israeli rhythmic gymnastics national team. Six of the gymnasts were from families that had immigrated to Israel from Eastern Europe. Some could speak Hebrew fluently, but others had difficulties with Hebrew and therefore had to use their native language. The other two gymnasts were born in Israel and developed their early careers in an Israeli gymnast club. The gymnasts practiced in a large city in the middle of the country and lived with their families in nearby cities. They practiced daily for 3 to 4 hours. The Elite Sport Department provided the team with the required professional support. As the sport psychologist who worked for this department, I was assigned to provide psychological services to the gymnasts.

As was the case with the football team, I used three kinds of sessions to deliver the psychological services: individual sessions, group sessions, and home assignments.

INDIVIDUAL SESSIONS

The objective of the individual sessions was to establish a map of goals for each gymnast (Lidor et al., 2007a). We used two stages to develop the map. In stage 1, the map was composed of conceptual goals, such as "What do I want to achieve during the upcoming year?", and practical goals, such as "What should I do to achieve this goal?" In stage 2, specific goals were set for each phase of the yearly training program. In this stage, we set goals to help the gymnasts cope with regional challenges such as discipline.

INDIVIDUAL INTERVENTIONS

I helped the Israeli-born gymnasts set specific goals for bridging the gap between themselves and the gymnasts who were not born in Israel. The gymnasts who were not born in Israel were more committed to gymnastics and were extremely self-disciplined. They sacrificed almost everything to achieve their personal goals, namely to be the best in the country and to qualify for the Olympic Games. The gymnasts who were born in Israel, on the other hand, demonstrated less commitment and self-discipline, so we set short- and long-term goals focusing on improving their attitude toward gymnastics and increasing self-discipline and commitment during practices and other team activities. The head coach, a woman with 25 years of experience in coaching elite rhythmic gymnasts, selected the gymnasts for the national team mainly based on their achievements in national and international competitions. However, she stressed discipline in her program and rewarded gymnasts who were highly disciplined.

Goal setting, imagery, and self-talk were also used in the individual sessions to help the gymnasts who were born in Israel to cope with the different mentality of the coaching staff, particularly the head coach. The head coach had emigrated from Belarus a few years before I began to work with the gymnasts. She treated her gymnasts differently from the way the Israeli-born gymnasts were used to being treated by their previous coaches, who had been born in Israel. For example, she demanded a high level of consistency during practices, prevented interference by the gymnasts' parents, and asked for full participation in every practice. In short, she was tough on the gymnasts regardless of background and experience.

The gymnasts who were not born in Israel handled this approach successfully; they were used to it in their native countries (Belarus, Russia, and Ukraine). However, for the gymnasts who were born in Israel it was not an easy task. Therefore, we set short- and long-term goals, such as "I will follow exactly the instructions given by the coach each time she approaches me" or "I will convince the coach that I am doing my best," to help them overcome this barrier. These goals focused primarily on compliance. I adopted this approach to help the Israeli-born gymnasts elevate their standards to those of the gymnasts who were not born in Israel.

In addition, the gymnasts practiced imagery and self-talk to increase their awareness of how they should perform during practice sessions. They imagined themselves performing the segments of the routine, used a self-talk technique to remember the specific order of the segments, and then evaluated the imagined routine in a short discussion with the sport psychology consultant. The gymnasts who were not born in Israel told me that they had practiced attention focusing, imagery, and self-talk before their immigration to Israel. They also reported that their coaches in their native countries had stressed the use of imagery, devoting a few minutes of almost every practice to imagining the routines.

GROUP SESSIONS

Group sessions with selected gymnasts were more common than sessions with the entire group. I met with two or three gymnasts each time, mainly at the coach's request. For example, I practiced imagery with those who needed to refine certain segments of their 90-second routine. Imagery was used for 90-second intervals to simulate the actual time of the routine. After each interval, the gymnasts provided feedback on their imagined routine. They exchanged ideas on how to improve their routines and what practical measures they could take to achieve this goal.

GROUP INTERVENTIONS

As indicated earlier, several of the gymnasts who were not born in Israel already had been exposed to some of the psychological interventions that I administered. I encouraged them to share their perspectives on the contribution of sport psychology to their performance. It was one of my strategies to enable the gymnasts who were born in Israel and those who were not born in Israel to acknowledge each other's backgrounds and experiences. I devoted a few minutes to an informal discussion among the gymnasts, and each time a different gymnast took the lead and talked about her previous experience in rhythmic gymnastics. For example, the gymnast might talk about how she achieved a balance between sport and schoolwork, how she overcame a serious injury, how she handled stress, or how she dealt with performance slumps. The other gymnasts could ask questions and share their views after listening to the gymnast's story.

I introduced two psychological techniques during these sessions: goal setting and self-talk. These techniques were matched to each athlete by taking into account her specific needs, physical and psychological states, and motivational state. The psychological interventions presented in this session complemented the interventions presented in the individual sessions and home assignments. In the meetings with the entire group, I encouraged the Israeli-born gymnasts to observe those who were not born in Israel in order to learn how to be consistent in practice and how to benefit from each practice session. However, I did this in a way that did not criticize the gymnasts but instead helped them change several undesirable habits in practices. For example, the entire team watched a video of one of the gymnasts who was not born in Israel performing her routine with the ball. They were asked to focus on her overt behavior after failing to catch the ball. At one point I stopped the film and stressed the gymnast's reaction to her failure. I wanted to emphasize that this gymnast did not stop her routine, but continued to perform as if nothing had happened. Her facial expression did not change. She did not give any indication that anything was wrong. I pointed out that this reaction was appropriate, and I asked the gymnasts, particularly those who were born in Israel, to learn from her behavior and try to handle this kind of event in a similar manner, namely to continue with their routines as she did if something like that ever happened to them.

Since the gymnasts lived with their parents, I did not spend time discussing military threats and terror attacks. I assumed that the families of the gymnasts would take care of these situations, if necessary. The gymnasts also told me that following a terror attack, the main topic discussed by their family was the attack. As a result, some athletes were tired of the discussion.

HOME ASSIGNMENTS

I asked the gymnasts to practice the psychological techniques at home in a quiet and relaxed atmosphere. The objective of the home assignments was to reinforce the use of psychological interventions that the gymnasts learned during the individual and group sessions.

The athletes were asked mainly to perform imagery and self-talk techniques. In some cases, they also listened to music while imagining their routines.

Due to their previous experience with imagery, this was the preferred method of the gymnasts who were not born in Israel. They mainly performed imagery while listening to the music that accompanied their routines. In some phases of the training program, particularly before a series of competitions, they performed imagery on a daily basis. The gymnasts who were born in Israel alternated daily between imagery and self-talk on alternate days.

HOME ASSIGNMENT INTERVENTIONS

As in the case of the football players, the effectiveness of the home assignments could not be assessed. I did not check on a regular basis to see if the gymnasts actually practiced the psychological techniques at home; it was their responsibility to practice at home. Instead, we saw the homework as an educational campaign.

SUGGESTIONS FOR PROVIDING SPORT PSYCHOLOGY CONSULTATION

We have provided psychological services to elite athletes in Israel for the past 15 years. We have experience working in the Elite Sport Department, as well as in the private sector, namely for professional basketball and football clubs. Based on our experience, we provide three practical tips for sport consultants who work in regions with similar challenges.

First, sport consultants should focus on the provision of the psychological services to their athletes. As indicated previously, the unique political situation of Israel makes it easy to start talking about politics, military actions, or the relations between the Arabs and Jews. In our early years as sport psychology consultants we were more liberal with our athletes and discussed topics with them that were not related to sport, such as Israeli politics, international politics, and financial matters. However, in time we realized that the athletes were too emotionally involved with these issues, so we decided not to bring them up in our discussions anymore. It is our advice that sport consultants should focus solely on their professional service without becoming involved in such discussions. Sport consultants should treat athletes of different religions or ethnic backgrounds equally, and they should keep their political opinions to themselves.

Second, sport consultants should use psychological techniques with which they are familiar. Sport consultants cannot present just any psychological intervention available in the sport psychology literature; instead, they should focus on what they

ISSUES AND STRATEGIES TO CONSIDER WHEN WORKING WITH ATHLETES IN ISRAEL

Our advice for working with Israeli and non-Israeli athletes in Israel is as follows:

- Full cooperation between the sport psychology consultant and other professionals working with the athletes is required. Professionals may include the club director, head coach and assistants, sport physician, athletic trainer, and strength and conditioning coach.
- The sport psychology consultant should treat all athletes equally, regardless of their nationality, ethnic background, or religion. Full respect should be given to each athlete.
- The sport psychology consultant should be familiar with the cultural backgrounds of all the athletes, particularly those of non-Israeli athletes.
- The sport psychology consultant should not get involved in any political discussions with either Israeli or non-Israeli athletes; instead, consultants should keep their political and social agendas to themselves.
- Psychological services should be given mainly in individual sessions in order to overcome language barriers.
- The sport psychology consultant should take an open-door approach, particularly with non-Israeli athletes.

do best. Sport consultants are advised to consider the knowledge and experience of elite athletes who have consulted sport psychologists in the past and may have been exposed to other sport-enhancement psychological interventions. However, consultants should instruct their athletes how to use the chosen psychological interventions and convince them that the sport psychology program they have developed will help the athletes achieve their best. Knowing the culture of the athletes or living in the same culture will help consultants select the most appropriate interventions for helping athletes to achieve their goals.

Third, sport consultants should encourage their athletes to consult them at any time, not only during formal consultations. In Israel, some players may prefer to meet sport consultants at their office or in a restaurant. Due to the language barrier, unfamiliarity with the Israeli mentality, and other challenges, it may be more effective for certain players to meet with consultants in a location other than the usual meeting place.

To enable the athletes to receive the best possible psychological services, sport consultants should sup-

port these requests. They can also use the cultural preferences of the athletes to improve the consultation process. For example, if the Arab athletes prefer to meet in informal settings, the sport consultant should agree to do so. If the Israeli-born athletes prefer to be part of an official individual or team consultation session, the sport consultant should be sensitive to their request. Although different cultural preferences may exist among a group of elite athletes, sport psychologists can benefit from the multicultural climate if they coordinate psychological interventions with the athletes' cultural needs in addition to their professional requirements.

Our objective in this chapter was to demonstrate how sport psychology services can be provided in a country with unique challenges. We believe that sport psychology services can be effective in such countries if the foundations of the services are professional and egalitarian and reflect the knowledge and experience of the consultant. It is our contention that psychological interventions for enhancing sport performance can also help elite athletes cope with regional challenges such as those outlined in this chapter.

A CANADIAN SPORT PSYCHOLOGIST IN KUWAIT

Shaun Galloway, PhD

The theoretical basis for this chapter can be summed up by the typical model of communication presented by Shannon and Weaver (1949), where it was suggested that communication follows a continuum: Source → transmitter → received signal (which may be affected by noise) → receiver → destination. This model has received both support and criticism; however, its practicality is revealed in its ease of application when entering a culture that widely uses English, though not as its first language. When I went to Kuwait, it was easy at times to forget that English is a second language there, and when a communication problem arose I had to step back and remind myself of this fact. Shannon and Weaver suggested that communication problems exist on three levels: the technical level, pertaining to the accuracy of the symbols used in communication; the semantics level, focusing on the precision of the symbols to deliver the meaning; and the effectiveness level, which is determined by how the meaning affects behavior in the desired way.

Where do sport psychologists begin when they meet an athlete for the first time and are presented with a world of possibilities—and a world of differences? In a chapter on cultural aspects of sport psychology, Parham (2005) maintained that understanding both your own context and that of the country in which you are practicing is essential. Sport psychologists practicing abroad will face a great many misbeliefs about their culture. These misbeliefs as well as those of the psychologists regarding the country in which they are practicing are the meat of the problems they will face. The present discussion assumes the validity of Parham's ideas and is framed in terms of my experiences consulting as a sport psychologist in Kuwait. The areas that will be covered include getting to know the culture, initial meetings, communication intervention, spirituality and self-actualization, a team intervention focusing on team cohesion, and an individual intervention focusing on perspective.

In keeping with Parham's views, and in order to orient readers to the context within which I have written this chapter, I will provide a brief description of my background. I grew up in a small Canadian city with first-generation Sikhs, Vietnamese, Croatians, and Israelis, as well as a few second-generation Irish, Germans, and Iranians. The mix of food, language, religion, and traditions gave me a flexibility that stood me in good stead during my past 16 years of living in six countries (Japan, Australia, Greece, Hungary, Kuwait, and the United Kingdom).

I would like to highlight one caveat before I go on. My experiences are my own, and though they may serve as basic guidelines for conducting sport psychology practice in an Islamic country such as Kuwait, perspectives of how to proceed or what to suggest may be different for someone else.

KUWAITI CONTEXT

An important consideration when visiting any country is an understanding of history, religions, and family structure. However, when the laws of

Author note: I would like to express my sincere gratitude to my two collaborators, Omar Lewis and Sager Al Armeli, who helped me greatly with my historical knowledge of Kuwait as well as with bringing up past memories of my time in Kuwait.

that country are based largely on religion, it is paramount that sport psychologists learn the religion as thoroughly as possible. This is definitely the case for working in Kuwait.

HISTORY

According to Dr. Abdallah Al-Ghoneim, the president of the Centre for Kuwaiti Research and Studies (Kuwait City, Kuwait), recent research proves that Kuwait existed as an independent political entity as early as 1613—not 1752, as formerly believed (Al-Durae, 2000). During the late 18th and early 19th centuries, Kuwait became a major port of call for international commerce and a crossroads of busy trading routes. Pearls were the only natural resource, and as a result, shipbuilding became an important industry. One of the most famous and influential rulers of Kuwait was HH (His Highness) Sheikh Abdullah Al-Sabah. During Al-Sabah's tenure from 1950 to 1965, Kuwait became an affluent and influential independent country.

Trade declined sharply in Kuwait from the 1920s onward due to the worldwide recession, reducing the importance of the country as a major commercial link in the 20th century. In the 1950s and 1960s, however, Kuwait underwent a transition from a small emirate to an internationally influential modern state because of the oil boom.

RELIGION AND CLASS

The majority of Kuwaiti nationals are Sunni Muslims; the minority are Shia. Figures have never been published on the number of Shia, but estimates in the 1980s ranged from 15% to 25% of the population. The Shia are diverse—some are descendants of immigrants from Ash Sharqiyah (Eastern Province) in Saudi Arabia or from Bahrain. Other Shia come from Arab families who moved from the Arabian side of the gulf to Iran, stayed awhile, and then returned to Kuwait. Still others are of Iranian origin and often speak Farsi as well as Arabic at home and maintain business or family ties with Iranians across the gulf.

After the Iranian Revolution of 1979 and the subsequent Iran-Iraq War from 1980 to 1988, the Shia community experienced a renewed sense of sectarian identification. The identification resulted from sympathy with their revolutionary coreligionists in Iran and from increasing government and social discrimination. During the 1980s, the tension between Sunnis and Shia, which had erupted occasionally in the past, became sharper.

Kuwaitis are also divided to a certain extent along class lines. Although the national population is generally well off because of generous state employment policies and social services for nationals, important divisions nonetheless exist between the economic elite and the rest of the population. The wealthiest Kuwaitis are members either of the ruling family or of what was once a powerful merchant class. Many of these are descendants of the Bani Utub, the original central Arabian tribe that settled Kuwait in the 18th century. The most important and wealthiest of the Bani Utub are members of the Al-Sabah, the ruling family of Kuwait. The economic elite are largely Sunni. However, some Shia families are also wealthy.

Despite these internal divisions, the population is also characterized by a strong sense of national identity. There are no key ethnic divisions; the national population is overwhelmingly Arab. The major sectarian divisions are subsumed in the larger shared Islamic identity. And unlike many of its neighbors, Kuwait is not a 20th-century colonial fabrication—it has been an autonomous political and social unit since the 18th century. In the intervening years, a strong sense of local identity has arisen. This sense of national unity was deeply reinforced by the Iraqi occupation in 1990 and 1991.

FAMILY

Kuwaitis tend to have strong attachments to their families. Houses are designed to show little to the outside world, and they often have a nearby structure, called a *diwaniyya*, for receiving guests. Men spend much of their evenings in the diwaniyyas with friends and associates while women stay inside the house. In large part because cultural life is centered on home and diwaniyya, there are few theaters or other places of public entertainment. Recently, however, shopping malls have become a prominent social meeting place.

<u>USING RESOURCES IN KUWAIT</u>

Cultural information such as that provided in the previous sections should be the starting point of anyone wanting to consult in another country. The ability to relate and develop rapport is greatly enhanced through knowledge of historical and cultural information. However, it is important to confirm that information with a few nationals with whom you feel comfortable. I have found that historical information is generally presented with a political slant, and if a

This shopping mall in Kuwait exemplifies shoppers' wealth and provides a social meeting place for families.

© Walter Bibikow/age fotostock

book talked about, for example, how the country you are working in was aggressive and militaristic during the 18th century, you would do best to learn about the local take on that history.

Another valuable resource, if you can find it, is other expatriates who have preceded you and who are assimilated to some extent into the local culture. During my time in Kuwait, one of my greatest sources of information was an African American physical education teacher and coach. Omar had played Division III basketball and was a good coach. Furthermore, he had converted to Islam and was able to help me with the cultural and religious nuances whenever I needed advice.

The following is pieced together from conversations we had during the first 3 months I was in Kuwait. These questions helped both of us. Because Omar had already been in Kuwait for 3 years before my arrival, I wanted him to tell me more about how

the religion and culture would influence sport psychology, and he wanted to use my services.

- *Shaun Galloway (SG): What did you have to do differently from coaching in the States to coach here in Kuwait?*

- Omar (O): In the States it was assumed that scheduled practices were not to be missed barring a legitimate excuse. Moreover, players would be on time. Every so often, any player who violated this rule would run the risk of some sort of consequence. In Kuwait, I found out early that to survive as a coach here, I would have to go with the flow in regard to players missing practices and coming late. Oftentimes, practices and even games take a back seat to whatever cultural activity the players are engaged in.

- *SG: What does it mean to go with the flow? Give me an example.*

- O: The flow is determined from the culture. For example, during Ramadan there are two conflicting views with regard to activity. The first is that life should continue as usual and that fasting challenges us and makes us stronger. Some even believe that you should become more active. However, others believe that you should conserve energy and be thoughtful about why you are fasting. The two contradictory views either work for a sporting team during Ramadan or they do not. In this case, going with the flow involves flexibility. You will have half the athletes at training and half not. Then you take into consideration that training cannot be as strenuous.

- *SG: What areas in sport psychology could be problematic for Islamic athletes?*

- O: In terms of motivation, some things would be problematic in an Islamic society. For example, many athletes use music as a motivational tool. We see this in many different sport venues, such as during boxing matches and basketball games. In an Islamic society, music is considered forbidden by many Muslims. If you come across a Muslim athlete who is diligent in his Islamic practices, he would most likely refuse to listen to any music.

- *SG: Can you think of any other main areas that might cause a problem—for example, the concept of self-actualization?*

- O: Well, self-actualization is definitely a problem. We believe that our God determines our future. Certainly we are to do our best, but believing that we can determine our own destiny is not something that should be considered. It would be bad for a sport psychologist to follow that route.

I found this information useful. For instance, some athletes used music before games, which posed a problem with some of the parents. To resolve this problem, we asked the athletes who were allowed to use music to only listen to it in the locker room.

- *SG: What do you think a sport psychologist can add to a sport team in Kuwait?*

- O: He could possibly assist teams in methods of relaxation. However, being that Kuwait is an Islamic society, he would need to be careful of what types of relaxation methods he recommends. The psychologist would be smart to do his homework in regard to the Kuwaiti culture before working with Kuwaiti athletes. This way he would have an idea as to what may be considered offensive and what may be considered suitable.

- *SG: What would be an example of proper relaxation in Kuwaiti society?*

- O: I think that the deep diaphragmatic breathing that you mentioned along with personal meditation (similar to our prayer) would be acceptable. It is normal to us, just a few differences in the breathing. The physical differences are acceptable reasons for using this type of relaxation. I'm not sure, but I believe hypnosis is not an acceptable form because there is something about losing control. I am not really sure, but that is an answer in itself. If it's questionable, then get more answers. So I would say stay away from hypnosis.

- *SG: How would you advise a sport psychologist find out more information? What sources would be best?*

- O: Well, I think that talking to a religious scholar or leader is a useful investment in time. I also think finding someone who is not Islamic and has lived in the country for at least 3 years would also be a useful source of information. Then I would use the Internet. I think that the best information I can give is that if you are in doubt, get a second opinion and a third opinion on any questionable actions.

In the whirlwind that was my first 3 months in Kuwait, I learned a great deal, in no small part due to the conversations that I had with Omar. I can't think of a better resource—someone from a similar culture who played sport, coached sport, and knew the country and the religion. Nevertheless, I was always looking for different views and I followed Omar's suggestion, contacting Islamic scholars and expats with experience. It worked well and I can say that I made it through my time in Kuwait without committing a cultural or religious mistake that offended. This was not always the case in other countries where I lived. My guess is that my previous expatriate experience prepared me well for Kuwait.

CROSS-CULTURAL EXCHANGES

In North America, introductions could be characterized by their slow pace and formality. However, I found that this was not the situation in Kuwait. The Kuwaiti athletes were straightforward, and it did not take long to develop open relationships. This proved to be both positive and negative. On the one hand, I could get to the source of a matter quickly and efficiently. On the other hand, I had to protect against this comfort because I was still learning what was OK and what was not acceptable for interventions.

INITIAL INTERVENTION

From my first day in Kuwait, the athletes were curious about everything: my understanding of sport, my country, my province, my city, and just what sport psychology was all about. Automatically, the athletes would assume that I was from the United States. When I told them that I was from Canada, opinions would change. I found that there were two prominent views on Americans: neutral or very positive. The opinion of Canadians was that they were the peaceful, polite neighbor of the United States. This set the basis for the intake meeting and introduction to sport psychology.

Though in most cases the Canadian stereotype of being nice was a positive start to the athlete–sport psychologist relationship, there were times when it posed a problem. One example was an ongoing situation that involved both the coaches and the athletes. The athletes wanted my opinions about how a Canadian coach would do things as opposed to the largely American coaching staff. My answer in every situation was that coaches are the same all over the world: Their philosophy determines the way that they handle a situation. Then the athletes would usually ask me what a Canadian coach with a performance-based philosophy would do in a certain situation. Sometimes I just had to plead that there was no clear answer to the question.

First Meeting represents a typical initial consultation with an athlete based on my experiences. Mohammed was a 16-year-old high school athlete who played on both the varsity football (soccer) team and volleyball team. Similar to most Kuwaiti athletes

I met, Mohammed was forward in his conversation. I had met him before with some of his fellow athletes at a diwaniyya, though we had little conversation. Apparently it was enough to get hit with blunt questions fairly quickly in our first real meeting.

Depending on time constraints, in first encounters I define sport psychology and what sport psychologists can do, and more to the point, what I can do. However, in this instance, the athlete was a leader on his team and would be a sounding board for most future contact with the team as well as the sport club. With that in mind, I needed a general idea of what the Kuwaiti athletes thought of sport psychologists and the roles that I might play; thus the probing. I ran into a sticky situation when I mentioned that you need to factor out physical and skill requirements before looking at the mental game as a problem, and I tried to diffuse the situation by redirecting to two other possibilities. The first was that I did not see the physical training conducted during practices, and the second was that individual performance is hard to measure in a team sport. I had heard of coaches in Kuwait who were relieved from coaching when a sport science expert had informed an athlete that the coach had some possible deficiencies. With that knowledge in mind, I filed the problem away with the intent of talking to the coach and then later with the athlete. It was definitely a potential tinderbox.

First Meeting

Mohammed (M): So, I heard you are from Canada?
Shaun Galloway (SG): Yes, originally, but it has been 14 years since I lived there.
M: Really? Why, I have lots of cousins living over there and they love it. I have heard it is cold.
SG: Well, it can be. It is definitely a lot colder than here.
M: So I came by to ask you what a sport psychologist is and what you are going to do for me.
SG: Well, Mohammed, what do you think a sport psychologist is?

From observing school classes and talking to the teachers, this approach to questions and answers seemed to be the most efficient way to communicate in a challenge-of-knowledge situation. I have found the process of watching teachers communicate with their students to be a valuable way of getting a feel for how to communicate with the student-athletes in other countries.

M: I'm not really sure. That's why I asked you.
SG: *(Waits for him to continue.)*

M: If I had to guess, I would say that a sport psychologist helps athletes when they have a bad performance so that they don't mess up again.
SG: That could be one of the things that a sport psychologist does. What else do think a sport psychologist could do?
M: I also know that they help you with your mental game. I am not too sure what that means. Could you tell me what that means?
SG: It's different for everyone, but when athletes are in good physical condition and have well-learned skills but are not able to compete to the best of their potential, it could be that some aspect of their mental game needs to be revised.
M: That makes a lot of sense to me. The coach is always blaming the team for the lack of our mental game, but I think that we don't have good physical training.
SG: I wouldn't know about that. I haven't seen your training, but the only way to be sure is to be tested physically. Another possibility that comes up in team sport is the team and how people work together. We may need to explore this at a later time.
M: Anyway, what can you do to help me?
SG: That depends on what you want help for.

Initially, I continued the approach of turning questions back to the questioners to learn how they were thinking and what they really meant. It took me 3 or 4 months before I starting trying various approaches to see if they had better efficacy. Though individualization of the approach was essential (as it is with every encounter), the direct approach was most often the best one during my tenure in Kuwait.

M: I can't seem to concentrate as well as I used to be able to. Could you help me with concentration?
SG: Well, the good news is that if you used to be able to concentrate in the past, it shouldn't be too hard to learn how to find your concentration again!

Communication Clarity

In every country I have lived in, I have noticed one consistent variable that determines the success of any expatriate: the ability to communicate. It sounds like common sense, but in this case I am not only talking about the language but the metacommunication (i.e., tone, pace, and body language), which has a profound effect on the communication process. I have met many expatriates who have learned roughly 15% of the language yet seem to communicate at nearly 100%.

This division of communication problems into technical, semantic, and effectiveness levels is the basis for a communication cleaning intervention that I have used in other countries to help foreign coaches (usually whose first language is English). An Intervention on Communication Cleaning briefly conveys how I used this intervention with a coach in Kuwait and how it fits into the Shannon and Weaver framework. This communication intervention was used for a U14 (under 14 years of age) basketball team and their American coach, who had been coaching for 8 years. The team was in the Kuwait private school league.

During my time in Kuwait, the communication cleaning strategy usually worked well. Some athletes, however, didn't like it. Though it was hard to figure out exactly why, it seemed that if the words that the coach used were clearly defined, the athlete would then be confronted with clear parameters that were to be kept, and some found it scary to have to deal with that kind of responsibility. A related possibility is that I experienced a tendency in Kuwaiti culture to avoid completely clear communication as a means of ensuring that one could not be found at fault for not following instructions to the letter.

Whatever the reason for resistance to communication cleaning, I found that when I dropped the terms the coach was using and changed the focus to actions developed through a communication cleaning intervention that was not labeled as such, the athletes generally accepted this solution. For example, when the coach and the team used the term *mental toughness*, they came to a group definition that focused on specific defensive actions: "Mental toughness is the ability to focus on defensive discipline no matter how tired we are." From this definition came two general actions for the team. Definition 1 was, "Mental toughness is the ability to come back on defense and catch the closest unmarked player ahead of you no matter how far ahead of you they are!" Definition 2 was, "Mental toughness is being aware of your defensive spacing and making sure you are able to rotate quickly to help fill the gap in defense." The team then went on to define mentally tough actions for each offensive and defensive position.

AN INTERVENTION ON COMMUNICATION CLEANING

Shaun Galloway (SG): How are you doing, Coach?
Coach (C): Pretty good. I liked the coaching psychology seminar today. You mentioned that you've done

some work with helping the communication process. I was wondering if you could walk me through that process.
SG: Sure. Let's pick three words you use all the time that might be misunderstood.
C: Well, that could be most of what comes out of my mouth, but I think the big three are *pride, trust,* and *heart.*
SG: Those are some fairly complex words; I can see how they could be misunderstood. OK, now that you have them, do you use them more in certain circumstances?
C: Hmm, I'm not sure if I do.
SG: How about situations such as offense and defense?
C: Actually, I use *pride* for both situations, *trust* more often for offensive situations, and *heart* for defensive situations. Now that I think of it, I use all three much more when we're behind in the score, and I use all three lots during training.
SG: OK, so now we have a lot of situations. What I want you to do is to have a team meeting and ask the players what these words mean to them. It's best to have them write it out on paper. After you've done that, give your definition for each one followed by three or four of the athletes' definitions. The goal is to come up with some sort of group definition.
C: So where does the situational information come in?
SG: You're quick! That would be the next line of questioning. You can ask them if the definition would change due to the environment. For example, does the word *pride* mean the same thing to the athletes when they are performing well as opposed to when they are falling short? Again, redefine and try to find a group consensus.

This first phase involved resolving the problems at the technical and semantic level across a number of predetermined domains. The next phase involved developing the effectiveness level.

SG: This may take some time and doesn't have to be completed during one meeting. You may also find it hard to get total agreement, but somewhere around 90% is good. If it's less than that, then the next phase usually helps bring everybody under the same umbrella. What you'll then do is ask your athletes how they would actualize each definition. How would they put that word into actions for each situation? Then go through the same steps. Again, you may not reach a specific action for each term due to positional differences and roles, but the terms will start to gain some momentum both for yourself and your athletes.

C: Hey, wow. I can see it now. So when I use these words there's an idea of what each one means as well as what an athlete needs to do to meet the requirements of the word.

SG: That's right. I'm not sure if communication is ever really 100% clear but the exercise should go a ways toward getting the results that you and your athletes want.

Spirituality Versus Self-Actualization

One of my major concerns coming to Kuwait was the ability to be culturally sensitive and more specifically, religiously sensitive. I had been long aware of the possible friction between religion and the tendency for sport psychology to focus on self-actualization, a concept reinforced by Watson and Czech (2005). Crust (2006) noted that "most sport psychology consultants (promoting self-regulation and internal control) are diametrically opposed to spiritual practices where faith is placed outside of the self" (p. 1).

Contrary to Watson and Czech's (2005) suggestions for integration of spirituality into sport psychology practice, it was my experience that awareness and sensitivity were of much more use than integration. I would never be able to understand Kuwaiti Islamic traditions, and as a result it was much better to leave spirituality to the religious scholars or imam. (The term *imam* can have various meanings, especially between Shia and Sunni interpretations, but for my purposes an imam is a religious leader, though not necessarily a cleric.) I confirmed this impression with the religious authorities in charge of the school and those who had an interest in the sport club where I worked. In both cases their primary concern was that sport and learning how to be better at it (physical and mental training) should not get in the way of prayer times. Although spirituality was always a concern, during my time in Kuwait it was sensitivity as well as common sense that served me best. Though it had never happened to me or anybody I knew, I had heard about a school teacher who had been misinterpreted while engaging in a religious conversation and ended up being dismissed. The dismissal was due in part to a lack of understanding of the culture, as well as misguided exploration with nonreligious leaders about religion.

Working With Teams

I chose the examples in this section for their ability to highlight some of the differences between working with teams in North America and working with teams in Kuwait. For example, in North America, I would not normally put myself in the situation of potential role conflict by being both a coach and a sport psychologist.

Unconventional Combination: Coach and Sport Psychologist

I performed a lot of jobs while I was in Kuwait, and one of them was coaching a boy's U16 (under 16 years of age) volleyball team in the Kuwait club championship. Prior to becoming a sport psychologist, I had always emphasized psychological skills; however, after my training I would generally find a sport psychologist to run that part of the program because I did not want problems with role clarity. In Kuwait, however, I could not assign sport psychology to someone else for two reasons: I did not know of any other sport psychologists in Kuwait, and it was a skill that I was hired for. So I had to be the sport psychologist as well as the coach.

The first thing I wanted to do was to make sure the athletes understood that the sport psychology sessions were not compulsory and that they would not gain or lose playing time depending on their attendance. I did mention that similar to extra conditioning, sport psychology could benefit them and their ability to compete against other teams in the conference. The next step I wanted to take was to use techniques that could be easily integrated and that would be useful outside of sport as well.

The first session was a brief introduction to sport psychology and what it might be able to offer. The athletes were fairly open and there was less apprehension than I thought there would be. From there, I told the athletes that I would be going through two skills. The first was how to set goals and the second was how to develop values into actions. A few of the athletes had done goal setting previously and looked as if they were not looking forward to learning about it again. I quickly asked if they would help those who had never done goal setting before, and this seemed to work. However, when I mentioned turning values into action, I got blank looks from the team as a whole. We explored the idea of values but without much progress. It was at this point that I decided to bring up religion. I asked them to think of the main principles of their religion and indicated that they would find values in their religious principles. From their numerous examples, I chose to examine humility. I asked them how they would act with humility. Again, there was not a lot of involvement, so I created various scenarios and we came up with action points. The one that resonated most was that after they scored a service ace, they would turn and wink at the server rather than come together in a circle and yell out "Ace!" (the usual celebration for a service ace).

DEVELOPING TEAM DYNAMICS

The dynamics of any team can be complicated to say the least, but Kuwait definitely offered unique difficulties. The teams that I worked with ranged from high school international teams (usually comprising embassy children and Kuwaiti elite) to teams with only Kuwaiti athletes (teams that sometimes revolved around tribal hierarchy as well as religious differences between Sunni and Shia). Using Carron and Hausenblaus' (1998) framework for cohesion, I will discuss some of the differences and similarities that I found when working with Kuwaiti athletes, beginning with the coach's first contact with me regarding the team. According to the framework, cohesion is made up of social and task goals related to the team and to the individual. The focus of this section is the U14 basketball team mentioned in the previous section on communication cleaning. See Team Building for a description of my experiences.

It seemed that most of the team building program had some effect. On review, there seemed to be no negative results and some baby steps were taken. Though I had lived in four countries up to this time, nothing had prepared me for Kuwait. I had relatives who worked in the Middle East, but the experience is hard to put into words. The environment alone is something to be experienced and words alone do not compare to experiencing 45° Celsius weather, or a sand storm, or 35° with 98% humidity while trying to do some sort of sport activity. With that in mind, I was still feeling my way around social interventions, and I was pleased with my first attempt.

Later in the season, the team had been doing well enough to make the final-four championships. The tournament was seeded where team 1 played 4 and 2 played 3. The winners played for first and second and the other teams played for third. Understandably the athletes were nervous about their upcoming matches. The coach asked if I could come in and help the team focus. I pointed out to him—as politely as I could—that sport psychology skills are similar to physical skills. You need to practice them or else they will not be usable, especially during stressful times. He responded by letting me know that anything I could do on such short notice would be appreciated. Prepping for a Crucial Game describes the preteam meeting before the first match.

IDENTITY AND VALUES

In the beginning, most of my time in Kuwait was spent trying to figure out what approach would work best. As is the case for most situations, there was no one approach that I could generalize. However, one framework seemed to recur many times during my tenure in Kuwait. Brown, Cairns, and Botterill (2001) called it *perspective*. At the time I was not aware of the model, but I was using most of the components to deal with a wide range of athletes and their situations. Brown and colleagues suggested that perspective consists of three components: identity, support, and values. Most of my work could be classified under developing identity and values. Support was rarely a problem, though there were times where guardians would show more support for academics than for athletics. In most cases, a short meeting with the athlete and the parents to talk about priorities resolved any shortcomings. I had many informal chats with student-athletes about developing both identity and values. See Establishing Identity and Values and also Exploring Roles for descriptions of meetings that I had with a 14-year-old high school student over the course of a basketball season playing in the Kuwait national club league and the Kuwait private school league.

There were a few areas that I needed to address in future meetings. The first was that Ahmed's passions seemed to border on obsession. Possibly we could work on refocusing obsession into a calculated focus. The second area for concern was peer pressure. This was an area for future examination because it could be connected to his identity as an athlete. The final area was that Ahmed was able to transfer his mastery skill to other areas of his life, indicating that positive transference should be possible. Many Kuwaitis aspire to own their own business if they don't already have a couple of businesses in the family. A recent trend has been the younger generation wanting to start their own businesses regardless of how many family businesses already exist. This was the case for Ahmed.

TEAM BUILDING

Coach (C): Hi, I was wondering if I could talk to you about developing more of a team atmosphere. We train OK but we're not really a team.

Shaun Galloway (SG): Sure. What do you want in terms of a team?

C: Well, I would like us to be closer. When things are going well we are fairly OK, but when we have a misstep or two then we become a group of individuals with no real focus.

SG: Do you think that has anything to do with team goals or is it that the team doesn't know each other very well?

C: Maybe a little of both. I know that I have set out team goals, but I'm not too sure that the team has really bought into them. I know that's important, but when I try to talk about goals in more depth, the team politely suggests that it is my decision and that they would like to get on to physical training. As far as being social, I think that most of them hang out and do other stuff than just play ball, but I do get the feeling that there are two separate camps.

Here I used the two basic groupings—task and social domains. It appeared that both areas were lacking. The fact that the coach had addressed the concept of buying into the goals was interesting but daunting. Certainly, personality and communication deficiencies could be attributed to the coach and could be the reason why the team didn't want to talk about goals. However, the players' statement proposing that he was the decision maker and that they would do what he told them to was important and definitely needed further exploration. My experience with education in Kuwait had shown me that the Kuwaiti population puts a big emphasis on education and a lot of trust in the educator. I had often heard parents tell their children that they should listen to the teacher without question.

SG: Well, Coach, it sounds like you have a few situations that could be resolved. I'm going to talk you through a couple of suggestions that might make a difference, and then after a couple weeks we can meet again to hear what you have to say. Would that be OK with you?

Most of the time I work this way because the coach usually has developed a good relationship with the team and thus is better able to communicate freely with the athletes compared with a sport psychologist, who has a limited relationship with the athletes.

In this case the team-building program was a good option because the coach had some experience with sport psychology in his undergraduate studies. The team-building program consisted of learning about each other's religions (similarities and differences), tribal customs, personal goals, how the personal goals connect to the team goals, differences in language and dialect, and an exercise in defining key sporting words used by the coach (as mentioned in the communication section). We met again 2 weeks later.

SG: So, how are things developing with the team?

C: Well, I think we are becoming stronger as a team. I still don't think we are really clear on the goals, but defining the terminology that I use has been really useful because a lot of the terms are part of the team goals. Most of my goals are philosophical and built on character, so in a way I guess we're moving in the right direction.

SG: How about the social aspects?

C: Again, I'm not sure how useful the social part of the team building went. When we did it, there was a lot of quiet and it took a big effort to get anything done. It was very awkward. From the results of the last game, I would say that there was less friction between subgroups and more of a team effort. I suppose that's positive, but I think we have a long way to go with the social development.

SG: Would you like me to come and see what I can do?

C: No, right now I like the idea of letting the athletes consider the information for a few days and then seeing if things improve.

SG: All right, that may be the best idea. Let me know if you want to talk about anything. Oh, hey Coach, just like when you defined the words with working actions, how about you put into actions what it means for your team to be social or not and at the level you want them to be?

C: That's a good idea. I'll make up my list and see how it goes over the next week or so.

PREPPING FOR A CRUCIAL GAME

Shaun Galloway (SG): Hi. I've been really enjoying your season so far. It's a really big accomplishment to make the final four in your first year in the league! You must all be really proud.

Team athlete 1 (TA1): Yeah, I never realized how much we had done until now.

Team athlete 2 (TA2): But it will be really disappointing if we don't win.

SG: What do you guys think?

(Silence.)

SG: Well, being successful can be measured in many ways, but one of the ways that I think is most important is that your team has been successful at walking the walk.

TA1: What do you mean?

SG: I mean that your team has values and that you know how to show those values on the court: pride, trust, and heart.

TA2: We do that stuff as best we can.

SG: And it is that stuff that I want you to focus on when you take to the court. Everyone has expectations, and sometimes those expectations can be blown up pretty big so that seeing what is most important is hard to do. I think that Coach and your team have done something special this year. Results are just one part of it. Your team has values, and if you keep your eyes on those values, then you should be able to do your best on the court. What do you think about that?

TA1: I think that's going to help, but we need to figure out a way to not forget about our values.

TA2: Hey, what if we made four signs on each side of each half with our values on them so that we can always see them?

SG: There you go. That's an outstanding idea! Let's finish the session with a big poster-building exercise.

Establishing Identity and Values

Shaun Galloway (SG): Hi, Ahmed, how are you doing today?

Ahmed (A): Pretty good, but I'm thinking about what I am going to do this coming summer. I think I want to go to a basketball camp in Canada or the States.

SG: That's a pretty big trip. Is your family going?

A: No, just me. They want me to ask you where I should go.

SG: That depends on you. What do you want to accomplish?

A: Well, I want to play basketball against good players and get a chance to be seen. I've been thinking about trying to get a scholarship.

Ahmed had been playing basketball for only a year, and though he was a hard worker, he was only 5 feet, 6 inches (168 centimeters) tall, with modest physical and technical skills. To complicate things further, Ahmed had bought into the basketball subculture. He was basketball. It was more than a sport for him. I didn't think it was my place to bring him back to reality, but I wanted him to have an

experience that added to his development holistically so that he could benefit no matter what the results. The dialogue that follows started about 5 minutes into the session.

SG: Ahmed, how do you view yourself?

A: I am ambitious; if I find something that I grow very fond of I pursue it until I have mastered it. I would not cross a line if I truly believed that it was wrong to cross; therefore I draw my own limits according to what I have experienced and what many other people have guided me toward (mostly parents). I am learning to be patient, at least in terms of the things that matter to me. As an example, I am a loyal friend; however, sometimes my peers can easily influence me. I occasionally do crazy stuff that has no real meaning. I also can be blinded by fun and as a result not see the consequences, but nothing extreme.

SG: So, you like to master your passions? Where else in life do you think this ability to pursue your passions might be useful?

A: I guess it could be useful if I found an area that I like to study. It would also be useful when I decide to get a job or start my own business.

Exploring Roles

Shaun Galloway (SG): What type of roles do you play in life?

Ahmed (A): I am known mostly for my basketball. I take pride being the all-around athlete of the year 5 years in a row. *(Ahmed had been on the national team for rifle shooting and had played football and track and field.)* After that, I would say some of the other roles I have are the friend, the average student, the eldest son, the bad boy, and the sensitive guy (but very few know that).

Here Ahmed has confirmed my suspicion of basketball playing a major role in his life. Some of the other roles appear to be the norm for the Kuwaiti student-athlete—friendship, student concerns, and being the eldest are all major factors in Kuwaiti life. The two areas that differ are the bad boy and sensitive guy. The bad boy seems to be related to the socioeconomic level of most Kuwaiti youth and the influence of teen movies. Teenage angst knows no cultural bounds, whether it is a result of real situations or manufactured, and both ends of the socioeconomic continuum have their share of bad boys. The role of sensitive guy is not one that is usually well received in a male-dominant society (and Kuwait is definitely such a society). Though I was fairly sure that the order that he listed his roles reflected the order of importance, there was a pos-

sibility that the first list was what others would want from him and that if I asked him his personal order, I would find that it differed. So I asked him.

SG: What importance do you give to each role?

A: I would put them in the following order: the friend, the basketball player, the athlete, the eldest son, the bad boy, the somewhat emotional guy, and the average student.

So there were differences, and I could explore them, focusing on personal and social perspectives. However, right now I was trying to create a holistic, interchangeable view of these roles. As a result, I decided to ask questions focusing on qualities, similarities, dissimilarities, and values.

SG: In each of those roles there are qualities that you need to be successful. What do you think are a few of those qualities?

A: The friend—knowing how to make you smile. The basketball player—ambition, fast decision making, goal seeking. The athlete—physically strong, being good at more than one thing. The eldest son—responsibility, problem organization. The bad boy—taking risks. The somewhat emotional guy—none that I can think of. The average student—organization of priorities, responsibility.

A number of qualities carried across the roles and would be useful for Ahmed to notice, so I followed up with a question about distinguishing similarities and dissimilarities.

SG: What are their similarities and dissimilarities? Compare your roles and the qualities against each other. For example, is decision making the quality of a good basketball player but also a quality of a good student?

A: The average student and the eldest son roles both have the quality of organization and responsibility. Also as a team captain in two sports, responsibility has a role. Risk taking could also be related to sport, mostly basketball, with taking risks to win, but on the other hand playing it safe sometimes is beneficial. I believe their dissimilarities are obvious.

SG: Are there also differences between the characteristics?

A: Well, responsibility and risk taking can be different.

SG: Give me an example.

A: In terms of responsibility, I sometimes consider others, and with risk taking, I usually just worry about what I want. My risks usually involve myself, and my responsibilities concern more than myself.

SG: I think that is a really useful differentiation.

I thought about rejoining with how risk and responsibility could also be interchangeable in regards to their focus. However, I decided to let Ahmed digest this point rather than add to the thought processing. I went on with examining values. Since the coach and I had worked on an understanding of value, I had hoped that the concept would be more easily understood. However, I noted to myself that values and qualities could possibly be understood as synonymous.

SG: What type of values do you need for each of those roles?

ISSUES AND STRATEGIES TO CONSIDER WHEN WORKING WITH ATHLETES IN KUWAIT

Although Kuwait is the focus of these considerations, many of them would apply to other Islamic athletes as well.

- Get many different points of view. The most important points of view come from the police and religious authorities. Err on the conservative side.
- Be careful with giving advice outside your area of expertise and take into consideration the ramifications of such advice.
- The speed with which a relationship can be developed in Kuwait may be different from the norm in Western society. Being unprepared for this situation can lead to problems.
- Consider turning questions back to the questioners to learn their points of view.
- Be aware of the potential friction between religion and the tendency for sport psychology to focus on self-actualization.

A: That's a hard one. I think that an athlete needs commitment and dedication. A friend needs loyalty, trustworthiness, and honesty. Playing sports taught me fairness, giving everyone a chance. I think I would also need that for being the eldest son. For being a student, I was respectful to others older than me.

I felt pretty confident that Ahmed had started to understand that roles, values, and qualities are interchangeable and that his total dedication to sport had given him skills that were transferable across all the roles and into new contexts. Next, I asked him how he viewed the roles with respect to his peers. Again, I did not make apparent to Ahmed the differences between his personal views and those of his significant others. My relationship with Ahmed was fairly good, and I had learned that he did best when he could think about matters on his own.

SG: To those who know you in each of those roles, what importance do you think they give to your role? In other words, if you were to ask your friends, family, teachers, and coaches, what order would they put them in?

A: That's hard because I have to include all the people I know and I think that some of them have different opinions of me. But if I had to make a list, this would be the list: the friend, the basketball player, the athlete, the eldest son, the somewhat emotional guy, the average student, and the bad boy.

SG: All right Ahmed, I think we had a really good session. What do you think?

A: I definitely learned a lot about myself. I didn't know I had so many roles!

CONCLUSIONS AND FUTURE DIRECTIONS

The speed with which a relationship can be developed in Kuwait needs to be considered; it is different from the norm in Western society. Being unprepared for this situation can lead to problems. Regardless, my time in Kuwait was one of my most interesting and challenging experiences. I went from a relaxed approach to a more abrupt—maybe even aggressive—style due to what I had learned from fellow teachers. I found that communication cleaning was a useful tool for both sport psychology and bridging the gap of cross-cultural understanding. I also decided after speaking to my sources that it was best to not involve spirituality during my sessions but rather be sensitive to it. The team-building sessions ran relatively well, but I would have needed to understand about tribal and intra-Islamic differences before applying a proper team-building program. My individual sessions with Ahmed were successful, and 4 years later, Ahmed has used his sport experience in all areas of his life. Finally, and maybe most importantly, I believe that knowing the country, traditions, and religion is the key to a successful transition in a country that has many differences from one's own.

One final note that I would like to make regards women sport psychologists and women in sport in Kuwait. During my time in Kuwait, there was sport for Islamic women. However, it was always pursued out of the sight of men. At the time a couple of sport and fitness clubs were being built for women in Kuwait City. I had conversations with some Kuwaitis about women's sport on an international level, and the response I received was that it would most likely not happen because women are expected to wear modest clothing in public settings, which would make participation in elite sport problematic. I am not entirely sure if this is the official word, but it was what was explained to me.

Another question pertaining to gender is whether a woman sport psychologist could be employed in Kuwait. There are many American schools throughout the Middle East, and many are affluent. Most of these schools are under the auspices of the American embassy and have an international student body. I could see where sport psychologists—men or women—would be able to at least work with their own gender. In addition, a number of high-performance sport clubs are opening throughout the Middle East. One such club in Qatar, called *Aspire*, has a full sport science support team, but I believe that there are no women on the team. Women's sport and the position of female sport psychologists in Kuwait are currently both uncertain topics.

Another important area for future inquiry would be a formal conversation with both Sunni and Shia religious leaders to talk about which areas of sport psychology would be acceptable and which areas would not be acceptable. I tried to get a detailed answer to this question, but I never got any information of which I could be certain. From discussions with Omar and the leaders with whom I did speak, I concluded that supporting self-actualization would not be a good idea.

It is my hope that this chapter will help future sport psychologists successfully navigate sport psychology services in Arabic countries (or at least Kuwait) and that some of the principles and concepts presented may be useful wherever sport psychology is practiced. See Issues and Strategies to Consider When Working With Athletes in Kuwait for a quick review of questions to explore in working not only with Kuwaitis but with other Islamic athletes as well.

WORKING WITH NIGERIAN ATHLETES

P.B. Ikulayo, PhD, and J.A. Semidara, MEd

In this chapter we introduce Nigerian culture. The chapter begins with a brief description of Nigerian history and geography. We then consider several customs of Nigeria and their variations. After the introduction of sport development and the role of sport in Nigeria, we discuss the influence of Nigerian customs on sport participation and performance. Although the use of sport psychology techniques and services is not widely accepted in Nigeria, examples of its successful introduction in sport situations are provided.

NIGERIAN CONTEXT

Before getting into the specifics of sport and sport psychology, it is useful to consider the history, geography, and customs of Nigeria. The country is diverse, with a variety of languages, religions, food, and dress.

HISTORY AND GEOGRAPHY

Although today Nigeria is a well-established country of roughly 140 million people, it was divided into distinct northern and southern regions before the arrival of European explorers and Christian missionaries in the 15th and 16th centuries. Between 1851 and 1918, the British systematically colonized the region. The northern and southern protectorates were combined into a single political entity in 1914 by Sir Frederick Lugard, the first governor general. This joining of the protectorates resulted in three regions—the Northern, Eastern, and Western Regions (Kukuru, 1997). British colonization lasted until October 1960, when Nigeria gained independence. Three years later, Nigeria became a republic.

The people of Nigeria originated from the Niger-Congo, Afro-Asiatic, and Nilo-Saharan groups, which have cultural characteristics indicative of the Western, Northern, and Eastern Regions, respectively. Sir Lord Lugard's wife, Flora, coined the name *Nigeria* from "Niger area" because of the country's proximity to the Niger River. The three regions have been split into six geopolitical zones comprising 36 states plus the Federal Capital Territory, Abuja, which is administered as a state but with a minister or a governor. Every geopolitical zone is under the administration of the federal government. At present, Nigeria is made up of more than 250 distinct social and ethnic groups (Kukuru, 1996).

European explorers invested a great deal of time, energy, and resources in opening up the Niger River for the trans-Atlantic slave trade. After the abolition of the slave trade, Portuguese trade merchants entered the hinterlands to trade in palm produce. British interest in Nigeria gained momentum after the abolition of the slave trade and its replacement by trade in palm produce in the 1930s and 1940s (Kukuru, 1996).

NATIVE ATTIRE AND FOODS

In some northern states of Nigeria, traditional attire for men includes the *babariga*, a long, flowing shirt that covers from the neck to the feet, and matching caps. Men also often wear long shorts. Women wear different dresses for everyday wear and for ceremonial occasions. In most cases, they wear dresses that cover almost every part of the body (especially Muslim women), and they also wear head ties that leave only the face exposed.

The southern states are home to greater variety in attire. In the states of Bayelsa, Rivers, and Delta, the men wear bowler hats, flowing shirts called *amayanabo*, and trousers, and the women wear wrappers around skirts, blouses, and head ties. Yoruba women wear a *buba*, a blouse with wide and long sleeves that covers the arms except the hands, on top of an *iro*, a cloth wrapper. They also wear a head tie, as well as necklaces and bangles.

During the opening and closing ceremonies of national sport festivals such as the Nigerian University Games and the Nigeria Polytechnic Games, it is customary for athletes and officials to wear their traditional dress in order to showcase their culture. The attire serves as a medium for comparing the diverse cultural heritages of the country, encourages those who are interested to copy different styles, and fosters a spirit of cooperation and integration.

The various ethnic groups in Nigeria also eat different foods. Among the Ibos, the native food is *akpu* (ground cassava, fermented and later boiled to dry). The native food of the Yorubas includes *iyan*, or pounded yam; *ewedu* soup (made from sliced or shredded green vegetables) and ground melon; and *egusi*, or vegetable soup. The Hausas and Fulanis, who traditionally raise cattle, mainly consume dairy products called *tuwo shikafa*. The Ijaws (Izon) are customarily known for soup made with fresh palm oil *(pilofiyah)* that is eaten with plantain, yam, or cassava. The regional differences in cuisine mean that athletes may need to adapt to changes in diet when traveling around Nigeria for competitions, not to mention internationally.

In the southern part of Nigeria, including the Delta Region, occupations include blacksmithing and carving iron, brass, ivory, and wood. The carvers produce beautiful ornaments, bells, lamp holders, doors, and pillars, and blacksmiths make cutlasses, knives, hoes, and shovels. Agriculture involves the production of cash and food crops. Some of the cash crops are cotton, rubber, cassava, and cocoa, and food crops include pepper, potatoes, tomatoes, and palm oil. Occupations in the northern part of Nigeria include agriculture, metalwork, weaving, dyeing, woodwork, pottery, and leatherwork. Agricultural products include millet, rice, and peanuts. In addition, dairy farming is common (Kukuru, 1996; Ogunniyi & Oboli, 2000). The national per capita income is $310 per year (www.nigeriabusinessinfo.com/opps.htm), which may spur people to pursue sport and the opportunities it provides.

Nigerian women often perform dances at opening and closing ceremonies of sports festivals to showcase Nigerian culture and dress.

© Liu Jin/AFP/Getty Images

Spiritual and Religious Orientation

Before the arrival of Christianity in the 15th and 16th centuries through Portuguese Catholic missionaries and the launching of Fulani jihad by Uthman Dan Fodio in 1841, traditional religion flourished. Diverse ethnic groups believed in the existence of a supreme being who created and owned all things animate and inanimate. Although they shared this common belief, Nigerians represented and worshipped God in different ways. Some worshipped through the river goddess Olokun and some through Sango, god of thunder. They believed that through these lesser gods and goddesses their prayers would reach the almighty God, and through these intermediaries God would grant their requests. Still today some people have faith in traditional religion and worship, and it is practiced in some parts of the country with worshipping at ancestral shrines (Ogunniyi & Oboli, 1996). Of course, this means that some athletes practice traditional religion.

With the arrival of Islam, many Northerners became Muslims. In the South, traditional religion also lost many followers with the arrival of Christianity. Nigeria now has three religions: Islam, Christianity, and traditional religion. Islam is dominant in the North, but Christianity has a considerable edge in the South, and traditional religion is practiced sparsely throughout the country.

The diverse ethnic groups of Nigeria endorse the existence of a supreme being (almighty God) from birth. Some ethnic groups worship God in churches, including Pentecostal, Orthodox Christian, and Cherubim and Seraphim churches. The worship of God is inculcated from an early age—parents bring their children to church to listen to teachings from the Bible, and thus the children become devoted Christians. Worship at the Cherubim and Seraphim Church involves a lot of music along with drumming, clapping, and dancing (Ogunniyi & Oboli, 1999). When the music reaches a frenzy, people speak in tongues by invoking the Holy Spirit. In most cases, the Cherubim and Seraphim wear white garments as their customary dress of worship. The Pentecostal and Orthodox churches also use music and clapping, but not as frequently. Pentecostal ministers and other church members who are spirit filled also speak in tongues and prophesy. Prayer is a vital aspect of the Christian belief system, with faith as a cardinal tenet of Christianity as a whole.

In the Islamic religion, norms are taught in mosques using the Koran under the guidance of imams and Islamic teachers. Imams are custodians of Islamic laws and norms and are knowledgeable in both the theory and practice of Islamic rites and functions in the day-to-day practice of Islam. Islamic teachers seek advice from imams when the occasion arises. Some of the most conservative Muslims do not allow women to take part in sport. The women in such households cover their faces with veils and seldom go out in public. If they do go out, their faces are fully covered and they wear flowing apparel that covers the body from the neck to the soles of the feet (Ogunniyi & Oboli, 2000). Muslims who practice this form of Islam tend to have an extremely negative attitude toward sport psychology.

Because of the almost universal Nigerian belief in the supremacy of God, most athletes profess faith and trust in God. Thus, many pray before serious competitions and also fast before the competition takes place in order to make their prayers effective. Many athletes believe that if they fast, God will answer their prayers and keep them from making mistakes.

Languages

Nigeria is home to more than 250 ethnic groups with distinct languages, but only three major languages—Hausa-Fulani, Yoruba, and Igbo—are nationally spoken and taught from primary school through university. Children are expected to learn at least one of the three major indigenous languages in school so that they will be able to communicate well and transact business in a language other than their mother tongue. In addition, the English language was brought to Nigeria by the British, who established it as the official language. The diverse athletes on a team are able to integrate well because they all have the ability to interact in pidgin, an adulterated form of English (see also chapter 15). Some state radio stations in Nigeria even read the news in pidgin in addition to their indigenous languages. The ability to communicate in English with people who have a different mother tongue fosters a spirit of tolerance, understanding, cooperation, and integration of the diverse ethnic groups to which athletes belong.

Family Structure

In Nigeria, the two main family structures are nuclear and extended families. Additionally, there are two types of marriages—monogamous and polygamous. The nuclear family includes a man, a wife or wives, and their children. The extended family is an extension of the nuclear family and consists of natal and conjugal families. The natal family is the family one is born into, and the conjugal family is the family in which one is a parent. Members of the extended family include aunts, uncles, cousins, nephews, nieces, grandfathers, grandmothers, stepsisters, stepbrothers, and stepmothers. The extended family can be simple when it originates from monogamous marriage and complex when it originates from polygamous marriage.

Another family structure is the compound family, which comprises the patrilineal and matrilineal families. The compound family consists of many families living in the same space, with the oldest man as the head of the compound. The patrilineal family is a family lineage based upon descendants in the male line and includes the extended family in the line of first, second, or third cousins, and the matrilineal family is the family lineage based upon descendants in the female line (Ikulayo, 2002). Some Christian denominations allow polygamous marriages, including the Cherubim and Seraphim and some Protestant denominations such as the First African Church. However, the Pentecostals discourage polygamy.

REALITIES OF NIGERIAN SPORT

Early participation in sport depends on some extent on children's level of education, their exposure to sport, their economic status, and their parents' interests. Parents need to provide any required equipment, so children whose parents cannot afford to purchase equipment are deterred from sport. The availability of equipment and facilities during primary school through university encourages interest in sport. In most cases, it is the influence of significant others during childhood that results in later participation in sport (Ipinmoroti & Ajayi, 2003).

CONTRIBUTIONS TO STABILITY

Sport as a social phenomenon is a universal language. Whether one is from the north or south does not matter because sport encourages fair play and positive socialization. In addition, it fosters international cooperation, bilateral relations, and understanding. The Nigerian sporting community is well aware of the positive gains that sport can bring. Thus, organization of and participation in sport competitions both nationally and internationally is regarded as paramount.

Sport allows athletes to travel to competitions outside their states of origin. During such occasions, athletes meet with competitors from other states with different cultural backgrounds and languages. Communication may begin with just one or two words in each others' languages. Eventually, true

friendship and interpersonal relationships are formed that occasionally metamorphose into courtship and cross-cultural marriages. These marriages may promote cultural understanding and accelerate effective communication in the sport community and beyond. Acculturation is also fostered by sport competitions held throughout the country. Through cultural diffusion, assimilation, and integration, different types of dress, food, and occupations have penetrated multiple geographic areas.

TRADITIONAL BELIEFS

Before formal education was introduced, there were many myths and taboos about female participation in sport, such as the beliefs that sport makes females masculine, unproductive, and promiscuous and delays marriage. When former athletes gave birth to twins in their first pregnancies, people began

Endurance Ojokolo, a two-time gold medal champion in the 100-meter race, has raised awareness of how powerful female athletes in Nigeria can be.

© Icon SMI

CULTURAL AWARENESS

Stephen Ikonta, an 18-year-old student at a secondary school in Lagos, was the only son of illiterate parents. His coach brought him to me (J.S.) because he was interested in throwing the discus, and he was the best in his school. However, Stephen's performance had started fluctuating. Upon questioning, he stated that because he was the only child in the family, his parents felt that participation in sport would affect his academics and therefore he should quit. His energy and interest waned quickly due to fear of failure in his studies coupled with disapproval by his parents.

Stephen was advised to explain to his parents the importance of sport and exercise (e.g., physical fitness, stress relief, mental alertness, strengthening of the heart and other organs, prevention of bone loss). During the intervention, I conducted a cultural awareness and blending session with the coach after inviting an interpreter who could speak the father's language. Thereafter, Stephen's father discussed the issue with the school, and it was resolved amicably by the school, Stephen, and his parents. Stephen happily came back to his sport with enthusiasm and determination, and an accelerated improvement was recorded in a short time. Eventually he won a gold medal in the 2006 Lagos State Sports Festival (Semidara, 2006).

to change their minds about women in sport, and today the old beliefs have changed for the better. More and more women are taking part in national and international competitions and winning recognition for Nigeria. For example, women such as Modupe Oshikoya (long-jump gold medalist, 1974 Commonwealth Games), Mary Onyali-Omagbemi (200-meter Olympic bronze medalist, 1996), and Endurance Ojokolo (100-meter gold medalist, 2002 and 2004 African Championships) are worthy of note. Also, with the dissemination of modern science, education, and enlightenment through the Nigeria Association for Physical, Health Education, Recreation, Sports and Dance (NAPHER-SD); the Sport Psychology Association of Nigeria (SPAN); and the publication of the proceedings of their conferences, seminars, symposia, and clinics, the populace has become more aware of the importance of women's participation in sport.

Another area in which traditional beliefs are still strong is credence in the existence and power of spirits. *Juju* is the term for the practice of invoking spirits to assist a person. Practitioners of juju believe that when these spirits are invoked, they can act negatively on opponents, causing them to make mistakes on the field to the advantage of those who called on the spirits. In other cases, believers assert that the supernatural powers of juju work on the senses of the opponents and distort vision, causing hallucinations and a general stupor, among other symptoms. When practitioners of juju believe they are seeing the aforementioned symptoms, they take advantage of the situation to outplay their opponents. Practitioners of traditional medicine who invoke spirits

have strong faith that the spirits will materialize (see Ikulayo, 1990, 2003).

Although Western sport professionals will have difficulty knowing how to deal with such beliefs, juju remains a significant force in Nigerian society. If Westerners wish to work in Nigeria, they must be prepared to deal with this phenomenon.

DEVELOPMENT OF NIGERIAN SPORT PSYCHOLOGY

Sport psychology is relatively new in Nigeria. Examining both the history of its progress and current challenges can give the non-Nigerian sport psychologist valuable insight into the unique aspects of practicing in Nigeria.

RECENT HISTORY

Techniques of modern psychology are numerous and can be found in general sport psychology textbooks (e.g., Cox, 2006; Weinberg & Gould, 2006; Williams, 2006). Building on the combination of modern and traditional indigenous practice, many relationships among athletes, coaches, and sport psychologists have developed through sport clinics, seminars, symposia, and conferences organized by NAPHER-SD and SPAN since the 1980s. Sport psychologists provide their services to national athletes in training camps free of charge. They love their country and sport in general but also want to showcase their relevance. Because the importance of sport psychology to skill acquisition and performance is not understood, coaches, athletes, and sport administrators need to learn about the benefits of sport psychology. When conferences and seminars are organized, national sport associations often foot the bill with the help of donations. Thus coaches and trainers are given ample chance to build their knowledge base and receive training so they can better deliver their services (Ikulayo, 2006).

The process of adopting new strategies has been slow to some extent. This is occasioned by the negative attitude of the sport establishment (i.e., the Federal Ministry of Youth and Sports and the National Sports Commission) toward sport psychology. This is one reason why the achievements of Nigerian athletes have fluctuated. The early 1980s, when the Sport Psychology Association of Nigeria was founded, may be considered the golden age of sport in Nigeria. In 1985, the National Sports Commission and the Federal Ministry of Youth and Sports were given the mission of helping Nigerian sport to achieve an enviable status both nationally and internationally. The National Sports Commission was separate from the Federal Ministry of Youth and Sports, so with its autonomy there was a direction and focus for sport development. Around this time, sport psychologists monitored athletes as they prepared for competitions. Services included counseling, assessment, and mental preparation leading to mental readiness for competition. Sport psychologists also taught stress management techniques. To avoid jeopardizing their physical and psychological capabilities, athletes were taught how to recognize when they were overstressed and manage their stress as each occasion demanded. To reinforce the techniques, sport psychologists accompanied Nigerian athletes whenever they went to international competitions.

In addition to providing direct services to athletes, sport psychologists trained coaches and trainers how to use their new knowledge. This service was provided through seminars, clinics, and workshops (Ikulayo, 1990, 2006).

Today, the situation has changed because the National Sports Commission has been put under the authority of the Ministry of Youth and Sports and its autonomy has eroded. It receives no direct vote or financial allocation from the federal government, and anything that has to do with sport is directly under the ministry. In summary, in the golden age of sport in Nigeria, sport psychologists were included in the training and competitions of athletes both at home and outside Nigeria. The practice of athletes working with sport psychologists for training and competitions is on the decline. The reasons for this may be both economical and political, as well as due to ignorance on the part of sport managers and administrators.

CURRENT SITUATION OF SPORT

Coaches, trainers, and even sport managers and directors in schools, colleges, higher institutions of learning, and national sport clubs and teams have not been able to blend the old coaching techniques with the psychological techniques that are practiced in technologically advanced countries such as those in North America and Europe. Most Nigerian coaches, trainers, or managers are unaware of psychological arousal-control techniques and cue words. In addition, they are unfamiliar with coping strategies, counseling services, autogenic training, desensitization, and anxiety- and arousal-reduction techniques for overaroused or overanxious athletes. These shortcomings limit the capacities of athlete handlers and consequently also limit the performance of Nigerian athletes.

An exception to the drought of psychological services to Nigerian athletes is worthy of mention here. In 2000, the first author (P.I.) used different approaches to introduce psychological services to Nigerian football (soccer) teams. Effective interventions used with the footballers included verbalization, individual and group counseling, team psyching up, and psychological skills. The sport psychology services were rendered before and after practice sessions and during breaks so that the athletes could practice their new skills. Pep talks were also encouraged, and talking back (feedback or response) was allowed to clarify procedures. For more details, see Interventions for Male Footballers.

With the female footballers on the national team, I (P.I.) employed counseling sessions and psyching processes consolidated for the Sydney 2000 Olympic Games and the second Women's African Football Championship, which they won. The intervention strategy was put to traditional music and is in the process of being adopted by national sport organizations, and the Union Bank of Nigeria, which sponsors elite teams in basketball and soccer, is already using the strategy. For more details, see Interventions for Female Footballers.

INTERVENTIONS FOR MALE FOOTBALLERS

Akporobaro was a 22-year-old undergraduate student and a member of the University of Lagos football team. During the preliminaries for the Nigerian University Games Association (NUGA) Games, the Lagos team was beaten by the University of Ibadan team. This defeat was a source of demoralization, discouragement, and dampened enthusiasm for

Akporobaro. These initial problems sparked off additional problems of nervousness, confusion, and muscle tightness, which culminated in hyperstress during critical times at competitions.

In the intervention schedule for Akporobaro, Semidara (2006) employed the Ikulayo Stress Management Approach (ISMA-MAIRTAR). Developed by Professor Ikulayo at the University of Lagos, this model has seven stages:

- M = Monitor the behavioral responses of the footballer in training and actual competition.

- A = Assess observed situations and overt reactions to such situations.

- I = Interview the athlete to substantiate the findings of stages 1 and 2.

- R = Recognize stressors and opportunities for interventions (identify situations of optimal stress and when the athlete becomes overstressed).

- T = Teach the athlete coping skills for concentration, relaxation, directional attention, mental rehearsal, and positive thinking.

- A = Acquire the coping skills through practice.

- R = Reinforce the athlete's successful coping efforts.

Specific strategies included relaxation (Jacobsen, 1958) and self-talk. For example, when the athlete realized he was going through a stressful situation and was starting to make mistakes or get distracted, he was to quietly and soothingly say to himself words such as *easy, quiet, relax,* and *focus* (Suinn, 1980). Before the end of every practice session, 10 to 15 minutes were spent on mental practice and rehearsal of specific skills (Syer & Connolly, 1984) such as shooting and accurate passing. In addition, Akporoparo was trained to use these intervention strategies during quiet time to harmonize his mental and physical skills. Eventually, he was able to get over the stress and nervousness that had hampered his performances on the football team. His coach happily testified that Akporoparo went on to help the university to win many matches against other teams.

INTERVENTIONS FOR FEMALE FOOTBALLERS

The education level of the female footballers was low, so it was necessary to use strategies they could understand and practice easily. The footballers needed to be psyched up because of low morale, lack of focus,

lack of commitment, lack of team cohesiveness, absence of mental toughness, lack of concentration, and lack of alertness. A psyching verse was used to help the athletes to focus, have directional attention, commit to the task at hand, and be mentally alert. It worked because the words are concise, enthusiastic, energizing, and intrinsically motivating. For example, the concluding line, "Success is ours!", is full of positivity related to the task to be undertaken. Here is the psyching verse, with the leader's words in bold and the group responses in the bulleted lists (Ikulayo, 2003):

Be eager, be anxious, be willing, be ever ready to always do better

- We can, we can, we can

- We will, we will, we will

- Success is ours.

We will succeed, we must win

- We are together to achieve success

- We are committed to win the Olympic football gold medal

- We can, we can, we can

- We will, we will, we will

- Success is ours.

We must cooperate with one another to strive and struggle to win

- We will put all our efforts to achieve greater for our nation for our families and for ourselves

- We can, we can, we can

- We will, we will, we will

- Success is ours.

We are determined to work harder

- To put our might in all our endeavors

- Toward the achievement of Olympic gold

- To prove the greatness of our nation

- We can, we can, we can

- We will, we will, we will

- Success is ours.

Although the athletes were all Nigerians and most had a strong belief in spiritual realities, they were from diverse cultures and their beliefs varied. For example, not all of them had faith in the efficacy of juju or in particular forms of prayer and fasting. Thus, it was only reasonable to use a nonreligious strategy to encourage cohesion and commitment. Athletes used the aforementioned verse before practice, during

ISSUES AND STRATEGIES TO CONSIDER WHEN WORKING WITH NIGERIAN ATHLETES

Practitioners working with Nigerian athletes may find it useful to keep in mind the following points:

- The literacy and education levels of athletes will vary. Do not rely on written materials (e.g., handouts, journals, diaries).

- Many languages are spoken in Nigeria, but the major ones are Yoruba, Igbo, and Hausa. It is not uncommon for athletes, coaches, and consultants to speak different primary languages. Most, however, will be able to speak English (the lingua franca) or at least pidgin English.

- Teams will include Christian and Muslim athletes as well as traditional worshippers. Consultants need to be aware of how religious beliefs might affect athletes and their behaviors (e.g., beliefs in juju or that fasting will be beneficial for performance).

- Homesickness is not a major concern for elite Nigerian athletes competing internationally. However, some less elite Nigerian athletes may experience homesickness when traveling within the country because of regional differences in food, dress, and language.

breaks, after practice sessions, and also during their free time so that it could be infused into their conscious and subconscious minds. After they started using the psyching verse, their season transformed. The team has since won the Women's African Football Championship five times. The most obvious changes in the team were as follows:

- They were energized and motivated to compete with zeal.

- They were more committed and willing to try harder.

- They were able to win more games and perform with greater confidence.

- Their facial expressions and body language expressed joy rather than discouragement about their abilities.

- They expressed happiness and willingness to interact.

CONCLUSIONS AND RECOMMENDATIONS

In the mid-1980s, when Nigeria was proving its worth in international sport, most of the higher institutions in the country had not started providing degree programs in sport psychology at the master's level. In 1987 under the supervision of Dr. Ikulayo, the University of Lagos became the first university in Nigeria to produce a class of master's-degree holders in sport psychology. From that time until the present, the university has produced many doctoral graduates in sport psychology. These sport psychologists are currently contributing to the educational development of Nigerian sport in various capacities, including practical and academic endeavors.

Despite this proliferation of professionally trained Nigerian sport psychologists, it has not been government policy to connect sport psychologists with athletes. This situation appears to be political to some extent, and we believe it has been a major cause of the downward trend in the achievements of Nigerian athletes. The use of sport psychology in every strata of sport is necessary if the country wants to regain its former glory. Nigeria has the practitioners trained in sport psychology to bring it back to sport greatness. The country should take a cue from North America, Australia, and Europe, where sport psychology is integrated in daily sport practice and international competitions.

WORKING WITH GHANAIAN ATHLETES

Caren D.P. Diehl, MEd; Anna Hegley, MSc; and Andrew M. Lane, PhD

For Western sport psychologists, working in Ghana represents an intriguing challenge. In an attempt to understand the differences between Ghanaian and Western cultures, this chapter begins with a brief overview of the Republic of Ghana. Although a plethora of cultural aspects could be examined, we have chosen to discuss a few factors that we perceive to be the most relevant:

- The history of Ghana (e.g., demographics, predominant races, past and present status of culture)

- Spiritual and religious orientation (e.g., primary religious and spiritual affiliations, religious practices, use of spiritual healing)

- Family structure (e.g., decision making, gender issues, caring roles, expectations of children, expectations of caregivers)

- Communication (e.g., nonverbal cues, greetings, tone of voice, orientation to time)

- Cross-cultural exchanges (e.g., circular and linear decisions, potential communication divides, how to foster understanding and support performance)

In the second part of the chapter, we discuss challenges and strategies related to working as a sport psychologist in Ghana, and we provide case examples that illustrate some of the challenges. Key aspects are the steep learning curve and the rewards that come from working in a culture other than one's own. Finally, we provide recommendations for practitioners.

OVERVIEW OF GHANA

The Republic of Ghana is a small country located in West Africa. Accra is the capital and largest city, followed by Kumasi and Tamale. In July, 2007, the population of Ghana was estimated to be 22,931,299 (Central Intelligence Agency [CIA], 2007).

In precolonial times, Ghana was home to a number of ancient kingdoms, such as the Asante kingdom. During the 15th century, the Portuguese became the first Europeans to develop trade with the country. Ghana, previously known as the Gold Coast, became a British colony in 1874, and in 1957 it became the first sub-Saharan country to gain independence from colonial rule (Salm & Falola, 2002). Ghana recently celebrated its 50th anniversary of independence and is regarded as one the most politically, economically, and socially stable countries in West Africa.

VERBAL AND NONVERBAL COMMUNICATION

Ethnologue, a publication on world languages, lists a total of 79 languages spoken in Ghana, although the main languages are English (the official language of the country) and a few tribal languages (Gordon, 2005). Nine languages are government sponsored (i.e., are supported by the Bureau of Ghana Languages): Akan or Asante, Dagaare or Wale, Dagbane, Dangme, Ewe, Ga, Gonja, Kasem, and Nzema. The Akan or Asante language (Twi) is the most dominant after English. Major ethnic groups in Ghana are Akan at 45.3% of the population, Mole-Dagbon at 15.2%, Ewe at 11.7%, Ga-Dangme at 7.3%, Guan at 4%, Gurma at 3.6%, Grusi at 2.6%, Mande-Busanga at 1%, other tribes at 1.4%, and other groups at 7.8% (CIA, 2007).

Although the official language of Ghana is English and schools teach in English, in the family home the local language is usually preferred. Most conversations are a hybrid of a local language mixed with some English. The traditional greeting in Ghana when meeting someone informally (e.g., walking past someone in the street) or formally (e.g., for business) is to say "Hello," followed by "How are you?" or *"Ete sea?"* (Twi translation). The answer is normally "I'm fine" or "I'm very fine" *("Eye* or *"Eye paa").* This is different from English culture, where a more enthusiastic response is typically delivered regardless of how the person is feeling.

Tone of voice is also important. With the previous example, the response of "I'm fine" may be delivered in a monotone that in another culture, such as in the United Kingdom, might indicate that something was wrong. In Ghana, however, it is simply a standard greeting that masks any personal feelings, positive or negative. Another feature of speaking in Ghana is that it can be loud and animated, which visitors may misinterpret as aggressive and confrontational. However we have found that loudness and animation in speech is frequently used because the loudest and most animated person is often the one who is listened to the most. Those who can shout over everyone else and become the most animated always command attention.

Communication is made up of both verbal and nonverbal cues. Ghanaian culture uses several nonverbal cues that differ from those in other cultures. Hall (1962, cited in Guardo, 1969) noted that the phenomenon of culture shock occurs when people from different cultures fail to interpret nonverbal communication cues. One such cue is personal space, which is "the area immediately surrounding the individual in which the majority of his interactions with others takes place" (Little, 1965, p. 237). Hall (1959) recognized that a variety of sensory cues are used to judge the social meaning of the interaction distance. When Ghanaians speak to each other, they tend to stand close together and often touch each other when making a point. In the past there has been little research into haptics, the use of touch to communicate (Jandt, 2007), but it is a feature of Ghanaian culture that could warrant further research to explore its influence on communication.

In Ghana, it is not uncommon to see adults of the same sex walking down the street holding hands. Although this behavior can be alien for visitors from Western cultures, Jandt (2007) highlighted that adult male friends walking hand in hand is common among a number of cultures. Further, in some cultures maintaining eye contact is an important part of communication, but this is not the case in Ghana and most other African countries. In Ghana it is a sign of respect to not look directly into someone's eyes.

GHANA MAYBE TIME

According to Hall (1959), time speaks more plainly than words. Hall stated that cultures vary in their concepts of time and that Western cultures have difficulty adapting and learning about other time concepts. For sport psychologists educated in the United Kingdom or United States, a limited understanding of different cultural perceptions of time can lead to problems, and Hall illustrated this with the following example. An American agriculturalist who was assigned to duty as an attaché of the American embassy in a Latin American country arrived promptly at the time arranged for a meeting with the minister. He ended up waiting 45 minutes. In the United States, this is the point at which one is likely to be offended by poor timekeeping. However, the minister was not likely to expect such a response—45 minutes was the beginning of the waiting scale in that country.

The orientation to time in many Latin countries is similar to the concept of time in Ghana, which many refer to as *Ghana maybe time* (GMT). Many Ghanaians are relaxed about the organization of events in relation to time. For example, if you arrange to meet with someone at 10 a.m., that person could show up an hour later and still be on time. Given Western expectations about time, GMT can make it difficult to plan meetings with players, coaches, and staff members. Visitors from cultures with a rigid orientation to time must adopt a more flexible and patient approach to their day in Ghana (see Dowuona, 2006).

RELIGION

Ghana is a deeply religious country—68.8% of Ghanaians are Christian, 15.9% are Muslim, 8.5% practice traditional religion, 0.7% practice other religions, and 6.1% practice no religion (CIA, 2007). The importance of religion is most evident on Sundays, when most Christians attend church (which is often the highlight of the week). Throughout the week, finding time to pray is important to the majority of Ghanaians who take their religion seriously. Religious orientation and finding time for religious practices structure the lives of most Ghanaians and have important implications for applied work.

When working as an applied practitioner in Ghana, it is important to understand the importance of indigenous beliefs and practices. Indigenous beliefs, especially juju (magic), are taken seriously by most Ghanaians. Juju even surfaces in national teams; one time the Black Stars, the national football (soccer) team, would not play another team because they believed their opponents had put a curse on the pitch. Juju is commonly credited to West African tribes and is associated with spirits. Car accidents, miscarriages, and any other unexplained circumstances are usually blamed on juju (witchcraft). Witches or witch doctors are real men and women who are purported to use supernatural powers for evil deeds. Juju can be used anywhere from sport competitions to political campaigns—wherever the goal is to eliminate the opponent (Salm & Falola, 2002).

Juju is particularly important in football, where juju men (i.e., men who practice juju) are commonplace at matches. For example, many Ivorians attributed the win by Ivory Coast in the African Cup of Nations in 1992, which followed a penalty shoot-out against Ghana, to a band of juju men enlisted by the sport minister to give the Ivorians an advantage (Maharaj, 2002). Winning or losing competitions and poor decisions by referees may be attributed to juju.

ECONOMY

As of 2008, the economy of Ghana continues to expand, experiencing an annual growth rate of 6% (UK Foreign Office, 2007). Ghana is regarded as one of the best-performing economies in Africa; overall poverty has declined from 52% in 1992 to 28% in 2006, and Ghana is on course to exceed the 2015 Millennium Development Goal of halving the poverty rate. Following successful debt relief in 2004 and further cancellations by donors, the external debt of Ghana (about $6 billion in 2001) has been almost entirely written off (World Bank, 2007). Although Ghana still has many challenges in the areas of education, health, water, sanitation, energy, and transport, and disparities still exist between rural and urban life and the north and the south of the country, the economy looks set to continue growing.

The average family has six children (DATA, 2005), and the gross national product per head of population was $430 per year in 1993 (World Write, 2003). These two factors can have one of two effects: Parents can pressure their children to stop sport participation so they can focus on their education and get jobs, or they can encourage them to work hard at sport because they see professional sport as a way out of poverty. Many children with a passion and talent for sport come under considerable pressure to contribute monetarily to their families. It is necessary to grasp the level of poverty in Ghana to recognize why many Ghanaians view sport—particularly football—in this light. A range of factors might influence the motivation of athletes in Ghana, particularly those who come from a deprived background.

GHANAIAN FOOTBALL

Many features of Ghanaian culture outlined thus far will be explored later in the chapter in relation to working as an applied sport psychology consultant in Ghana. In the following section we focus on the importance of football in Ghana. Any practitioner working in Ghana needs to understand the importance of sport in Ghanaian culture, especially football. The passion for football goes beyond the ordinary—it's almost a religion.

Football is the number one sport in Ghana in terms of participation, television coverage, audience figures, and investment by governmental and non-governmental organizations. The importance of the sport to Ghanaian culture was highlighted during the 2006 World Cup when Ghana progressed to the last 16. After every match played by Ghana, thousands of people took to the street parading, cheering, and celebrating the achievements of their team, even after the last match when Ghana lost 4 to 1 to Brazil and was knocked out of the competition. The popularity of football creates intensely competitive environments for matches at all levels, from matches between villages to the Premier League, from youth to adult football. From a young age, football players have to learn to play in a pressurized and competitive environment where every mistake is on display and often ridiculed by the crowd.

FOOTBALL AND POVERTY

Although football is the top sport in Ghana, the average wage of a professional football player is still relatively small. A professional player in the Premier League can expect to earn a basic monthly salary of US$100 (without win bonuses). However, most football players in the second and third division are not paid. Win bonuses can help to increase the players' average earnings, but few sponsorship opportunities such as those enjoyed by professional athletes in the Western world are available.

As a result, professional athletes are eager to play in Western countries, where they can earn much larger salaries and can send money home to their families. The majority of top athletes in Ghana come from underprivileged, poverty-stricken families. Most athletes know what it is like to train on an empty stomach, and many have to walk miles to their training venue. Athletes are prepared to endure such hardships because they believe that sport offers the opportunity for a better quality of life.

This drive to succeed also appears to make it harder for athletes to assess their performance. Regardless of their age or the level of football, most players believe that they will make it to the top leagues of the world. This belief means that they find it difficult to accurately assess their performances, which can be a challenge in applied sport psychology because they may deny that any areas of their performances could be improved.

Ghanaian soccer fans run through the streets of Accra, Ghana, celebrating their World Cup 2-1 win against the USA, played in Germany, Thursday, June 22, 2006.

©AP Photo/Olivier Asselin

FOOTBALL AND AGE

One important feature of football in Ghana relates to the age of footballers, who often lie about their date of birth. Many clubs don't know how old their players are. While conducting research in Ghana, we had to ask the athletes to report their real age and not their football age. It turned out that many were older than they had indicated on their club card.

The phenomenon of footballers misrepresenting their age occurs not just in Ghana but across Africa in countries including Kenya, Nigeria, Cameroon, Morocco, and Egypt, and also around the world, including Brazil and Argentina (Aforo, 2007). In a few high-profile cases, players have been caught lying about their age. For example, Phillip Osundo, a well-known Nigerian footballer, was prosecuted for lying about his age in Belgium (Onmonya, 2007). On an international scale, this issue is being addressed with magnetic resonance imaging (MRI) technology (Dvorak, George, Junge, & Hodler, 2007).

The problem of players lying about their age has been created in part by the European football market. European football clubs are looking for 17- and 18-year-olds so that they can sign them for their first contract, develop them for 5 years, and then sell them when they are supposedly at their prime at 22 years old. European clubs are therefore not looking for players aged 22 to sign their first contract. This approach is biased toward European players because it does not take into account that African players typically develop their skills at a later age. Whereas the career span of a European player may be from 17 to 31 years of age, the career span for an African player is typically from 22 to 36 years of age. With clubs not willing to give older players a first contract, it is understandable why some talented players lie about their age in order to be given the same opportunity as European players to sign a professional contract. For instance, the U-17 World Cup organized by the Fédération Internationale de Football Association (FIFA) is an opportunity for professional clubs to view and sign the best young talent. From an African point of view, this tournament for players under the age of 17 is a golden opportunity for players to secure their first contract.

CHALLENGES FOR EXPATRIATE SPORT PSYCHOLOGISTS

Increasing globalization and labor migration in sport have led to more and more athletes crossing cultures to ply their trade. A sport psychologist wishing to identify literature on providing consulting services to athletes from different cultures is likely to find limited resources. A method proposed by Kontos and Argeullo (2005) to overcome this lack is to approach athletes as culturally unique individuals and to alter services to meet individual needs. Consultants should explore cultural factors with the same degree of rigor that they investigate the demands of the sport. The following section explores some of the cultural challenges we experienced while working with athletes in Ghana.

COMMUNICATION

Few Ghanaians use English as their first language but instead use their local language. All schools teach in English and Ghana is working toward the Millennium Development Goal of ensuring that all children complete a full course of primary schooling (United Nations [UN], 2007), but the total adult literacy rate remains at about 58% (UNICEF, 2007). Although primary school is free, other costs associated with school (e.g., uniforms) are prohibitive for many families, and as a result, attendance is sporadic for many children. Thus, a significant number of athletes are limited in their ability to use English.

Jambor (1996) described communication barriers encountered when a swimming instructor in the United States tried to teach nonswimmers whose second language was English. Students in the swimming class were from Argentina, China, Korea, Mexico, Nigeria, and Vietnam. Jambor identified three tools for overcoming verbal communication obstacles: task analysis, creativity, and peer teaching. For task analysis, the stroke was broken down into its components, such as the arm movements, the leg movements, and breathing. Examples of creativity included developing new words to explain the skill the students were trying to learn. Because the students played a part in developing these words, it gave the words more meaning. For example, instead of using the terminology *flutter kick*, the students used *flap-*

ping kick. Finally, the author mentioned that peer teaching was one of the most valuable techniques. A few of the students spoke better English and could therefore understand the instructions better than their compatriots. These students increased the effectiveness of the instruction significantly by serving as interpreters.

Most adults in Ghana speak English, but they have their own version: pidgin English, also known as broken English. Pidgin English does not use standard grammar and sentence structure. For instance, "I de go come" means "I am going to go and come back again," and "Where from you?" means "Where have you come from?"

From our consultancy experiences, we found that it is necessary to determine the client's level of English before planning any intervention in detail. English ability is quickly gauged during the first intake interview and by hanging out with the athletes (as we'll discuss later, hanging out can also be a valuable way of gaining acceptance by the group and learning its values and beliefs). Practitioners will probably have difficulty understanding athletes' efforts to express themselves because, as mentioned earlier, not only is English typically pidgin, it is also often delivered in a monotone. This robs Western English speakers of the clues that they are used to picking up from tone and expression. In the beginning, it is often necessary to apologize and ask athletes to repeat themselves and then to check your understanding by rephrasing back to the athletes what they have said, usually in pidgin English that both athlete and consultant understand. The athletes are likely to be understanding and supportive when they notice that you are making an effort.

We also found from our experiences that being able to use basic phrases in the local language to start a conversation (before switching to English as the main language) can help to open up the conversation. This type of approach can build rapport because it allows the practitioner to demonstrate commitment to developing the client–consultant relationship.

Further challenges are presented when trying to use paper-and-pen English assessments. Montgomery and Orozco (1985) demonstrated that the use of English-based psychological assessments can erroneously pathologize Latin Americans athletes who speak English as a second language. Additionally, few instruments have been translated into languages other than English. In African nations, this problem is exacerbated by the significant number of local dialects in each country. As a result of these language challenges, we found it best to base our consulting on qualitative assessment methods such as behavioral

Initial Assessment of an Adolescent Footballer

The client was a 16-year-old male Ghanaian based at a residential football academy in Ghana. The player had been at the academy for 4 years and was due to graduate at the end of the summer and begin playing full time on a football team. The academy director referred the client to me (Anna) for individual sport psychology work aimed at helping the client to become assertive in situations such as heading the ball, tackling for the ball, and attacking the ball.

Given the student's level of English, I could not assess his needs with the tools I would have used had he been from the British Isles. I needed a multimethod assessment program to understand not only the client but also the cultural constraints that existed. As Andersen (2000) highlighted, hanging out and immersing yourself in a sport is an important part of entrance into service delivery. Hanging out allowed for many informal conversations with the athlete and academy staff, and these conversations helped me develop a detailed understanding of the athlete, as well as good rapport. Other useful tools were an intake interview, semistructured interviews with academy staff, and observations.

Another important element of the assessment strategy was the use of a training diary. Although such diaries are common in the United Kingdom and not likely to encounter resistance from athletes or coaches, it is a relatively unfamiliar concept in Ghana. In Ghanaian culture, athletes are not generally encouraged to analyze their own performances or to adopt a problem-solving approach to weaknesses. In addition, athletes can be reluctant to express their views and take responsibility for their behavior, instead relying on coaches to provide feedback. Thus, I felt that the diary would increase the client's ownership of and commitment to the consultation process. In addition, because he was fairly introverted, I hoped the diary would encourage him to express his opinions and that we would both gain greater understanding of his perceptions regarding his performance.

Due to the client's level of English and to help him avoid overanalyzing his performance, I devised a simple version of a training diary. It asked him to reflect on four main questions each day: What went well in training (or a match) that day and why? What new things did he learn that day? What didn't go so well in training (or a match) that day and why? What areas would he like to work on in the next training session? The diary was used to identify strengths and weaknesses and therefore areas for improvement. I worked through the first entry of the diary with the player to provide him with an example to refer to in subsequent entries.

The use of English-based questionnaires as part of a client needs analysis is problematic when the client's level of understanding and use of language differs from that on the questionnaire. When I administered the Test of Performance Strategies (TOPS) (Thomas, Murphy, & Hardy, 1999), I had to explain many of the terms on the test and give many examples to aid his understanding, which raised questions over interviewer-presence bias. Thus, I found that I needed to take a more qualitative approach to determining the use and quality of existing mental skills and monitoring the use, improvement, and evaluation of his mental skills.

To assess mental imagery, I used the TOPS results as a basis for an introductory discussion, but as my understanding of the client's use and level of English developed, I rejected the use of another questionnaire. Instead, I used practical exercises alongside discussions to develop a detailed picture of the client's use of imagery and the quality of his imagery skills, which I used as a basis to work on image clarity. I took exercises from Hale (2004) that involve imaging progressively more complex scenarios (e.g., first the ball, then the training venue, then a skill) to explore his use of various senses (e.g., visual, tactile, audio, kinesthetic) to create an image. After each exercise, I asked the player to rate his ability to generate a vivid image (figure 15.1).

Although the player had been using mental imagery regularly, it is possible that his responses were an attempt to provide the answers that he thought I wished to hear. Following the first attempt at the exercises, we discussed what a rating of 5 meant (i.e., the image was completely perfect and couldn't be improved). The second attempt at all four exercises saw a slight decrease in his rating on each exercise, which again could have been a result of his desire to provide the answers he thought I wanted.

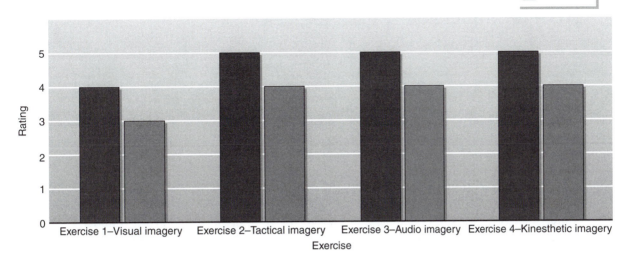

FIGURE 15.1 Measuring mental imagery: The graph compares a 16-year-old Ghanaian footballer's first attempt to rate his ability to create strong images with his second attempt to rate this ability.

observations, semistructured interviews, and video analysis (see Initial Assessment of an Adolescent Footballer).

As Anna continued to work on mental imagery with her adolescent client, she used the initial ratings as a baseline by which to examine his skills, providing some indication of areas to work on. Importantly, these responses were used as a basis for discussion on the importance of developing the ability to realistically assess all aspects of performance (physical, mental, and technical) and taking personal responsibility for improving performance. In summary, the multimethod needs analysis highlighted a number of important issues:

- The client's self-awareness of his own performance was fairly low (e.g., early entries into his training diary noted, "Everything went perfectly today."). This was likely due to the traditional authoritarian approach to coaching adopted in youth teams in Ghana, which can discourage athletes from analyzing their performance and is reliant on the coach providing performance-related feedback.

- The client was already using some psychological skills in both training and performance (e.g., mental imagery).

- The client had low self-confidence that was situation dependent and translated into observable behavior on the pitch (e.g., avoidance of one-on-one situations for fear of losing the ball).

For a discussion of the interventions used with this client, see Interventions and Their Assessment With an Adolescent Footballer.

The multifaceted assessment strategy contributed to a detailed understanding of the client that helped facilitate the development of client–consultant rapport. This point is important when the consultant is seeking to understand the influence of culture on the client. For example, through observing client behavior it was possible to understand how religion influenced his preparations for playing football. The client would pray before and after a match and would discuss his performance in relation to God, noting on more than one occasion that "I will play well if God wishes it so." (For more discussion, see Religion in Sport on page 181.) One of the most important goals from the outset was to raise the client's self-awareness of his behavior early on in the consulting process, and so the introduction of a training diary (along with video analysis) was important.

POWER DIFFERENTIALS AND CANDOR

Although being a female working in a traditional patriarchal society such as Ghana could be viewed as difficult, we found that gender was not an issue when working with young football players. In Ghana, people with seniority are automatically respected regardless of whether they have earned it. Moreover, Ghanaians tend to respect the expertise associated with the position of sport psychologist. The problem

INTERVENTIONS AND THEIR ASSESSMENT WITH AN ADOLESCENT FOOTBALLER

The range of interventions used to address the needs uncovered by the initial assessment included stopping negative thought, using positive self-talk, and using concentration cues, goal setting, and imagery. Determining the effectiveness of the interventions was problematic without the use of quantitative measures (ruled out by the player's poor English and interview-presence bias). Moreover, the player would often say something worked well simply because he believed that was what I (Anna) wanted to hear. So to determine the effectiveness of the intervention, I relied on behavioral observations of the player in training and matches; the player's self-report on the use of the interventions; detailed conversations with the player; listening carefully to how he described his use of an intervention and the effect he felt it had on his performance; and the training diary.

Evaluation of the interventions was clearly subjective, but the client reported progress toward goals relating to aggression levels in certain situations on the pitch, an increase in the structured use of preexisting mental skills (e.g., imagery), and the use of interventions that were introduced in the support work (e.g., concentration cues to help him focus on his goal of being more aggressive in certain situations and to improve his self-confidence). Additionally, the coaches noted observable differences in the player's behavior.

---

this creates for applied work is that athletes are so eager to please the sport psychologist that they will often tell you that they understand you when they don't, or they will say an intervention is working when it isn't. They tend to ask few questions and find it harder than most Western athletes to have a discussion; it would appear that they are more comfortable with being told what to do. In comparison to consultations with Western athletes, the practitioner has to work much harder at developing a relationship of trust and creating an atmosphere in which athletes feel comfortable speaking their minds.

Thus, as a practitioner you need to observe the athlete to see if an intervention is working and learn to be clever in assessing interventions, incorporating qualitative techniques in addition to the traditional quantitative tools of Western assessment. The earlier section on assessing the 16-year-old footballer provides examples of such creativity in the multimethod assessment approach. Reviewing how Anna adapted unconventional tools to assess her Ghanaian client may prove helpful as you begin to work with athletes for whom English is a second language or for whom giving the answers they think others want to hear is more common than giving the answers they truly believe. Our work in Ghana did not always require creative or unconventional approaches. Sometimes only small steps were needed to take into account possible cultural differences (see Elite Goalkeeper).

TRANSFERENCE

Evaluation of the psychological strategies taught to clients can be problematic. The greatest challenge is avoiding situations where the clients simply provide answers they think the consultant wants to hear. This problem is not limited to Ghana, and more research is required that examines assessment of the use and effectiveness (in both the short and long run) of psychological strategies for enhancing performance.

One of the biggest challenges that we confronted repeatedly was transference, the redirection of the athlete's feelings associated with a significant person toward the consultant. Andersen (2000) highlighted how transference isn't necessarily negative. When athletes like their sport psychologists, enjoy meeting with them, feel better from the attention they receive, and work hard at the psychological skills training (in part to please the psychologist), they can emerge from the relationship feeling better about themselves and their sport. The outcome is that the athletes have learned mental and communication skills and have been exposed to a healthy model of human behavior. The athletes' transference to their sport psychologist and their good feelings toward the consultant fuel the positive changes that they are experiencing.

Similar situations sometimes developed with our Ghanaian clients, influenced in part by Ghanaian culture. In Ghana, the authoritative value system

ELITE GOALKEEPER

I (Caren) worked with a goalkeeper of the Benin national team who played at a club in Ghana. He experienced anxiety when playing against the top teams in the league, but the anxiety settled if he started the game well. For example, if he held the ball and made a decent save early on, he was fine for the rest of the game. However, if he perceived his performance in the initial stages of the game to be poor, his anxiety grew worse, leading him to magnify small mistakes, which increased his anxiety even more. Further, he would worry about his performance, lying awake at night thinking about what he had done wrong and putting himself down. This sequence of cognitive and affective states typically meant he woke up feeling exhausted, which in turn made him worry further that he could not control his emotions.

The intervention was designed to first tackle his ability to control his physiological responses to emotions. The effectiveness of the intervention depended on teaching the athlete self-regulation strategies to manage unpleasant thoughts and emotions, and we had only a short window of opportunity to demonstrate effectiveness. The first strategy was to teach breathing exercises that he could use before and during the game. The intervention was explained to the athlete and a multisensory approach was used to demonstrate changes in psychological and physiological states during the intervention. In this instance, I asked him to put his hands on his abdomen so that he could feel the difference between breathing normally and deep breathing.

We also used other relaxation exercises. I wrote several scripts for him after talking to him and discovering what he found relaxing. With this information, I wrote the scripts in English, they were then read to the athlete, and he chose the script that suited him best. The script was not translated into his language because his English was good and he felt he understood everything.

I suggested that he record the script onto a tape and listen to it every night before he went to sleep. Athletes will ascribe greater personal meaning to such scripts when the dialect and the presentation are similar to their own. An important part of this work was to encourage the athlete to fully engage with the process by indicating personal preferences and being open about himself and his culture. Tools developed for one population might not be readily accepted by another, so it was necessary to invest this time engaging with the individual athlete in order to develop an appropriate intervention.

Results of the intervention indicated that the consistency of his performance improved, particularly against the top clubs in Ghana. He reported that he was sleeping better and therefore felt more relaxed, which in turn made him feel he could play better. I trusted what he reported to me about performance improvements because he came to me for help, and just by observing him I saw that he seemed more relaxed and his performance was improving. When I talked to him before games he seemed less stressed, and he was joking around instead of sitting by himself and worrying about his performance. In addition, he started opening up to me by talking about his homesickness, his family, and other personal concerns, which showed that he trusted me—and therefore I trusted his reports about the intervention.

means that few people receive individual attention. Those who do, tend to thrive from the attention and work hard to maintain that attention. The danger of this process of transference is that the athletes can become dependent on support from the consultant, which poses problems when that support is withdrawn. To avoid this situation, we continually emphasized the importance of the clients taking responsibility for their own skill learning and development, the personal reasons why they were

working on mental skills, and the personal benefits they would receive.

RELIGION IN SPORT

As previously highlighted, Ghana is a religious country. In football, Ghanaians will pray before team meetings; before training sessions; before, during, and after games; before they drive to a game; and once they have arrived at their destination. In the context of sport psychology, praying can form an important part of group cohesion practices, such as when a team comes together to pray before a match.

Awareness of religious beliefs is important when consulting with athletes from Ghana, particularly when encouraging athletes to take personal responsibility for aspects of their performance over which they have some degree of control. In our consultancy experiences, Ghanaian athletes frequently indicated that they would play well "if God wanted me to" or that "God will help me play better." We found it was important to accept the players' beliefs while helping them to develop a sense of personal responsibility for performance.

When I (Anna) was working with the Ghanaian football club, I asked one of the players what he would like to work on, and he told me that God helped him perform his best. I am not a religious person, which I was honest about, and we discussed the matter of God helping him play better. I asked him if God was helping all footballers play their best. I suggested that if he worked on his skills, techniques, and fears, he might play a lot better. He smiled at that idea and told me some things he wanted to work on, although he might have done so simply because he thought that was what I wanted to hear.

Another incident happened after we had lost a match due to a referee's poor call. The flag was up, indicating that the opponent had been offside, and the linesman kept the flag up for quite some time, but the referee allowed the goal and the linesman quickly put down his flag as if nothing had happened. The players were angry and tried to talk to the linesman, but he refused to listen. During our team meeting afterward, a few of the players said the devil was involved in the game. At first I did not know how to respond, so I asked them why they thought the devil would want them to lose the game. Had they done something to deserve to lose the game after playing so well? After discussing these questions, they came to believe that instead of it being the devil's fault, the other team had bribed the referees.

RECOMMENDATIONS FOR PRACTITIONERS

In this chapter we have highlighted the importance of understanding Ghanaian culture and its role in applied sport psychology. As in any country, many aspects of Ghanaian culture influence sport psychology practice, including societal values and the importance of religion and language.

Ghana is a developing country, and at times there is a lack of water and electricity. Any consultants looking to practice in Ghana should be flexible and always prepared for the unexpected. The need to be prepared and creative is important whether the electricity goes off when you're working or you lack resources and need to be creative in setting up a drill to illustrate a point.

For example, early on in my applied work in Ghana, I (Anna) would often use a video camera to record athlete behavior and use it as a basis for further discussion. This helped players develop a more realistic approach to assessing their performances. However, frequent power cuts that lasted days and the camera breaking on a regular basis meant that I had to find other methods to accomplish the same result. An alternative was putting athletes in pairs and having them take turns observing each other and giving structured feedback about specific elements.

ISSUES AND STRATEGIES TO CONSIDER WHEN WORKING WITH GHANAIAN ATHLETES

Practitioners working with Ghanian athletes may find it useful to keep in mind the following points:

- Take time to immerse yourself in the training and competitive environment to better understand the unique features of Ghanaian culture and sport.
- Develop an understanding of how religion and indigenous beliefs influence the preparation of athletes.
- Be prepared to come up with creative examples to aid athlete understanding; the onus is on the consultant to overcome language barriers and other challenges.
- Recognize the limitations of traditional Western assessment methods and be prepared to come up with creative alternatives.

As another example of flexibility and creativity, when I was creating drills that involved the players practicing the skills they were working on at the time, we had to be flexible in the timing of the sessions, which could be affected by torrential rain and reseeding. These circumstances would render the pitch unusable and the next closest one was a 20-minute run away. Getting upset would not have solved anything; instead, I just had to adjust what I doing by trying a new technique, waiting patiently, or adapting my original plans to new circumstances.

Do not underestimate the value of immersing yourself in the sport and culture of Ghana. A consultant needs to take the time to just hang out and understand the environment in which the athlete lives. You will learn a lot in general about how to communicate, build rapport, and work together with an athlete. If possible, also take time to get to know and observe other personnel such as the coach, manager, and physiotherapist. Sometimes you will be lucky and encounter someone who has a bit of knowledge about sport psychology and can help you with the transition into working in the culture.

Reflective practice should be a key component in all applied work, but it becomes critical when working with athletes from a different culture. When so many factors can influence the consulting process, reflective practice is imperative. Carrying out reflective practice ensures that key lessons can be applied to consulting practices.

WORKING WITH AUSTRALIAN ABORIGINAL ATHLETES

Stephanie J. Hanrahan, PhD

Australian Aborigines, similar to many other native populations in the world, experienced death and destruction at the hands of invaders. This chapter begins with a brief summary of the long Aboriginal history. The majority of the chapter describes general aspects of Aboriginal culture (e.g., Dreamtime) and specific aspects of communication (e.g., the use of narration instead of questions and answers). The chapter is interspersed with case studies to demonstrate how these cultural concerns are relevant to the field of sport psychology.

HISTORICAL OVERVIEW

Australia celebrated its bicentennial in 1988, suggesting a fairly young nation when compared with many European countries. The original people of the Australian continent, however, have one of the longest histories known. Evidence exists of inhabitation 120,000 years ago and use of stone tools 60,000 years ago (Dudgeon, Garvey, & Pickett, 2000). Before colonization by the British (mostly by convicts), an estimated 300,000 to more than 1 million Aboriginal people were living on the continent now known as Australia ("Australian Aborigine Traditional Sociocultural Patterns," 2007). The continent was populated by many Aboriginal nations, culturally distinct groups of people associated with culturally defined regions. About 500 clans (subsets of nations) existed and had their own territories, histories, dialects, and cultures.

In 1770, Captain James Cook claimed possession of the entire East Coast of Australia for the British Empire. Aboriginal land was deemed unoccupied and was taken without negotiations or treaties. This unilateral claiming of land that had been inhabited by others for thousands of years was only the beginning

of a series of events that have resulted in the desecration and marginalization of the Australian Aboriginal people. There is not space in this chapter to list all of these events, but I will provide two examples. First, the foreign invaders brought smallpox and other diseases that decimated Aboriginal populations in certain areas. One could argue that this spread of disease that caused harm to the indigenous population was accidental. However, one can make no such claim for the second example. In 1804, settlers in Tasmania (the island state to the south of mainland Australia) authorized the shooting of Aborigines. As a result, the majority of Aborigines in Tasmania were slaughtered.

In addition to outright atrocities, there are also many examples of Aboriginal Australians being treated as second-class citizens. For instance, Aborigines served in the Australian military in World War II, but they were refused membership to the Returned Services League (RSL) upon their return from war. The main role of the RSL is to ensure the well-being, compensation, and commemoration of military members and their dependants, but the Aboriginal servicemen were not entitled to these services.

Only in the last 40 or 50 years have Aborigines begun to be recognized as people. Aboriginal people were first able to vote in Australia in 1962, and in 1967 they were counted in the census for the first time. It was not until 1969 that the practice of taking indigenous children away from their families officially ended. Before 1969, children were removed from families and placed in government-run institutions, adopted by White parents, or fostered in White families. The children were often trained as domestic servants or farm laborers. The main purpose seemed to be to cut them off from their culture and raise them to think and act White. These children became known as the Stolen Generations. Some of them, who are now in their 40s and 50s, are still trying to track down their original families.

An example from sport indicating that the future might be heading in a better direction comes from the Olympic Games that have been held in Australia. In 1956, the Olympic Games were held in Melbourne, and there were no indigenous athletes on the Australian team. In the 2000 Olympic Games held in Sydney, not only were there indigenous athletes on the team, but possibly the most well-known Australian Olympian from the Sydney Games was an Aboriginal runner. Cathy Freeman lit the Olympic flame in the opening ceremony and won gold in the 400-meter event (cathyfreeman.com.au).

ABORIGINAL CULTURE

Categorizing people as Aboriginal is overly simplistic due to the great diversity within the Aboriginal population. The majority of Australian Aborigines, however, have extensive family and kinship networks in a collectivist society. Additionally, Spirit Ancestors and the land are both strong elements in Aboriginal culture. The rich cultural history, however, is countered by the notably short life expectancy of today's Aboriginal people.

DREAMTIME

According to Aboriginal culture, land was created by the journeys of the Spirit Ancestors during a time known as the Dreaming or Dreamtime (NSW Department of Health, 2004). The stories of the Dreamtime have been passed down through generations using songs, dance, poetry, drama, dance, and, of course, storytelling. Each Spirit Ancestor is symbolized by an animal that is the totem of a clan. The Spirit Ancestors gave life to the land and determined the societal structure, rituals to maintain the life of the land, and rules for human behavior. The Dreamtime explains the origin of the universe, the cycle of life and death, and the workings of nature and humanity. Dreamtime stories provide shape and structure to Aboriginal life and prescribe relations between the sexes as well as the obligations of Aborigines to people, land, and spirits. According to the Dreamtime, Aboriginal people do not own the land but instead belong to the land. Land is more than a place to hunt and gather; it is the basis of spiritual life. The law determined in the Dreamtime is guarded by elders, who make important decisions, give advice, organize learning and ceremonies, and arbitrate disputes (NSW Department of Health, 2004).

Aboriginal protesters wait for Britain's Queen Elizabeth II to arrive for an official luncheon in Melbourne in March 2006. They were among approximately 200 demonstrators claiming that British colonizers stole the land that became Australia from its original inhabitants more than 200 years ago.

©AP Photo/Rick Rycroft

HEALTH

The life expectancy of Australian Aborigines is approximately 20 years shorter than that of nonindigenous Australians. When combined with the complex kinship system, this shorter life expectancy means it is likely that indigenous athletes will attend more funerals than nonindigenous athletes (see Absences From Training Sessions).

Aborigines tend to have a holistic view of health (Riley, 1998). Unlike the biomedical model of health, which tends to focus on the physical, the Aboriginal perspective includes physical, mental, emotional, spiritual, and cultural states of being. This view is similar to the biopsychosocial model of health, which

ABSENCES FROM TRAINING SESSIONS

An Aboriginal athlete, whom I'll call Marcus, was a member of an Australian Football League (AFL) team that was competing one level down from the top professional level of competition in Australia. The coach and manager, who were White, were upset because Marcus had missed numerous training sessions—not just one here and there, but 2 or 3 days in a row on three separate occasions. Each time Marcus told the coach that he had to miss training sessions because he had to go home to attend a funeral.

The coach believed Marcus the first time and was willing to give him the benefit of the doubt the second time, but he judged the third time to be an excuse to cover for laziness, a poor attitude, or the need to go walkabout. Some non-Aboriginal Australians believe that Aborigines have the tendency to leave where they are, wander around, and eventually (maybe) return. Such people sometimes inaccurately attribute this behavior to laziness and the inability to stay focused rather than recognizing walkabouts as traditional spiritual journeys to renew relationships with the Dreamtime and the land.

The coach believed Marcus was outright lying when he phoned during a training session to explain that he was on his way to another funeral and that he'd be back in 3 days. The coach became angry (possibly exacerbated by the fact that this time Marcus would be missing a game, not just training) and told Marcus to not bother coming back. The coach felt that Marcus did not care about the sport or the team if he felt free to not only miss training but to miss a game as well. The coach did not believe it was possible for a relatively young athlete to have four different family members die during the same sporting season, let alone that the athlete felt obligated to attend all the funerals. Greater cultural awareness about health and the size of Aboriginal families on the part of the coach or the intervention of a culturally aware sport psychologist might have resulted in a different outcome for Marcus and his team.

came to the fore of health psychology in the 1980s and 1990s. For Aboriginal people, health is an intertwining of spirituality and relationships with family, land, and culture (Westerman, 2004), and ill health is considered payback for transgressions.

Although the focus of this book is cultural sport psychology (CSP), it is worth providing an example of the role culture can play in clinical psychology. In Australian Aboriginal culture, hallucinations may be seen as a spiritual rather than a psychotic phenomenon. For example, hearing voices of the dead is widely accepted in some Aboriginal communities (Queensland Health, 1996).

CULTURAL DIVERSITY

It is almost misleading to talk about Australian Aboriginal culture because doing so implies it is a single culture. As mentioned earlier, the Aboriginal people came from diverse nations (most nations contain multiple clans) with their own traditions and languages. There is no one homogenous Aboriginal culture—Aboriginal cultures are many and varied (e.g., the Murri in Queensland and the Anangu of Central Australia).

Many Aboriginal people also have a non-Aboriginal ancestry that is just as diverse, although perhaps less evident in their cultural identity. For example, in a psychological skills training program I conducted with Aboriginal performing artists, 12 participants were of Aboriginal or Torres Strait Islander (i.e., indigenous to the islands of the Torres Strait) descent. Of these 12 participants, 10 also had Irish, South Sea Islander, Scottish, Spanish, Venezuelan, Indonesian, German, English, Chinese, or Italian heritage (Hanrahan, 2004). The majority, however, identified themselves as Aborigines.

Another source of diversity in the current Aboriginal population is the extent to which they have maintained links with their culture (Ralph, 1997) or have acculturated to mainstream Australian society. Dudgeon and Oxenham (1989) outlined broad examples including urban Aborigines (i.e., those who live in cities and have largely acculturated to mainstream society), traditionally oriented Aborigines (i.e., those who have maintained strong links with their Aboriginal culture), and settlement or reserve Aborigines who live on established reserves. See Being the Only Aboriginal Athlete on a Team for an example of how teammates from

BEING THE ONLY ABORIGINAL ATHLETE ON A TEAM

Although the following compilation focuses on the experiences of athletes as the only Aboriginal member of a team, it might apply to any athlete who is the single representative of a particular culture on a team. The focus is not on the behavior of the single Aboriginal athlete but on the behavior of the non-Aboriginal teammates. These responses typically fall into one of three categories: prejudice, color blindness, and expecting the person to be a cultural expert.

Prejudice

Prejudice is prejudging an individual or group based on untested assumptions and sticking with those judgments however inaccurate they are shown to be. Prejudice can result in negative behaviors such as name-calling, limitation of opportunities, or physical violence. Most professional sports in Australia have regulations in place regarding racial vilification, and breaking such regulations has resulted in large fines as well as suspension for repeat offenders. How Aboriginal athletes respond to racial taunts varies:

> Well, it does hurt in fact, you know, your feelings. All you want to do is play football, you just want to have a kick of the ball and not have some idiot attack you because of your color. And I know different players react in different ways. Some are able to accept it—well, even though it does hurt them, they're able to accept it and get on with the game. Others aren't able to accept it and in fact do retaliate. (Maurice Riolo, ABC Radio, April 1999)

Prejudice, however, also can exist in seemingly well-meaning people. For example, understanding that Aboriginal Australians have been oppressed is a possible first step toward cultural understanding, but assuming that all the problems of an Aboriginal athlete on the team stem from being a member of this minority group is still a form of prejudice. Another example of prejudice experienced by some Aboriginal athletes is that their athletic skills are perceived as something they were lucky enough to be born with. Effort, practice, and hours of training are not acknowledged as having contributed to their current level of skill. In a way, such assumptions divorce the athletes from their achievements.

Color or Culture Blindness

Assuming all people are alike regardless of color or culture may be better than being overtly prejudiced against others because of their race or culture. But thinking that all people are the same no matter their cultural backgrounds dismisses the existence—let alone the importance—of their cultures. One Aboriginal athlete told me that other Aborigines had referred to him as an Oreo cookie—Black on the outside, White in the inside. He felt frustrated and confused. To fit in with his team, he felt he had to join in their activities (e.g., going clubbing with friends on weekends) instead of doing something he preferred (e.g., going out bush, otherwise known as spending time outdoors). Not once had anyone on the team asked him what he liked to do or considered that he was ignoring his other friends. He believed his teammates meant well when they said things such as "He's just one of us" or "We don't even think of him as being Aboriginal." However, he was an Aboriginal athlete, and he was not the same as everyone else on the team. He feared that if he mentioned anything relating to his culture, the racist treatment he had received in a previous team would become the norm with his current team. He wanted to be himself, but he worried that by doing so he would become an outcast.

Assuming Cultural Expertise

A third common response to an Aboriginal team member is assuming that the athlete will know everything there is to know about Aboriginal culture. It is ludicrous to think that the opinion of one Aboriginal athlete can represent all Aboriginal people. Yet I have heard a Caucasian athlete ask an Aboriginal athlete, "So how do Aboriginal people feel about that?", as if the athlete can speak for the entire group.

the mainstream Australian culture sometimes fail to recognize the individuality of an Aboriginal teammate.

Particularly for those who are not strongly entrenched in either traditional or mainstream culture, bicultural competence is an issue. They learned to switch between indigenous and nonindigenous ways of being with changing social environments. The uniqueness of individual people who share a historical background has been aptly summarized by Dudgeon (2000):

> The history of most Aboriginal people in the region is one of exploitation, racism, hardship, tragedy, and cultural genocide woven into a social fabric that is expressed through durability, strength, adaptation, extended family, and affinity with the land. The outcomes, expectations and effects of this historical concoction can vary tremendously within the individual. (p. 265)

COLLECTIVE NATURE OF SOCIETY

In Australian Aboriginal society, family and kinship networks are extensive and are supported by an intricate pattern of responsibility and obligations. People have extra mothers, brothers, sisters, and other relatives (Smith, 2004). For example, when I attended the wedding of two friends of mine (she was Caucasian and he was a Torres Strait Islander), the family network was mentioned in a couple of the speeches at the reception. After her father welcomed the groom into their family, one of the groom's cousins welcomed the bride into their family and made a point of saying that she had not only acquired a few brothers and cousins, but a lot of new relatives—probably hundreds. Another example demonstrating the obligations to an extensive family is that the couple needed to invite the entire family. Because there was not enough room for the entire extended family at their relatively small wedding, they compromised by indicating that there was only space for the first 40

A DECREASE IN MOTIVATION

Darren (not his real name) was a track-and-field athlete who had performed well at school and at state-level competitions for junior athletes. A school coach saw Darren compete and knew that he had achieved a lot with little formal training. The coach decided to train Darren and had high expectations of his ability to compete at the national and even the international level. The coach recognized that Darren's family had little money, and he paid Darren's track fees himself (there was a small charge to use the local track). He even arranged to take Darren home after training in order to save bus fare.

During the first 2 months of training, Darren seemed to be highly motivated and took to the drills with lots of energy and effort. The coach referred Darren to me, however, after Darren started missing sessions, making excuses, and demonstrating inconsistent levels of effort when he did go to training. The coach told me he thought Darren had an attitude problem and needed to get motivated.

I only met with Darren for three sessions. In the sessions I encouraged him to tell me his story. Although at times I wanted to jump in with suggestions of a cognitive-behavioral intervention such as goal setting or self-talk, I was patient, and with a few clarifications and prompts I learned that Darren enjoyed running, liked the coach, and even looked forward to training. The problem was that he wondered if he was casting aside his Aboriginal culture to participate in competitive athletics. He described the feeling of selling out his own people by entering into White sport and by putting himself first. He questioned whether it was appropriate to train to improve his performance when doing so did not have any obvious benefit for his community. (This consultation took place in the 1990s, before the international publicity and acceptance of Cathy Freeman.) I believe that having the opportunity to tell his story helped Darren clarify what was going on in his life. I suggested that he might want to speak with an indigenous counselor (I did not know any indigenous sport psychologists at the time), but he decided to instead discuss the situation with members of his family.

A month or so after my sessions with Darren, the coach told me he was happy with Darren's level of motivation. It may have been the talk he had with his family, the sessions with me, some unknown cause, or simply the passage of time that lead to this perceived change in behavior, but I doubt that the standard cognitive-behavioral intervention I have used with many other athletes would have been effective.

PUNISHMENT OR REWARD?

This example comes from a nonsport environment but is applicable to a sport environment. During a cultural awareness training workshop I attended, a presenter provided the following example of how a system designed to increase punctuality backfired because White bosses in a mining company were not aware of a particular aspect of Aboriginal culture.

The mining company employed a large number of Aboriginal workers, and the managers were not happy with what they perceived as an increasing problem with tardiness. They decided to address the problem by docking the pay of employees who were late to work. However, the managers were surprised when tardiness dramatically increased after the introduction of this policy. What they were not aware of was that in the Aboriginal community, there was neither total individual ownership of objects nor a complete communal sharing of assets but rather a synthesis of the two. When it became known in the Aboriginal community that certain workers were not receiving their full pay, there was less pressure for these workers to provide money to other members of the community. Individuals who had their pay docked ended up with more money than those who received full pay, because fewer community members asked them for money. The managers had unknowingly promoted the behavior they were trying to eliminate.

Whenever a system of rewards or punishments is created, it is important to determine how the rewards and punishments are perceived by those for whom they are intended. Just as rewarding a child with chocolate won't do much good if the child doesn't like chocolate or is allergic to it, basing rewards and punishments on an incorrect understanding of individuals' values is likely be ineffectual. Thus, systems of rewards and punishments in sport need to take into account the cultural values of the people involved.

or 50 family members who RSVP'd. It would have been culturally inappropriate to selectively invite certain members of the family, because doing so would have insulted any family members who were not invited.

In Aboriginal society, potentially contentious decisions are based on consensus of all family members rather than a majority view or the opinion of key individuals (Ralph, 1997). The collective nature of this society also dictates that family responsibilities take priority over individual interests. Some Aboriginal athletes have at times questioned the dedicated nature of training for elite sport because it seems to put their individual interests above those of the family or community (See A Decrease in Motivation). The importance of family is demonstrated by the responses of Aboriginal performing artists to the question, "What are the real loves in your life?" The majority of responses related to family or nature (Hanrahan, 2004). Responses from similar non-Aboriginal groups mentioned family but tended to center on dance, theater, sport, or whatever the focus of performance was for the person.

Being a member of a collective-oriented culture, however, does not mean that one lives in a pure socialist society where everyone works for the common good and all assets are shared equally.

Hundreds of years ago that may have been the case, but as mentioned in the section on diversity, there have been varying levels of acculturation to mainstream society. What results is a complex, and to some people, confusing social order. Punishment or Reward? illustrates this fusion of individualism and collectivism.

RECOMMENDATIONS FOR CLEAR COMMUNICATION

To be effective, sport psychology professionals need to be able to communicate with the athletes and teams with which they are working. All the knowledge in the world is useless unless the consultant can convey that information to others. Many of us may have learned about communication in counseling courses or through experience, but we need to remember that culture can influence what is considered to be appropriate or understandable when conversing.

LANGUAGE

As previously mentioned, there are many Aboriginal nations and clans that speak different languages and dialects. Although many of the languages have been lost, multiple Aboriginal languages continue to exist. In some traditional communities, the original languages are still spoken, but most Aborigines today speak some form of Aboriginal English, a continuum of English ranging from forms close to standard Australian English to Aboriginal Kriol (an English-based creole language). Aboriginal English and standard English differ in pronunciation, grammar, vocabulary, style, and meaning (Ralph, 1997). An example of difference in meaning is that *yes* may be used in response to a question to indicate that you are obliging and want the questioner to think well of you, not that the you agree with the content of the question. It can be considered rude to say no. My way around this potential confusion was to avoid asking yes-or-no questions. For example, instead of asking athletes whether they were going to the team dinner on Friday, I'd ask what they were doing on Friday night.

NARRATION INSTEAD OF QUESTIONS AND ANSWERS

Aboriginal culture has a strong oral tradition. Storytelling has long been the main venue for passing on history and information from the Dreamtime. Therefore, when working as a sport psychologist with Aborigines, a narrative style is often more suitable than direct questions. For example, when meeting with athletes for the first time and conducting intake interviews, it is appropriate to allow them to tell their story in their own words without interrupting. Not only does listening without interrupting demonstrate genuineness and sensitivity, the practitioner is also more likely to get meaningful information than by firing questions at the athlete. In Aboriginal culture, indirect questions, hinting, and inviting are more appropriate than direct questions. This approach to communication may seem roundabout and at times frustrating for non-Aboriginal consultants, but it can be more efficient than the standard direct questioning.

SILENCES

Hopefully most practitioners reading this book have already learned the value of listening, an effective technique no matter who the client is. When I first started to work with clients, I was uncomfortable with silences and felt compelled to fill them. I've since learned the value of silence, which can be even more important when working with Aboriginal athletes. Allowing the person to pause, to collect thoughts, and to speak again indicates a relaxed atmosphere and genuine interest. Practitioners need to be comfortable with silences and not jump to fill in the space.

Not allowing silences can be perceived as pressure (Dudgeon, 2000).

STATING OPINIONS AND MAKING DECISIONS

Aboriginal athletes may be reluctant to express a firm opinion, especially if it is perceived to be in conflict with the opinion of someone else. When working in a team environment, consultants need to be aware of this possible reluctance. Failing to respond to a comment may mean that athletes don't have an opinion on the topic or that they don't feel they are in a position to make a comment (Dudgeon, 2000). Forcing a response can be perceived as antagonistic and result in a nongenuine response.

Group or team decisions work best when made by consensus. Decisions are typically not made until all relevant parties have had input into the decision-making process. Deadlines are traditionally not of concern. This apparent devaluation of time may actually be the result of a different concept of time. The traditional concept of time was cyclical rather than continuous (Dudgeon, 2000). Activities were dictated by need and seasons, not routines or schedules. This different concept of time often means that non-Aboriginal practitioners need to be patient.

EYE CONTACT, PROXEMICS, AND SETTING

Some Aboriginal people may not use direct eye contact, especially when meeting someone for the first time. Staring may be seen as intrusive or even an attempt at seduction (Dudgeon et al., 2000), and prolonged eye contact may be considered offensive (Dudgeon, 2000). However, other Aboriginal people will engage in direct eye contact and may think a practitioner is uncomfortable working with them if eye contact is avoided. Therefore, a basic rule of thumb is to use discretion and take cues regarding eye contact from the client.

The term *proxemics* refers to personal space. Some Aboriginal people may prefer to sit at a distance or at an angle beside the other person in a one-on-one situation such as counseling (Dudgeon et al., 2000). The distance between the client and the practitioner that is perceived as comfortable may change with time. In addition, rather than meeting in a practitioner's office, it may be preferable to meet in a different setting (e.g., outdoors or at the training venue). Office settings may be uncomfortable, and going to a psychologist's office may make the person feel shame for having to seek help. Although counseling is usually one on one in Western culture, some

ISSUES AND STRATEGIES TO CONSIDER WHEN WORKING WITH AUSTRALIAN ABORIGINES

Practitioners working with Australian Aboriginal athletes may find it useful to keep in mind the following points:

- The life expectancy of Australian Aborigines is about 20 years shorter than that of nonindigenous Australians.
- Indigenous athletes are likely to attend significantly more funerals than nonindigenous athletes.
- Illness (and perhaps injuries) may be seen as payback for wrongdoing.
- Treating all people the same regardless of cultural background dismisses the existence and importance of culture.
- Contentious issues are decided by consensus, not by the majority or a few key people.
- Most Australian Aborigines have extensive family and kinship networks.
- Training for elite sport may be perceived as selfish.
- Aboriginal English and standard English may differ in pronunciation, grammar, vocabulary, style, and meaning.
- A narrative style of communication may be more appropriate than direct questions.
- Silence in a conversation may mean genuine interest, not indifference.
- Sometimes eye contact may be appropriate, and sometimes it may be perceived as confrontational or seductive.
- The uniqueness of individual Aboriginal athletes needs to be recognized.

Aboriginal people may feel more comfortable if they bring another person (usually a family member) to the meeting, especially the first one. For all of these considerations, the best option is ask clients what their preferences are in terms of the consultation location, the seating arrangements, and whether they want to bring someone with them to the session.

SUMMARY

This chapter is designed to help readers be aware of the history, values, structure, and beliefs of indigenous Australian culture, all of which may influence the effectiveness of applied sport psychology practice with members of this population. It is by no means conclusive or complete. As mentioned in part II of this book, consultants also need to be aware of their own cultural values, biases, and stereotypes. The process of becoming culturally aware is a combination of self-awareness and learning about the culture of a client. The individual athlete, however, always needs to be foremost in the mind of the practitioner. No single individual is ever completely defined by a cultural stereotype.

Singaporean Athletes in a Multicultural Society

Kaori Araki, PhD, and Govindasamy Balasekaran, PhD

Singapore is a tiny island located south of the Malay Peninsula. At 697 square kilometers, it is the smallest country in Southeast Asia, but throughout history it has been valued for its strategic location, and it has been colonized repeatedly for this reason. Since its independence from Malaysia in 1965, Singapore has developed into a multicultural society that revels in its diversity. Its amalgamation of cultural traditions and rapid progress to a high standard of living has created a unique environment for sport and physical activities.

This chapter introduces the major ethnicities of Singapore and their languages, religions, and customs. It continues with the politics and economy of the country, which are related to the educational systems as well as the sporting culture. Lastly, the chapter highlights sport psychology in Singapore and uses case studies to illustrate the adaptation of psychological skills training in this multicultural society.

INTRODUCTION TO SINGAPORE

The small size of Singapore and its rich ethnic diversity have contributed to the development of a unique culture. In the following sections we explore how the multiplicity of ethnicities and languages has affected education, government, economy, social constructions, and religious life, all of which compose the environment in which Singaporean sport exists.

ETHNICITIES AND LANGUAGES

The population of Singapore was 4.48 million in 2006 (Singapore Department of Statistics). Based on the Singapore 2000 census report, the majority of Singaporeans are Chinese (76.8%), followed by Malays (13.9%) and Indians (7.9%). The remaining 1.4% of the population includes Eurasians and non-permanent residents working in Singapore.

The official languages in present-day Singapore are English, Mandarin, Tamil, and Malay. About 28% of Singaporeans speak English at home (Singapore Department of Statistics), and 36% of Singaporean Chinese speak Mandarin (Singapore Department of Statistics) due to the emphasis of the government on this language during the 1990s (in the 1980s, all education was taught in English). The promotion of Mandarin was a calculated policy by the government to allow Singaporeans to reap economic benefits from the fast growth of China as an economic powerhouse. This proved to be a viable gamble for sustaining economic success since the country lacks natural resources. In addition to Mandarin, Singaporean Chinese speak Cantonese (23.9%), Hokkien (48.5%), Teochew (20.1%), and other dialects (7.5%).

The majority of Indians in Singapore are Tamils who emigrated from South India, and 77% of Singaporean Indians speak Tamil (Singapore Department of Statistics). Other Indians who immigrated to Singapore include Bengalis from North India.

The Malays were the early settlers in Singapore and are mainly from the Malay Peninsula and neighboring Indonesian islands. The Malay language spoken in Singapore is similar to the Malay spoken in present-day Malaysia, but the enunciation, accent, and speed differ somewhat. Some of the Chinese immigrants have assimilated into the Malay lifestyle. Known as *Peranakan,* they speak Chinese as well as Malay, but they have adopted aspects of the local Malay lifestyle, such as food, clothing, and mannerisms.

In addition, some of the early settlers in Singapore married Caucasians, which created a new group, Eurasians. The Eurasians primarily speak English. In addition, the multicultural Singaporean identity has influenced the spoken English language, which has been transformed into a local language called *Singlish,* a mix of English, Chinese dialects (mostly Hokkien), and Malay. The loss of the Queen's English in Singapore has led to various debates—the government encourages the use of proper English, and the proponents of Singlish argue that it gives Singaporeans an identity that is valuable because of its distinctiveness.

POLITICS AND ECONOMY

Singaporean politics have been dominated by one political party, the People's Action Party (PAP), since 1959. Lee Kuan Yew was prime minister from 1959 to 1990. In 2008, the PAP held 82 out of 84 seats and

Lee Kuan Yew's son, Lee Hsien Loong, was serving as prime minister.

Singapore has strong roots in Asian and Confucian values, so the PAP's adoption of an Eastern liberalism entrenched with strict Asian values was supported by the population and the party was elected to power at every election. The few opposition parties that exist in Singapore have not been able to break the stronghold of the PAP. The no-nonsense approach of the PAP government to enforcing strict law and order has prevented riots, strikes, and other forms of chaos. This strong stability of racial and cultural harmony has helped Singapore become a prosperous society.

Singapore has enjoyed great economic success since its independence. Its growth has been comparable to that of Hong Kong, Macau, and Taiwan. However, the Singaporean economy has been recovering from a global recession since 2001, and its gross domestic product (GDP) has been growing ever since. In 2006, the GDP grew by 7.7 % and the manufacturing sector grew by 11.4% (Singapore Department of Statistics).

In a clear sign of economic success, cranes fill the skyline in late 2007 in Singapore, where construction jumped 15.5% that year.
© AP Photo/Wong Maye-E

This economic success has had huge repercussions on society. Singaporeans have been enjoying a good life, and their success is a cornerstone of their philosophy. Their strong work ethic and thirst for success have been transmitted even to sport. The push to succeed in sport as well as the economy has been evident in the last decade. The number of high-level athletes is increasing, and sport associations are engaging in systematic training to achieve athletic success. To support these efforts, the sport sciences are being emphasized more and more. The government is providing more funding to sport and has targeted a number of policies to achieve success in sport.

Social Constructions

By the mid-1980s, Singapore was a newly born metropolitan city with an affluent middle class. As the country developed a high standard of living, material goods and status inevitably became the vehicle by which people measure success (Bastion, 2007). Singaporean Chinese have a drive to be successful, and materialism is influenced by traditional Chinese teachings of wealth and prosperity (Trocki, 2006). Thus, materialism became part of the Singaporean dream of being successful, wealthy, and beyond self-sufficient (Chua, 1995). In Singapore, parents expect children to excel in education because success will then be guaranteed for life. The increase in wealth from this success satisfies basic survival needs and enables people to spend extra money on hobbies, sport, and traveling. Owning a car in a country with the most expensive taxes and restrictions in the world is embraced by Singaporeans because of its status and convenience (Trocki, 2006). Bastion (2007) and McNeill, Sproule, and Horton (2003) indicated that pragmatism is one of the dominant Singaporean national values. People easily depend on the government for their social and economic security. Pragmatism in this case is considering what will bring benefits, success, and fame in a short amount of time. It also makes people goal oriented with an emphasis on individual success. Bastiam stated that

> the common phrases associated with pragmatism are, "What's in it for me?"; "How much does this job pay?"; "What is coming out in the exam?"; "Let's get married because we can get a flat"; "It's free—quick grab it, just shove aside the little old lady in front of you." (p. 130)

Related to pragmatism, education is one way for guaranteed success, particularly if one excels in the subjects necessary for future security. Physical education and extracurricular sport are not the right subjects to concentrate on because they will not lead to success in society. (Successful people are defined as those with enough resources to sustain a high quality of life with enough money to splurge on hobbies and other recreational activities.) Thus, pragmatism does not favor participation in economically nonviable subjects such as sport and physical education because they do not lead to achieving the Singaporean dream.

The traditional family structure in Singapore has mainly consisted of the male as the breadwinner and the female taking care of the children and household duties. This traditional concept is changing because of Western influence and the affluence of the society. In 2006 (Ministry of Manpower), 89% of male residents and 63% of female residents were employed. Even though the female employment rate is still lower than the United States, United Kingdom, Sweden, and Japan, it has significantly increased.

The desire to earn more money to gain additional status in society by buying luxury goods or to pay for the increased expenses in an average household may have contributed to the women in Singapore joining the workforce. Children are usually cared for by maids, mothers-in-laws, or grandmothers. Thus, the nurturing of values and discipline in children has been passed to others as time spent with the parents, especially the mother, has dwindled.

Spiritual and Religious Life

The rich ethnicity of Singapore has not only contributed to an array of languages but also has provided a mixture of religious faiths. Based on a Singapore Department of Statistics survey, the main religions are Buddhism (51%), Islam (15%), Christianity (15%), and Hinduism (4%). In addition, 15% of Singaporeans are without religious affiliation. Religion is important to the people of Singapore and plays a pivotal role in everyday life.

The Singaporean Chinese include Taoists, Buddhists, and Christians, but they all share a common belief in Confucianism, which extols ancient Chinese values such as filial piety, benevolence, care, and concern. These beliefs intertwine with daily life, including the work environment and personal relationships.

Almost all Malays are Muslims (Singapore Department of Statistics Census) and belong to the Sunni sect of Islam, which plays a major role in everyday life. Most Malays pray five times a day and attend a mosque prayer session on Fridays, so no classes or meetings are scheduled on Friday from 12:30 to 14:30 in Singapore. The observance of Ramadan requires fasting from dawn to sunset for a month. Even Malay athletes observe Ramadan and maintain their training during this time. The other main religion in Singapore is Christianity. Christianity has been growing steadily in Singapore, with 16.5% of Chinese, 12.1% of Indians, and other races practicing it.

About 55.4% of Singaporean Indians practice Hinduism. The belief in karma (the law of action and consequence) is a cornerstone of the religion. The concept of reincarnation and attaining release from the cycle of birth and rebirth is a daily reality in the life of a Singaporean Hindu. For example, there can be the realization that friends and enemies are associates of eternity, thereby leading individuals to see relationship issues as their own problem that they should fix, rather than a problem of the environment.

OVERVIEW OF SPORT AND EXERCISE

In 1973, Prime Minister Lee Kuan Yew stated at the Singapore National Stadium opening ceremony, "Our purpose is to generate healthy, vigorous exercise for the whole population, enhancing the valuable qualities we have in our people—keen, bright, educated and more productive if they are fit" (Lee, 1973). This landmark speech may have been interpreted by some to mean that the main purpose of Singaporeans is to be productive and have economic success, and thus sport is a vehicle for creating productive citizens who contribute to the economy.

NATIONAL ATTITUDES TOWARD SPORT

Singaporeans commonly value the seven Cs (computer, cash, career, condominium, club, credit card, and car) because of the rise in affluence and materialism. Recognizing this trend, the government responded with new policies, one of which is to introduce exercise values and to carry out a national campaign for a healthy lifestyle. The Health Promotion Board (HPB) was founded in 2001 to promote fit and healthy Singaporeans. The HPB encourages people to engage in physical activity 30 minutes a day, five or more times a week. This campaign and the launching of the HPB have made Singaporeans more physically active than ever.

The Singapore Sports Council (SSC), the governing body of sport in Singapore, conducts survey research every 5 years to examine sport and physical activity participation in Singapore. The latest annual report (SSC, 2007) shows that Singaporeans aged 15 and older are relatively active and enjoy various sports and physical activities. More males reported being

regularly active (55%) than sedentary (40%), but more females reported being sedentary (53%) than regularly active (42%).

The survey showed that regardless of race and ethnicity, many Singaporeans participate in regular sport activities—53% of Indians and others reported being regularly active, as well as 48% of Chinese and 46% of Malays. The top three activities among Singaporeans are jogging (21.1%), swimming (14.4%), and walking (10.5%). The government policy of constructing walking trails and swimming pools has led to increased accessibility of recreational sport, so it is no surprise that jogging, walking, and swimming are the top recreational activities. Overall, Singaporeans are more involved in physical activity compared with past years.

PHYSICAL EDUCATION

As mentioned, parents are more willing to encourage children to excel in academics rather than sport because of the perceived path to greater success in society. In Singapore, few children play on the street, in the park, or in the field after school or on weekends compared with other Asian or Western countries. On the other hand, the educational system encourages some students to participate in sport. For example, all the students who desire to enter preuniversity programs or university are required to participate in cocurricular activities (CCA), which are sport activities outside the school curriculum. Students receive extra points for admission into preuniversity by participating in one of the CCA programs offered at school.

The two kinds of CCA programs are nonsport and sporting. Those who choose or are chosen to participate in sporting CCAs must attend training sessions two or three times a week. The schools offer various sports (table 17.1) and compete at interschool competitions. The interschool competitions allow the Ministry of Education to monitor and rank the schools. Schools placing in the first to fourth positions consecutively in the same sport or activity are acknowledged with the Sustained Achievement Award (SAA), which adds prestige to the school.

NATIONAL PHYSICAL FITNESS AWARDS

The National Physical Fitness Awards (NAPFA) program was launched in 1982. An annual fitness test is conducted during physical education in August for primary schools and in April for secondary schools. Students perform six health and fitness tasks, which include pull-ups, a 2.4-kilometer walk or run (1.6 kilometers for primary school students), the standing jump, sit-ups, the sit and reach, and the shuttle

TABLE 17.1   CCA SPORTING ACTIVITIES OFFERED BY SCHOOLS

Sport	Male	Female
Badminton	+	+
Basketball	+	+
Bowling	+	+
Canoeing	+	+
Cricket	+	–
Football (soccer)	+	–
Golf	+	+
Gymnastics	+	+
Hockey	+	+
Judo	+	+
Netball	–	+
Rugby	+	–
Sailing	+	+
Sepak takraw	+	–
Shooting	+	+
Softball	+	+
Squash	+	+
Swimming	+	+
Table tennis	+	+
Tennis	+	+
Track and field	+	+
Volleyball	+	+
Water polo	+	–
Wushu	+	+

run. Performances are graded from A to F, with F being failure. The Ministry of Defence awards the junior colleges up to S$3,000 (US$2,225) if a certain number of senior students obtain a gold (at least a C grade performance on all tasks) or silver (at least a D grade performance on all tasks) grade in the NAPFA test. The NAPFA test is actually a dry run for male Singaporeans, who must serve at least 2 years in the military. The grade or level of physical fitness affects the length of basic training. A minimum of a silver grade allows 18-year-old males to participate in 2 months of basic training during their national service. Those who fail to obtain a silver grade usually must undergo 3 months of basic training, and the obese must attend a 4-month training program.

Because of the reward systems based on the fitness test and the ranking of schools, physical education is used to prepare students to perform well on the test. This push for fitness results means there is little emphasis on fun activities. Even though the government is promoting sport for life, it has been difficult for children to simply enjoy physical education and learn basic physical skills such as throwing and catching.

TRIM AND FIT

Trim and Fit (TAF) was launched in 1992 to reduce obesity and improve the physical fitness of students from primary to preuniversity levels. To attain respectable obesity rates in schools, physical activities for obese children increased; for instance, it was common to see children running before school and during recess. However, there was no scientific evidence supporting the effectiveness of the TAF program, and approximately 10% of students in the program reported experiencing eating disorders (Lee, Lee, Pathy, & Chan, 2005). Eventually the government decided to do away with the program and to introduce a holistic approach to tackle the problem of obesity.

CURRENT STATE OF SPORT PSYCHOLOGY

Sport psychology in Singapore is still in a developmental phase. There is no official sport psychology organization and only a few professionals have earned a PhD in exercise and sport science. These professionals are actively teaching and conducting research in sport and exercise psychology at the university level. Consulting with athletes and teams also has been provided by only a few trained professionals. Because demands for sport psychology services are increasing due to the greater emphasis on winning international competitions and on CCA, sport psychology professionals in Singapore are trying to educate practitioners in sport psychology and psychological skills training.

The sport psychology profession suffers from a number of problems in Singapore. Myths about psychological skills training abound, including ideas such as "PST [psychological skills training] is for problem athletes only; PST is for elite training only; PST provides a quick fix; and PST is not useful" (Weinberg & Gould, 2007, p. 253). Because of the increase in competitive sport participation, there is not enough supply to meet the demand, so it is common for people to refer to themselves as sport psychologists without the proper qualifications. Sport psychology professionals in the United States usually have a doctoral degree in the field and some are also certified practitioners, but this is not the case in Singapore. This lack of structured training could be due to low interest in the field until recently. Despite this predicament, a few educational sport psychology professionals in Singapore have been successful in delivering quality services to both local and international-level athletes.

UNDERSTANDING ELITE ATHLETES

Elite athletes in Singapore are a diverse group, reflecting the multitude of ethnicities represented in the population. The cultures of these groups have significantly shaped athletes' attitudes. In addition, these potential champions cannot be understood apart from the historic attitudes toward sport, the current emphasis on economic success, and the government's determination to be number one in as many areas as possible. The failure of coaches to understand their athletes can have serious consequences for the national effort to arrive at the forefront of international sport accomplishment. A Loss for Singapore illustrates how this can happen.

INCENTIVES FOR ELITE ATHLETES

Developing both local and elite talent has been an uphill struggle in Singapore, where it is rare for young students to commit to a lifetime of competitive sport. One way the government encourages participation is by awarding scholarships, sponsorships, and attractive incentives. For example, the Multi-Million Dollar Award programme (MAP) was launched for the 15th Asian Games in 2006. Gold medalists received S$250,000 (US$185,400) for individual events and S$400,000 (US$296,600) for team events, silver medalists received S$125,000 (US$92,700) for individual events and S$200,000 (US$148,300) for team events, and bronze medalists received S$62,500 (US$46,300) for individual events and S$100,000 (US$74,100) for team events. Twenty-seven medalists received a total incentive of S$4.75 million (US$3.5 million) in recognition of achievements in the Asian Games, and half of the recipients were teenagers.

The Singapore National Olympic Council (SNOC) is the governing body in Singapore that provides support for elite athletes. Project 0812 has been launched, a S$7 million (US$5.2 million) funding project to help athletes win Olympic medals in 2008 and 2012. Twenty-two athletes are chosen from the sports of sailing, shooting, and table tennis. These targeted athletes are allowed to take official leave from work or school so that they can concentrate on full-time training for the Olympic Games. In addition

A LOSS FOR SINGAPORE

Kumar was an Indian and a native of Singapore. He was a long-distance runner who competed at the national level. Singaporean coaches were in short supply, and although foreign coaches were abundant, they lacked knowledge of Singaporean culture and had difficulty relating to local athletes. The turnover rate for such coaches was high, and the frequent changes of coaches were disruptive for athletes. Kumar tried to cope by concentrating solely on his training, but he could not deal with the psychological aspects needed to perform at a high level on his own.

Finally he packed his bags and headed to a foreign land where he had never been before—the United States. Kumar was accustomed to community-based living and experienced huge culture shock upon arrival. Some professionals and teammates did not even know of the existence of Singapore. Their humor, although not malicious or targeted specifically at him, was at times insensitive to his culture and ethnicity. Food was a huge problem since Kumar was used to a simple diet of rice, vegetables, and meat as opposed to the Western style of bread, salads, and large portions of meat. He had never seen snow in his life and was not used to the cold temperatures in the northeastern part of the country.

Kumar coped by developing a less sensitive attitude toward people's comments and concentrating on his performance. Excelling in his sport helped him assimilate into American culture. He also relied on social support from some of his teammates. This peer-group support was vital and eventually contributed to his qualifying in the regional and NCAA championships in the United States.

to Project 0812, the government is giving scholarships and jobs to athletes so that they are not left to fend for themselves once they retire. These kinds of incentives have resulted in greater participation in sport.

From April 2007 to March 2008, S$31.9 million (US$23.6 million) was available to the local national sports associations (NSAs). The chief executive officer of the SSC stated the following:

> Singapore has recorded historical highs in the medal tally in the last three consecutive Major Games—SEA Games, Commonwealth Games, and Asian Games. As we plot the path forward, the outcome-based funding model encourages NSAs to be more disciplined and purposeful in the way we design our programmes and invest our resources. . . . [I]t is about stretching every dollar and prioritising limited resources into programmes that can best deliver the Sporting Singapore vision. (SSC, 2007)

ATTITUDINAL RESULTS OF INCENTIVES

Such financial incentives may reinforce outcome-oriented behavior rather than a process orientation among elite athletes, encouraging them to search for answers to questions such as "What's in it for me?" and "How much does this job pay?" As a further reflection of the focus on winning, the Foreign Sports Talents (FST) scheme was recently established to raise the competitive level in local and international levels:

> Foreign sports talent should be part of an integrated plan to develop sports excellence in Singapore. It is therefore important for NSAs to show us that they indeed have a good long-term plan to develop their sports, which will include the nurturing of our young local talents. (Ministry of Community Development and Sports, 2003)

Sport has been counting increasingly on foreign talent. Foreign students from China, Thailand, and Indonesia have been dominating table tennis and badminton at interschool events. Similarly, at the Commonwealth and Asian Games, many foreign-born athletes compete for Singapore's national team to bring home medals. This trend is seen even in coaching supporting staff. For example, all of the coaches and support personnel working with the sailing team, which brought back the most medals (5 gold, 3 silver, and 2 bronze) from the Asian Games in 2006, were expatriates from Australia, China, and Peru.

The strong emphasis on winning that has developed in Singapore appears to have had equally strong effects on elite athletes' attitudes toward their efforts to become winners, as we shall see in the next section.

CONSULTING WITH ELITE ATHLETES

Singaporean history, economic pressures, ethnic makeup, and cultural and religious values have strongly affected athletes' attitudes toward training for and competing in sport. What follows are discussions of three issues that sport psychology professionals who work with elite Singaporean athletes are likely to encounter:

- Strong emphasis on winning
- Balancing of academics and sport
- Leadership styles of foreign coaches

EMPHASIS ON WINNING

Parents, relatives, teachers, coaches, and supporting staff shape athletes' self-perceptions, affect, and motivation. However, parents sometimes support their children in negative ways, including setting unrealistically high standards, expecting winning, criticizing performance, and comparing them with other children. Pressure from parents generally affects athletes' enjoyment and anxiety levels (Brustad, 1993, 1996; Weiss, Wiese, & Klint, 1989). In Singapore, these expectations are magnified by parents putting strong pressure on their children to succeed at everything they do. In addition, government-funded projects such as Project 0812 place coaches under extreme pressure to produce champion athletes. With the dual pressure from parents and coaches, precompetitive anxiety is a typical problem among most Singaporean athletes. Given constant monitoring of their progress and pressure from both parents and coaches to excel in sport, athletes struggle to please by winning competitions. Elite sport has just started growing, and a general lack of winning experiences at international competitions has been one of the major concerns of staff and coaches.

Thus, psychology professionals working on goal setting with Singaporean athletes must be aware that their clients will tend to focus only on the results of major competitions. Typically, athletes include avoiding mistakes as a process goal because if they make a mistake, they won't win and the coach won't be happy. Many athletes also report that they do not feel competent in sport because they make mistakes.

It is typical for Singaporean athletes to show an all-or-nothing attitude, which means if they don't win, they don't feel competent.

Usual recommendations for athletes in Singapore include strategies for coping with adversity. Accepting the fact that every athlete will make mistakes either in training or competitions may be a breakthrough moment for Singaporean athletes. Thus, the sport psychologist will need to focus on dealing with mistakes already made rather than on not making a mistake. This approach will help the athletes have a constructive attitude toward training and competition. As the focus shifts from avoiding mistakes to process and performance goals, athletes should be able to develop a healthier perspective toward competition.

Parental education also should help lessen athletes' negative self-perceptions and improve the overall motivational climate. Tremendous media attention, especially regarding endorsements, can give both athletes and parents a false sense of success. Parents should instead keep winning in perspective and help athletes set realistic process and outcome goals. They should encourage their children in sport and reinforce preparation and hard work, which will eventually lead to their children becoming responsible athletes. To enhance positive parental behavior, communication among coaches, staff members, and sport psychology professionals is imperative.

BALANCING ACADEMICS AND SPORT

As mentioned earlier, academic demands in Singapore are high, and excelling in examinations generally secures one's future. Athletes are expected to excel in academics as well as in their sport because sport alone rarely pays. Thus, athletes are constantly under stress, and their stress levels dramatically increase about a month before examinations. Travel demands also affect submission of assignments and contributions to group projects. In addition, some athletes take a break from training to focus on preparing for the examinations. Missing training due to examinations is often detrimental for athletes and coaches and causes stress for both parties. Physical fitness and technique suffer from diverging priorities even though many aspiring athletes attempt to balance both competition and examination demands.

Sport psychologists can help athletes apply coping strategies to this difficult situation. Problem-focused coping strategies that have proven effective among Singaporean athletes include time management and study planning. Exam dates are usually fixed by the school and athletes have to work their training around the examination timetable. Thus, annual planning for training and competitions is crucial. Athletes may have to prioritize certain competitions and forego others that clash with their examinations. Careful planning of training phases and selecting the right competitions are critical for success.

The government has recognized this dilemma and has allowed some flexibility for athletes sitting for examinations at the university level. Additionally, sport psychology professionals can help the athletes think about how important the competition could be in terms of their sport career. Questions such as "What are the consequences of not competing at one or two competitions?" can be discussed with the athletes.

If it is impossible to skip competitions (for example, qualifying events), it is important to help athletes plan early for both competitions and exams. Early and diligent preparation for examinations might give athletes more training time as the examinations approach. It is also common for athletes to ask for extensions for assignments because of training and competition schedules; thus, athletes need to learn how to negotiate with their teachers and principals. Lastly, it is imperative to equip athletes with a weekly plan incorporating schoolwork, tutoring, sport-specific training, general fitness and weight training, meetings with athletic trainers, medical checkups, debriefing with coaches and staff members, psychological skills training, and time for rest or relaxation. A thorough plan incorporating such details will help athletes to worry less and reduce the stress brought on by the demands of juggling academics and sport.

Project 0812 (see page 198) is extremely important for athletes because elite athletes often lack social support during exams. The project allows them to focus on training for international competitions without having to keep up with academic work at the same time. Even with that program, however, many elite athletes still struggle with balancing academics and sport.

LEADERSHIP STYLES AND FOREIGN COACHES

Coaching behavior has a significant effect on athletes' performances and psychological well-being (Horn, 2002). Recent government support of elite sport is reflected by the influx of foreign coaches. In Singapore it is common for elite athletes to work closely with coaches from, for example, Australia, China, South America, and the United Kingdom. As a consequence, Singaporean athletes have dramatically improved their skills, techniques, and tactics.

TRAIN AND STUDY SMART

Amanda was a student in secondary school who was training for an upcoming international table-tennis event. The annual standardized academic exam was a week before she was to compete. Her teacher and parents asked her to study for the exam instead of competing, but she believed that competing at the event was crucial for her athletic career.

Amanda, her coaches and staff, and her sport psychology consultant needed to find a solution. First, Amanda and her coach and staff sat down with her parents to ask their permission for her to compete, helping her parents to understand that she had great potential as a player and competing at the event would help her gain experience. Second, Amanda and her coach modified the training schedule as follows: training less during weekdays to reduce traveling time to and from the training center, finding space and time at home to fulfill fitness and conditioning training, and studying before the start of training over the weekend. Third, her sport psychology consultant helped her to come up with a specific timetable for each day that included studying, training, relaxing, and sleeping. Fourth, Amanda, her coach, and her sport psychology consultant discussed specific goals for training, fitness and conditioning, studying, and preparing for the trip (e.g., packing).

Social support from her parents, staff, coach, and sport psychology consultant helped Amanda to cope with the stress before and during the exam and prepared her well for the competition. Since then, it has become more acceptable for athletes to train before exams, and other athletes on the team also have started to create a balance between academics and sport.

The medal counts from recent international competitions have increased, reflecting improvement of Singaporean athletes in the international scene. On the other hand, athletes have raised concerns about communication, mainly because the leadership styles of foreign coaches are often different from Singaporean sport practice.

Singaporean values adhere to a hierarchical relationship that comes from Confucian teachings and Eastern religious practices of respect for people of higher status such as elders, parents, teachers, and bosses (Meriwether, 2001). The hierarchical relationship can be explained by power distance, which refers to social acceptance of inequality in power between people. Based on surveys among 50 countries and 3 regions, Singapore was ranked 13th on power distance, the United States was ranked 38th, and Australia was ranked 41st (Hofstede, 2001). In lower-ranked countries, teachers and students treat each other as equals and students initiate some communication in class. However, in higher-ranked countries, students treat teachers with respect and defer to teachers. Teachers initiate communication in class and students tend not to ask or answer questions openly (Hofstede, 2001; Meriwether, 2001).

Horn's (2002) working model of coaching effectiveness explains that the sociocultural context, organizational climate, and coaches' personal characteristics may influence coaching behavior. Coaching behavior may be mediated by coaches' characteristics, values, beliefs, and goals, which in turn may affect athletes' performance and behavior as well as perceptions, interpretation, and evaluation of their coaches' behavior. Applying Horn's model to the current situation in Singapore suggests that an understanding of the culture, especially its hierarchical aspects, is an asset when working with athletes.

At present, coaches mainly come from Western cultures or have been trained in Western countries, so their values, beliefs, and goals are slightly different than those of Singaporean athletes. For example, some coaches with Western values provide instruction during training and competitions and encourage athletes to make their own decisions about tactics and strategies. This democratic style of leadership tends to make Singaporean athletes feel insecure because they prefer to be given quick strategies that will lead to immediate success. An autocratic style of coaching involves the coach making decisions with little or no input from the athletes. Although an autocratic style is less challenging for the athletes due to the lack of responsibility in making decisions, during the competition they must make critical decisions on their own. If they have not practiced decision making during training, it is likely they won't perform well in international arenas.

Helping foreign coaches adjust their leadership style to the Singaporean context may be helpful. As mentioned, the Singaporean value system focuses on respect and team thinking; thus, athletes prefer

WESTERN COACH AND EASTERN ATHLETES

Eric was an experienced Australian sailing coach and had been coaching the sailing team in Singapore for about a year. He felt that the Singaporean sailors were good listeners but lacked the courage to act spontaneously. On the other hand, the sailors thought that Eric was a great coach but lacked in giving specific advice about their performance.

For example, during training Eric felt that the sailors were capable of implementing tactics and techniques he taught them. When he debriefed the training session, the sailors seemed to understand what Eric was saying and provided perfect answers to his questions. They also could give specific strategies to follow on the water. Thus, Eric felt that the sailors were capable of making appropriate decisions during a regatta without his input.

The sailors felt that Eric taught good sailing techniques and tactics, as demonstrated in their improvement under his coaching. At the same time, they did not know what tactics or techniques to use if the scenario changed from what Eric had taught them. The sailors also felt guilty if they made unnecessary mistakes. However, sailing is a unique sport with constantly changing conditions, which means decision making is crucial. Without quick and appropriate decision-making processes, it would be hard for the Singaporean sailors to compete against international-level sailors.

A sport psychology consultant helped Eric understand that in Singaporean culture, athletes are not comfortable questioning teachers, coaches, and parents. They also are not used to making spontaneous decisions on their own and are sometimes afraid to make decisions, thinking that it might hurt their relationships with the coaches. Therefore, Eric needed to be supportive and patient for his sailors to learn to make appropriate decisions at crucial moments. The sport psychology consultant also helped the sailors by conducting sessions about being independent and responsible sailors by making decisions on their own. The sailors were also encouraged to ask Eric questions as necessary.

Both Eric and the sailors have been slowly learning about each other. This progress has shown in the sailors' performances, which have been excelling under Eric's guidance.

ISSUES AND STRATEGIES TO CONSIDER WHEN WORKING WITH SINGAPOREAN ATHLETES

If you are working with Singaporean athletes, keep the following points in mind.

- Athletes in Singapore tend to have high expectations to win and as a result are afraid to make mistakes. Athletes must learn how to cope with the fear of making mistakes.
  - Sport psychology professionals can help athletes by teaching them skills such as goal setting, especially process and performance goals.
  - Parental education, including realistic expectations for children's performance and positive behavior toward coaches and staff, should be helpful.
- Athletes in Singapore are expected to excel in both sport and academics, and their stress increases tremendously before examinations. Sport psychology professionals can help athletes
  - learn time management for studying and training,
  - prioritize examinations and competitions, and
  - learn how to negotiate with teachers.
- Coaches from non-Asian countries have been improving the quality of athletic performances in Singapore. At the same time, communication between foreign coaches and local athletes can be improved. Sport psychology professionals should
  - conduct coaching education sessions for better understanding of values, beliefs, and goals in Singapore; and
  - help athletes lean how to communicate with coaches to maximize their learning experiences with foreign coaches.

an autocratic leadership style in sport. Singaporean athletes are not used to decision making and prefer authority figures to be the decision makers. In addition, abdicating the decision-making process to others absolves them from taking responsibility when mistakes are made, which somewhat lessens the societal pressure they feel to succeed. Coaches should learn how these factors lead Singaporean athletes to think less spontaneously and want to follow their coaches' strategic plans instead of developing their own.

Learning is a two-way process of communication between coaches and athletes, and thus sport psychology professionals are needed to help athletes learn how, what, and when to ask about technique, tactics, or strategies. It is also important for athletes to inform their coaches about physical and psychological conditions so coaches will have a chance to adjust the training and competition plans. Thus, sport psychology professionals may be in a position to educate Singaporean athletes and foreign coaches and thereby help improve coach–athlete relationships.

SAMURAI AND SCIENCE: SPORT PSYCHOLOGY IN JAPAN

Yoichi Kozuma, MPE

Most coaches and athletes seek practical solutions that can enhance performance. In Japan, however, accepting scientific methods in sport has not been easy. Coaches are generally unfamiliar with sport psychology because of a long-standing tradition of basing their athletes' training programs on their personal experiences. Athletes typically follow their coaches' training methods and later perpetuate the cycle when they become coaches. In addition, other cultural factors influence the acceptance of sport psychology by both coaches and athletes.

Although many Western sports exist in Japan, strong Japanese traditions and culture often hinder the progress of applied sport psychology. The application of sport psychology in Japan needs to combine both Eastern and Western approaches. In this chapter I will explore the historical traditions of Japan and how they have influenced the introduction of sport psychology to Japanese elite athletes.

CULTURE OF FEUDAL JAPAN

Although Japanese history goes back more than 2,000 years, many people in the West are most familiar with feudal Japan, when the ruling class consisted of samurai and shoguns. The West has glorified feudal Japan in movies and literature for the loyalty, bravery, and honor of the samurai class.

From the 12th to the 19th centuries, Japan was organized under a feudal system where the emperor was the ceremonial ruler of the country. The political and military powers were in the hands of the shogun, a military warlord whose rank and title were hereditary. The shogunate system was a military dictatorship that established a rigid social caste system. Under the shogun were powerful regional feudal lords,

called *daimyo*, who had autocratic control over their domains. The samurai were a noble class of warriors who were the military retainers of a daimyo and who vowed absolute allegiance to their lord. Members of the samurai class were afforded many social and financial privileges that were not available to commoners. Only the samurai could carry swords, which became emblems for their swordsmanship skills as well as their status in society. For the samurai, the sword was their identity.

The samurai class lived by an ethical code of behavior known as *Bushido*, or the way of the warrior. The Bushido tenets emphasize duty, loyalty, courage, justice, chivalry, spirit, and honor in death (Yamamoto, 2001). The idea was to develop not only the martial skills necessary for battle but also to strengthen one's true warrior character. This ethical code of behavior, which was founded in teachings from Buddhism, Zen, Confucianism, and Shintoism, was instilled from a young age and all members of the samurai class were required to abide by it. Violations of the code were often met with the death penalty for both the samurai warrior and his family. Any actions or thoughts deemed unworthy of a samurai warrior would result in purging the family line from nobility and the family would simply cease to exist.

HISTORY OF JAPANESE SPORT PSYCHOLOGY

The history of sport in Japan is strongly connected with the samurai. Although sport psychology is a modern Western concept, the mental outlook of Japanese athletes has always been influenced by samurai values.

SAMURAI VALUES IN MODERN JAPANESE SPORT

Many have described Bushido as the essence of modern Japanese culture, and the influence of the samurai can still be seen today. One example can be found in Japanese sport, namely martial arts. During the Meiji era (1868-1912), judo became the first Japanese sport introduced to physical education in schools. Around the same time, many other martial arts (i.e., kendo, karate, and aikido) reorganized themselves into competitive sports; however, their foundation and philosophy retained the original martial arts methods of training to develop martial skills and character. The new martial art sports also maintained the ethical codes instilled in the samurai warriors of the past. In addition, the rigid elitist hierarchy of the samurai was preserved. The upper echelons of the hierarchy had absolute authority and often treated those who were lower ranked in a tyrannical manner. Lower-ranking athletes did not question authority, loyalty and alliance to the team was the utmost, and the coach was the supreme ruler of the athletes.

As Japan started to adopt various Western sports, the philosophy of training, practice, and sportsman-

Samurai ideals remain an important element of Japanese culture and are key to understanding Japanese athletes.

© AP Photo/Tsugufumi Matsumoto

ship still reflected the samurai culture of the past. One such sport introduced during the Meiji era was baseball. The Japanese viewed baseball as a perfect fit for their culture. According to Whiting (1989), the one-on-one battle between the pitcher and the batter is similar to battles in martial arts, and mental and physical strength as well as harmony and split-second timing are required in both. The Ministry of Education encouraged the growth of baseball, believing that it would be good for the development of the national character.

Thus, the foundation of baseball in Japan is based on the training of a warrior. Warrior training included the notion that the more you train, the better you become. This stems from the days when the samurai would train constantly to perfect their martial skills. Samurai were professional warriors, so becoming skilled was their only goal when they were not fighting a war. Similarly, athletes dedicate an enormous amount of time to training for a game or competition. Participation in sport becomes a year-round commitment to consecutive days of training with long hours. In addition, a military style of psychological training has emerged where orders are obeyed without question. Coaches have become more like drill sergeants, using techniques such as shouting, anger, punishment, and negative coaching.

When various other sports were introduced around the turn of the 20th century, the underlying function of sport was not to provide leisure and exercise but to provide mental discipline to create a strong character (Guttman & Lee, 2001). Before the 1890s, track and field, football (soccer), and rugby were introduced into the school system and competition between schools was encouraged. Competition was viewed as the new battlefield and the samurai code was still enforced through sport. In addition to samurai training techniques, the teachings of famous martial artists from the samurai era still influenced how sport was played, practiced, and coached because the teachings were integrated into the newly introduced Western sports.

Musashi Miyamoto was a famed samurai swordsman in the 1600s who wrote books to teach his students tactics, strategies, and philosophy in the art of swordsmanship. His famous book, *The Book of Five Rings*, emphasizes mental preparation and discipline for fighting in the field (Miyamoto, 2001). His method included meditation before practice or battle to clear the mind so the warrior could focus on the sword-to-sword battle. Another samurai, Yamaoka Tesshu, who lived in the 19th century, focused on the importance of combining martial arts (physical training) and Zen prayer and meditation (psychological training). The traditional philosophies and training techniques that originated with these two men can still be seen in sport today. For example, many professional athletes go to Zen temples to meditate before the start of their season.

KONJO VERSUS SPORT PSYCHOLOGY

Japanese society has often been described as having strong traditions that do not easily incorporate new ideas, especially ideas that do not originate from Japan. The first Japanese sport psychology book was published in 1923 (Tokunaga, 2005), but the readership was limited to researchers and scholars in higher education. Not until 1960 was there movement toward sport psychology, when researchers proposed to study how Japanese Olympic athletes handled pressure during competition in preparation for the 1964 Tokyo Olympic Games. The project was called *Sport Psychology Practices With Elite Athletes in Japan*, and the researchers were all from the field of clinical psychology (Japan Sport Association, 1960). The project was limited to shooting, gymnastics, and swimming, and it was not well received. The problem was that the researchers used techniques from clinical psychology that were simply not suitable for sport. After the Tokyo Games, sport psychology practice was suspended and did not restart until 1985, after the 1984 Olympic Games in Los Angeles (Inomata, 1997).

One major hurdle to the use of any scientific approach to elite sport is the predominance of *konjo*. Many generations of athletes and coaches have been influenced by the notion of konjo, which comes from the strong influence of the samurai world on sport. Konjo has been loosely translated into English as "guts," but it has a much deeper meaning, including high physical endurance, courage under adversity, and the tenacity to face pain and hardship for the good of the team. Konjo became a catch phrase in Japanese sport and was highlighted in the mass media when the gold-medal win of the national volleyball team at the 1964 Tokyo Olympic Games was attributed to the team's konjo. Winning teams or athletes were believed to accomplish their goals solely because of their konjo. Teams or athletes who did not succeed were reprimanded because they did not put in enough effort to show their konjo (i.e., did not practice enough, did not give it their all, or did not sacrifice enough). Echoing the samurai code of ethics, konjo was perceived as the only reason why a team would win or lose, and it is still prevalent in many sports today.

LONGITUDINAL MENTAL TRAINING PROJECT

Remnant beliefs from the samurai warrior class and faith placed on konjo in the sport community are still strong and often difficult to overcome. The introduction of Western ideas is often viewed with suspicion, as was the case with a longitudinal mental training project for elite athletes that continued from 1985 to 2002 (Kozuma, 2003). In 1985, the Japan Sport Association initiated a five-step longitudinal mental management project to provide psychological support in order to enhance the performance of the national teams who would compete in the 1988 Seoul Olympic Games.

More than 50 sport psychologists from various academic settings participated in the first step of the project (1985-1989). Because mental training was a new concept in Japan, the focus of the project was collecting material on mental training and surveying the Japanese athletes and coaches on their current psychological conditions and training. Information on mental training was collected from around the world, and the data were consolidated and tailored to the Japanese elite athletes. A 10-week basic mental training program was produced on audiotapes that included concentration, imagery, relaxation, and positive thinking. In addition, sport-specific programs for gymnastics, tennis, shooting, boxing, and marathon runners were produced. The audiotapes were distributed to the national team members for the 1987 Asian Games and the 1988 Seoul Olympic Games.

A post-Olympic survey showed that the majority of the sport associations would not accept mental training as a scientific approach to enhance the performance of elite athletes. They felt that it was not effective, not important, and not necessary. The same survey results were found after the Team Sport Project (1990-1993) for the 1992 Barcelona Olympic Games. The nonacceptance of mental training continued until the Junior Athletes Project (1994-1996) postgame survey, which found a slight change in the attitudes of coaches. The coaches thought that psychological factors were important for athletes but did not think it was necessary to provide any support or training for psychological skills. The coaches of the 1998 Nagano Winter Games expressed similar beliefs. The coaches realized that psychological skills were important, but they did not have any experience teaching psychological skills to athletes. They also did not know who to turn to for assistance. At the time, the majority of the sport psychologists in Japan were involved strictly in research and only a few sport psychologists were practicing in the field.

GROWING ACCEPTANCE

It was not until the turn of the century that the door to the acceptance of sport psychology slowly opened. For the 2000 Olympic Games in Sydney, a letter was sent to all Olympic teams to offer a mental training program for the athletes. Fourteen teams responded and participated in a mental training program, which consisted of a lecture and a workshop just before the start of the Games. Although the response was small, the sport community began to become aware of the possibility of sport psychology techniques.

Hoping to increase this trend, the Japanese Institute of Sport Science (JISS) opened in 2001 to provide support to national team members. To fill the gap in the market, various businesses joined the bandwagon and started to offer psychological support to all athletes. The problem was that the majority of these businesses did not have sport psychology backgrounds and were simply in business for the profit. The high prices they charged and the uncertain qualifications of the programs they sold made the coaches and athletes wary of incorporating sport psychology in their training.

To educate the general public and to establish the credibility of psychological support, the Japanese Society of Sport Psychology (JSSP) created a certified two-tier consultant system: the Certified Mental Training Consultant in Sport and the Certified Mental Training Assistant Consultant in Sport. In 2007, 37 certified consultants and 57 certified assistant consultants were working in Japan. The JSSP sends a list of the certified mental training consultants to every professional team, sport association, and school athletic department throughout Japan. Around the same time, the JISS also established a certification system for those who consult with national team members.

Before a nationwide certification system was established, the Japanese Society of Mental Training and Applied Sport Psychology (JSMTASP) educated coaches and athletes. Founded in 1994 under the auspices of the International Society of Mental Training and Excellence (ISMTE), the purpose of this organization was to hold monthly workshops to introduce psychological skills and techniques for performance enhancement and to provide consultations for athletes, coaches, and teams of all ages and levels. Members were required to meet certain criteria before they were able to go into the field to provide support. One factor in the success of the JSMTASP was that it was open to anyone who was interested in mental training. Thus, it was able to educate parents, coaches, athletes, and anyone else who worked with teams or individual athletes.

Following this development, Tokai University started an academic education system to certify mental training consultants in sport. The university designed an undergraduate and graduate curriculum that incorporates applied sport psychology and mental training studies in addition to fieldwork with the university teams. Graduates from the program work with professional, national, college, secondary, and elementary school teams and athletes.

Awareness of sport psychology is slowly growing throughout the sport community, but it still faces many obstacles. Not only are there cultural traditions to overcome, but there are also financial restraints. Psychological support is considered important, but funding for an athlete or team to hire full-time sport psychologists is rare. In addition, for those who do have an opportunity to work with a team or athlete, the payment is minimal. As an example, when I worked with a national athlete for the 2000 Sydney Olympic Games I volunteered my consultation work and had to pay for my own travel expenses and accommodation at the Games. For my work with a national team for the 2004 Athens Games, I received approximately US$20 a day. Because of this low pay, sport psychologists in Japan are often faculty members at universities and are more proactive in the research field than in the applied field. Consequently, theories posited from the research field do not always transfer easily to the applied field due to the limited access of the sport psychologists to athletes and teams. With these restrictions, fieldwork application becomes difficult; however, there are some examples of successful programs that have been implemented with Japanese elite athletes. See pages 212-213 for examples of mental training in the field in Japan.

The practice of applied sport psychology with elite Japanese athletes is expanding. Due to strong traditions and culture, the process may seem slow to those outside of Japan, but interest in sport psychology is growing in a positive direction. The number of people studying in the field is also increasing. Now there are young graduate students who are seeking to be certified as sport psychology consultants. More and more institutions of higher education are designing programs that encompass sport psychology and mental training. In addition, many sport teams and athletes are now aware of the importance of the mental aspect of sport and are becoming more open to integrating psychological skills in their training and practice. It is my hope that the contributions from sport psychology and mental training specialists become as recognized by the sport community in Japan as they are in the West and become accessible to all sports at all levels.

WORKING
WITH JAPANESE ATHLETES

For applied practitioners outside of Japan who are interested in working with Japanese athletes, it is important to realize that although sport may appear on the surface to be the same, underneath lies a strong culture still influenced by samurai traditions. The samurai code of Bushido still exists in the world of sport and can be seen at all levels, from junior organizations to professional sport.

Needless to say, one must also be aware of the language barrier. Although English is taught as a foreign language in secondary schools and colleges, this does not mean that many Japanese can speak English. There was a case where a professional baseball team retained the service of a sport psychologist from the United States; however, due to the language gap, the consultation did not last long. Because the American sport psychologist did not speak Japanese, it became expensive for the team to hire a translator, and the program did not go over well because concepts and skills were lost in translation. Although the language barrier does not seem to be a concern for Japanese athletes overseas, it is still a problem for those who are active in their sport in Japan.

More importantly, one must recognize the role of coaches in Japan. There are few coaches whose coaching job is their career. With the exception of professional teams and athletes, coaches are volunteers, and it is often difficult for a volunteer coach to hire any supporting staff, much less a sport psychologist. Furthermore, although it is slowly changing, the coach is often the authoritative figure similar to the daimyo and rules over the team with an iron fist. The rigid hierarchy of coach and athlete is strictly enforced, and it is the coach who seeks information and makes final decisions for the team.

This authority could be a challenge because Japan has no coaching education system in higher education. Coaches do not formally learn coaching theories, skills, or techniques and therefore rely heavily on the tradition of the sport. Most base their coaching on past experience and do not feel comfortable modifying their coaching style, which they consider to be tried and true. The incorporation of mental training can only be successful if it is fully supported by the coach, so the introduction of sport psychology concepts must be culturally sensitive to the sport as well as to the coach.

Many other unique aspects of the Japanese approach to life influence sport in Japan. Some of the most important are addressed in the following examples.

EXAMPLE 1:
MEN'S FOOTBALL TEAM
IN THE 1995 UNIVERSIADE GAMES

In 1995, Japan hosted the Universiade Games, also known as the World University Games or World Student Games, in Fukuoka. For the first time, the Japanese team won a gold medal for football in an international competition. It was also the first time a national team followed a mental training program as a scheduled part of training. Three months before the Universiade Games, the National University Football Team requested a mental training program. This request was most likely due to strong interest expressed by the coaching staff and administrators of the team. Three mental training specialists in sport psychology and a football coach from a university team were selected to provide mental training. The program was administered during a weeklong training camp held 2 months before the competition, 1 week before the competition, and during the actual competition. Throughout the 2 weeks of the competition, a sport psychologist was available to the team at practice, at the actual competition, and at the athlete's village to provide support (Kozuma, 2002). Following is the detailed schedule and mental training program provided to the national football team.

STAGE 1

Two months before the Universiade Games, a weeklong training camp was held. The training camp consisted of 15 hours of mental training instruction, which was administered four times a day. I was the sport psychologist for the team and requested that all athletes and coaches participate in the mental training program.

The second segment consisted of mental preparation training that was administered 10 minutes before the daily practice session. The 10-minute package for practice preparation included relaxation, psyching up, visualization, self-talk, concentration, positive thinking, and other techniques that were applicable to the practice session that day. The psyching-up skills were especially important for developing group dynamics and cohesion. For their psyching-up routine, the team did shadowboxing and shadow karate fighting to upbeat dance music. Using music before and during practice was a new experience for the team. Practice time was serious, and the idea of using music to help the team focus and relax was foreign to them. Through trial and error, European club music was introduced to different segments of the practice. Based on my advice, the coaching staff supported the use of music during practice and the idea was well received by the athletes. Later the team developed an original warm-up routine for psychological and physiological preparation using the football skills of a Brazilian exercise.

After practice, a psychological cool-down session was held after the athletes physically cooled down. The 10-minute cool-down included relaxation, visualization, meditation, and emotional control. I designed the segment so that the athletes could switch their feelings from the events that had happened during practice to their personal lives. After dinner, an hour-long mental training seminar was held in a classroom setting. The classroom setting provided the athletes with an opportunity to increase their theoretical understanding of mental training and to record in journals personal data and their reactions to the techniques they had learned. Ending the day in this manner would be a breakthrough for any Japanese team, because designated sessions for mental training and self reflection are not typical.

STAGE 1 INTERVENTIONS

The mental training practice started before breakfast with 30 minutes of exercise and self-conditioning skills. Previously, the team would conduct morning exercise before breakfast, but it simply consisted of a walk. The difference this time was that the walk had a purpose of mental and physical conditioning. Self-conditioning skills were introduced as a package of relaxation techniques, including relaxing music, smiling, self-massage, breathing control, stretching, progressive relaxation techniques, autogenic training, meditation, and a 10- to 20-minute walk. During the morning exercise, each athlete carried a heart-rate monitor to check his physiological reactions and emotional states. After the morning exercise, the athletes and coaches were alert, relaxed, and felt good about themselves. From these sessions, the athletes learned self-control and mental preparation techniques that they were able to apply to their practice sessions and practice games. The skills acquired during these sessions were transferable and became part of their daily lives as they prepared for the competition.

STAGE 2

I was with the team every day during stage 1. At the end of the training camp, the team members were allowed to go home for 2 days before reconvening at the airport for a trip abroad. Since I could not be with the team for the trip to their pregame camp, I instructed the athletes to continue their daily writings in their mental training journals and to continue implementing the relaxation and psyching-up skills during practice.

STAGE 2 INTERVENTIONS

The team traveled to Russia for 11 days in preparation for the Universiade Games. The trip to Russia was designed to provide the experience of playing against a foreign team at a foreign location. During the trip, the athletes continued their mental preparation routine of writing in their journals as well as practicing their relaxation and psyching-up skills.

The team members gathered for a pregame camp held 1 week before the Universiade Games. As part of their mental preparation, a video of the competition site and the athlete's village was shown to the team. The athletes were instructed to visualize the event through the images of the video. This visualization helped the team become familiar with the actual stadium and the field.

STAGE 3

The day before the competition, I met with the team again. I was available at their practice session and at the athletes' village to consult with them individually. By this time, the team had evolved and created an original mental preparation and psyching-up program.

Sixteen teams from around the world competed in the football championship at the 1995 Universiade Games. The Japanese team won its first gold medal that year and continued to win gold medals in 1999, 2001, and 2003. For the subsequent Universiade Games, some of the coaching staff was retained, allowing the continuation of the mental training program for the succeeding teams. Several members of the 1995 team went on to become professional footballers, and about one-third were still active as of 2007.

This particular team had several landmark achievements. They were the first Japanese team to incorporate the support of a sport psychologist for mental training. A total of 120 hours of mental training support was provided for the Universiade Games. More importantly, the coaches and athletes developed an unusual relationship not readily found in a traditional Japanese team. The rigid hierarchy and training techniques left over from the samurai days did not apply to this team. Both coaches and athletes participated in the mental training program side by side. The coaching staff showed great interest in mental training and incorporated the program into their practice schedule, training camp, and free time. In addition, positive communication skills were established. The coaches encouraged the athletes in a positive manner and did not fall into the traditional method of giving negative remarks and instructions. The coaches were also open to new ideas such as using music before and during practice and establishing routines before the game that supported the athletes rather than threatening them into doing their best. The athletes were also accepting of new ideas.

For both the coaching staff and the athletes, participating in a mental training program was a new experience. Some of the steps involved in mental training were confusing and hard for them to understand at first. One example was goal setting. The team was told to focus on a goal to win, but the concept of winning at an international event was unfamiliar to them. The team faced the Universiade Games at a time when no Japanese team had ever won an international competition for football. The players were dedicated to playing their best, but they never considered the possibility that they could win the gold medal.

Another new experience involved the athletes becoming responsible for their training. After the initial introduction to the mental training program, the athletes took it upon themselves to continue mental training both during practice time and during their free time. They were never forcibly told what to do. This was a divergent approach from the military style of keeping the chain of command intact where the athletes had no say in team matters and blindly obeyed orders. They all kept journals and were encouraged to express their personal reflections on the coaches, practice, or mental training. The football players realized that mental training was beneficial for them as well as the team and took the responsibility to continue the program.

STAGE 3 INTERVENTIONS

I was with the team for the entire 2 weeks of the competition. At the competition site, I waited for the team bus to arrive from the athletes' village. I observed the team members' faces, expressions, attitudes, and general feelings before the game. When the athletes entered the locker room, psyching-up music was already playing. The athletes were smiling and relaxing in the locker room an hour before the game. At the team meeting, the coaches used many positive words to encourage the athletes to play their best and to discuss the game plan. After the meeting, as the team prepared for the competition, each athlete performed his own relaxation, visualization, self-talk, positive thinking, meditation, and psyching-up techniques.

Dance music was used to signal the start of the warm-up session. The music was playing while the team walked to the area designated for their warm-up practice. The warm-up area was closed to the public; only the team and the staff had access. The team warmed up using the routine they created from the Brazilian football exercise and dance music. After 10 minutes, the music stopped, and the athletes did some stretching for 10 minutes without any music. Once again, the dance music started, cueing the team to commence a 10-minute warm-up session with a football. The purpose of this warm-up session was to combine physical and mental aspects in preparation for the competition.

At the end of the warm-up session, each team member counted off in a loud voice to raise his competitive spirit, a technique used by many Japanese teams. The athletes formed a circle holding hands, and the coach stood in the middle. The purpose of the circle was to help the team focus on the game and to increase the feeling of being a team. The team huddled closer together and clapped in rhythm with the coach to create a sense of oneness. After the huddle, the team changed locations and did some precompetitive practice on the actual playing field. Music played during the entire time.

When the team returned to the locker room, they again were greeted with upbeat music. The music was played at a low volume while the athletes changed into their uniforms and prepared for the game. During this time, I gave specific signs to individual athletes to encourage them to relax, smile, do self-massage, or do deep breathing exercises. I accomplished this through mimicking—when I took a deep breath, the athlete would take a deep breath; when I smiled, the athlete would smile back. I also used a camera to encourage the athletes to relax because they would automatically pose and smile when their picture was being taken.

A few minutes before the game, everyone in the locker room, including the coaches, staff, team doctor, trainers, and mental training support staff, formed a circle by joining hands to symbolize teamwork. The team captain shouted out words of encouragement and the team headed to the field with the music blaring in the background. The coaches and the staff met with the athletes at the door before they entered the field. They gave high fives to each player and shouted encouragement. Shouting is often used because it is a breath-control technique that can enhance concentration and help athletes focus on the competition at hand. The players walked onto the field hand in hand until they reached the center and bowed to the audience. At halftime, the players came back to the locker room and had quiet relaxation time for about 3 minutes, and the coaches gave some advice to the athletes as they rested. During halftime, the players had time to refocus and recharge their energy for the last half of the game.

The act of walking onto the field was a combination of both Japanese and Western cultures. The idea of walking onto the field hand in hand was borrowed from the Brazilian national football team, who entered the field in a similar manner during the 1994 World Cup. Walking hand in hand is not generally seen among Japanese adults, but it was suggested that they should show their unity as a team that is determined to win by entering the field in the same manner as the 1994 World Cup champions. Before the start of the game, the team bowed to the audience and to the other team. The Japanese tradition of bowing is a social gesture with many meanings; it can be used to greet, to apologize, to show respect, to show appreciation, and to show acknowledgment. In feudal Japan, the samurai would bow to show respect to the battlefield and would bow to acknowledge the enemy before the battle commenced. Since the outcome of a battle could result in death, the samurai would be able to leave this world without any regrets because he had shown his respect to life and death as he performed his warrior duty. In the same manner, all sport games in Japan start and end with a bow.

EXAMPLE 2: MEN'S OLYMPIC JUDO TEAM

In April 2000, the head coach of the national judo team requested that I consult with a prospective Olympic judo athlete. The athlete was a university student majoring in physical education at the same university where I teach, so as part of the consulting process, I advised the judo player to enroll in two of my university courses: sport psychology and mental training in applied sport psychology. I also asked him to see me once or twice a week for personal sessions. Some of the basic psychological skills that I introduced to the athlete were goal setting, relaxation, psyching up, visualization, concentration, positive

thinking, self-talk, and mental preparation for competition. During this consultation, the judo athlete won the national tournament for the 100-kilogram weight division and placed second in the open weight national tournament in Japan, thereby qualifying for selection for the 2000 Sydney Olympic Games.

During the weeklong summer camp for the national judo team just before the Olympic Games, I consulted with the judo athlete on a daily basis. I also gave a talk to the coaching staff that provided them with background on mental preparation and what they could do for their athletes. I traveled with the judo team to Sydney as an independent member of the support staff because I was not recognized as an official member of the Olympic team. Before the start of the Olympic Games, I provided the judo athlete with psychological support during his daily practice at the Olympic site. The athlete ultimately won the gold medal for his weight class.

After the Sydney Olympic Games, the new head coach of the judo national team wanted to extend psychological skills support to the entire team for the 2004 Athens Olympic Games. At the Athens Games, the men's national team won three gold medals and one silver medal, an outstanding record in the history of the Japanese national judo team.

Providing psychological support for the 2004 national judo team was a 4-year process that started at a national judo team camp held at the end of 2000. I provided consultation on goal setting, relaxation, psyching up, visualization, concentration, positive thinking, self-talk, and metal preparation for competition. I participated in all of the national judo team training camps, which were held four or five times a year for 4 years. In addition, I traveled with the team and provided consultation at the various Japan championship and international world championship sites where the team was competing.

INTRODUCING MENTAL TRAINING

At the beginning of judo camp, data from all the team members were collected using two standardized Japanese sport psychology tests that evaluated motivation and other psychological factors. Since mental training was a new concept for many, both the athletes and coaches attended an introductory workshop on mental training that I conducted. At this workshop, reading material consisting of a mental training textbook and workbook (Kozuma, 1995) was provided to both athletes and coaches. The study of mental training continued at every training camp, where I held mental training and sport psychology seminars for the entire team and provided individual study sessions for the athletes.

DAILY MENTAL TRAINING SCHEDULE

Every morning the athletes would gather at 7:00 at a designated place to perform morning exercises for psychological conditioning, including attitude training, smiling, relaxing music, positive conversations with a partner, breath control through karate techniques, stretching with breath control, progressive relaxation, simple autogenic training, meditation, 10 seconds of visualization for their best performance, and physically reenacting their best performance in slow motion. The best-performance visualization was practiced several times both mentally and physically to create a clear image of the athlete's personal best. After the morning exercises, everyone took a walk for about 15 minutes. The walk was an important segment of the morning exercise and created an opportunity for informal discussion with the athletes. Open communication was important to maintain, so after the walk I ate breakfast with the athletes and even went to the practice site an hour before the start of practice so that the they would have ample opportunities to speak with me in a nonstructured environment.

At the training camps, the judo team had morning and afternoon training sessions. From 2000 to 2002, I worked with all of the athletes for 15 minutes at the beginning of every training session to practice their mental preparation skills. After 2 years, the athletes were able to perform the mental preparation on their own and were able to integrate the practice into their own preperformance routine. During the training sessions, I monitored the athletes' psychological attitudes and mental states. I provided feedback that the players could use on-site to help them refocus on their task. After the afternoon practice, time was set aside for the athletes to communicate with each other about the mental aspects of their sport, reflect on practice for that particular day, and express any comments or concerns.

Before dinner, I would bathe with the judo athletes in the local hot spring. The purpose of soaking in a bath is not only cleaning the body but also resting. Hot springs are high in mineral content and are said to have certain health benefits in addition to offering a place to relax the mind and body. Bathing at a hot spring in groups is a traditional Japanese style of bathing. It is believed that bathing together creates a strong communion in a relaxing environment. However, this type of bonding experience may be difficult to replicate outside of Japan where communal public bathing is not customarily practiced.

After the bath, the athletes and I would have dinner together. The purpose of bathing and eating together was not simply socialization but to give the athletes numerous opportunities to communicate with me in an informal atmosphere. Every night after dinner, the athletes would visit the trainer's room for their sport massages. The trainer's room was open every night until midnight and was a place where the athletes and consulting staff could communicate in a friendly, casual environment.

USING EMOTIONS

The judo team had several cultural barriers to overcome in accepting the idea of mental training. Although I implemented similar techniques as those used for the national football team, judo is not a Western sport but a Japanese martial art steeped in culture and tradition. Even as judo became more of a sport, it still retained the samurai code of behavior. The spirit of Bushido was ingrained in the fabric of judo, and it was revered by all who participated in the sport. One feature of Bushido is approaching your duty as a judo athlete in a somber and disciplined manner. In martial arts, emotions are not shown because they reveal weakness to the opponent. Whether they experience joy or pain, martial artists are taught to be detached from their emotions during competition.

BREAKING THE EMOTIONAL BARRIER

When you work with a sport where the athletes are purposely emotionless, psychological skills such as psyching up, relaxation, and self-talk have to be introduced in a manner that makes them acceptable to the athletes. One example is smiling, which is basically forbidden during practice and competition. Smiling, which comes naturally to most people, had to be taught as a relaxation technique to the players. This was an unfamiliar expression for them; often throughout the training sessions and competitions they had to be reminded to smile or to feel free to enjoy the sport. Another obstacle to overcome was resistance to music during practice. The judo athletes viewed music as a distraction that minimized the seriousness of the sport. Using music for psyching up or cooling down had never been done before, especially at the level of the national team. Although using music may be a simple method in Western cultures, it was an innovative move in the world of judo in Japan.

USING EVERY MOMENT

Another revolutionary change for the judo team was productive time management. Judo athletes spend most of their time at a tournament waiting for their match. During the qualifying round, a judo athlete warms up, is called to the arena, waits until the previous match finishes, and finally enters the mat to compete. If the athlete wins the round, he competes several times again to qualify for the finals, and he must go through a cycle of warming up and cooling down for the successive rounds. The national judo team was taught to follow a routine of light exercises and psychological skills during their wait time. When the wait time was not used in a productive manner, it was easy for the athletes to psychologically wander from the task at hand and start to have negative thoughts leading to impatience, anxiety, or frustration. Having an established routine helped alleviate these negative thoughts and directed the athletes to focus on their match and the goal of the team.

The support from the head judo coach played an important role in the success of the mental training program. The head coach was a former Olympic gold medalist who trained under the traditional konjo style of training. As he learned more about mental training, he realized that he used similar mental techniques. Although he unconsciously used psychological skills when he was an active competitor, he realized that not everyone approached judo in a similar manner. He wanted the members of his team to learn these techniques, so he searched for a sport psychologist who could help. In Japan, where the head judo coach is considered to be a deity, it was rare for a head coach to seek this kind of help. It was a bold move on his part, and without his support the mental training program would not have continued in the manner that it did.

Other members of the support staff also accepted me as a member of the coaching staff. Instead of the military style of high command where orders are simply given and obeyed, the staff members of the national judo team had an open approach and were willing to exchange ideas to benefit the team. The support staff included the team's doctor, athletic trainer, strength and conditioning coach, nutrition specialist, and sport psychologist. We met together to exchange information at each training camp and competition site in order to gain a holistic perspective of the athletes so that we could give them appropriate advice. This type of open communication is unusual in a Japanese setting. Not only were the coaching staff members given opportunities to communicate with each other, the athletes were also given access to the coaching staff in an informal manner.

Open communication among the athletes, coaching staff, and the sport psychologist was a key to the success of the program. By the fourth year of the mental training program, which was a year before the Athens Games, the judo athletes were so well versed in the mental training program that they were able to perform mental training skills on their own.

TEACHING PRODUCTIVE TIME MANAGEMENT

Every moment of the training schedule was used to enhance performance. Instead of simply waiting in a nonproductive manner when they were not actually competing, the judo athletes were taught how to effectively use their wait time during practice and competitions.

In traditional judo sparring practice, the weaker or smaller athletes approach the stronger athletes and request to spar for a 5- to 6-minute round. Since judo is a one-on-one sport, only one athlete is selected as an opponent for that particular round, and the others wait until the end of the round before seeking the stronger athletes again. Instead of simply waiting for the round to end, the athletes were specifically instructed to do imagery training. They would visualize the opponent's weak points and imagine what techniques they would use against the opponent. Although they were not actually sparring on the mat, they were able to use their off-mat time productively.

It was important to recreate the actual wait times of a typical tournament so that the athletes could practice their waiting routines in real time. To prepare for international competitions, the entire team would go through a simulation training the day before. Every aspect of the actual tournament was recreated, including the meet schedule, an audio recording of noise from the fans in the arena, and announcements made in a foreign language. The scheduled times to wake up, weigh in, eat breakfast, and travel to the competition site were also included and observed. Practice time was reconfigured to recreate the tournament schedule so that the team would physically and psychologically experience every moment of the tournament beforehand.

Both the simulation training and the wait-time routines were novel ideas never incorporated in judo training before. In addition to being a sport psychologist, I am also a martial artist, and I knew that making any changes in a tradition that has been observed for generations would be met with distrust and resistance. The acceptance of these suggestions depended on the approach to the sport. The purpose was not to radically change the training practices but to adapt the psychological skills and techniques so that they would complement the existing training style.

ISSUES AND STRATEGIES TO CONSIDER
WHEN WORKING WITH JAPANESE ATHLETES

Following is a summary of aspects of Japanese culture that are important for practitioners to grasp, as well as strategies that will help them be successful in their work with Japanese athletes and coaches.

Social Factors

The following points address some social factors to consider:

• **Honne and tatemae:** *Honne* (real face) and *tatemae* (public face) are important factors in Japanese society. Behavior is dictated by position or social status in a particular group. In public, the Japanese will conduct themselves as they are expected to behave in their social roles. Tatemae is the public face that is shown to these social groups. The behavior is always polite and nonconfrontational. Honne is the true face of a person and is rarely shown in public; it is only revealed to close family members or intimate friends.

• **Social hierarchy:** Japan has a complicated social hierarchy. A person's social status is influenced by a combination of age, gender, education, employment affiliation, and position. Language usage is determined by the social status of the speaker and the listener. A polite form of the language is used in speaking to those who are socially higher than you, and a plain form is used with those who are your peers.

• **Language barrier:** The Japanese study English as a foreign language from junior high school through high school. Although they have had a minimum of 6 years of English education, English is not widely spoken or used. Additionally, translating from English to Japanese or vice versa is not an easy task. Just because a person speaks both languages, it does not necessarily mean that the person can translate well.

• **Dress:** Athletes and coaches from different sports are expected to dress in a certain way on the field, at practice, or at competition sites. Some sports even require athletes to have a certain type of haircut.

  - Being involved with the team may require the sport psychologist to dress accordingly.
  - Removing ones' shoes before entering a home is a well-known Japanese custom. However, shoe removal is required at many gymnasiums and at schools as well. Be prepared to bring a separate pair of indoor shoes that you can change into when working at schools or at a gymnasium.

• **Time management:** Japan has a monochromatic view of time—everything starts on time with no delays. Athletes train, practice, and compete year-round. No centralized sport authority exists to regulate athletes' training and competing. Depending on the sport, athletes rarely have downtime. Weekends and holidays are always used for competition, tournaments, or practice.

  - It is customary to be at practice before the coach arrives and not leave until the coach leaves.
  - Practice schedules will fluctuate. The starting time will always be on time; however, the ending time will be at the discretion of the coach.

• **Socializing:** The Japanese place emphasis on eating and drinking. Having drinks with others is a social practice that builds trust and forges relationships. With alcohol, people are able to speak freely or commiserate with each other within their social group. It is an opportunity to see each other's honne (true self). Having drinks together is strongly associated with the sport world.

Working With Athletes and Coaches

Japanese coaches and athletes present a unique combination of characteristics and challenges. Many of the most important are listed here, in some cases with specific strategies for the non-Japanese cultural sport psychologist.

» *continued*

» *continued*

- Adhere to social hierarchy practices.
  - If the athletes or coaches are older than the sport psychologist, this presents a difficult situation. It requires the use of the polite form of the language but with an authoritative approach.
  - Always have business cards with you. When meeting someone for the first time, business cards are exchanged. The exchange is not simply for information, but to determine social status so they will know what role they will have and what language they will use in the conversation.
- Athletes will not ask questions or talk to the coaching staff.
  - Coaches are at the top of the social hierarchy for the team. They are treated with the utmost respect and their orders are obeyed without question.
  - Athletes have a low status on the team and will not talk to anyone who has a higher status, including their parents. They are more willing to speak to their peers.
  - If you appear to be close to the coach, then the athletes will identify you as a member of the higher echelon and will not be willing to talk to you.
  - Many Japanese have a fear of talking to foreigners. They do not want to embarrass the team or lose face by not being able to speak English well.
- Athletes will not make eye contact.
  - Japanese do not usually make direct eye contact when speaking to another person, so lack of eye contact is not necessarily a sign of disrespect.
  - Sometimes eye contact is an indication that the dynamics between the team and the coach have been disrupted. The relationship is frayed but the team members are expected to show respect, so they are showing their tatemae (public face).
- Athletes will not seek the advice of a sport psychologist.
  - Japanese athletes will not do anything independently without the approval of the coach.
  - Athletes will follow the cultural requirement of maintaining team harmony. The team is more important than the individual. Because of this, individual athletes will purposely not outperform their fellow teammates.
  - Seeking help to improve one's performance will be viewed as disrupting team harmony.
- It is hard to use motivational skills with the athletes.
  - The Japanese are conditioned through extrinsic motivation techniques from their social environment. Switching to intrinsic motivational techniques may be difficult.
  - Traditionally, punishment and the coach's reprimand or long lecture were used to motivate the athletes. Athletes may not initially respond well to positive feedback or instructions.
- Teams usually are not receptive to a sport psychologist.

  Male teams and athletes prefer to work with a male psychologist, and female teams and athletes prefer to work with a female psychologist.
  - Teams and athletes prefer to work with someone who has experience in the same sport.
  - The concept of hiring a full-time sport psychologist is foreign. It will take time for them to realize the contribution that the sport psychologist will be able to make.
  - Personnel are generally selected through personal recommendations from social and organizational networks. Unsolicited personnel usually are not trusted.
  - Professional teams prefer that the sport psychologist has not worked with another team in their league.
  - Due to language barriers and cultural differences, most teams and athletes prefer to work with a Japanese sport psychologist.

RECOMMENDATIONS

Through both direct discussion and extensive examples, this chapter has introduced important aspects of the culture that characterizes the Japanese sport community. These discussions and examples provide the aspiring culturally sensitive practitioner with a great deal of useful information. Issues and Strategies to Consider When Working With Japanese Athletes summarizes many of these points and provides specific strategies that will be useful for sport psychologists practicing in Japan or working with expatriate Japanese athletes.

So What?

Stephanie J. Hanrahan, PhD, and Robert Schinke, EdD

What happens now that this book has been written and read? Rather than simply summarizing the chapters or the main points (a redundant exercise in our opinion), we decided it would be more useful to share our personal reflections on the book as a whole and our ideas about how its information might be used in research, teaching, and applied practice.

We are sharing how working on this book has affected us in the hope that—to misquote a famous American astronaut—this book will be one small step for individuals that will point the way toward one giant leap for humankind. We live in a global society. If we continue to ignore culture, our research findings will not be generalizable to the majority of the world, our applied practice will not be as efficacious as it could be, and our students will continue to follow the narrow path we have taken in the past.

What We Got From This Book

In this book, a number of contributing authors bared their souls (or at least admitted to mistakes they learned from or situations in which they were less than comfortable). It is now our turn to engage in a bit of self-reflection.

Stephanie's Thoughts

It really hit home that I am not consistent in my appreciation and acknowledgment of culture. I travel a lot, and I like to believe that I'm not the kind of traveler who's always thinking, "At home, that would never happen," or "In my country, this is better," although I definitely admit to a preference for indoor plumbing. I have traveled to more than 40 countries, worked in 5 (excluding stays of less than 2 months), and am likely to strike up conversations with strangers on public transport while traveling. I have had graduate students from more than 10 different countries, and for years I have included diversity topics and assignments in the master's program in sport and exercise psychology at the University of Queensland.

Thus, I have understood myself as someone who wants to move well beyond the idea of tolerance (merely putting up with others who are different from ourselves) to a genuine appreciation of cultural variety. In putting this book together, however, I have realized that I have not been proactive in incorporating this sense of multiculturalism from my private life into all aspects of my work as a sport psychologist. Although my introductory undergraduate sport psychology course includes a section on socialization through sport that considers cultural differences, I have not purposefully included multicultural examples when covering traditional sport psychology topics such as motivation, competition, and team cohesion. This book has inspired me to actively consider culture in all my classes.

From an applied perspective, I have had the good fortune to work with Aboriginal Australians as well as to spend time working with teenagers in Mexico. When I was the minority in these situations, I was hugely aware of culture. I am also usually aware of culture when working with an individual client from a different culture. I am not so quick, however, to acknowledge culture when I am working with a team or group in Australia. Although in some instances they may all have a similar skin color, chances are great that they vary in cultural background. When working with groups, I need to actively consider how culture may influence communication, learning, and being.

The place where I fail the most is research. I have published qualitative research about Aboriginal performing artists, quantitative research about Mexican teenage orphans, and both qualitative and quantitative research about athletes with disabilities. I have gone outside the traditional focus of investigating White, subelite or elite, usually male, able-bodied athletes. I have developed and implemented programs designed to enhance life satisfaction, self-worth, and in some instances performance in sport. However, I have not considered how my personal biases inform the research questions I ask, and I have not looked to other cultures for theories, measurement instruments, or ways of doing research.

When working in Mexico, for example, I used questionnaires that had been psychometrically validated in Spanish, but I never even considered searching the Spanish research literature for instruments developed within Hispanic culture. I went with instruments from English-speaking culture that someone had already translated into Spanish and validated. Why had people bothered to translate them? Perhaps they used them because they are good instruments that are applicable across cultures. But maybe they used them because of the belief that research published in top journals in English is more rigorous than anything published in another language. Perhaps using preexisting questionnaires simply increases the chances of getting the work published.

Another way in which I fail to consider culture in my research is that I have not collaborated with Aboriginal Australians or Mexicans in my research. Although I have taught skills and hopefully left them with something useful (rather than having them simply answer questions for me), I have not developed the intervention programs hand in hand with people from the culture. During my most recent project in Mexico, two social workers and a psychologist took part in the program, and I provided them with all of the resources I used. This may have given them new information and techniques, but I did not incorporate their knowledge and skills into my program. I definitely need to develop some true multicultural partnerships.

I have other research that is perceived by many in my university to be my *real* research, and it is not the service-related research I have done in other cultures. The research that has drawn the big grant dollars has related to achievement goal orientations, attributions, motivational climate, and persistence and performance in sport and work. Although I consider the different subcultures of sport and work, I have not considered how culture might affect many of the variables investigated. I've been sucked into believing that I am finding the truth about how goal orientations, attributions, and motivational climate predict persistence and performance.

Now I'm not convinced a single truth exists. Moreover, I'm not sure I'm asking the right questions. This puts me in a bit of a quandary. The powers that be in my university believe that the research that in no way considers culture is my best research, and funding organizations tend to agree. It has a strong (culturally mainstream) theoretical base with straightforward hypotheses that can be tested to determine their so-called truth. My research on using games and psychological skills to enhance the life satisfaction and self-worth of marginalized populations is good enough for the university glossy magazine but is frowned upon by many of those in power. One such person actually told me that if I wanted to continue to do that type of project, I would need to take leave without pay.

The obvious answer is to either get smarter about how I play the game (i.e., find funding for the research I really want to do and write at least some of it up in journals that the university perceives as quality) or give up the traditional academic career and find another avenue that will allow me to spend more time working to enhance the quality of life of marginalized populations. My lack of financial savings (largely due to my travel addiction) makes me hesitant to give up my university salary, and I also genuinely enjoy working with sport psychologists in training. I will most likely pursue alternative funding sources, develop multicultural partnerships, and for the near future at least, remain in academia.

ROB'S THOUGHTS

My exposure to different cultures started early in life. As a 5-year-old, I lived with my mother and sister on a kibbutz in Israel for an entire year. A few years later, my family and I went to Israel a second time and spent another year there, part on a kibbutz, and part living near Tel Aviv. During my second visit, I became acutely aware of different cultures within and across regions. My father was employed in a luxurious country club as an equestrian coach. One evening after a long day's work, we had a barbecue on-site, just my family and I. While my parents were preparing the meal, a Palestinian who worked for the same employer as my father happened upon us. My mother immediately invited him to join us for dinner, and his response was an uneasy yes. He was concerned that he would be seen by his employer dining with our Jewish family. At that moment I learned that there are mainstream and marginalized cultures the world over.

Many years later, I was hired as a faculty member at Laurentian University, the institution for which I continue to work because of its strong multicultural approach (Laurentian is federally funded as a bilingual and tricultural institution). Laurentian University is located in Northern Ontario, Canada, a region where there are three predominant cultures: mainstream Anglophones, mainstream Francophones, and Canadian indigenous people.

The two latter cultures have slowly gained rights under the Canadian constitution, though especially in the case of Canada's indigenous people, challenges continue with poor living conditions and a history of systemic racism. Their experiences were similar to my family's history; both sides of my family are Eastern European Jews. When I first met the people from Wikwemikong, the community members wanted to know about my family background. After I explained who I was in relation to my ancestry, both parties agreed that I was a good match to work with their community. From the ongoing contact with my friends from Wikwemikong, many of whom now coresearch with me, my perspective of sport psychology has become increasingly reflexive. I will speak more about reflexive research shortly, but first I'm going to follow Stephanie's lead and discuss how the present book has influenced me.

When I began teaching at Laurentian University, I adopted the same strategy that I was taught throughout my formal education—my students and I engaged in discussions about mental training skills. The skills covered in my first few years of teaching could have been gained by the students anywhere in North America and Europe. Last year, though, I started delivering two courses that targeted cultural diversity in earnest. Both courses were special topics, one at the undergraduate level and the other at the graduate level. When we decided to offer the undergraduate course, there was some concern that students wouldn't be interested. When I entered the small classroom in early January for the first class, however, I was surprised to find that the course was overbooked! At the request of faculty and students, I will be teaching those cultural diversity courses again this year.

How did the courses come to be? Last year I used the courses as an excuse to become familiar with the expanse of cultural and cross-cultural literature that was required when developing and coediting this book. Having been introduced to new material by the authors, I am looking forward to integrating it into discussions about my own and my students' cultural assumptions. I am now keenly aware that I am a cultural being and that my need to fill silence and assert my individual interests is part of who I am—my perspective. Mine is one of many perspectives, and as Stephanie recognized already, there are many perspectives and many truths. Yes, there is such a thing as White privilege, and I have been perpetuating it in my classes for too long.

Similar to Stephanie, I continue to practice applied sport psychology. Over the last 5 years, some of that time has been allotted to working with professional boxers. As part of my role, I meet with athletes, many of whom immigrated to Canada from Eastern Europe and Africa. In addition, I work with several Quebecois athletes, though at present, no Anglophone Canadian athletes. In the professional boxing context, I am in the minority. Similar to Stephanie's experiences when traveling abroad, when I am situated in the boxing context, I am aware of my cultural tendencies and values. My challenge is to listen to athletes and build consulting practices based on who they are and what they desire.

It is now clear to me that I have farther to go than I thought in meeting that challenge. Sometimes I misstep and sit across from clients when I should have sat to the side. Other times, I am either too aggressive or too passive. At the end of a recent meeting with me, a professional boxer from Eastern Europe was asked by his coach to reflect upon the experience. The athlete responded that our first encounter felt much the same as a doctor taking his pulse. Was I not aware that the athlete had a pulse and that he wanted to engage in intense discussion from the beginning? Earlier experiences with athletes from the same country indicated a pattern whereby initial discussions were meant only to build rapport. Yet after this encounter, I walked away with the distinct impression that I was a little too passive during our initial meeting. Cultural strategies are loose guidelines, and there are as many within-group differences as general cultural strategies. Reflecting the views proposed by the authors in this book, I now approach applied practice with general guidelines that I use as tools when developing relationships with athletes and coaches. Those tools are imperfect, but they are better than proceeding blindly without any cultural competence.

I have engaged in research with cultures other than my own for a few years. As part of my first externally funded research grant, I worked with colleagues from Laurentian and Wikwemikong and interviewed elite Aboriginal athletes from across Canada. In some ways, the research was reflexive. For example, the interview guide was created with consultation from the local Aboriginal community, and afterward, it was coanalyzed and coauthored with a mixed team that included community-appointed members. Although the aforementioned grant was a step in the right direction, it was not an entire shift to cultural sensitivity. One does not typically arrive at the final destination of culturally reflexive research, at least not in the first few attempts.

More recently, my White colleagues and I have taken a few more positive steps toward better cultural research. Our research strategy when working with people from a marginalized population is to have them develop the general research question based on their community needs. As a consequence, my White coauthors and I have been taken out of our comfort zone, and we are currently trying to help our community partners uncover why their young people drop out of sport during their early teenage years. Our main method of gathering data involves talking circles in place of interviews, and the data coding is done by community members who decide what data go into what category and what each theme should be called. Also, there are monthly discussions in Wikwemikong where we talk about the ongoing development of the project.

Gradually, I have noticed that the community coresearchers have taken on leadership roles during our most recent collaboration. Mistakes have been made along the way as community members lead data collections—for example, ineffective probing—but mistakes lead to enhanced capacity over the long-term above and beyond a better portrayal of participants' standpoints. I suppose that much like an effective sport psychology consultant, I am slowly working myself out of a job at Wikwemikong, and research has become a vehicle through which community determination is being enhanced. As a team, my colleagues and I are uncertain where we will go next in our research, but with time, more answers will come.

USING THE INFORMATION IN THIS BOOK

Aside from inspiring us to reflect on our awareness and consideration of culture, this book has also motivated us to think about how we might use the information in this book in our research, teaching, and applied practice. The following points we make are by no means exhaustive, but we hope they might serve as a starting point for the development of readers' action plans.

RESEARCH

A few years ago, one of us (Rob) was fortunate to have a submission rejected by the editor of a well-known peer-reviewed journal. Rejections sting at the receiving end, but within a few days of the initial blow, there is also the opportunity to learn. In that submission, individual interviews, content analysis, and frequent community involvement in the wording of questions, coding, and coauthoring were employed. However, the community had not been involved in the inception of the research project or with the general lines of questioning. Essentially, the

feedback from one prized reviewer was that we had taken a predominantly White mainstream approach to the qualitative study and the methods were not culturally reflexive. Often, the term *cultural research* is used in the literature when researchers are targeting a culture other than their own. From that early lesson and after a few discussions, the research team came to the agreement that there is sometimes a distinction between cultural studies and studies that integrate culture. With the latter approach, one can employ conventional White mainstream methods with a variety of cultural populations. In a cultural studies approach, the methodological strategies are derived from within the intended culture and are not based on the researcher's cultural values.

Under the general umbrella of cultural research, one can adopt or develop many strategies. It is our perspective that there is no one correct strategy that can be used to answer all cultural questions. That being said, a few general suggestions can be considered as guidelines for any approach to cultural studies:

- Allocate time to working with the intended cultural community before developing, or at least finalizing, research questions. For example, studies that involve theories of self (e.g., self-determination, self-efficacy, self-concept) in a collective culture will provide data, but not necessarily the sort of data important to a collective-minded client. Discussing the relevance of the topic with cultural community members will often distinguish what is meaningful from what isn't.

- Consult and even include coresearchers from within the intended culture. Oversights sometimes occur when researchers develop rigorous methods without integrating culturally specific aspects.

- Ensure that the wording of assessment instruments is relevant to the intended audience. Doing otherwise will provide data, but they might not be meaningful in the cultures being studied.

- If qualitative data are part of the research project, invite coresearchers from the intended cultural community to assist with coding before verifying data with the participants. Doing so will enhance the presentation of views that are representative of another's cultural perspective.

- Should you be interested in developing a study where the intended population has been marginalized as a culture, at least ensure that their voices are brought to the fore. Further, as indicated earlier in this section, research can become an effective strategy for empowering a community.

TEACHING AND TRAINING

People in academic positions vary in the amount of freedom they have in the courses they teach and their content, structure, and evaluation. We don't expect instructors to have the time or inclination to take on board all of our examples, nor do we think that the list provided here is in any way exhaustive or complete. What we do hope is that all people who teach sport psychology or supervise practical experiences of trainees ask their students to actively consider culture. If you are a student reading this book out of personal interest, you may want to consider how you can create a cultural spin on an existing assignment or create multicultural applied opportunities. Of course, constructively and diplomatically worded suggestions to instructors could potentially spur them to include culture in their courses. What follows are some ideas that might aid the process of including culture in sport psychology education:

• Encourage (or require) students to complete a course related to sociocultural foundations of sport or psychology.

• Check that examples in sport psychology courses come from multiple cultures. Many examples can be taken from the chapters of this book.

• Encourage students to become self-aware regarding their own cultures. Challenge them to discover the norms, values, and beliefs that guide their interactions with others, their understanding of success, and their day-to-day behavior.

• Give assignments that require students to explore different cultures. Grading criteria could include familiarity with the culture, practical considerations for someone new to the culture, and making the exploration real (encourage interaction and personal experience, not just surfing the Web). With the globalization of society, no one needs to travel far to meet people from different cultures.

• When supervising practical placements, ensure that the student considers the client's worldview.

• Students in internships, externships, or other supervised practice should always experience the supervision of more than one practitioner so that they fully recognize there is never a single way of doing things. Where possible, supervisors should come from different cultures.

• Create practical experiences for students that force them to engage with clients from other cultures. Perhaps arrange for them to be involved with an exercise program for adult refugees or a sport program in schools with a high percentage of minority children.

• Promote travel and work experience in other countries during the summer or before or between degrees. You might also explicitly consider multicultural experience as a factor when deciding whom to accept into your academic program.

• Encourage international student exchange or study abroad programs and accept international students into your program. When you have a multicultural classroom, it may be easier to have discussions about culture. Granted, many classrooms are already multicultural and may not require any intentional action on your part to create this environment. Of course, you need to avoid treating students as if they are the single voice or representative of their cultures.

APPLIED PRACTICE

If culture is a standard component of education, there may be less need to specifically consider culture in applied practice, because hopefully it will become an integral facet of applied practice. In the meantime, here are a few suggestions about how to be culturally aware when working with clients:

• During intake interviews with individual clients, take time to explore the cultures with which the client identifies. Avoid just filling in a blank on a form. For example, the person may be Latino, but there are many Latino cultures. In addition, if you are working in a country outside of Latin America, people will vary in how much they identify with their Latino culture and the mainstream culture of the country in which they now find themselves.

• Celebrate diversity when working with a team. Instead of having teammates simply tolerate each other, help them appreciate the unique contributions of each team member. Team-building activities can help participants consider different ways of communicating and solving problems. The structure of the activities themselves or the debriefing process can include culture as part of the process.

• When working with athletes who are to travel to another county, hold a cultural awareness session. As an example, Stephanie had a graduate student who was working with a synchronized (precision) skating team as part of her externship. The team won the national championship and as a result qualified to compete at the world championship, which was being held in Croatia. As luck would have it, another graduate student in the program, although born in Australia, had a Croatian family. Together the students created an interactive session to familiarize the team with Croatia. They provided a list of Croatian facts (e.g., population, currency, geography, common foods), as well as a list of seven or eight phrases in English and Croatian such as "I am from Australia," "Please take me to the skating rink," and "It's great to be here." Subgroups of the team then created skits that had to include at least three phrases in Croatian (the artistic nature of the sport made this activity popular with the athletes). The session finished with a few basic steps of a traditional Croatian dance along with a typical Croatian yell or yodel. The athletes had fun, learned a little about Croatia, and became a hit in Croatia when they spontaneously used the yell in their preperformance routine.

FINAL WORDS

We hope this book has reinforced positive ideas and actions regarding culture in sport psychology, and perhaps more importantly, we hope it has inspired people in the field who previously may not have been convinced of the importance of culture to engage in the process of becoming culturally competent educators, researchers, and practitioners. None of us is or ever will be an expert on the hundreds of cultures that exist in this world, but we can use the tools in this book to aspire to become culturally reflexive professionals.

REFERENCES

Chapter 1

Andersen, M.B. (1993). Questionable sensitivity: A comment on Lee and Rotella. *Sport Psychologist, 7,* 1-3.

Butryn, T.M. (2002). Critically examining white racial identity and privilege in sport psychology consulting. *Sport Psychologist, 16,* 316-336.

Catina, P.D. (2006). A cross-cultural analysis of positive illusion and sport performance. Retrieved December 20, 2006, from www.athletinsight.com/Vol8Iss3/Crosscultural.htm.

Cowlishaw, G.K. (2000). Censoring race in postcolonial anthropology. *Critique of Anthropology, 20,* 101-123.

Danish, S.J., Petipas, A.J., & Hale, B.D. (1993). Life development interventions for athletes: Life skills through sports. *Counseling Psychologist, 21,* 352-385.

Duda, J.L., & Allison, M.T. (1990). Cross-cultural analysis in exercise and sport psychology: A void in the field. *Journal of Sport & Exercise Psychology, 12,* 114-131.

Duda, J. L., & Hall, H. (2001). Achievement goal theory in sport: Recent extensions and future directions. In R.N. Singer, H.A. Hausenblas, & M.C. Janelle (Eds.), *The handbook of sport psychology* (2nd ed., pp. 417-443). New York: Wiley.

Duda, J.L., & Hayashi, C.T. (1998). Measurement issues in cross-cultural research within sport and exercise psychology. In J.L. Duda (Ed.), *Advances in sport and exercise psychology measurement* (pp. 471-484). Morgantown, WV: Fitness Information Technology.

Fisher, L.A., Butryn, T.M., & E.A. Roper (2003). Diversifying (and politicizing) sport psychology through cultural studies: A promising perspective. *The Sport Psychologist, 17,* 391-406.

Gill, D.L. (2000). Feminist sport psychology: A guide for our journey. *Sport Psychologist, 15,* 363-372.

Greenfield, P.M. (1997). Culture as process: Empirical methods for cultural psychology. In J.W. Berry, Y.H. Poortinga, & J. Pandey (Eds.), *Handbook of cross-cultural psychology* (Vol. 1, pp. 301-346). Boston: Allyn and Bacon.

Hall, E.T. (1966). *The hidden dimension.* New York: Doubleday.

Hanrahan, S.J. (2004). Sport psychology and indigenous performing arts. *Sport Psychologist, 18,* 60-74.

Hanrahan, S.J. (2005a). Using psychological skills training from sport psychology to enhance the life satisfaction of adolescent Mexican orphans. *Athletic Insight.* Retrieved December 20, 2006, from www.athleticinsight.com/Vol7Iss3/PsychologicalSkills.htm.

Hanrahan, S.J. (2005b). On stage: Mental skills training for dancers. In M.B. Andersen (Ed.), *The practice of sport psychology* (pp. 109-127). Champaign, IL: Human Kinetics.

Hill, T.L. (1993). Sport psychology and the collegiate athlete: One size does not fit all. *Counseling Psychologist, 21,* 436-440.

Holmes, P. (2006). Problematizing intercultural communication competence in the pluricultural classroom: Chinese students in a New Zealand classroom. *Language and Intercultural Communication, 6,* 18-34.

Hooks, B. (2000). *Feminism is for everybody: Passionate politics.* Cambridge, MA: South End.

Kashima, Y., Yamaguchi, S., Kim, U., Choi, S.C., Gelfand, M.J., & Yuki, M. (1995). Culture, gender, and self: A perspective from individualism–collectivism research. *Journal of Personality and Social Psychology, 69,* 925-937.

Kontos, A.P., & Arguello, E. (2005). Sport psychology consulting with Latin American athletes. *Athletic Insight.* Retrieved December 20, 2006, from www.athleticinsight.com/Vol7Iss3/LatinAmerican.htm.

Kontos, A.P., & Breland-Noble, A.M. (2002). Racial/ethnic diversity in applied sport psychology: A multicultural introduction to working with athletes of color. *Sport Psychologist, 16,* 296-315.

Kral, M.J., Burkhardt, K.J., & Kidd, S. (2002). The new research agenda for a cultural psychology. *Canadian Psychology, 43,* 154-162.

Levine, R.V. (1988). The pace of life across cultures. In J.E. McGrath (Ed.), *The social psychology of time: New perspective* (pp. 39-60). Newbury Park, CA: Sage.

Maguire, J. (1999). *Global sport: Identities, societies, civilizations.* Cambridge, UK: Polity Press.

Martens, M.P., Mobley, M., & Zizzi, S.J. (2000). Multicultural training in applied sport psychology. *Sport Psychologist, 14,* 81-97.

Miller, J.G. (1984). Culture and the development of everyday social explanation. *Journal of Personality and Social Psychology, 46,* 961-978.

Myers, D.G., & Spencer, S.J. (2003). *Social psychology* (Canadian ed.). Toronto: McGraw-Hill Ryerson.

Norenzayan, A., & Nisbett, R.E. (2004). Culture and causal cognition. In J.R. Ruscher & E.Y. Hammer (Eds.), *Current directions in social psychology* (pp. 55-60). Upper Saddle River, NJ: Pearson.

Peterson, C. (2000). The future of optimism. *American Psychologist, 55,* 44-55.

Reber, A.S. (1995). *Dictionary of psychology* (2nd ed.). Victoria, Australia: Penguin.

Rettew, D., & Reivich, K. (1995). Sports and explanatory style. In G. McClellan Buchanan & M.E.P. Seligman (Eds.), *Explanatory style* (pp. 173–186). Hillsdale, NJ: Erlbaum.

Ryba, T.V., & Wright, H.K. (2005). From mental game to cultural praxis: A cultural studies model's implications for the future of sport psychology. *Quest, 57,* 192-212.

Schinke, R.J. (2007). A four-year chronology with national team boxing in Canada. *Journal of Sport Science and Medicine, 6,* 1-7.

Schinke, R.J., Eys, M.A., Danielson, R., Michel, G., Peltier, D., Pheasant, C., et al. (2006). Cultural social support for Canadian Aboriginal elite athletes during their sport development. *International Journal of Sport Psychology, 37,* 1-19.

Schinke, R.J., & Hanrahan, S.J. (2006, September). *Understanding challenges and working effectively with marginalized populations: Recommendations for effective practice.* Symposium conducted at the meeting at the annual congress of the Association for the Advancement of Applied Sport Psychology. Miami.

Schinke, R.J., Michel, G., Gauthier, A., Danielson, R., Pickard, P., Peltier, D., et al. (2006). Adaptation to the mainstream in elite sport: A Canadian aboriginal perspective. *Sport Psychologist, 20,* 435-448.

Seeley, K.M. (2000). *Cultural psychotherapy: Working with culture in the clinical encounter.* Northvale, NJ: Aronson.

Seligman, M.E.P. (1991). *Learned optimism.* New York: Knopf.

Shweder, R.A. (1990). Cultural psychology: What is it? In J.W. Stigler, R.A. Shweder, & G. Herdt (Eds.), *Cultural psychology: Essays on comparative human development* (p. 143). Cambridge, UK: Cambridge University Press.

Thomason, T.C. (1991). Counseling Native Americans: An introduction for non-Native American counselors. *Journal of Counseling and Development, 69,* 321-327.

Triandis, H.C. (1994). *Culture and social behavior.* New York: McGraw-Hill.

Williams, J.E., Satterwhite, R.C., & Saiz, J.L. (1998). *The importance of psychological traits: A cross-cultural study.* New York: Plenum Series in Social/Clinical Psychology.

Chapter 2

Barona, A., & Santos de Barona, M. (2003). Recommendations for the psychological treatment of Latino/Hispanics populations. In Council of National Psychological Associations for the Advancement of Ethnic Minority Interests (Ed.)., *Psychological treatment of ethnic minority populations* (pp. 19-23). Washington, DC: Association of Black Psychologists.

Basow, S.A. (1984). Ethnic group differences in educational achievement in Fiji. *Journal of Cross-Cultural Psychology, 15,* 435-451.

Bernal, G., & Saez-Santiago, E. (2006). Culturally centered psychosocial interventions. *Journal of Community Psychology, 34,* 121-132.

Berube, M.S., Castello, R.B., Prichard, D.R., Jost, D.A., Ellis, K., Severnse, M., et al. (1994). *The American heritage dictionary* (3rd ed.). New York: Houghton Mifflin.

Boykin, A.W. (1983). The academic performance of Afro-American children. In J. Spence (Ed.), *Achievement and achievement motives: Psychological and sociological approaches* (pp. 321-371). San Francisco: W.H. Freeman.

Chang, L., Arkin, R.M., Leong, F.T., Chan, D.K.S., & Leung, K. (2004). Subjective overachievement in American and Chinese college students. *Journal of Cross-Cultural Psychology, 35,* 152-173.

Chelladurai, P., Imamura, H., Yamaguchi, Y., Oinuma, Y., & Miyauchi, T. (1988). Sport leadership in a cross-national setting: The case of Japanese and Canadian university athletes. *Journal of Sport and Exercise Psychology, 10,* 374-389.

Cheung, F.M., & Leung, K. (1998). Indigenous personality measures: Chinese examples. *Journal of Cross-Cultural Psychology, 29,* 233-248.

Church, A.T., & Katigbak, M.S. (1992). The cultural context of academic motives: A comparison of Filipino and American college students. *Journal of Cross-Cultural Psychology, 23,* 40-58.

Constantine, M.G. (2002). Predictors of satisfaction with counseling: Racial and ethnic minority clients' attitudes toward counseling and ratings of their counselors' general and multicultural counseling competence. *Journal of Counseling Psychology, 49,* 255-263.

Constantine, M.G. (2007). Racial microaggressions against African American clients in cross-racial counseling relationships. *Journal of Counseling Psychology, 54,* 1-16.

Duda, J.L., & Allison, M.T. (1990). Cross-cultural analysis in exercise and sport psychology: A void in the field. *Journal of Sport & Exercise Psychology, 12,* 114-131.

Eaton, M.J., & Dembo, M.H. (1997). Differences in the motivational beliefs of Asian American and non-Asian students. *Journal of Educational Psychology, 89,* 433-440.

Echeverry, J.J. (1997). Treatment barriers: Assessing and accepting professional help. In G. Garcia & M.C. Zea (Eds.), *Psychological interventions and research with Latino populations* (pp. 94-124). Boston: Allyn & Bacon.

Eklund, R.C. (1996). Preparing to compete: A season-long investigation with collegiate wrestlers. *Sport Psychologist, 10,* 111-131.

Fryberg, S.A., & Markus, H.R. (2008). Models of education in American Indian, Asian American, and European American cultural contexts. Manuscript submitted for publication.

Gano-Overway, L.A., & Duda, J.L. (1999). Interrelationships between expressive individualism and other achievement goal orientations among African and European American athletes. *Journal of Black Psychology, 25*, 544-563.

Geisler, G., & Kerr, J. H. (2007). Competition stress and affective experiences of Canadian and Japanese futsal players. *International Journal of Sport Psychology, 38*, 187-206.

Gill, D.L. (2004). Gender and cultural diversity across the lifespan. In Weiss, M.R. (Ed.), *Developmental sport and exercise psychology: A lifespan perspective* (pp. 475-501). Morgantown, WV: Fitness Information Technology.

Gould, D., Eklund, R.C., & Jackson, S.A. (1992). 1988 U.S. Olympic wrestling excellence: I. Mental preparation, precompetitive cognition, and affect. *Sport Psychologist, 6*, 358-382.

Hayashi, C.T., & Weiss, M.R. (1994). A cross-cultural analysis of achievement motivation in Anglo-American and Japanese marathon runners. *International Journal of Sport Psychology, 25*, 187-202.

Heine, S.J. (2001). Self as cultural product: An examination of East Asian and North American selves. *Journal of Personality, 69*, 881-906.

Heine, S.J., Kitayama, S., Lehman, D.R., Takata, T., Ide, E., Leung, C., et al. (2001). Divergent consequences of success and failure in Japan and North America: An investigation of self-improving motivations and malleable selves. *Journal of Personality & Social Psychology, 81*, 599-615.

Heine, S.J., Lehman, D.R., Markus, H.R., & Kitayama, S. (1999). Is there a universal need for positive self-regard? *Psychological Review, 106*, 766-794.

Helms, J.E., & Cook, D.A. (1999). *Using race and culture in counseling and psychotherapy: Theory and process.* Needham Heights, MA: Allyn & Bacon.

Highlen, P.S., & Bennett, B.B. (1979). Psychological characteristics of successful and nonsuccessful elite wrestlers: An exploratory study. *Journal of Sport Psychology, 1*, 123-137.

Hofstede, G.H. (1980). *Culture's consequences, international differences in work related values.* Beverly Hills, CA: Sage.

Iyengar, S.S., & Lepper, M.R. (1999). Rethinking the value of choice: A cultural perspective on intrinsic motivation. *Journal of Personality and Social Psychology, 76*, 349-366.

Jackson, J. (1989). Race, ethnicity, and psychological theory and research. *Journal of Gerontology: Psychological Sciences, 44*, 1-2.

Kamal, F.A., & Blais, C. (1992). Noncontingent positive and negative feedback during maximal exercise. *Perceptual and Motor Skills, 75*, 203-210.

Kim, B.J., Williams, L., & Gill, D.L. (2003). A cross-cultural study of achievement orientation and intrinsic motivation in young USA and Korean athletes. *International Journal of Sport Psychology, 34*, 168-184.

Kirkby, R.J., Kolt, G.S., & Liu, J. (1999). Participation motives of young Australian and Chinese gymnasts. *Perceptual and Motor Skills, 88*, 363-373.

Kitayama, S. (2002). Cultural psychology of the self: A renewed look at independence and interdependence. In C. Hofsten, & L. Backman (Eds.), *Psychology at the turn of the millennium* (Vol. 2, pp. 305-322). Florence, KY: Taylor & Frances/Routledge.

Kochman, T. (1981). *Black and White styles in conflict.* Chicago: University of Illinois.

Kontos, A.P., & Arguello, E. (2005). Sport psychology consulting with Latin American athletes. *Athletic Insight.* Retrieved April 04, 2007, from www.athleticinsight.com/Vol7Iss3/LatinAmerican.htm.

Kwok, D.C. (1995). The self-perception of competence by Canadian and Chinese children. *Psychologia, 38*, 9-16.

Maehr, M. (1974). Culture and achievement motivation. *American Psychologist, 29*, 887-896.

Maehr, M.L., & Nicholls, J.G. (1980). Culture and achievement motivation: A second look. In N. Warrens (Ed.), *Studies of cross cultural psychology* (pp. 221-265). New York: Academic Press.

Martens, M.P., Mobley, M., & Zizzi, S.J. (2000). Multicultural training in applied sport psychology. *Sport Psychologist, 14*, 81-97.

Martin, D.J., Garske, J.P., & Davis, M.K. (2000). Relations of the therapeutic alliance with outcome and other variables: A meta-analytic review. *Journal of Consulting and Clinical Psychology, 68*, 438-450.

McPherson, S.L. (2000). Expert-novice differences in planning strategies during collegiate singles tennis competition. *Journal of Sport & Exercise Psychology, 22*, 39-62.

Morgan, K., Sproule, J., McNeill, M., Kingston, K., & Wang, J. (2006). A cross-cultural study of motivational climate in physical education lessons in the UK and Singapore. *International Journal of Sport Psychology, 37*, 299-316.

Myers, D.G. (2005). *Social psychology.* Boston: McGraw-Hill.

Nicholls, J.G. (1984). Conceptions of ability and achievement motivation. In R. Ames & C. Ames (Eds.), *Research on motivation in education: Student motivation.* (pp. 39-73). New York: Academic Press.

Peters, H.J., & Williams, J.M. (2006). Moving cultural background to the foreground: An investigation of self-talk, performance, and persistence following feedback. *Journal of Applied Sport Psychology, 18*, 240-253.

Ram, N., Starek, J., & Johnson, J. (2004). Race, ethnicity, and sexual orientation: Still a void in sport and exercise psychology? *Journal of Sport & Exercise Psychology, 26*, 250-268.

Ramirez, M., & Price-Williams, D.R. (1976). Achievement and motivation in children of three ethnic groups in the United States. *Journal of Cross-Cultural Psychology, 7*, 49-60.

Rudolfa, E., Rappaport, R., & Lee, V. (1983). Variable related to premature terminations in a university counseling service. *Journal of Counseling Psychology, 30*, 87-90.

Salili, F. (1996). Learning and motivation: An Asian perspective. *Psychology and Developing Societies, 8,* 55-81.

Salili, F., Chiu, C., & Lai, S. (2001). The influence of culture and context on students' achievement orientations. In F. Salili, F. Chiu, & Y. Hong (Eds.), *Student motivation: The culture and context of learning* (pp. 221-247). Dordrecht, Netherlands: Kluwer Academic.

Si, G., & Lee, H. (2007). Cross-cultural issues in sport psychology research. In S. Jowette, & D. Lavallee (Eds.), *Social psychology in sport.* (pp. 279-288). Champaign, IL: Human Kinetics.

Steinberg, L., Dornbusch, S.M., & Brown, B.B. (1992). Ethnic differences in adolescent achievement: An ecological perspective. *American Psychologist, 47,* 723-729.

Stevenson, H.W., & Stigler, J.W. (1992). *The learning gap: Why our schools are failing and what we can learn from Japanese and Chinese education.* New York: Summit.

Stigler, J.W., Smith, S., & Mao, L. (1985). The self-perception of competence by Chinese children. *Child Development, 56,* 1259-1270.

Sue, S. (2006). Cultural competency: From philosophy to research and practice. *Journal of Community Psychology, 34,* 237-245.

Sue, D.W., Bingham, R.P., Porche-Burke, L., & Vasquez, M. (1999). The diversification of psychology: A multicultural revolution. *American Psychologist, 54, 1061-1069.*

Sue, D.W., & Sue, D. (1999). *Counseling the culturally different: Theory and practice* (3rd ed.). New York: Wiley.

Thompson, C.E., & Jenal, S.T. (1994). Interracial and intraracial quasi-counseling interactions when counselors avoid discussing race. *Journal of Counseling Psychology, 41,* 484-491.

Van Raalte, J.L., Brewer, B.W., Lewis, B.P., Linder, D.E., Wildman, G., & Kozimor, J. (1995). Cork! The effects of positive and negative self-talk on dart throwing performance. *Journal of Sport Behavior, 18,* 50-57.

Van Raalte, J.L., Brewer, B.W., Rivera, P.M., & Petitpas, A.J. (1994). The relationship between observable self-talk and competitive junior tennis players' match performances. *Journal of Sport & Exercise Psychology, 16,* 400-415.

Williams, J.M., & Leffingwell, T.R. (2002). Cognitive strategies in sport and exercise psychology. In J.L. Van Raalte & B.W. Brewer (Eds.), *Exploring sport and exercise psychology* (pp. 75-98). Washington, DC: American Psychological Association.

Yan, J.H., & McCullagh, P. (2004). Cultural influence on youth's motivation of participation in physical activity. *Journal of Sport Behavior, 27,* 378-390.

Yan, J.H., & Thomas, J.R. (1995). Parents' assessment of physical activity in American and Chinese children. *Journal of Comparative Physical Education and Sports, 17,* 38-49.

Yan, W.F., & Gaier, E.L. (1994). Causal attributions for college success and failure: An Asian-American comparison. *Journal of Cross-Cultural Psychology, 25,* 146-158.

Zinsser, N., Bunker, L., & Williams, J.M. (2001). Cognitive techniques for building confidence and enhancing performance. In J.M. Williams (Ed.), *Applied sport psychology: Personal growth to peak performance* (4th ed., pp. 284-311). Boston: McGraw-Hill.

Chapter 3

Barker, C. (2003). *Cultural studies: Theory and practice.* Thousand Oaks, CA: Sage.

Berger, B.G., Pargman, D., & Weinberg, R.S. (2002). *Foundations of exercise psychology.* Morgantown, WV: Fitness Information Technology.

Brewer, B., Van Raalte, J., & Petitpas, A. (2000). Self-identity issues in sport career transitions. In D. Lavallee & P. Wylleman (Eds.), *Career transitions in sport: International perspectives* (pp. 29-48). Morgantown, WV: Fitness Information Technology.

Brustad, R. (2002). A critical analysis of knowledge construction in sport psychology. In T. Horn (Ed.), *Advances in sport psychology* (2nd ed., pp. 21-38). Champaign, IL: Human Kinetics.

Chun, C.A., Enomoto, K., & Sue, S. (1996). Health care issues among Asian Americans: Implications of somatization. In P.M. Kato & T. Mann (Eds.), *Handbook of diversity issues in health psychology* (pp. 347-365). New York: Plenum Press.

Clifford, J. (1999). On collecting art and culture. In S. During (Ed.), *The cultural studies reader* (2nd ed., pp. 57-76). London: Routledge.

Coakley, J.J. (2007). *Sports in society: Issues and controversies* (9th ed.). Boston: McGraw-Hill.

Cox, R.H. (2006). *Sport psychology: Concepts and applications* (5th ed.). Boston: McGraw-Hill.

Delgado, R., & Stefancic, J. (2001). *Critical race theory: An introduction.* New York: NYU Press.

Duda, J.L. (1998). *Advances in sport and exercise psychology measurement.* Morgantown, WV: Fitness Information Technology.

Duhacek, D. (2006). Ethics and/in politics: Toward citizenship as responsibility to the other. In E. Skaerbaek (Coord.), *Common passion, different voices: Reflections on citizenship and intersubjectivity* (pp.15-25). York, England: Raw Nerve Books.

Eitzen, D.S. (2000). Slaves of big-time college sports. *USA Today Magazine, 129,* 26-30.

Fernandes, L. (2003). *Transforming feminist practice.* San Francisco: Aunt Lute Books.

Fisher, L.A. (2001). Book review of *Career Transitions in Sport: International Perspectives* by David Lavallee and Paul Wylleman. *Sport Psychologist, 15,* 450-452.

Fisher, L.A., Butryn, T.M., & Roper, E.A. (2003). Diversifying (and politicizing) sport psychology through cultural studies: A promising perspective. *Sport Psychologist, 17,* 391-406.

Fisher, L.A., Butryn, T.M., & Roper, E.A. (2005). Diversifying (and politicizing) sport psychology through cultural studies: A promising perspective revisited. *Athletic Insight.* Retrieved March 20, 2007, from www.athleticinsight.com/Vol7Iss3/DiversifyingPoliticizing.htm.

Foucault, M. (1976). *Mental illness and psychology.* New York: Harper & Row.

Giardina, M.D., & McCarthy, C. (2005). The popular racial order of urban America: Sport, identity, and the politics of culture. *Cultural Studies-Critical Methodologies, 5,* 145-173.

Gill, D. (2000). *Psychological dynamics of sport and exercise* (2nd ed.). Champaign, IL: Human Kinetics.

Giroux, H. (1994). Doing cultural studies: Youth and the challenge of pedagogy. *Harvard Educational Review, 64,* 278-308.

Green, M. (1996). The centre for contemporary cultural studies. In J. Storey (Ed.), *What is cultural studies? A reader* (pp. 49-60). London: Arnold.

Hall, M.A. (1996). *Feminism and sporting bodies: Essays on theory and practice.* Champaign, IL: Human Kinetics.

Hall, S. (1992). Cultural studies and its theoretical legacies. In L. Grossberg, C. Nelson, & P. Treichler (Eds.), *Cultural studies* (pp. 277-294). New York: Routledge.

Haug, F. (1986). *Female sexualization: A collective work of memory.* London: Verso.

HBO Home Video. (1995). *Fields of fire: Sport in the 60s* [Documentary]. United States: HBO Home Video.

Hughes, G. (2004). Managing Black guys: Representation, corporate culture, and the NBA. *Journal of Sport and Social Issues, 25,* 20-30.

Kiefer, D. (2007, January 17). The changing face of basketball: Monta Vista is a rarity in boys basketball—a team that starts five Asian-Americans. *San Jose Mercury News,* pp. 1D.

Kontos, A.P., & Breland-Noble, A.M. (2002). Racial/ethnic diversity in applied sport psychology: A multicultural introduction to working with athletes of color. *Sport Psychologist, 16,* 296-315.

Krane, V., Waldron, J., Michalenok, J., & Stiles-Shipley, J. (2001). Body image concerns in female exercisers and athletes: A feminist cultural studies perspective. *Women in Sport and Physical Activity Journal, 10,* 17-54.

Lee, S. (Director). (1998). *He got game* [Motion picture]. United States: Touchtone Pictures.

Majors, R. (1998). Cool pose: Black masculinity and sports. In G. Sailes (Ed.), *African Americans in sport* (pp. 15-22). New Brunswick, NJ: Transaction.

Markula, P. (2003). The technologies of the self: Sport, feminism and Foucault. *Sociology of Sport Journal, 20,* 87-107.

Martens, R. (1987). Science, knowledge, and sport psychology. *Sport Psychologist, 1,* 29-55.

Ryba, T.V., & Wright, H.K. (2005). From mental game to cultural praxis: A cultural studies model's implications for the future of sport psychology. *Quest, 57,* 192-212.

Schinke, R.J., & Hanrahan, S.J. (2006, September). *Understanding challenges and working effectively with marginalized populations: Recommendations for effective practice.* Symposium conducted at the meeting at the annual congress of the Association for the Advancement of Applied Sport Psychology, Miami.

Smith, J.D. (Producer), & Smithee, A.F. (Director). (2001). *Really Big Disaster Movie* [Motion picture]. United States: Paramount Pictures.

Storey, J. (1996). *What is cultural studies? A reader.* London: Arnold.

Thomas, J., & Nelson, J. (1996). *Research methods in physical activity* (3rd ed.). Champaign, IL: Human Kinetics.

Walton, T.A. (2001). The Spreewell/Carlesimo episode: Unacceptable violence or unacceptable victim? *Sociology of Sport Journal, 18,* 345-357.

Ward, G. (1997). *Postmodernism.* Blacklick, OH: McGraw-Hill.

Weinberg, R.S., & Gould, D. (2003). *Foundations of sport and exercise psychology* (3rd ed.). Champaign, IL: Human Kinetics.

Weinberg, R.S., & Gould, D. (2007). *Foundations of sport and exercise psychology* (4th ed.). Champaign, IL: Human Kinetics.

Williams, R. (1960). Culture and society: 1780-1950. Harmondsworth: Penguin.

Wright, H.K. (2007, October). Cultural studies of sport psychology and the formation of a multicultural, socially just sport studies. Paper presented at the Association of Applied Sport Psychology (AASP) Annual Congress, Louisville, Kentucky.

Chapter 4

Association for Applied Sport Psychology (AASP). (2006). What is applied sport psychology? Retrieved April, 2006, from http://aaasponline.org/asp/faq.php.

Braidotti, R. (1994). *Nomadic subjects: Embodiment and sexual difference in contemporary feminist theory.* New York: Columbia University Press.

Buss, A.H., & Perry, M. (1992). The Aggression Questionnaire. *Journal of Personality and Social Psychology, 63,* 452-459.

Coakley, J. (1992). Burnout among adolescent athletes: A personal failure or social problem? *Sociology of Sport Journal, 9,* 271-285.

Coakley, J. (2004). *Sport in society: Issues and controversies* (8th ed.). Boston: Irwin McGraw-Hill.

Conroy, D.E. (2006). Commentary on Walker, Kremer, and Moran. *Sport and Exercise Psychology Review, 2,* 39-40.

Du Bois, W.E.B. (1953). *The souls of Black folk.* New York: Fawcett.

Foucault, M. (1972). *The archaeology of knowledge* (A.M. Sheridan Smith, Trans.). London: Routledge.

Foucault, M. (1995). *Discipline and punish: The birth of the prison* (A. Sheridan, Trans., 2nd ed.). New York: Vintage Books.

Freire, P. (1970). *Pedagogy of the oppressed.* New York: Continuum Press.

Freire, P. (1985). *The politics of education: Culture, power, and liberation.* South Hadley, MA: Bergin & Garvey.

Gill, D. (2000). Psychology and the study of sport. In J. Coakley & E. Dunning (Eds.), *Handbook of sports studies* (pp. 228-240). London: Sage.

Glesne, C. (2006). *Becoming qualitative researchers* (3rd ed.). Toronto: Pearson.

Gramsci, A. (1978). *Selection from the prison notebooks.* London: Lawrence and Wishart.

Hardy, L. (2006). Commentary on Walker, Kremer, and Moran. *Sport and Exercise Psychology Review, 2,* 40-43.

Harris, D.V. (Ed.). (1972). *Women in sport: A national research conference.* State College, PA: Pennsylvania State University.

Hoberman, J. (1992). *Mortal engines: The science of performance and the dehumanization of sport.* New York: The Free Press.

Ingham, A.G., Blissmer, B.J., & Davidson, K. (1999). The expendable prolympic self: Going beyond the boundaries of sociology and psychology of sport. *Sociology of Sport Journal, 16,* 236-285.

Kincheloe, J., & McLaren, P. (2000). Rethinking critical theory and qualitative research. In N.K. Denzin & Y.S. Lincoln (Eds.), *Handbook of qualitative research* (2nd ed., pp. 279-313). Thousand Oaks, CA: Sage.

Kral, M.J., Burkhardt, D.J., & Kidd, S. (2002). The new research agenda for a cultural psychology. Retrieved March 21, 2007, from http://findarticles.com/p/articles/mi_qa3711/is_200208/ai_n9145557.

Martens, R. (1979). From smocks to jocks: A new adventure for sports psychologists. In P. Klavora & J.V. Daniel (Eds.), *Coach, athlete, and the sport psychologist* (pp. 56-62). Toronto: School of Physical Education, University of Toronto.

Martens, R. (1987). Science, knowledge, and sport psychology. *Sport Psychologist, 1,* 29-55.

Migeod, F.W.H. (1926). *A view of Sierra Leone.* New York: Trench, Trubner.

Moghaddam, F.M., & Studer, C. (1997). Cross-cultural psychology: The frustrated gadfly's promises, potentialities, and futures. In D. Fox & I. Prilleltensky (Eds.), *Critical psychology: An introduction* (pp. 185-201). Thousand Oaks, CA: Sage.

Pettifor, J.L. (1996). Ethics: Virtue and politics in the science and practice of psychology. *Canadian Psychology, 37,* 1-12.

Ponterotto, J.G. (2005). Qualitative research in counseling psychology: A primer on research paradigms and philosophy of science. *Journal of Counseling Psychology, 52* (2), 126-136.

Ryba, T.V. (2004, March). Searching for the "true" self. Paper presented at the International Gay and Athletics Conference, Boston.

Ryba, T.V. (2005). Sport psychology as cultural praxis: Future trajectories and current possibilities. Retrieved March 21, 2007, from www.athleticinsight.com/Vol7Iss3/CulturalPraxis.htm.

Ryba, T.V., & Wright, H.K. (2005). From mental game to cultural praxis: A cultural studies model's implications for the future of sport psychology. *Quest, 57* (2), 192-212.

Sage, G.H. (1993). Sport and physical education in the New World Order: Dare we be agents of social change? *Quest, 45,* 151-164.

Sage, G.H. (1998). *Power and ideology in American sport: A critical perspective* (2nd ed.). Champaign, IL: Human Kinetics.

Schön, D. (1983). *The reflective practitioner: How professionals think in action.* London: Temple Smith.

Schutt, R. (1999). *Investigating the social world* (2nd ed.). Thousand Oaks, CA: Pine Forge.

Schwandt, T.A. (1997). *Qualitative inquiry: A dictionary of terms.* Thousand Oaks, CA: Sage.

Schwandt, T.A. (2000). Three epistemological stances for qualitative inquiry: Interpretivism, hermeneutics, and social constructionism. In N.K. Denzin & Y.S. Lincoln (Eds.), *Handbook of qualitative research* (2nd ed., pp. 189-213). Thousand Oaks, CA: Sage.

Seve, L. (1978). *Man in Marxist theory and the psychology of personality.* Atlantic Highlands, NJ: Humanities Press.

Sherif, C.W. (1979). Bias in psychology. In J.A. Sherman & E.T. Beck (Eds.), *The prism of sex: Essays in the sociology of knowledge* (pp. 99-133). Madison: University of Wisconsin Press.

Sherif, C.W. (1982). Needed concepts in the study of gender identity. *Psychology of Women Quarterly, 6,* 375-398.

Silva, J.M., & Weinberg, R.S. (Eds.). (1984). *Psychological foundations of sport.* Champaign, IL: Human Kinetics.

Sloan, T. (1997). Theories of personality: Ideology and beyond. In D. Fox & I. Prilleltensky (Eds.), *Critical psychology: An introduction* (pp. 87-103). Thousand Oaks, CA: Sage.

Smith, D. (1990). *Conceptual practices of power: A feminist sociology of knowledge.* Toronto: University of Toronto Press.

Sparkes, A.C. (1998). Validity in qualitative inquiry and the problem of criteria: Implications for sport psychology. *Sport Psychologist, 12,* 363-386.

Spielberger, C.D., Reheiser, E.C., & Syderman, S.J. (1995). Measurement of the experience, expression and control of anger. In H. Kassinove (Ed.), *Anger disorders: Definitions, diagnosis, and treatment* (pp. 49-67). Washington, DC: Taylor and Francis.

Vealey, R.S. (2006). Smocks and jocks outside the box: The paradigmatic evolution of sport and exercise psychology. *Quest, 58,* 128-159.

Weedon, C. (1997). *Feminist practice and poststructuralist theory* (2nd ed.). Cambridge: Blackwell.

Wright, H.K. (2007, March 8). Is this an African I see before me? Paper presented at the Global Dialogue: Representations of Africa, Vancouver, BC.

Chapter 5

American Psychological Association (APA). (2003). Guidelines on multicultural education, training, research, practice and organizational change for psychologists. *American Psychologist, 58*, 377-402.

Barber, H., & Krane, V. (2005). The elephant in the locker room: Opening the dialogue about sexual orientation on women's sport teams. In M.B. Anderson (Ed.), *Sport psychology in practice* (pp. 265-285). Champaign, IL: Human Kinetics.

Basow, S.A., & Rubin, L.R. (1999). Gender influences and adolescent development. In N.G. Johnson, M.C. Roberts, & J. Worell (Eds.), *Beyond appearance: A new look at adolescent girls* (pp. 25-52). Washington, DC: APA.

Beilock, S.L., & McConnell, A.R. (2004). Stereotype threat and sport: Can athletic performance be threatened? *Journal of Sport & Exercise Psychology, 26*, 597-609.

Carpenter, L.J., & Acosta, R.V. (2006). *Title IX.* Champaign, IL: Human Kinetics.

Contrada, R.J., Ashmore, R.D., Gary, M.L., Coups, E., Egeth, J.D., Sewell, A., et al. (2000). Ethnicity-related sources of stress and their effects on well-being. *Current Directions in Psychological Science, 9*, 136-139.

Crespo, C.J. (2005, June). Physical activity in minority populations: Overcoming a public health challenge. *President's Council on Physical Fitness and Sports Research Digest, 6* (2).

Crespo, C.J., Ainsworth, B.E., Keteyian, S.J., Heath, G.W., & Smit, E. (1999). Prevalence of physical inactivity and its relations to social class in U.S. adults: Results from the Third National Health and Nutrition Examination Survey, 1988-1994. *Medicine & Science in Sports & Exercise, 31*, 1821-1827.

Devine, P.G., & Baker, S.M. (1991). Measurement of racial stereotype subtyping. *Personality and Social Psychology Bulletin, 17*, 44-50.

Duda, J.L., & Allison, M.T. (1990). Cross-cultural analysis in exercise and sport psychology: A void in the field. *Journal of Sport & Exercise Psychology, 12*, 114-131.

Fredericks, J.A., & Eccles, J.S. (2004). Parental influences on youth involvement in sports. In M.R. Weiss (Ed.), *Developmental sport and exercise psychology: A lifespan perspective* (pp. 145-164). Morgantown, WV: Fitness Information Technology.

Fredericks, J.A., & Eccles, J. S. (2005). Family socialization, gender and sport motivation and involvement. *Journal of Sport & Exercise Psychology, 27*, 3-31.

Gill, D.L. (2002). Gender and sport behavior. In T.S. Horn (Ed.), *Advances in sport psychology* (2nd ed., pp. 355-375). Champaign, IL: Human Kinetics.

Gill, D.L. (2007). Gender and cultural diversity. In G. Tenenbaum & R. Eklund (Eds.), *Handbook on research on sport psychology* (3rd ed., pp. 823-844). Hoboken, NJ: Wiley.

Gill, D.L., Jamieson, K.M., & Kamphoff, C. (2005). *Final report: Promoting cultural competence among physical activity professionals.* American Association of University Women Scholar-in-Residence award, 2003-2004.

Gill, D.L., Morrow, R.G., Collins, K.E., Lucey, A.B., & Schultz, A.M. (2005). Climate for minorities in exercise and sport settings. *Journal of Sport & Exercise Psychology, 27* (Suppl.), S68.

Gill, D.L., Morrow, R.G., Collins, K.E., Lucey, A.B., & Schultz, A.M. (2006). Attitudes and sexual prejudice in sport and physical activity. *Journal of Sport Management, 20*, 554-564.

Guthrie, R.V. (1998). *Even the rat was White: A historical view of psychology* (2nd ed.). Boston: Allyn & Bacon.

Hall, R.L. (2005, October). Experiences with and training in diversity: AAASP 2002 survey. In R. Hall, D. Gill, C. Kamphoff, & E. Claspell, Where are our voices? The status of diversity in AAASP. Symposium conducted at the meeting of the Association for the Advancement of Applied Sport Psychology, Vancouver, Canada.

Harris, O. (2000). African American predominance in sport. In D. Brooks & R. Althouse (Eds.), *Racism in college athletics: The African-American athlete's experience* (2nd ed., pp. 37-51). Morgantown, WV: Fitness Information Technology.

Herek, G.M. (2000). Psychology of sexual prejudice. *Current directions in psychological science, 9*, 19-22.

Heyman, S.R. (1993). Affirmation of diversity. *ESPN: Exercise and Sport Psychology Newsletter, 7* (Spring), 2.

Human Rights Watch. (2001). Hatred in the hallways: Violence and discrimination against lesbian, gay, bisexual, and transgender students in U.S. schools. *American Journal of Health Education, 32*, 302-306.

Hyde, J.S. (2005). The gender similarities hypothesis. *American Psychologist, 60*, 581-592.

Kamphoff, C.S. (2006). *Bargaining with patriarchy: Former women coaches' experiences and their decision to leave coaching.* Doctoral dissertation, University of North Carolina at Greensboro.

Kamphoff, C. Araki, K., & Gill, D. (2004 Fall). Diversity issues in AAASP. *AAASP Newsletter, 19* (3), 26-27.

Kane, M.J., & Snyder, E. (1989). Sport typing: The social "containment" of women. *Arena Review, 13*, 77-96.

Kimm, S.Y.S., Glynn, N.W., Kriska, A.M., Barton, B.A., Kronsberg, S.S., Daniels, S.R., et al. (2002). Decline in physical activity in black girls and white girls during adolescence. *New England Journal of Medicine, 347*, 709-715.

Krueger, J. (1996). Personal beliefs and cultural stereotypes about racial characteristics. *Journal of Personality and Social Psychology, 71*, 536-548.

Lapchick, R. (2005). *The 2004 Racial and Gender Report Card: College sports.* Retrieved July 2005 from www.tidesport. org/RGRC/2004/RGRC_2004.pdf.

Lapchick, R. (2006). *The 2005 Racial and Gender Report Card: College sports*. Retrieved May 2007 from www.tidesport. org/RGRC/2005/FINAL_2005_RGRC.pdf.

Maccoby, E., & Jacklin, C. (1974). *The psychology of sex differences*. Stanford, CA: Stanford University Press.

Mio, J.S., Barker-Hackett, L., & Tumambing, J. (2006). *Multicultural psychology: Understanding our diverse communities*. Boston: McGraw-Hill.

Morrow, R.G., & Gill, D.L. (2003). Perceptions of homophobia and heterosexism in physical education. *Research Quarterly for Exercise and Sport, 74*, 205-214.

Parham, W.D. (2005). Raising the bar: Developing an understanding of athletes from racially, culturally, and ethnically diverse backgrounds. In M.B. Anderson (Ed.), *Sport psychology in practice* (pp. 201-215). Champaign, IL: Human Kinetics.

Pratt, M., Macera, C.A., & Blanton, C. (1999). Levels of physical activity and inactivity in children and adults in the United States: Current evidence and research issues. *Medicine and Science in Sport and Exercise, 31*, 526-533.

Ram, N., Starek, J., & Johnson, J. (2004). Race, ethnicity, and sexual orientation: Still a void in sport and exercise psychology. *Journal of Sport & Exercise Psychology, 26*, 250-268.

Rankin, S.R. (2003). Campus climate for gay, lesbian, bisexual, and transgender people: A national perspective. Retrieved June 6, 2005, from www.thetaskforce. org/reports_and_research/campus_climate.

Rivers, I., & D'Augelli, A.R. (2001). The victimization of lesbian, gay, and bisexual youth. In A.R. D'Augelli & C.J. Patterson (Eds.), *Lesbian, gay and bisexual identities and youth: Psychological perspectives* (pp. 199-223). New York: Oxford University Press.

Sailes, G. (2000). The African American athlete: Social myths and stereotypes. In D. Brooks & R. Althouse (Eds.), *Racism in college athletics: The African-American athlete's experience* (2nd ed., pp. 53-63). Morgantown, WV: Fitness Information Technology.

Steele, C.M. (1997). A threat in the air: How stereotypes shape intellectual identity and performance. *American Psychologist, 52*, 613-629.

Steele, C.M., Spencer, S.J., & Aronson, J. (2002). Contending with group image: The psychology of stereotype and social identity threat. In M.P. Zanna (Ed). *Advances in Experimental Social Psychology* (Vol. 34, pp. 379-440). New York: Academic Press.

Stone, J., Lynch, C.I., Sjomeling, M., & Darley, J.M. (1999). Stereotype threat effects on black and white athletic performance. *Journal of Personality and Social Psychology, 77*, 1213-1227.

Stone, J., Perry, Z.W., & Darley, J.M. (1997). White men can't jump: Evidence for the perceptual confirmation of racial stereotypes following a basketball game. *Basic and Applied Social Psychology, 19*, 291-306.

Sue, S. (1999). Science, ethnicity, and bias: Where have we gone wrong? *American Psychologist, 54*, 1070-1077.

Sue, D.W. (2004). Whiteness and ethnocentric monoculturalism: Making the "invisible" visible. *American Psychologist, 59*, 761-769.

Trickett, E.J., Watts, R.J., & Birman, D. (Eds.). (1994). *Human diversity: Perspectives on people in context*. San Francisco: Jossey-Bass.

U.S. Department of Health and Human Services (USDHHS). (2000). *Healthy people 2010*. Washington, DC: DHHS.

USDHHS. (2003). *National healthcare disparities report*. Washington, DC: DHHS.

Yali, A.M., & Revenson, T.A. (2004). How changes in population demographics will impact health psychology: Incorporating a broader notion of cultural competence into the field. *Health Psychology, 23*, 147-155.

Chapter 6

Austin, S.B. (1999). Fat, loathing, and public health: The complicity of science in a culture of disordered eating. *Culture, Medicine, and Psychiatry, 23*, 245-268.

Bernard, H.R. (2000). *Social research methods*. Thousand Oaks, CA: Sage.

Brandl-Bredenbeck, H.P., & Brettschneider, W.D. (1997). Sport involvement and self-concept in German and American adolescents. *International Review for the Sociology of Sport, 32*, 357-371.

Butryn, T.M. (2002). Critically examining white racial identity privilege in sport psychology consulting. *Sport Psychologist, 16*, 316-336.

Caglar, E., & Asci, F.H. (2006). Gender and physical activity level differences in physical self-perception of university students: A case of Turkey. *International Journal of Sport Psychology, 37*, 58-74.

Cerulo, K.A. (1997). Identity construction: New issues, new directions. *Annual Review of Sociology, 23*, 385-409.

Crotty, M. (1998). *The foundations of social research: Meaning and perspective in the research process*. London: Sage.

Cruickshank, D. (1985, June). Uses and benefits of reflective teaching. *Phi Delta Kappan*, 704-706.

Culver, D.M., Gilbert, W.D., & Trudel, P. (2003). A decade of qualitative research in sport psychology journals: 1990-1999. *Sport Psychologist, 17*, 1-15.

Curry, T.J., & Weiss, O. (1989). Sport identity and motivation for sport participation: A comparison between American college athletes and Austrian student sport club members. *Sociology of Sport Journal, 6*, 257-268.

Dagkas, S., & Benn, T. (2006). Young Muslim women's experiences of Islam and physical education in Greece and Britain: A comparative study. *Sport, Education and Society, 11*, 21-38.

Deci, E.L., & Ryan, R.M. (1985). *Intrinsic Motivation and Self-Determination in Human Behavior*. New York: Plenum Press.

Denzin, N.K., & Lincoln, Y.S. (1994). *Handbook of qualitative research*. London: Sage.

Denzin, N.K., & Lincoln, Y.S. (2000). Introduction. In N.K. Denzin & Y.S. Lincoln (Eds.), *Handbook of qualitative research* (2nd ed., pp. 1-29). London: Sage.

Denzin, N.K., & Lincoln, Y.S. (2005). *Handbook of qualitative research* (2nd ed.). Thousand Oaks, CA: Sage.

Dewey, J. (1910). *How we think*. Boston: D.C. Heath & Co.

Donnelly, P., & Young, K. (1988). The construction and confirmation of identity in sport subcultures. *Sociology of Sport Journal, 5,* 223-240.

Duda, J.L., & Allison, M.T. (1990). Cross-cultural analysis in exercise and sport psychology: A void in the field. *Journal of Sport & Exercise Psychology, 12,* 114-131.

Duda, J.L., & Hayashi, C.T. (1998). Measurement issues in cross-cultural research within sport and exercise psychology. In J.L. Duda (Ed.), *Advances in sport psychology measurement* (pp. 471-483). Champaign, IL: Human Kinetics.

Ellis, C.S., & Bochner, A.P. (2006). Analyzing analytic autoethnography: An autopsy. *Journal of Contemporary Ethnography, 35,* 429-449.

Fisher, L.A., Butryn, T.M., & Roper, E. (2003). Diversifying (and politicizing) sport psychology through cultural studies: A promising perspective. *Sport Psychologist, 17,* 391-405.

Fisher, L.A., Butryn, T.M., & Roper, E. (2005). Diversifying (and politicizing) sport psychology through cultural studies: A promising perspective revisited. *Athletic Insight.* Retrieved February 5, 2007, from www.athleticinsight.com/Vol7Iss3/DiversifyingPoliticizing.htm.

Fox, K.R. (1997). *The physical self: From motivation to well-being.* Champaign, IL: Human Kinetics.

Fox, K.R., & Corbin, C.B. (1989). The Physical Self-Perception Profile: development and preliminary validation. *Journal of Sport and Exercise Psychology, 11,* 408-430.

Gano-Overway, L.A., & Duda, J.L. (2001). Personal theories of achievement motivation among African and white mainstream American athletes. *International Journal of Sport Psychology, 32,* 335-354.

Gergen, M., & Gergen, K. (2000). Qualitative inquiry. In N.K. Denzin, & Y.S. Lincoln (Eds.), *Handbook of qualitative research* (2nd ed., pp. 1025-1046). London: Sage.

Gilbert, W.D., & Trudel, P. (2001). Learning to coach through experience: Reflection in model youth sport coaches. *Journal of Teaching in Physical Education, 21,* 16-34.

Gould, D., Feltz, D., & Weiss, M. (1985). Motives for participating in competitive youth swimming. *International Journal of Sport Psychology, 16,* 126-140.

Grenz, S.J. (1996). *A primer on postmodernism.* Grand Rapids, MI/Cambridge, UK: William B. Eedermans.

Guba, E.G. (1990). The alternative paradigm dialog. In E.G. Guba (Ed.), *The paradigm dialog* (pp. 17-30). Newbury Park, CA: Sage.

Guba, E.G., & Lincoln, Y.S. (2005). Paradigmatic controversies, contradictions, and emerging confluences. In N.K. Denzin & Y.S. Lincoln (Eds.), *The Sage handbook of qualitative research* (3rd ed., pp. 191-215), Thousand Oaks, CA: Sage.

Hanrahan, S.J. (2004). Sport psychology and indigenous performing arts. *Sport Psychologist, 18,* 60-74.

Harter, S. (1981). Development of competence motivation in the mastery of cognitive and physical skills: Is there still a place for joy? In Roberts, G.C., & Landers, D.L. (Eds). *Psychology of Motor Behavior and Sport, 1980* (pp. 3-29). Champaign, IL: Human Kinetics.

Hatton, N., & Smith, D. (1994). Reflection in teacher education: Towards definition and implementation. *Teaching & Teacher Education, 11,* 33-49.

Heron, J., & Reason, P. (1997). A participatory inquiry paradigm. *Qualitative Inquiry, 3,* 274-294.

Hertz, R. (1997). Introduction. In R. Hertz (Ed.), *Reflexivity and voice* (pp. vii-xviii). London: Sage.

Hofstede, G. (1991). *Cultures and organizations: Software of the mind.* London: McGraw-Hill.

Holt, N. (2003). Representation, legitimation, and autoethnography: An autoethnographic writing story. *International Journal of Qualitative Methods, 2,* 1-22.

Jegatheesan, B.I. (2006). I see start: An auto-ethnographer speaks on fieldwork and flashbacks. *Qualitative Inquiry, 11,* 667-688.

Kane, R., Sandretto, S., & Heath, C. (2004). An investigation into excellent tertiary teaching: Emphasizing reflective practice. *Higher Education, 47,* 283-310.

Kimiecik, J., Horn, T., & Shurin, C. (1996). Relationships among children's beliefs, perceptions of their parents' beliefs, and their moderate to vigorous physical activity. *Research Quarterly for Exercise & Sport, 67,* 324-336.

King, S.J. (2005). Methodological contingencies in sports studies. In D.L. Andrews, D.S. Mason, & M.L. Silk (Eds.), *Qualitative methods in sports studies* (pp. 21-38). New York: Berg.

Krane, V. (1996). Lesbians in sport: Toward acknowledgment, understanding, and theory. *Journal of Sport & Exercise Psychology, 18,* 237-246.

Krane, V. (2001). One lesbian feminist epistemology: Integrating feminist standpoint, queer theory and feminist cultural studies. *Sport Psychologist, 15,* 401-411.

Krane, V., Andersen, M.B., & Strean, W.B. (1997). Issues of qualitative research methods and presentation. *Journal of Sport & Exercise Psychology, 19,* 213-218.

Krane, V., Barber, H., & McClung, L.R. (2002). Social psychological benefits of gay games participation: A social identity theory explanation. *Journal of Applied Sport Psychology, 14,* 27-42.

Lally, P. (2007). Identity and athletic retirement: A prospective study. *Psychology of Sport and Exercise, 8,* 85-99.

Markus, H. (1977). Self-schemata and processing information about the self. *Journal of Personality and Social Psychology, 35,* 63-78.

Marsh, H. (1990). A multidimensional hierarchical model of self-concept: Theoretical and empirical identification. *Educational Psychology Review, 2,* 77-172.

Martens, R., Mobley, M., & Zizzi, S.J. (2000). Multicultural training in applied sport psychology. *Sport Psychologist, 14,* 81-97.

McGannon, K.R., & Mauws, M. (2000). Discursive psychology: An alternative approach for studying adherence to exercise and physical activity. *Quest, 52,* 148-152.

McGannon, K.R., & Mauws, M. (2002). Exploring the exercise adherence problem: An integration of ethnomethodological and poststructuralist perspectives. *Sociology of Sport Journal, 19,* 67-89.

McGinley, M., Kremer, J., Trew, K., & Ogle, S. (1998). Socio-cultural identity and attitudes to sport in Northern Ireland. *Irish Journal of Psychology, 19,* 464-471.

Mills, C.W. (1940). Situated actions and vocabularies of motive. *American Sociological Review, 5,* 904-913.

Nicholls, J. (1984). Achievement motivation: Conceptions of ability, subjective experience, task choice, and performance. *Psychological Review, 91,* 328-346.

Osterman, K.F. (1990). A new agenda for education. *Education and Urban Society, 22,* 133-152.

Phinney, J.S. (1992). The Multigroup Ethnic Identity Measure: A new scale for use with diverse groups. *Journal of Adolescent Research, 7,* 156-176.

Ponterotto, J.G. (2005). Qualitative research in counseling psychology: A primer on research paradigms and philosophy of science. *Journal of Counseling Psychology 52,* 126–136.

Ram, N., Starek, J., & Johnson, J. (2004). Race, ethnicity, and sexual orientation: Still a void in sport and exercise psychology? *Journal of Sport & Exercise Psychology, 26,* 250-268.

Richardson, L. (1995). Writing stories: Co-authoring "The Sea Monster," a writing-story. *Qualitative Inquiry, 1,* 189-203.

Richardson, L. (1998). Writing: A method of inquiry. In N.K. Denzin & Y.S. Lincoln (Eds.), *Collecting and interpreting qualitative materials* (pp. 345-371). Thousand Oaks, CA: Sage.

Richardson, L. (2000a). New writing practices in qualitative research. *Sociology of Sport Journal, 17,* 5-20.

Richardson, L. (2000b). Writing: A method of inquiry. In N.K. Denzin & Y.S. Lincoln (Eds.), *Handbook of qualitative research* (2nd ed., pp. 923-948). Thousand Oaks, CA: Sage.

Richardson, L., & St. Pierre, E.A. (2005). Writing: A method of inquiry. In N.K. Denzin & Y.S. Lincoln (Eds.), *The Sage handbook of qualitative research* (3rd ed., pp. 959-978). Thousand Oaks, CA: Sage.

Roper, E. (2001). The personal becomes political: Exploring the potential of feminist sport psychology. *Sport Psychologist, 15,* 445-449.

Roper, E., Fisher, L.A., & Wrisberg, C.A. (2005). Professional women's career experiences in sport psychology: A feminist standpoint approach. *Sport Psychologist, 19,* 32-50.

Ryba, T.V., & Wright, H.K. (2005). From mental game to cultural praxis: A cultural studies model's implications for the future of sport psychology. *Quest, 57,* 192-212.

Saukko, P. (2003). *Doing research in cultural studies: An introduction to classical and new methodological approaches.* London: Sage.

Schinke, R.J., Hanrahan, S.J., Eys, M.A., Blodgett, A., Peltier, D., Ritchie, S., et al. (in press). The development of cross-cultural relations with a Canadian Aboriginal community through sport psychology research. *Quest.*

Schinke, R.J., Michel, G., Gauthier, A.P., Peltier, D., Pheasant, C., Enosse, L., et al. (2006). The adaptation to the mainstream in elite sport: A Canadian aboriginal perspective. *Sport Psychologist, 20,* 435-448.

Schinke, R.J., & Tabakman, J. (2001). Reflective coaching interventions for athletic excellence. Retrieved March 22, 2007, from www.athleticinsight.com/Vol3Iss1/Reflective_Coaching.htm.

Shavelson, R.J., Hubner, J.J., & Stanton, G.C. (1976). Self-concept: Validation of construct interpretations. *Review of Educational Research, 46,* 407-441.

Silk, M., Andrews, D.L., & Mason, D. (2005). Encountering the field: Sports studies and qualitative research. In Andrews, D.L., Mason, D.S., & Silk, M.L. (Eds.), *Qualitative methods in sports studies* (pp. 1-20). New York: Berg.

Smith, B., & Sparkes, A.C. (2005). Analyzing talk in qualitative inquiry: Exploring possibilities, problems and tensions. *Quest, 57,* 213-242.

Sparkes, A.C. (1996). The fatal flaw: A narrative of the fragile body self. *Qualitative Inquiry, 2,* 463-494.

Sparkes, A.C. (2002). *Telling tales in sport and physical activity: A qualitative journey.* Champaign, IL: Human Kinetics.

Tierney, W. (1997). Lost in translation. In W. Tierney & Y. Lincoln (Eds.), *Representation and the text* (pp. 22-36). Albany, NY: SUNY Press.

Weedon, C. (1997). *Feminist practice & poststructuralist theory* (2nd ed.), Cambridge, MA: Blackwell.

Weinberg, R., Tenenbaum, G., McKenzie, A., Jackson, S., Anshel, M., Grove, R., et al. (2000). Motivation for youth participation in sport and physical activity. *International Journal of Sport Psychology, 31,* 321-346.

Chapter 7

Andersen, M.B. (1993). Questionable sensitivity: A comment on Lee and Rotella. *Sport Psychologist, 7,* 1-3.

Andersen, M.B. (Ed.). (2000). *Doing sport psychology.* Champaign, IL: Human Kinetics.

Anderson, A., Knowles, Z., & Gilbourne, D. (2004). Reflective practice for sport psychologists: Concepts, models, practical implications, and thoughts on dissemination. *Sport Psychologist, 18,* 188-203.

Anshel, M.H., Williams, L.R.T., & Hodge, K. (1997). Cross-cultural and gender differences on coping style in sport. *International Journal of Sport Psychology, 28,* 141-156.

Baruth, L.G., & Manning, M.L. (1999). *Multicultural counseling and psychotherapy: A lifespan perspective.* Upper Saddle River, NJ: Prentice-Hall.

Bolkiah, S., & Terry, P.C. (2001). Coaching preferences of athletes in Brunei Darussalam and Great Britain: A cross-cultural test of the path-goal theory. In Papaioannou, A., Goudas, M., & Theodorakis, Y. (Eds.), *Proceedings of the International Society of Sport Psychology 10th World Congress* (pp. 8-10). Thessaloniki, Greece: Christodoulidi.

Buchanan, L. (2006, September). Impostor syndrome. *Inc. Magazine,* 37-38.

Chelladurai, P., Inamura, H., Yamaguchi, Y., Oinuma, Y., & Miyauchi, T. (1988). Sport leadership in a cross-national setting: The case of Japanese and Canadian university athletes. *Journal of Sport & Exercise Psychology, 10,* 374-389.

Cox, R.H., & Liu, Z. (1993). Psychological skills: A cross-cultural investigation. *International Journal of Sport Psychology, 24,* 326-340.

Cushion, C.J., Armour, K.M., & Jones, R.L. (2003). Coach education and continuing professional development: Experience and learning to coach. *Quest, 55,* 215-230.

Fisher, L.A., Butryn, T., & Roper, E.A. (2003). Diversifying (and politicizing) sport psychology through cultural studies: A promising perspective. *Sport Psychologist, 17,* 391-405.

Ford, M.G. (2003). Working toward cultural competence in athletic training. *Athletic Therapy Today, 8,* 60-66.

Gibbs, G. (1998). *Learning by doing: A guide to teaching and learning.* Oxford: Oxford Polytechnic Further Education Unit.

Hale, B.D., James, B., & Stambulova, N. (1999). Determining the dimensionality of athletic identity: A 'Herculean' cross-cultural undertaking. *International Journal of Sport Psychology, 30,* 83-100.

Hallahan, M., Lee, F., & Herzog, T. (1997). It's not just whether you win or lose, it's also where you play the game: A naturalistic, cross-cultural examination of the positivity bias. *Journal of Cross-Cultural Psychology, 28,* 768-778.

Hanrahan, S. (2005). Using psychological skills training from sport psychology to enhance the life satisfaction of adolescent Mexican orphans. *Athletic Insight.* Retrieved March 30, 2007, from www.athleticinsight.com/Vol7Iss3/UsingSportPsych.htm.

Heishman, M.F., & Bunker, L. (1989). Use of mental preparation strategies by international elite female lacrosse players from five countries. *Sport Psychologist, 3,* 14-22.

Hoedaya, D., & Anshel, M.H. (2003). Coping with stress in sport among Australian and Indonesian athletes. *Australian Journal of Psychology, 55,* 159-165.

Holt, N.L., & Strean, W.B. (2001). Reflecting on initiating sport psychology consultation: A self-narrative of neophyte practice. *Sport Psychologist, 15,* 188-204.

Isogai, H., Brewer, B.W., Cornelius, A.E., Etnier, J., & Tokunaga, M. (2003). A cross-cultural analysis of goal orientation in American and Japanese physical education students. *International Journal of Sport Psychology, 34,* 80-93.

Isogai, H., Brewer, B.W., Cornelius, A.E., Komiya, S., Tokunaga, M., & Tokushima, S. (2001). Cross-cultural validation of the Social Physique Anxiety Scale. *International Journal of Sport Psychology, 32,* 76-87.

Knowles, Z., Gilbourne, D., Borrie, A., & Nevill, A. (2001). Developing the reflective sports coach: A study exploring the processes of reflective practice within a higher education coaching programme. *Reflective Practice, 2,* 185-207.

Kolt, G.S., Kirkby, R.J., Bar-Eli, M., Blumenstein, B., Chadha, N.K., Liu, J., & Kerr, G. (1999). A cross-cultural investigation of reasons for participation in gymnastics. *International Journal of Sport Psychology, 30,* 381-398.

Kontos, A.P., & Arguello, E. (2005). Sport psychology consulting with Latin American athletes. *Athletic Insight.* Retrieved March 30, 2007, from www.athleticinsight.com/Vol7Iss3/LatinAmerican.htm.

Kontos A.P., & Breland-Noble, A.M. (2002). Racial/ethnic diversity in applied sport psychology: A multicultural introduction to working with athletes of color. *Sport Psychologist, 16,* 296-315.

Martens, M.P., Mobley, M., & Zizzi, S.J. (2000). Multicultural training in applied sport psychology. *Sport Psychologist, 14,* 81-97.

Martin, S.B., Lavallee, D., & Kellmann, M. (2004). Attitudes toward sport psychology consulting of adult athletes from the United States, United Kingdom, and Germany. *International Journal of Sport and Exercise Psychology, 2,* 146-160.

Martindale, A., & Collins, D. (2005). Professional judgement and decision making: The role of intention for impact. *Sport Psychologist, 19,* 303-317.

Mesquita, B., & Frijda, N.H. (1992). Cultural variations in emotion: A review. *Psychological Review, 112,* 179-204.

Munroe, K., Terry, P.C., & Carron, A.V. (2002). Cohesion and teamwork. In B.D. Hale & D. Collins (Eds.), *Rugby tough* (pp. 135-151). Champaign, IL: Human Kinetics.

Nelson, L.J., & Cushion, C.J. (2006). Reflection in coach education: The case of the National Governing Body Coaching Certificate. *Sport Psychologist, 20,* 174-183.

Papaioannou, A.G. (2006). Muslim and Christian students' goal orientations in school, sport, and life. *International Journal of Sport and Exercise Psychology, 4,* 250-282.

Pope, M. (1995). The "salad bowl" is big enough for us all: An argument for the inclusion of lesbians and gay men in any definition of multiculturalism. *Journal of Counseling and Development, 73,* 301-304.

Schinke, R.J. (2005). Editorial. *Athletic Insight.* Retrieved March 30, 2007, from www.athleticinsight.com/Vol7Iss3/Editorial.htm.

Schön, D.A. (1987). *Educating the reflective practitioner.* San Fransisco: Jossey-Bass.

Si, G., Rethorst, S., & Willimczik, K. (1995). Causal attribution perception in sports achievement: A cross-cultural study on attributional concepts in Germany and China. *Journal of Cross-Cultural Psychology, 26,* 537-553.

Stambulova, N., Stephan, Y., & Jäphag, U. (2007). Athletic retirement: A cross-national comparison of elite French and Swedish athletes. *Psychology of Sport and Exercise, 8,* 101-118.

Terry, P.C. (1984). Coaching preferences of elite athletes competing at Universiade '83. *Canadian Journal of Applied Sports Sciences, 9,* 201-208.

Terry, P.C. (1997). The application of mood profiling with elite sport performers. In R. Butler (Ed.), *Sport psychology in performance* (pp. 3-32). Oxford: Butterworth-Heinemann.

Xinyi, Z., Smith, D., & Adegbola, O. (2004). A cross-cultural comparison of six mental qualities among Singaporean, North American, Chinese, and Nigerian professional athletes. *International Journal of Sport and Exercise Psychology, 2,* 103-118.

Chapter 8

Aboriginal Diabetes Initiative. (2004). Introduction. Retrieved March 22, 2007, from www.hc-sc.gc.ca/fnihb/cp/adi/introduction.htm.

Adrian, M., Payne, N., & Williams, R.T. (1991). Estimating the effects of Native Indian population on county alcohol consumption: The example of Ontario. *International Journal of the Addictions, 2,* 731-765.

Borden, A., & Coyote, S. (2006). The smudging ceremony. www.asunam.com/smudge_ceremony.html.

Brant, R., Forsyth, J., Horn-Miller, W., Loutitt, J., Sinclair, C., Smith, M., et al. (2002). *North American Indigenous Games Sport Research Panel.* In R. Brant & J. Forsyth (Eds.), 2002 North American Indigenous Games Conference Proceedings (pp. 67-70). Winnipeg, Canada: University of Manitoba Press.

Danielson, R., Schinke, R.J., Peltier, D., & Dube. T. (2006, June 30). Role modeling sources and activities of elite Canadian Aboriginal athletes. Paper presented at the North American Indigenous Games Educational Symposium, Colorado.

Dickason, O.P. (2006). *A concise history of Canada's First Nations.* Toronto: Oxford University Press.

Hanrahan, S.J. (2004). Sport psychology and indigenous performing arts. *Sport Psychologist, 18,* 60-74.

Hill, T.L. (1993). Sport psychology and the collegiate athlete: One size does not fit all. *Counseling Psychologist, 21,* 436-440.

Kontos, A.P., & Breland-Noble, A.M. (2002). Racial/ethnic diversity in applied sport psychology: A multicultural introduction to working with athletes of color. *Sport Psychologist, 16,* 296-315.

Nelles, H.V. (2004). *A little history of Canada.* Toronto: Oxford University Press.

Peltier, D., Danielson, R., Schinke, R.J., Michel, G., & Dube, T.V. (2006, June 30). Cultural sport psychology: The Wikwemikong perspective. Paper presented at the North American Indigenous Games Educational Symposium, Colorado.

Ross, R. (1985). *Dancing with a ghost: Exploring Aboriginal reality.* Toronto: Penguin.

Running Wolf, P., & Rickard, J.A. (2003). Talking circles: A Native American approach to experiential learning. *Multicultural Counselling and Development, 31,* 39-43.

Ryba, T.V., & Wright, H.K. (2005). From mental game to cultural praxis: A cultural studies model's implications for the future of sport psychology. *Quest, 57,* 192-212.

Schinke, R.J., Eys, M.A., Michel, G., Danielson, R., Peltier, D., Pheasant, C., et al. (2006). Cultural social support for Canadian Aboriginal elite athletes during their sport development. *International Journal of Sport Psychology, 37,* 1-19.

Schinke, R.J., Hanrahan, S.J., Peltier, D., Michel, G., Danielson, R., Pickard, P., et al. (2007). The precompetition and competition practices of Canadian Aboriginal elite athletes. *Journal of Clinical Sport Psychology, 1,* 147-165.

Schinke, R.J., Michel, G., Gauthier, A., Pickard, P., Danielson, R., Peltier, D., et al. (2006). The adaptation to the mainstream in elite sport: A Canadian Aboriginal perspective. *Sport Psychologist, 20,* 435-448.

Schinke, R.J., Ryba, T.V., Danielson, R., Michel, G., Pickard, P., Peltier, D., et al. (2007). Canadian Aboriginal elite athletes: The experiences of being coached in mainstream cultures. *International Journal of Sport and Exercise Psychology, 4,* 123-141.

Schnarch, B. (2004, January). Ownership, control, access, and permission or self-determination applied to research: A critical analysis of contemporary First Nations research some options for First Nations communities. *Journal of Aboriginal Health,* 80-95.

Scott, K. (1995). *Indigenous Canadians: Substance abuse profile 1995.* Prepared for the Kisht Anaquot Health Research and Program Development, for the National Native Alcohol and Drug Abuse Program.

Thomason, T.C. (1991). Counseling Native Americans: An introduction for Non-Native American counsellors. *Journal of Counseling and Development, 69,* 321-327.

Winther, N., Nazer-Bloom, L., & Petch, V. (1995). A comprehensive overview of development, the North American Indigenous Games and provincial/territorial Aboriginal sport bodies. Retrieved May 05, 2007, from www.pch.gc.ca/progs/sc/pol/aboriginal/2005/6_e.cfm.

Chapter 9

American Psychological Association (APA). (1993). Guidelines for providers of psychological services to ethnic, linguistic and culturally diverse populations. *American Psychologist, 48,* 45-48.

APA. (2001). *Publication manual of the American Psychological Association* (5th ed.). Washington, DC: American Psychological Association.

Andersen, M.B. (1993). Questionable sensitivity: A comment on Lee and Rotella. *Sport Psychologist, 7*, 1-3.

Bemak, F., & Greenberg, B. (1994). Southeast Asian refugee adolescents' implications for counseling. *Journal of Multicultural Counseling and Development, 22*, 115-124.

Berry, J.W. (1993). Ethnic identity in plural societies. In M.E. Bernal & G.P. Knight (Eds.), *Ethnic identity: Formation and transmission among Hispanics and other minorities* (pp. 271-296). Albany, NY: State University of New York Press.

Brooks, L.J., Haskins, D.G., & Kehe, J.V. (2004). Counseling and psychotherapy with African American clients. In T. Smith (Ed.), *Practicing multiculturalism: Affirming diversity in counseling in psychotherapy* (pp. 145-166). Boston: Pearson.

Butryn, T.M. (2002). Critically examining White racial identity and privilege in sport psychology consulting. *Sport Psychologist, 16*, 296-315.

Casas, J.M., & Pytluk, S.D. (1995). Hispanic identity development: Implication for research and practice. In J.G. Ponterotto, J.M. Casas, L.A. Suzuki, & C.M. Alexander (Eds.), *Handbook of multicultural counseling* (pp. 155-180). Thousand Oaks, CA: Sage.

Chung, R.C., Bemak, F., & Okazaki, S. (1997). Counseling Americans of Southeast Asian descent: The impact of refugee experience. In C. Lee (Ed.), *Multicultural issues in counseling: New approaches to diversity* (2nd ed., pp. 207-231). Alexandria, VA: American Counseling Association.

Chung, R.C., & Kagawa-Singer, M. (1996). Southeast Asian refugees' symptom expression. *Journal of Nervous Disease, 183*, 639-648.

Coakley, J. (2004). *Sport in society: Issues and controversies* (8th ed.). New York: McGraw-Hill.

Comas-Díaz, L. (1989). Culturally relevant issues and treatment implication for Hispanics. In D.R. Koslow & E. Salett (Eds.), *Crossing cultures in mental health* (pp. 31-48). Washington, DC: Society for International Education Training and Research.

Constantine, M.G., & Ladany, N. (2001). New visions for defining and assessing multicultural competence. In J.G. Ponterotto, J. Manuel Casas, L.A. Suzuki, & C.M. Alexander (Eds.), *Handbook of multicultural counseling* (pp. 491-492). Thousand Oaks, CA: Sage

Cox, R.H. (2002). *Sport psychology: Concepts and applications* (5th ed.). Boston: McGraw-Hill.

Cross, W.E., Jr. (1995). The psychology of nigrescence: Revising the Cross model. In J.G. Ponterotto, J.M. Casas, L.A. Suzuki, & C.M. Alexander (Eds.), *Handbook of multicultural counseling* (pp. 93-122). Thousand Oaks, CA: Sage.

Deloria, V., Jr. (1983). Indians today, the real and the unreal. In D.R. Atkinson, G. Morten, & D.W. Sue (Eds.), *Counseling American minorities: A cross-cultural perspective* (2nd ed., pp. 47-76). Dubuque, IA: Brown.

Duda, J.L., & Allison, M.T. (1990). Cross-cultural analysis in exercise and sport psychology: A void in the field. *Journal of Sport & Exercise Psychology, 12*, 114-131.

Erickson, C.D., & Al-Timimi, N.R. (2004). Counseling and psychotherapy with Arab American clients. In T. Smith (Ed.) *Practicing multiculturalism: Affirming diversity in counseling and psychology* (pp. 234-254). Boston: Pearson.

Evans, R.C., & Evans, H.L. (1995). Coping: Stressors and depression among middle-class African American men. *Journal of African American Men, 1*, 29-40.

Ford, D.Y. (1995). *Correlates of underachievement and achievement among gifted and nongifted Black students.* Storrs, CT: National Research Center on the Gifted and Talented, University of Connecticut.

Ford, D.Y. (1997). Counseling middle class African Americans. In C. Lee (Ed.) *Multicultural issues in counseling: New approaches to diversity* (2nd ed., pp. 81-108). Alexandria, VA: American Counseling Association.

Gloria, A.M., Ruiz, E.L., & Castillo, E.M (2004). Counseling and psychotherapy with Latino and Latina clients. In T. Smith (Ed.) *Practicing multiculturalism: Affirming diversity in counseling and psychology* (pp. 167-189). Boston: Pearson.

Hoberman, J. (1997). *Darwin's athletes: How sport has damaged black America and preserved the myth of race.* Boston: Houghton Mifflin.

Jackson, M. (1997). Counseling Arab Americans. In C. Lee (Ed.), *Multicultural issues in counseling: New approaches to diversity* (2nd ed., pp. 333-349). Alexandria, VA: American Counseling Association.

Kehe, J.V., & Smith, T.B. (2004). Glossary. In T. Smith (Ed.), *Practicing multiculturalism: Affirming diversity in counseling and psychology* (pp. 325-337). Boston: Pearson.

Kontos, A.P., & Arguello, E. (2005). Sport psychology consulting with Latin American athletes. *Athletic Insight, 7* (3).

Kontos, A.P., & Breland-Noble, A.M. (2002). Racial/ethnic diversity in applied sport psychology: A multicultural introduction to working with athletes of color. *Sport Psychologist, 16*, 296-315.

Lapchick, D. (2004). *2004 race and gender report card.* Orlando, FL: University of Central Florida.

Lee, C.C., & Bailey, D.F. (1997). Counseling African American male youth and men. In C. Lee (Ed.), *Multicultural issues in counseling: New approaches to diversity* (2nd ed., pp. 123-170). Alexandria, VA: American Counseling Association.

Lloyd, A.P. (1987). Multicultural counseling: Does it belong in a counselor education program? *Counselor Education and Supervision, 26*, 164-167.

Marín, G. (1992). Issues in the measurement of acculturation among Hispanics. In K.F. Geisinger (Ed.), *Psychological testing of Hispanics* (pp. 235-251). Washington, DC: American Psychological Association.

Marín, G., & Marín, B.V. (1991). Research with Hispanic populations. Newbury Park, CA: Sage.

Martens, M.P., Mobley, M., & Zizzi, S.J. (2000). Multicultural training in applied sport psychology. *Sport Psychologist, 14*, 81-97.

Martin, S.B., Wrisberg, C.A., Beitel, P.A., & Lounsbury, J. (1997). NCAA Division I athletes' attitudes toward seeking sport psychology consultation: The development of an objective instrument. *Sport Psychologist, 11*, 201-218.

Morrissey, M. (1997, October). The invisible minority: Counseling Asian Americans. *Counseling Today, 1*, 21-22.

National Collegiate Athletic Association (NCAA). (2003). *1999-2000-2001-2002 NCAA student-athlete ethnicity report*. Indianapolis, IN: National Collegiate Athletic Association.

Nydell, M. (1987). *Understanding Arabs: A guide for westerners*. Yarmouth, ME: Intercultural Press.

Parham, W.D. (2005). Raising the bar: Developing an understanding of athletes from racially, culturally, and ethnically diverse backgrounds. In M. Andersen (Ed.), *Sport psychology in practice* (pp. 201-216). Champaign, IL: Human Kinetics.

Patton, J.M. (1995). The education of African American males: Frameworks for developing authenticity. *Journal of African American Men, 1*, 5-27.

Pope-Davis, D.B., & Coleman, H.L.K. (1997). *Multicultural counseling competencies: Assessment, education and training, and supervision*. Thousand Oaks, CA: Sage.

Ram, N., Starek, J., & Johnson, J. (2004). Race, ethnicity, and sexual orientation: Still a void in sport and exercise psychology? *Journal of Sport & Exercise Psychology, 26*, 250-268.

Red Horse, J.G. (1982). Clinical strategies for American Indian families in crisis. *Urban and Social Change Review, 2*, 17-19.

Robinson, T.L., & Howard-Hamilton, M.F. (2000). *The convergence of race, ethnicity, and gender: Multiple identities in counseling*. Upper Saddle River, NJ: Merrill.

Sage, G.P. (1997). Counseling American Indian adults. In C. Lee (Ed.), *Multicultural issues in counseling: New approaches to diversity* (pp. 35-52). Alexandria, VA: American Counseling Association.

Sue, D.W., Carter, R.T., Casas, J.M., Fouad, N.A., Ivey, A.E., Jensen, M., et al. (1998). *Multicultural counseling competencies: Individual and organizational development*. Thousand Oaks, CA: Sage.

Sue, D.W, & Sue, D. (1999). *Counseling the culturally different: Theory and practice* (3rd ed.). New York: Wiley.

U.S. Census Bureau (2001). *Census briefs*. Washington, DC: U.S. Census Bureau, Census 2000 Redistricting (Public Law 94-171) Summary.

Vontress, C.E., & Epp, L.R. (1997). Historical hostility in the African American client: Implications for counseling. *Journal of Multicultural Counseling and Development, 25*, 170-184.

Watkins-Duncan, B. (1992). Principles for formulating treatment with Black patients. *Psychotherapy, 29*, 452-456.

Wrisberg, C.A., & Martin, S.B. (1994, October). *Attitudes of African American and White athletes toward sport psychology consultants*. Paper presented at the annual conference of the Association for the Advancement of Applied Sport Psychology, Incline Village, NV.

Chapter 10

Ericsson, K.A., Krampe, R.T., & Tesch-Römer, C. (1993). The role of deliberate practice in the acquisition of expert performance. *Psychological Review, 3*, 363-406.

Janelle, C.M., & Hillman, C.H. (2003). Expert performance in sport: Current perspectives and critical issues. In J.L. Starkes & A.K. Ericsson (Eds.), *Expert performance in sports* (pp. 19-48). Champaign, IL: Human Kinetics.

Luxemburgo, V. (2004). É Campeão! A montagem de um time campeão [They are champions! The building of a champion team]. Rio de Janeiro: Gryphus.

MacArthur, D.G., & North, K.N. (2005). Genes and human elite athletic performance. *Human Genetics, 116*, 331-339.

Ministério do Planejamento, Orcamento e Gest o. (2007, June 23). Ultimos resultudos [Last results]. Retrieved June 23, 2007, from www.ibge.gov.br/home.

Moraes, L.C., Rabelo, A.S., & Salmela, J.H. (2004). Papel dos pais no desenvolvimento de jovens futebolistas [Role of parents in the development of young footballers]. *Revista Psicologia: Reflexão e Crítica, 17*, 211-222.

Moraes, L.C., Salmela, J.H., Rabelo, A., & Vianna, N. (2004). Le rôle des parents dans le développment des jeunes joueurs [The role of parents in the development of young players]. *International Journal of Sport Science & Physical Education, 25*, 109-123.

Salmela, J.H., & Marques, M.P. (2004). Religion, superstition and football in Brazil. *Insight, 3* (7), 22-23.

Salmela, J.H., Marques, M.P., & Machado, R.F. (2004). The informal structure of football in Brazil. *Insight, 7* (1), 17-19.

Salmela, J.H., Marques, M.P., Machado, R., & Durand-Bush, N. (2006). Perceptions of the Brazilian football coaching staff in preparation for the World Cup. *International Journal of Sport Psychology, 37*, 139-156.

Salmela, J.H., & Moraes, L.C. (2003). Development of expertise: The role of coaching, families and cultural contexts. In J.L. Starkes & A.K. Ericsson (Eds), *Expert performance in sports* (p. 272-291). Champaign, IL: Human Kinetics.

Zanoteli, E., Lotuffo, R.M., Oliveira, A.S., Beggs, A.H., Canovas, M., Zatz, M., & Vainzof, M. (2003). Deficiency of muscle alpha-actinin-3 is compatible with high muscle performance. *Journal of Molecular Neurosciencef, 20*, 39-42.

Chapter 11

Alexeev, A.V. (1978). *Sebya preodolet* [Overcome yourself]. Moscow: FiS.

Berry, J.W., & Triandis, H.C. (2004). Cross-cultural psychology: Overview. In C. Spielberger (Ed.), *Encyclopaedia of applied psychology* (Vol. 1, pp. 527-538). New York: Elsevier.

Borg, G. (1998). *Borg's perceived exertion and pain scale.* Champaign, IL: Human Kinetics.

Bronfenbrenner, U. (1979). *The ecology of human development: Experiments by nature and design.* Cambridge, MA: Harvard University Press.

Forsberg, A. (2005). Forskningsrapport nr 27 [Research report # 27]. Centrum för Idrottsforskning, Stockholm.

Gill, D. (2007). Gender and cultural diversity. In G. Tenenbaum and R.C. Eklund (Eds.), *Handbook of sport psychology* (3rd ed., pp. 712-736). New York: Wiley.

Gorbunov, G. (1986). *Psihopedagogika sporta* [Psycho-pedagogy of sport]. Moscow: FiS.

Greenfield, P.M., & Keller, H. (2004). Cultural psychology. In C. Spielberger (Ed.), *Encyclopedia of applied psychology* (vol. 1, pp. 545-554). New York: Elsevier.

Hanin, Y.L. (1980). *Psihologiya obscheniya v sporte* [Psychology of communication in sport]. Moscow: FiS.

Iliin, E.P., Kiselev, Y.Y., & Safonov, V.K. (1989). *Psihologiya sporta: Novye napravleniya v psihologii* [Sport psychology: New directions in psychology]. Leningrad: LGU.

Johnson, U. (2000). Short-term psychological intervention: A study of long-term injured competitive athletes. *Journal of Sport Rehabilitation, 9*, 207-218.

Johnson, U. (2006). Sport psychology past, present, and future: Perceptions of Swedish sport psychology students. *Athletic Insight.* Retrieved September 25, 2006, from www.athleticinsight.com/Vol8Iss3/PastPresentFuture.htm.

Johnson, U., & Fallby, J. (2004). Idrottspsykologisk rådgivning—en kritisk discussion [Sport psychology consulting—critical thinking]. *Svensk Idrottspsykologisk årsskrift.* Örebro: Örebro University.

Johnson, U., & Stambulova, N. (2006, July). Performance enhancement issues in sport psychology consulting: Seventeen cases summary. Paper presented at the 11th European College of Sport Sciences Congress, Lausanne, Switzerland.

Leontiev, A.A. (1990). *L.S. Vygotsky.* Moscow: Prosveschenie.

Moran, A.P. (1996). *The psychology of concentration in sport performers.* Hove, England: Psychology Press.

Puni, A.Tc. (1969). *Psihologicheskaya podgotovka k sorevnovaniyu v sporte* [Psychological preparation for a competition in sport]. Moscow: FiS.

Puni, A.Tc. (1973). *Nekotorye psihologicheskie voprosy gotovnosti k sorevnovaniyam v sporte* [Some psychological aspects of readiness for a competition in sport]. Leningrad: GDOIFK.

Rodionov, A.V. (1983). *Vliyanie psihologicheskih faktorov na sportivnyi resultat* [Impact of psychological factors upon sport result]. Moscow: FiS.

Rosenberg, M. (2006). Population decline in Russia. Retrieved May 29, 2007, from http://geography.about.com/od/obtainpopulationdata/a/russiapop.htm.

Ryba, T., Stambulova, N., & Wrisberg, C. (2005). The Russian origin of sport psychology: A translation of an early work of A.Tc. Puni. *Journal of Applied Sport Psychology, 17*, 157-169.

Sandemose, A. (1934). *En flykting korsar sitt spår* [A fugitive crosses his tracks]. Stockholm: Tiden.

Stambulova, N., Wrisberg, C., & Ryba, T. (2006). A tale of two traditions in applied sport psychology: The heyday of Soviet sport and wake-up call for North America. *Journal of Applied Sport Psychology, 18*, 3, 173-184.

Swedish Sport Federation (2002). *Sports in Sweden.* Riksidrottsförbundet, Idrottens Hus, Farsta.

Unestähl, L.-E. (2001). *Den nya livsstilen.* Veje International, AB.

Viatkin, B.A. (1981). *Upravlenie psihicheskim stressom v sportivnyh sorevnovaniyah* [Coping with psychological stress in sport competitions]. Moscow: FiS.

Vygotsky, L.S. (1983). Istoriya razvitiya vysshih psihicheskih funkcii [History of the development of higher mental functions]. In A.V. Zaporozhets (Ed.), *L.S. Vygotsky: Complete works* (Vol. 3, pp. 5-328). Moscow: Pedagogika.

Vygotsky, L.S. (1984). *Problema vozrasta* [Problem of an age]. In A.V. Zaporozhets (Ed.), *L.S. Vygotsky: Complete works* (Vol. 4, pp. 244-268). Moscow: Pedagogika.

Woo, E. (2005, September 29). Urie Bronfenbrenner: Co-founder of HeadStart urged closer family ties. *Los Angeles Times*, p B10.

Zagainov, R.M. (1984). *Psiholog v komande* [Psychologist in the team]. Moscow: FiS.

Chapter 12

Bar-Eli, M., & Blumenstein, B. (2004). Performance enhancement in swimming: The effect of mental training with biofeedback. *Journal of Science and Medicine in Sport, 7*, 454-464.

Bar-Eli, M., & Lidor, R. (2000). Sport psychology as a tool for regional cooperation in the Mediterranean Basin. In R. Bar-El, E. Menipaz & G. Benhayoun (Eds.), *Regional cooperation in a global context* (pp. 301-312). Paris: L'Harmattan.

Ben-Porat, A. (1993). *State and capitalism in Israel.* Westport, CN: Greenwood Press.

Blumenstein, B. (1992). Music before starting. *Fitness and Sport Review International*, April, 49-50.

Blumenstein, B., & Lidor, R. (2004). Psychological preparation in elite canoeing and kayaking sport programs: Periodization and planning. *Applied Research in Coaching and Athletics Annual, 19,* 24-34.

Blumenstein B., Lidor, R., & Tenenbaum, G. (2005). Periodization and planning of psychological preparation in elite sport programs: The case of judo. *International Journal of Sport and Exercise Psychology, 3,* 7-25.

Estabrooks, P.A., & Dennis, P.W. (2003). The principles of team building and their applications to sport teams. In R. Lidor & K.P. Henschen (Eds.), *The psychology of team sports* (pp. 99-113). Morgantown, WV: Fitness Information Technology.

Hall, C.R. (2001). Imagery in sport and exercise. In R.N. Singer, H.A. Hausenblas, & C.M. Janelle (Eds.), *Handbook of sport psychology* (2nd ed., pp. 529-549). New York: Wiley.

Henschen, K. (2005). Mental practice: Skill oriented. In D. Hackfort, J.L. Duda, & R. Lidor (Eds.), *Handbook of research in applied sport and exercise psychology: International perspectives* (pp. 19-34). Morgantown, WV: Fitness Information Technology.

Lidor, R., & Bar-Eli, M. (1998). Physical education in Israel: An overview. *Chronicle of Physical Education in Higher Education, 9,* 7, 14-15.

Lidor, R., & Bar-Eli, M. (2001). Israel. In R. Lidor, T. Morris, N. Bardaxoglou, & B. Becker (Eds.), *The world sport psychology sourcebook* (3rd ed., pp. 61-67). Morgantown, WV: Fitness Information Technology.

Lidor, R., Blumenstein, B., & Tenenbaum, G. (2007a). Periodization and planning of psychological preparation in individual and team sports. In B. Blumenstein, R. Lidor, & G. Tenenbaum (Eds.), *Psychology of sport training* (pp. 137-161). Oxford: Meyer & Meyer Sport.

Lidor, R., Blumenstein, B., & Tenenbaum, G. (2007b). Psychological aspects of training programs in European basketball: Conceptualization, periodization, and planning. *Sport Psychologist, 21,* 353-367.

Moran, A. (2005). Training attention and concentration skills in athletes. In D. Hackfort, J.L. Duda, & R. Lidor (Eds.), *Handbook of research in applied sport and exercise psychology: International perspectives* (pp. 61-73). Morgantown, WV: Fitness Information Technology.

Police Report (2002). Retrieved May 1, 2007, from www.fresh.co.il/dcforum/dcboard/cgi.

Reshef, N., & Paltiel, J. (1989). Partisanship and sport: The unique case of politics and sport in Israel. *Sociology of Sport Journal, 6,* 305-318.

Simri, U., Tenenbaum, G., & Bar-Eli, M. (1996a). The governmental sports policy of the State of Israel. In L. Chalip., A. Johnson., & L. Stachura (Eds.), *National sports policies: An international handbook* (pp. 241-252). Westport, CT: Greenwood.

Simri, U., Tenenbaum, G., & Bar-Eli, M. (1996b). Israel. In P. DeKnop, L-M. Engstrroem, B. Skirstad, & M.R. Weiss (Eds.), *Worldwide trends in youth sport* (pp. 59-66). Champaign, IL: Human Kinetics.

"Statistical aspects of Israel." (2006). Retrieved March 15, 2007, from www.cbs.gov.il.

"Terror attacks." (2007). Retrieved May 1, 2007, from http://he.wikipedia.org/wiki.

Weinberg, R., & Butt, J. (2005). Goal setting in sport and exercise domains: The theory and practice of effective goal setting. In D. Hackfort, J.L. Duda, & R. Lidor (Eds.), *Handbook of research in applied sport and exercise psychology: International perspectives* (pp. 129-144). Morgantown, WV: Fitness Information Technology.

Chapter 13

Al-Durae, M.O. (Ed.). (2000). *Kuwait pocket guide.* Kuwait City: Kuwait Publishing House.

Brown, M., Cairns, K., & Botterill, C. (2001). The process of perspective: The art of living well in the world of elite sport. *Journal of Excellence, 1* (5), 5-38.

Carron, A.V., & Hausenblas, H. (1998). *Group dynamics in sport.* Morgantown, WV: Fitness Information Technology.

Crust, L. (2006). Challenging the 'myth' of a spiritual dimension in sport. *Athletic Insight,* Retrieved March 02, 2007, from www.athleticinsight.com/Vol8Iss2/Spiritual.htm.

Parham, W.D. (2005). Raising the bar: Developing an understanding of athletes from racially, culturally and ethnically diverse backgrounds. In M.B. Andersen (Ed.), *Sport psychology in practice* (pp. 201-215). Leeds: Human Kinetics.

Shannon, C., & Weaver, W. (1949). *The mathematical theory of communication.* Urbana, IL: University of Illinois Press.

Watson, N.J., & Czech, D.R. (2005). The use of prayer in sport: Implications for sport psychology consulting. *Athletic Insight,* Retrieved March 02, 2007, from www.athleticinsight.com/Vol7Iss4/PrayerinSports.htm.

Chapter 14

Cox, R.H. (2006). *Sport psychology: Concepts and applications* (6th ed.). Boston: McGraw-Hill.

Ikulayo P.B. (1990). *Understanding sports psychology.* Lagos, Nigeria: EA/TCN Press.

Ikulayo, P.B. (2001). Psychological skills training. Paper presented at 10th World Congress of Sport Psychology, Skiathos Island, Greece.

Ikulayo, P.B. (2002). *Family life and sex education.* Lagos, Nigeria: University of Lagos Press.

Ikulayo, P.B. (2003). *The mind in the body sports psychology as the cornerstone to sports achievements and greatness.* Lagos, Nigeria: University of Lagos Press.

Ikulayo, P.B. (2006). *Sports psychology digest.* Lagos, Nigeria: University of Lagos Press.

Ipinmoroti, O.A., & Ajayi, M.A. (2003). Effects of significant others on sports: Involvement of athletes in Nigerian tertiary institutions. *Journal of International Council of Health Physical Education and Recreation, 34,* 56-59.

Jacobson, E. (1958). *Progressive relaxation.* Chicago: University of Chicago Press.

Kukuru, J.D. (1996). *A handbook of social studies: Discourses on man's origin and Nigeria as a nation.* Lagos, Nigeria: Turns Gam Enterprises.

Kukuru, J.D. (1997). *A handbook of social studies: Discourses on social services and changes in Nigerians.* Lagos, Nigeria: Ade Azeez.

NigeriaBusinessInfo. (2001). The Nigerian economy: Peeping out of the woods. Retrieved June 29, 2007, from www.nigeriabusinessinfo.com/opps.htm.

Ogunniyi, D., & Oboli, H.O.N. (1996). *Spectrum social studies for secondary schools book I.* Ibadan: Spectrum Books.

Ogunniyi, D., & Oboli, H.O.N. (1999). *Spectrum social studies for secondary schools book II.* Ibadan: Spectrum Books.

Ogunniyi, D., & Oboli, H.O.N. (2000). *Spectrum social studies for secondary schools book III.* Ibadan: Spectrum Books.

Semidara, J.A. (2006). *Psychological intervention for Nigerian elite athletes.* Paper presented at Department of Human Kinetics and Health Education, University of Lagos, Nigeria.

Suinn, R.N. (1980). *Psychology in sports, methods and application.* Minneapolis: Burgess.

Syer, J., & Connolly, C. (1984). *Sports body and sporting mind: An athlete's guide to mental training.* Cambridge, England: Cambridge University Press.

Weinberg, R., & Gould, D. (2006). *Foundations of sport and exercise psychology* (4th ed.). Champaign, IL: Human Kinetics.

Williams, J.M. (2006). *Applied sport psychology: Personal growth to peak performance* (5th ed.). New York: McGraw-Hill.

Chapter 15

Aforo D.A. (2007). Age cheating marring football. *Ground Report.* Retrieved May 15, 2007, from www.groundreport.com/articles.php?id=2833765.

Andersen, M.B. (2000). Beginnings: Intakes and the initiation of relationships. In M.B. Andersen (Ed.), *Doing sport psychology* (pp. 3-16). Champaign, IL: Human Kinetics.

Central Intelligence Agency (CIA). (2007) World Factbook. Retrieved December 13, 2007, from https://www.cia.gov/library/publications/the-world-factbook/geos/gh.html.

DATA. (2005). Ghana: Results from the demographic and health survey. *Studies in Family Planning, 36,* 158-162.

Dowuona, N.N. (2006). The culture of Ghana maybe time. Retrieved April 21, 2007, from www.ghanaweb.com/GhanaHomePage/NewsArchive/artikel.php?ID=116409.

Dvorak, J., George, J., Junge, A., & Hodler, J. (2007). Age determination by magnetic resonance imaging of the wrist in adolescent male football players. *British Journal of Sports Medicine, 41,* 45-52.

Gordon, R.G., Jr. (Ed.). (2005). *Ethnologue: Languages of the world* (15 ed.). Dallas: SIL International. Retrieved December 13, 2007, from www.ethnologue.com.

Guardo C.J. (1969). Personal space in children. *Child Development, 40,* 143-151.

Hale, B. (2004). *Imagery training: A guide for sports coaches and performers.* Leeds, UK: sports coach UK.

Hall, E.T. (1959). *The silent language.* New York: Anchor Books.

Jambor, E.A. (1996). Beyond language barriers: Teaching techniques for swimming. *Journal of Physical Education, Recreation and Dance, 67,* 34-36.

Jandt, F.E. (2007). *An introduction to intercultural communication identities in a global community* (5th ed.). London: Sage.

Kontos, A.P., & Arguello, E. (2005). Sport psychology consulting with Latin American athletes. *Athletic Insight.* Retrieved April 21, 2007, from www.athleticinsight.com/Vol7Iss3/LatinAmerican.htm.

Little, K.B. (1965). Personal space. *Journal of Experimental Social Psychology, 1,* 237-247.

Maharaj, D. (2002). Soccer and the Juju men. *LA Times.* Retrieved May 6, 2007, from www.arthurmag.com/magpie/?p=190.

Montgomery, G.T., & Orozoco, S. (1985). Mexican Americans' performance on the MMPI as a function of level of acculturation. *Journal of Clinical Psychology, 41,* 203-212.

Onmonya, G. (2007). Overage syndrome in Nigerian football. *Nigerian Village Square.* Retrieved May 12, 2007, from www.nigeriavillagesquare.com/articles/george-onmonya/overage-syndrome-in-nigerian-foo.html.

Salm, S.J., & Falola, T. (2002). Culture and customs of Ghana. Westport, CT: Greenwood Press.

Thomas, P.R., Murphy, S.M., & Hardy, L. (1999). Test of performance strategies: Development and preliminary validation of comprehensive measure of athletes' psychological skills. *Journal of Sports Sciences, 17,* 697–711.

UK Foreign Office. (2007). UK foreign office country profile: Ghana. Retrieved June 18, 2007, from www.fco.gov.uk/en/about-the-fco/country-profiles/sub-saharan-africa/ghana.

UNICEF. (2007). At a glance: Ghana. Retrieved June 18, 2007, from www.unicef.org/infobycountry/ghana_1878.html.

United Nations. (2007). Africa and the Millennium Development Goals 2007 update. United Nations Department of Public Information. Retrieved June 19, 2007, from www.un.org/millenniumgoals/docs/MDGafrica07.pdf.

World Bank. (2007). Ghana and the World Bank: 50 years of a reliable partnership. Retrieved December 17, 2007, from www.worldbank.org/ghana.

World Write. (2003). Ghana: Economy world write. Retrieved May 23, 2007, from www.worldwrite.org.uk/ghana/ghanaeconomy.html.

Chapter 16

"Australian Aborigine traditional sociocultural patterns." (2007). Retrieved June 15, 2007, from www.britannica.com/eb/article-256935.

Dudgeon, P. (2000). Counselling with indigenous people. In P. Dudgeon, D. Garvey, & H. Pickett (Eds.), *Working with indigenous Australians: A handbook for psychologists* (pp. 249-271). Perth, Western Australia: Gunada Press.

Dudgeon, P., Garvey, D., & Pickett, H. (Eds.). (2000). *Working with indigenous Australians: A handbook for psychologists.* Perth, Western Australia: Gunada Press.

Dudgeon, P., & Oxenham, D. (1989). The complexity of Aboriginal diversity: Identity and kindredness. *Black Voices, 5* (1), 22-39.

Hanrahan, S.J. (2004). Sport psychology and indigenous performing artists. *Sport Psychologist, 18,* 60-74.

NSW Department of Health. (2004, May). *Communicating positively: A guide to appropriate Aboriginal terminology.* North Sydney: Author.

Queensland Health. (1996). *Last night I heard a voice: Working with indigenous mental health clients* [Video recording]. Queensland: Author.

Ralph, S. (1997). Working with Aboriginal families: Issues and guidelines for family and child counsellors. *Australian Institute of Family Studies, 46* (Autumn), 46-50.

Riley, R. (1998). From exclusion to negotiation: Psychology in Aboriginal social justice. *InPsych 20* (2), 12-19.

Smith, C. (2004). *Country, kin and culture: Survival of an Australian Aboriginal community.* Kent Town, South Australia: Wakefield Press.

Westerman, T. (2004). Engagement of indigenous clients in mental health services: What role do cultural differences play? *Australian eJournal for the Advancement of Mental Health, 3* (3). Retrieved June 15, 2007, from www.auseinet.com/journal/vol3iss3/westermaneditorial.pdf.

Chapter 17

Annual report 05/06. (2006). *Match report.* Singapore Sport Council.

Bastion, A. (2007). *Singapore in a nutshell* (4th ed.). Singapore: Pearson Education South Asia.

Brustad, R.J. (1993). Who will go out and play? Parental and psychological influence on children's attraction to physical activity. *Pediatric Exercise Science, 5,* 210-223.

Brustad, R.J. (1996). Attraction to physical activity in urban schoolchildren: Parental socialization and gender influences. *Research Quarterly for Exercise and Sport, 67,* 316-323.

Chua, B.H. (1995). *Communication ideology and democracy in Singapore.* London: Routledge.

Hofstede, G.H. (2001). *Culture's consequences: Comparing values, behaviors, institutions and organizations across nations* (2nd ed.). Thousand Oaks, CA: Sage.

Horn, T. (2002). Coaching effectiveness in the sport domain. In T. Horn (Ed.), *Advances in sport psychology* (2nd ed., pp. 309-354). Champaign, IL: Human Kinetics.

Kaya, B. (1960). *Upper Nankin Street Singapore: A social study of Chinese households living in a densely populated area.* Singapore: University of Malaya Press.

Lee, H.Y., Lee, E.L., Pathy, P., & Chan, Y.H. (2005). Anorexia nervosa in Singapore: An eight-year retrospective study. *Singapore Medicine Journal, 46,* 275-281.

Lee, K.Y. (1973). Prime Minister's address. Official opening of the National Stadium, Singapore.

McCullagh, P., Matzkanin, K.T., Shaw, S.D., & Maldonado, M. (1993). Motivation for participation in physical activity: A comparison of parent–child perceived competencies and participation motives. *Pediatric Exercise Science, 5,* 224-233.

McNeill, M., Sproule, J., & Horton, P. (2003). The changing face of sport and physical education in post-colonial Singapore. *Sport, Education, and Society, 8,* 35-56.

Meriwether, J.C. (2001). *Culture shock! A guide to customs and etiquette.* Singapore: Time Media.

Ministry of Community Development and Sports (2003). Foreign talent remains part of sports scene—plans to develop sports talents, including local ones. Retrieved June 15, 2007, from http://app.mcys.gov.sg/web/corp_press_story.asp?szMod=corp&szSubMod=press&qid=232.

Ministry of Manpower, Manpower Research and Statistics Department Singapore. (2006). *Employment rate in Singapore.*

Singapore Department of Statistics. (2001). Census of population 2000 statistical release 2: Education, language and religion. Retrieved June 15, 2007, from www.singstat.gov.sg/pubn/census.html#c2000sr2.

Singapore Department of Statistics. (n.d.). Gross domestic product. Retrieved June 15, 2007, from www.singstat.gov.sg/stats/themes/economy/hist/gdp2.html.

Singapore Department of Statistics. (n.d.). Population (midyear estimates). Retrieved June 15, 2007, from www.singstat.gov.sg/stats/themes/people/hist/popn.html.

Singapore Sports Council (SSC). (2007). $31.9 million grant in FY07 to national sports associations. Retrieved June 25, 2007, from www.ssc.gov.sg/publish/Corporate/en/news/media_releases/2007_media_releases/0.html.

Trocki, C.A. (2006). *Singapore: Wealth, power, and the culture of control.* London: Routledge.

Weinberg, R.S., & Gould, D. (2007). *Foundations of sport and exercise psychology* (4th ed.). Champaign, IL: Human Kinetics.

Weiss, M.R., Wises, D.M., & Klint, K.A. (1989). Head over heels with success: The relationship between self-efficacy and performance in competitive youth gymnastics. *Journal of Sport and Exercise Psychology, 11,* 444-451.

Yeoh, B.S.A. (2007). Singapore: Hungry for foreign workers at all skill levels. Retrieved April 18, 2007, from www. migrationinformation.org/feature/display.cfm?ID=570.

Chapter 18

Guttman, A., & Lee, T. (2001). *Japanese sports: A history.* Honolulu: University of Hawaii.

Inomata, K. (1997). *A mental management manual for athletes and coaches.* (In Japanese). Tokyo: Taishukanshyoten.

Japan Sport Association. (1960). *Nihon Taiku Kyokai supotsu kagaku kenkyu houkokushu* [Reports of the Japanese Association of Physical Education and Sport Sciences]. Tokyo: Japan Sports Association Sports Science Committee.

Kozuma, Y. (1995). *Asukara sukaeru mentaru toreiningu* [Mental training you can use from tomorrow]. (In Japanese). Tokyo: Baseball Magazine.

Kozuma, Y. (2002). *A mental training program for athletes in Japan.* (In Japanese). Tokyo: Baseball Magazine.

Kozuma, Y. (2003). *A mental training program for coaching in Japan.* (In Japanese). Tokyo: Baseball Magazine.

Miyamoto, M. (2001). *A book of five rings: A classic guide to strategy* (V. Harris, Trans.). New York: Square One.

Tokunaga, M. (2005). *Kyouyou toshite no supotsu shinrigaku* [Sport psychology as general knowledge]. (In Japanese). Tokyo, Japan: Taishukanshyoten.

Whiting, R. (1989). *You gotta have wa.* New York. Vintage.

Yamamato, T. (2001). *Bushido: The way of the samurai* (M. Tanaka and J.F. Stone, Trans.). New York: Square One.

INDEX

ABOUT THE EDITORS

Courtesy of Cherie Harris.

Robert Schinke, EdD, is an associate professor of sport psychology in the School of Human Kinetics at Laurentian University in Sudbury, Ontario, Canada, where he teaches cultural sport studies at the undergraduate and graduate levels. As a coach and a Canadian Sport Psychology Association certified practitioner, Schinke has extensive experience working with national teams and professional athletes of North America, South America, Europe, Asia, Africa, and the Caribbean.

Schinke has authored more than 100 academic and applied articles in publications, including The Sport Psychologist, International Journal of Sport and Exercise Psychology, International Journal of Sport Psychology, Journal of Clinical Sport Psychology, and the Journal of Sport Science and Medicine. His research is supported by the Social Sciences and Humanities Research Council of Canada and the Canadian Foundation for Innovation. In addition, Schinke serves as editor of Athletic Insight.

A former Canadian equestrian team member and Pan American Games medalist, Schinke still enjoys equestrian pursuits in addition to hiking and cross-country running. He and his wife, Erin, reside in Sudbury.

Stephanie Hanrahan, PhD, is an associate professor in the Schools of Human Movement Studies and Psychology and the director of the sport and exercise psychology program at the University of Queensland in Brisbane, Australia. As an author and researcher, Hanrahan has obtained 15 grants and published five books, 17 book chapters, and over 80 articles. She also serves as editor of the Journal of Applied Sport Psychology.

Hanrahan is a fellow of the Australian Sports Medicine Federation and a member of the Association for Applied Sport Psychology, Australian Psychological Society, Sports Medicine Australia, and the International Society of Sport Psychology. As a registered psychologist, she has worked with individuals and teams from all levels of sport (both with and without disabilities), Aboriginal performing artists, Mexican orphans, and teenagers living in poverty.

Hanrahan resides in Queensland and enjoys traveling within Australia and abroad.

ABOUT THE CONTRIBUTORS

Kaori Araki, PhD, is originally from Kyoto, Japan, and competed as a sprinter at the national level. After receiving her PhD from University of North Carolina at Greensboro in the United States, she moved to Singapore. Currently, she is an assistant professor at the National Institute of Education, Nanyang Technological University. She teaches sport and exercise psychology, applied sport psychology, and track and field. Her research interests are perfectionism in sport and gender and cultural diversity in sport. She has consulted with professional, national-level, and college-level athletes and teams in Japan and the United States and is now consulting with the Singapore Sailing Federation Olympic Squad. During her free time, she enjoys surfing in Southeast Asian countries.

Govindasamy Balasekaran, PhD, earned his doctorate from the University of Pittsburgh in the United States. He was born in Singapore and lived in the United States a number of years during his graduate education. He was educated in Singapore until high school, and he has also represented Singapore in long-distance running events and has won medals in various international meets. He also competed for his university in the United States. The experience gained in competitive sport allows him to be familiar with competitive athletics, especially the local sport scene in Singapore. At present he is an assistant professor at the National Institute of Education, Physical Education, and Sports Science, Nanyang Technological University, in Singapore. His research projects involve human performance and physiological responses such as endocrinology and performance, obesity, postprandial lipidemia, and human genetics. Dr. Bala also has a strong interest in coaching and holds the level 1 and level 2 International Amateur Athletic Federation (IAAF) coaching certificates. He is also a certified American College of Sports Medicine (ACSM) Health and Fitness Director.

Amy Blodgett, MA candidate, was born and raised in Peterborough, Canada. She is currently a graduate student in the School of Human Kinetics at Laurentian University in Sudbury, Canada. Her research and practical interests pertain to culturally reflexive approaches, where at present she is part of a multicultural team working with aboriginal youth and community sport programming in Wikwemikong First Nation Reserve. Her research is supported by the SSHRC. In addition, she has presented her research at national and international conferences, and she is currently a cochair of the 2008 Eastern Canada Sport and Exercise Psychology Symposium.

Boris Blumenstein, PhD, is director of the Department of Behavioral Sciences at the Ribstein Research Center of the Wingate Institute in Israel. He is author and coauthor of more than 90 publications and senior editor of the recent books *Brain and Body in Sport and Exercise: Biofeedback Applications in Performance Enhancement* and *Psychology of Sport Training*. He has given more than 60 scientific presentations and workshops in the United States, Canada, China, Germany, South Korea, and others. He was a sport psychology consultant to the Soviet Olympic teams, and since 1990 he has been a consultant to the Israeli Olympic teams (Atlanta 1996, Sydney 2000, Athens 2004). Dr. Blumenstein teaches at the Zinman College at Wingate. His current research interests include psychological skills training for Olympic performance and profiles of successful coaching.

Ted Butryn, PhD, is an associate professor of sport psychology and sociology in the Department of Kinesiology at San Jose State University in the United States. He received his PhD in sport and cultural studies from the University of Tennessee in 2000. His research interests include the intersections between critical sport sociology and applied sport psychology; sport, Whiteness, and multiculturalism; and the growing subcultures of professional wrestling and mixed martial arts. Along with several book chapters, he has published in the *Sport Psychologist, Sociology of Sport Journal, Journal of Sport and Social Issues, Journal of Sport Behavior,* and *Athletic Insight.* Ted teaches graduate courses in sport sociology and research methods (qualitative), undergraduate courses in sport sociology and psychology of coaching, and several courses in general education, including diversity, stress, and health. He is a member of the AASP Diversity Committee.

Peter Catina, PhD, earned his doctorate in human performance psychology in 2000 at the University of Maryland in the United States. He is an assistant professor in the Department of Health and Human Development at Pennsylvania State University. He is a world-class athlete and has been competing and coaching in the sport of powerlifting for 27 years. He is a 16-time national champion and has won the world championship title 6 times. Dr. Catina combines his academic and athletic backgrounds to direct his research toward the collectivistic and individualistic components of human performance and to develop a taxonomy that can be used to construct methods for maximizing athletic potential in multiple paradigms and cultures.

Caren Diehl, MEd, was born in Germany and moved to Ghana at the age of 1 with her family. She and her family lived in northern Ghana near Tamale for 2 years, after which she and her family moved to Tanzania. Caren completed both her primary and secondary education at an international school in Tanzania, and after completing her international baccalaureate, she moved to Wales. She completed her bachelor of science in sport psychology at Glamorgan University and attended Temple University to get her master's in education in sport and exercise psychology. Once she completed her master's, she joined her parents in Ghana for 6 months and did an internship with one of the soccer teams based in Accra, the capital city. While in Ghana, she applied to do her PhD at the University of Wolverhampton in the United Kingdom, where she is currently completing her PhD in sport psychology.

Lawrence Enosse, BA, is a former elite athlete in both ice hockey and track and field. As a community member from Wikwemikong, Lawrence has been the assistant coach for the Manitoulin Wild and the Blind River Bears, both Junior A ice-hockey teams. In addition to his interests in coaching, he is a sport and activity enthusiast. He has also worked with Duke Peltier and Robert Schinke in several federally funded research grants. He has coauthored publications in the *Sport Psychologist, International Journal of Sport and Exercise Psychology, International Journal of Sport Psychology,* and *Journal of Clinical Sport Psychology.*

Leslee A. Fisher, PhD, is an associate professor of sport psychology in the Department of Exercise, Sport, and Leisure Studies at the University of Tennessee, Knoxville, in the United States. She received a PhD in sport psychology from the University of California at Berkeley and a master's degree in counselor education from the University of Virginia. She

is a Certified National Counselor (National Board of Certified Counselors) and a Limited License Professional Counselor (State of Michigan). Her research focuses on the role of gender and other identities in sport and exercise performance, postmodern theory, cultural studies, eating disorders, and exercise addiction. She has published her work in refereed journal articles and book chapters and has presented numerous papers at national and international meetings. Leslee is the current secretary-treasurer of the AASP.

Shaun Galloway, PhD, is a senior lecturer and course leader for the coaching degree program at the University of Wolverhampton in the United Kingdom. He has worked, lived, and competed in seven countries, living abroad for the past 16 years. He was certified under the Canadian Mental Training Registry (CMTR) and is awaiting certification with the Canadian Sport Psychology Association (CSPA). In addition to applied psychology, his research interests are communication models in sport and issues in psychophysiology. He is currently the head of the coaching special interest group for the AASP.

Diane L. Gill, PhD, is a professor in the Department of Exercise and Sport Science at the University of North Carolina at Greensboro in the United States. She received her PhD from the University of Illinois, her undergraduate degree from SUNY at Cortland, and held faculty positions at the University of Waterloo and the University of Iowa. Her research emphasizes social psychology and physical activity, with a focus on physical activity and psychological well-being. Recent projects follow two related lines: cultural competence in physical activity settings, and physical activity and well-being across the lifespan. Her scholarly publications include the text, *Psychological Dynamics of Sport and Exercise,* several book chapters, and more than 100 journal articles. She is former editor of the *Journal of Sport and Exercise Psychology,* a former president of APA Division 47 (Exercise and Sport Psychology) and of NASPSPA, and an AASP charter member and fellow.

Anna Hegley, MSc, was born and raised in the United Kingdom. She studied at Loughborough University in Leicestershire for both her bachelor of science in physical education and sport science and her master of science in sport science. Upon graduation, she joined a specialist sport and business management consultancy company and spent nearly 3.5 years working in the United Kingdom and Ireland on a range of strategic-level projects. Meanwhile, she continued to develop her interest in sport and exercise psychology by working through the process of British

Association of Sport and Exercise Sciences (BASES) supervision in sport and exercise psychology (support). During this time, she took a 3.5-month sabbatical from her full-time job to work as a volunteer sport psychologist in Ghana, where she spent the majority of her time at a nonprofit youth football academy in the south of Ghana. She also spent time working with professional golfers and senior footballers. Following this experience, she returned to the United Kingedom for 6 months before moving to Ghana full time to continue working for the academy.

Philomena Bolaji Ikulayo, PhD, is the immediate past vice president of the ISSP and a physical education specialist with a PhD in education and sport psychology. She is the head of the Department of Human Kinetics and Health Education, a senate member of the University of Lagos, and former chairperson of the Department of Physical and Health Education Postgraduate Committee. She is the founder and foundation president of SPAN, a former vice president and treasurer of NAPHER-SD, and an executive member of the Nigeria Association of Sports, Science, and Medicine (NASSM). She is the first professor of sport psychology in Nigeria and the first indigenous author on sport psychology, with many books to her credit.

Christina Johnson, PhD, earned her doctorate in health and sport studies with an emphasis in sport psychology at the University of Iowa in the United States. She also holds an MA (cultural studies of sport), a BS (psychology), and a BA (Spanish) from the University of Iowa. Her research interests include self and identity issues in sport and physical activity and qualitative methodologies (e.g., narrative analysis). As a visiting assistant professor at the University of Iowa, she teaches research methods and courses in applied sport psychology and theoretical sport psychology. In addition to her research she has provided relaxation training for elite gymnasts. She also holds a black belt in taekwondo and serves as an assistant coach for the University of Iowa taekwondo team.

Urban Johnson, PhD, is an associate professor in sport and exercise psychology at Halmstad University, Sweden. After gaining an elite trainer certificate, he worked for several years as a professional trainer in handball. Since 1990, he has been a lecturer and then an associate professor in sport psychology and sport sciences at Halmstad University. His main area of research is psychological aspects of sport injuries, focusing on rehabilitation, prevention, and intervention. Dr. Johnson also has extensive experience as an applied sport psychologist, especially for athletes in

team sport. He is a member of the European Forum of Applied Sport Psychologists.

Cindra S. Kamphoff, PhD, is an assistant professor in the Department of Human Performance at the Minnesota State University, Mankato, in the United States. She received her MS and PhD from the University of North Carolina at Greensboro and her BS from the University of Northern Iowa. Her research has focused on gender and cultural diversity, including projects on male and female athletes' interest in the coaching profession, cultural competence in physical activity settings, diversity content in AASP conference programs, and an analysis of softball media guides. Her dissertation, *Bargaining With Patriarchy: Former Women Coaches' Experiences and Their Decision to Leave Collegiate Coaching,* received the 2006 NASPE Sport and Exercise Psychology Academy Dissertation Award. She is an active member of the American Alliance for Health, Physical Education, Recreation and Dance (AAHPERD), the North American Society for the Sociology of Sport (NASSS), and the AASP and has presented more than 20 papers at national and international conferences. She works regularly as a consultant teaching mental skills to youth and collegiate athletes, and she received two national awards for her work in academic advising in a retention program using sport psychology principles with students on academic probation.

Anthony P. Kontos, PhD, is an associate professor at Humboldt State University in California, where he teaches courses in sport and exercise psychology and works as a sport psychology consultant. Previously, he was an associate professor at the University of New Orleans, where he was the sport psychology consultant for the university sports medicine team. Dr. Kontos received his PhD in kinesiology and sport psychology from Michigan State University, where he also received master's degrees in counseling and exercise science. He completed his BA in psychology at Adrian College. His research includes sport concussion, psychology of injury, and multicultural sport psychology. Dr. Kontos has published more than 25 articles and chapters and has delivered more than 40 professional presentations. He is a member of APA Division 47 and the AASP. In his spare time, he enjoys surfing, playing American football, landscaping, cooking, hiking, and spending time with his wife, Danna, and their children, Constantine and Marina.

Yoichi Kozuma, MPE, is a professor in the Department of Competitive Sports of the College of Physical Education at Tokai University in Japan, where he teaches undergraduate and graduate courses in applied sport psychology. He received his master of physical education at Thukyo University in Japan. He is a nationally (in Japan) certified Mental Training Consultant in Sport and is also director of the applied sport and mental training psychology lab at Tokai University. In addition, he is the founder of the JSMTASP. He works with professional, national, and Olympic athletes, as well as junior and senior high school teams. He holds a sixth-degree black belt in karate and is a former All-Japan Champion. Professor Kozuma is widely published in Japan and is pleased to have this opportunity to share his information with English readers.

Andy Lane, PhD, was born in and educated in the United Kingdom. Before completing his sport studies degree, he worked for several years as a self-employed builder while competing nationally as an amateur boxer. After completing his undergraduate degree at the West London Institute of Higher Education, he completed a professional teaching qualification and became a secondary school teacher in Harrow, Middlesex. After completing his master's degree, he studied full-time as a doctoral student at Brunel University, and after completing his PhD, he worked as a lecturer in sport psychology and as a consultant sport psychologist. He moved to the University of Wolverhampton in 2000 and became a professor in sport psychology in 2003. He has published more than 90 articles in peer-refereed academic journals, has given more than 200 conference presentations, has published a book on mood and performance, and is on the editorial board of several sport science journals.

Ronnie Lidor, PhD, is an associate professor at the Zinman College of Physical Education and Sport Sciences at the Wingate Institute and a member of the faculty of education at the University of Haifa in Israel. His main areas of research are cognitive strategies, talent detection, and early development in sport. He has published more than 90 articles, book chapters, and proceedings chapters, in English and in Hebrew. He is the senior editor of several books, among them *Sport Psychology: Linking Theory and Practice* (1999) and *The Psychology of Team Sports* (2003), published by Fitness Information Technology. A former basketball coach, Dr. Lidor now provides psychological consultation to young and adult elite basketball players. He focuses mainly on attentional techniques used before the execution of free-throw shots. He lives in Tel Aviv with his wife and three children.

Kerry McGannon, PhD, received her doctorate in health and exercise psychology from the University of Alberta after receiving a BA (psychology) and an MA (sport and exercise psychology) from the University of Victoria in Canada. She is an assistant professor in the Department of Health and Sport Studies at the University of Iowa. Her research provides a bridge between traditional epidemiological approaches and cultural studies approaches in order to understand physical activity participation. Her specific interest is the social construction of the self and critical interpretations of physical activity using social theory and qualitative methodologies (e.g., narrative, discourse analysis). The journals where her work is published, such as *Qwest, Sociology of Sport Journal, Journal of Sport and Exercise Psychology,* and *International Journal of Obesity,* underscore the interdisciplinary nature of her research.

Ginette Michel, MA, is the coordinator of the health promotion program and assistant professor in the School of Human Kinetics at Laurentian University in Sudbury, Canada. Her areas of expertise include exercise and health, stress management, and adaptive physical education. She recently received the Presidential Advisory Committee on the Status of Women Award for her involvement in health promotion, particularly related to special projects she has developed in Costa Rica and Zimbabwe. Her areas of research include the adaptation to elite sport by aboriginal athletes and program development in sport and physical activity for aboriginal youths and their coaches. Both projects are part of SSHRC grants.

Luiz Carlos Moraes, PhD, is adjunct professor in the School of Physical Education, Physical Therapy, and Occupation Therapy at Federal University of Minas Gerais, Brazil. He teaches sport psychology for undergraduate and graduate students. In 1999, he earned his PhD in education in the area of psychopedagogy from the University of Ottawa. Dr. Moraes is vice president of the Brazilian Society of Sport Psychology (SOBRAPE). He is a former national team champion in judo in Brazil, and his research interests are sport expertise, emotion in sport, and coaching processes in different sports in Brazil. He works with athletes from archery and taekwondo and has been the mental trainer of the Brazilian national team of taekwondo since 2002.

Duke Peltier is the sport and recreation director at Wikwemikong First Nations Indian Reserve in Manitoulin, Canada. A former elite ice-hockey athlete, Duke currently is a member of Wikwemikong's Band

and Council, and he devotes much of his time to developing effective sport and activity programs for young people in his local community. In addition, Duke has been the community lead on two external research grants funded by the SSHRC. The first uncovered the sport strategies of Canadian elite athletes, and the second—currently in process—involves designing and testing youth sport programming with members of his community. He has coauthored publications in *The Sport Psychologist*, *International Journal of Sport and Exercise Psychology*, *International Journal of Sport Psychology*, and *Journal of Clinical Sport Psychology*.

Heather J. Peters, PhD, is an assistant professor of psychology at the University of Minnesota-Morris in the United States, where she teaches a multicultural psychology course. She received her PhD from the University of Arizona, emphasizing sport psychology, and completed a predoctoral internship and a postdoctoral fellowship at the University of California-Davis, with emphases in sport psychology, eating disorders, and culture. Her research focuses on cultural background and self-talk. She participated in the International Relations Committee for the AASP from 2000 until 2005, when she began serving as the association's student representative. She is first author of publications in the *Journal of Applied Sport Psychology* and the *Journal of Exercise and Sport Psychology*. Her applied interests include facilitating multicultural discussion groups and providing sport psychology services to coaches and athletes.

Chris Pheasant, BEd, is a secondary school vice principal in Wikwemikong First Nations Indian Reserve. In relation to sport psychology, he has been appointed by his community to assist with two sport psychology research grants codeveloped with Duke Peltier and Robert Schinke. He has coauthored publications in *The Sport Psychologist*, *International Journal of Sport and Exercise Psychology*, *International Journal of Sport Psychology*, and *Journal of Clinical Sport Psychology*.

Patricia Pickard, PhD, is the coordinator of the sport and physical education program and associate professor in the School of Human Kinetics at Laurentian University in Sudbury, Canada. A former athletic director and university coach for 24 years, her areas of expertise are teaching and coaching strategies, risk management, and sport history. She has held a number of administrative positions in Ontario and Canadian university sport. Her research areas include crowd behavior in professional sport and at the Olympics. In addition, she is currently a member of

a research team supported by the SSHRC developing sport programming initiatives for aboriginal youths and their coaches.

Stephen Ritchie, MA, is currently an assistant professor and coordinator of the Outdoor Adventure Leadership Program at Laurentian University in Sudbury, Canada. In addition to working in the outdoor field as a guide and teacher, Stephen's 25-year career also includes working with diverse populations in a facilitating role. From presentations to backcountry debriefing to problem solving to strategic planning, Stephen has developed a unique approach to facilitating experiences that has been employed in the corporate boardroom as well as in some of the most remote areas of the world. Stephen is a coapplicant and facilitator in the first year of a 3-year research project funded by the SSHRC. This initiative is in partnership with Wikwemikong First Nation and is focused on understanding and improving youth adherence to sport programming.

Emily A. Roper, PhD, is an assistant professor in the Department of Health and Kinesiology at Sam Houston State University in the United States. She earned her master's degree in community health from the University of Toronto and her doctorate in cultural studies and sport psychology from the University of Tennessee. She has taught a variety of courses in health and kinesiology, including Women, Sport, and Culture; Contemporary Issues in Sport; Psychosocial Bases of Human Movement; Foundations of Community Health; and Minorities in American Sport. Her research interests focus on the intersection of sport psychology, women's studies, and cultural studies. Her research has been published in *The Sport Psychologist*, *Women in Sport and Physical Activity Journal*, *Journal of Applied Sport Psychology*, *Journal of Aging and Physical Activity*, *Sex Roles*, *Journal of Sport Behavior*, and *Athletic Insight*. She is a member of several professional associations and was recently appointed chair of the AASP Diversity Committee.

Tatiana V. Ryba, PhD, was born and raised in a Soviet sporting family (her parents are former elite coaches). She is currently a postdoctoral fellow in the School of Human Kinetics, University of British Columbia. She undertakes research in the intersecting areas of cultural studies of sport, sport psychology, identity, cultural history, and qualitative research, and is interested in the epistemology and politics of the formation of disciplinary knowledge. In a recent project she explored the cultural history of applied sport psychology in the former Soviet Union. She has written and taught extensively on questions of sociocultural diversity and research methodology in sport psychology. In addition to her research and teaching contributions, Dr. Ryba serves as chair of the AASP International Relations Committee.

John H. Salmela, PhD, has been involved in cross-cultural research since he carried out a behavioral observation study out across all gymnastic competitions at the 1976 Montreal Olympic Games. This study was followed by a joint project with Adbou Baria using a similar protocol at the African Games in Morocco. After taking early retirement and moving to Brazil, he was able to collect data on soccer, volleyball, and gymnastics using mental skills profiling and making comparisons with Canadian athletes. Most recently, he has spent 3 months in Iran working with the national delegation in preparation for the 2006 Asian Games. While in Iran, he has compared the mental skills profiles of these high-level athletes, including several world and Olympic champions, with their Canadian counterparts, and has established a hierarchy of mental skills proficiency among Iranian athletes and among medalists versus nonmedalists.

Johnson Aletile Semidara, MEd, has been a member of SPAN since 1986, when he enrolled in the master of education program with specialization in sport psychology. He received a master's degree in physical and health education with specialization in sport psychology in 1987 at the University of Lagos, Nigeria. He was one of the first set of master's-degree holders produced by P.B. Ikulayo and the Department of Human Kinetics and Health Education at the University of Lagos. He was the first Nigerian male graduate teacher at the International School, University of Lagos, and taught there from 1984 until 2006. He is enrolled in the MPhil and PhD program in sport psychology at the University of Lagos.

Alexander Stambulov, PhD, is a coach in the wrestling club Allians in Halmstad, Sweden. His professional experiences include both coaching and applied sport psychology in Russia and Sweden. In the 1970s, he was among the first applied sport psychologists in the U.S.S.R. to work with national teams on a full-time basis. In 1980, he served as a psychologist of the Soviet Olympic diving team. In the 1980s and 1990s, he combined coaching and psychological consulting in working with individual Russian athletes and teams and coaches in wrestling, swimming, diving, rowing, figure skating, artistic and rhythmic gymnastics, and ski jumping at the junior and senior elite levels. His specialization in applied work is performance enhancement and individual counseling.

Natalia Stambulova, PhD, is a professor in sport and exercise psychology at Halmstad University, Sweden. She has worked for 25 years as a teacher, researcher, and consultant in Russia and since 2001 in Sweden. Her athletic background is in figure skating at the level of the U.S.S.R. national team. Her research and publications relate mainly to athletic careers with an emphasis on career transitions and crises. In applied work, her specialization is helping athletes in crises and consulting athletes and coaches on various issues. She is a leader of the course, How to Work as an Applied Sport Psychologist, at Halmstad University. She is also a recipient of the AASP Distinguished International Scholar Award (2004).

Peter Terry, PhD, is professor and head of the psychology department at the University of Southern Queensland in Australia. He has been a team psychologist at seven Olympic Games and nearly 100 other international competitions. He has lived and worked as an applied practitioner in several countries, including England, Canada, Brunei, and Australia, and in 2005 he was a visiting professor at the National Institute of Education in Singapore. He is currently providing specialist support for several international shooting teams. A former state-level athlete, he is the author of more than 150 publications, a fellow of the British Association of Sport and Exercise Sciences (BASES), and past president of the Australian Psychological Society's College of Sport Psychology.

Mary Jo Wabano is the director for the Youth Center at Wikwemikong First Nations Indian Reserve. She has been involved in sport activities at Wikwemikong since childhood. At present, she has developed an initiative in which youths from Wikwemikong engage in sport with elders from the same community. The goal is to facilitate increased cultural awareness among young people while also creating closer ties across generations. She lives in Wikwemikong with her husband, Mike, and their children, Wahss and Paygibe.

Clifton Wassangeso George, BPHE, is a sport and physical education graduate from Laurentian University in Sudbury, Ontario. As a member of the Wikwemikong Unceded Indian Reserve Band, he has been involved with Robert Schinke and his colleagues at Laurentian University and stakeholders from Wikwemikong as a research assistant since October 2006. In his role,

Clifton has led culturally reflexive data collections, and he has assisted with data analyses, academic presentations, and publications. His contributions to the Wikwemikong project will continue as he attends teacher's college in September 2007. He has been actively involved in the Wikwemikong community since childhood, and his ambition is to become a physical education teacher within the community. He is a lacrosse enthusiast and a part-time strength and conditioning trainer.

Jean Williams, PhD, is a professor in the Department of Psychology at the University of Arizona in the United States. She currently teaches courses in stress and coping and psychology of excellence, and she has also taught sport psychology courses in social psychology, health and exercise psychology, and performance enhancement. She has been an active sport psychology researcher and consultant for more than 30 years and has authored more than 100 scholarly publications. She has also edited two books and coauthored a third. She has served on the editorial boards of four research journals, and she is a founding board member and past president of the AASP.